EXPLORING psychology

for AS Level AQA 'A'

Matt Jarvis and **Julia Russell**

with Jean-Marc Lawton

© 2008 Folens Limited, on behalf of the authors.

United Kingdom: Folens Publishers, Waterslade House, Thame Rd, Haddenham, Buckinghamshire HP17 8NT.

www.folens.com

Ireland: Folens Publishers, Greenhills Road, Tallaght, Dublin 24.

Email: info@folens.ie

Folens publications are protected by international copyright laws. All rights are reserved. The copyright of all materials in this publication, except where otherwise stated, remains the property of the publisher and the author. No part of this publication may be reproduced, stored in a retrieval system, or transmitted, in any form or by any means, for whatever purpose, without the written permission of Folens Limited.

Matt Jarvis and Julia Russell hereby assert their moral rights to be identified as the authors of this work in accordance with the Copyright, Designs and Patents Act 1988.

Project development: Rick and Samantha Jackman (Jackman Publishing Solutions Ltd)

Concept design: Patricia Briggs

Layout artist: GreenGate Publishing Services

Illustrations: Derek Griffin, Barking Dog Art, Alex Machin, GreenGate Publishing

Cover image: James Cant/Getty Images

First published 2008 by Folens Limited.

Every effort has been made to contact copyright holders of material used in this publication. If any copyright holder has been overlooked, we should be pleased to make any necessary arrangements.

British Library Cataloguing in Publication Data. A catalogue record for this publication is available from the British Library.

ISBN 978-1-85008-258-3

Contents

Introduction

Exploring Psychology is a new and completely different resource for the 2008 AQA-A Psychology specification from the authors of the hugely successful *Angles on Psychology*. Matt and Julia have several decades of teaching and examining experience between them and Matt is particularly well versed in the new specifications having been part of the Major Stakeholders Group that advised all the Awarding Bodies. This has put us in an excellent position to develop a textbook that really meets the changing needs of psychology students and their teachers. But what makes *Exploring* so special as a book?

The text is clearly written to make reading easy. It contains all the essential information required by the AQA-A specification and is enhanced by the use of much up-to-date, interesting research. Matt and Julia *enjoy* Psychology and want their readers to as well! The text also includes interactive features that are designed to teach students to think psychologically – to construct their own understanding of the subject rather than echo that of the authors. These extend their learning, enabling them to go beyond the information provided so that they can become competent researchers. In short it aims to produce students who not only have knowledge and understanding but who think and act like psychologists too.

The text contains the following features, designed to develop higher-level thinking and research skills:

To develop higher level psychological thinking skills:

Thinking *practically* about psychology: an interactive feature providing cues and requiring students to use psychological theory and research a range of real-life situations.

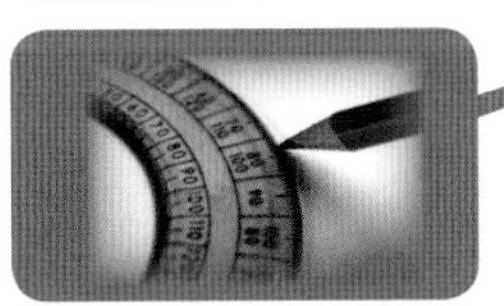

Thinking *critically* about psychology: an interactive feature requiring students to use the 'critical thinking toolkits' provided to evaluate theories and studies.

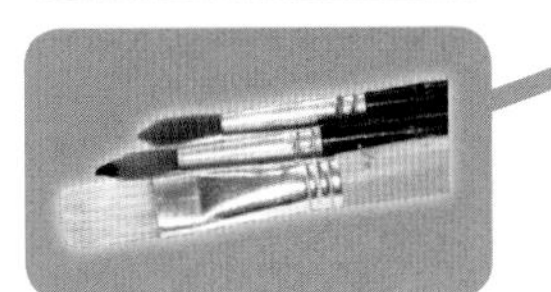

Thinking *creatively* about psychology: an interactive feature requiring students to design studies to test ideas, to consider alternative ways of investigating a phenomenon and to combine narrow explanations for psychological phenomena to come up with eclectic understandings.

To develop advanced secondary research skills:

Looking further: an interactive feature in which students are guided through the process of researching a topic, for example making general enquiries about psychological issues, using on-line databases and specialist search engines to locate additional studies to add to their notes.

Problem-solver: an interactive feature requiring students to gather information using on-line sources and use them to solve a problem, for example making a case for the defence of a friend falsely accused of a crime based on eyewitness testimony.

To develop examination skills:

What do I know?: a feature based on examination-style questions to help students to practise using their newly-acquired knowledge to develop good understanding of the format of testing they will encounter in their module examinations

Research in Action: a feature that uses real examples of studies described in the first two chapters to help students to understand specific ideas in research methods.

- **Your examinations:** an entire chapter devoted to developing a good examination technique. Written by an experienced AQA-A examiner, this section provides example questions, worked answers and examiner commentary.

The overall content is structured closely around the AQA-A specification so you won't waste a lot of time reading material you don't need to know. However, we have made sure that, within the demands of the specification, we have provided you with as much interesting, up to date and relevant to real life material as possible to study. This is because motivation is incredibly important in learning; we want you to share our love of psychology, work hard at it and do well. Happy exploring!

Acknowledgements

Matt and Julia would like to thank Rick Jackman who, as always, has been an excellent guide on this project, also the team at Folens who have provided terrific support.

Dedications

JR to Em with love

MJ to Clare with love

CHAPTER 1
Exploring Psychology

Thinking ahead

By the end of this chapter you should be able to:

- **define psychology**
- **outline the five major areas of psychology**
- **distinguish between theories and studies**
- **understand the importance of beginning to think 'psychologically'**
- **be aware of some key questions to ask about studies and theories**
- **recognise the importance of developing research skills**
- **understand how to use the learning features of this book**

In this introductory chapter we take a look at some of the things you should know a bit about before going too much further with studying psychology. We define psychology and introduce you to its key areas. We also explain the differences between theories and studies in psychology. Knowing about the subject matter of psychology, however, is only half the story. Psychology is as much a way of thinking, and one of our aims in this book is to get you thinking like a psychologist. In this chapter we begin this process by introducing you to how to think critically, creatively and practically about psychological material. Finally, we explain our ideas about the place of a book like this in studying psychology, and offer some advice on where else to look for information on psychology.

WHAT IS PSYCHOLOGY?

Psychology is often defined as the 'science of mind and behaviour'. By this we mean that it is the scientific study of how people (and sometimes animals) behave, and how their minds work. The subject matter of psychology is extremely wide-ranging, covering everything from why chewing gum might improve your exam results (Chapter 2) to why pilots crash planes (Chapter 6). The British Psychological Society recognises five core approaches to psychology. These are cognitive psychology, developmental psychology, biological psychology, social psychology and the psychology of individual differences. These are briefly summarised in Table 1.1.

Table 1.1 Five major approaches to psychology

Approach	Description	Examples of real-life applications
Cognitive	Concerned with the workings of mental processes such as thinking and memory, which we use to make sense of information	Understanding and improving the accuracy of eyewitness testimony
Developmental	Concerned with the ways the mind and behaviour change and develop with age	Understanding the effects of day care on young children
Biological	Concerned with the relationship between biological processes and psychological functions, for example in stress	Understanding how people cope with stress and how stress can be treated
Social	Concerned with how people interact, and how individuals, groups and society and culture at large influence us	Understanding how to make people more resistant to social pressure
Individual differences	Concerned with the ways in which people differ from one another, for example in personality, intelligence and mental disorder	Understanding how we can treat mental disorder and psychological distress

Some psychologists work very much within a framework of one particular approach. Thus, social psychologists may think very much in social terms and bring social-psychological theory and research to bear on a range of problems. Others draw freely on a range of approaches and are said to be *eclectic*.

THEORIES AND STUDIES

We have said already that psychology is a science. Science involves theories and studies. It is well worthwhile being clear before you go any further about the difference between the two ideas. As examiners, we have seen many students who knew their stuff fail to achieve what they should have, because in the exam they wrote about a theory when the question asked for a study or vice versa.

What is a theory?

A theory is an *explanation* for a psychological phenomenon. For example, we have theories of how memory works (Chapter 2), how mothers and babies form attachments (Chapter 3) and why people obey orders (Chapter 6). There is often more than one theory to explain something. Our job as psychologists is to look at the evidence for each theory and decide how credible it is. It is, however, *not* necessary to choose a single correct theory and discard the others. Often, different theories are concerned with different aspects of the same broad area. For example, in Chapter 7 we look at several explanations for mental disorder. In fact, all these approaches are useful for explaining some cases of mental disorder. However, none of them gives us a complete explanation for all cases.

What is a study?

A study is any exercise where data (information) is gathered and analysed. This is quite a different idea from a theory. There are a huge number of studies in psychology, and you will encounter more studies than anything else as you learn about psychology.

Some studies aim to test a theory. Others just gather information about a psychological phenomenon. A classic example of a study is Hofling *et al.*'s investigation of nurses' obedience to doctors (p167). This involved gathering two types of data from nurses. First, they were asked how they thought they would behave if ordered by a doctor to do something that would harm a patient. Second, they were actually put in that position and their behaviour recorded.

Studies should tell us something useful. For example, Hofling *et al.*'s study showed how nurses tended to follow doctors' orders unquestioningly and that this obedience could sometimes pose a danger to patients.

BEGINNING TO THINK LIKE A PSYCHOLOGIST

Psychology is not just a set of theories and studies to learn and reproduce in your exams. To succeed in psychology at A level – and even more so if you go on to study the subject at university – you need to learn to think like a psychologist. In fact one of the key aims of the new 2008 AS and A levels is to push you to think in more advanced ways and prevent you getting high grades just by rote learning. Don't be put off by this. If you learn to think more like a psychologist, the subject will be all the more interesting for you and you will actually have less to learn for your exams!

So how does a psychologist think? Psychologists are scientists, and remember that the lifeblood of science is research and theory. Psychologists need to be able to put together their own theories and design and carry out studies. As scientists, they also need to be able to think critically about their own and other people's studies and theories. Psychologists also need to be able to make their work relevant to people's lives. Leading educational psychologist Robert Sternberg has crystallised these points into three types of advanced thinking needed to learn psychology:

- **critical thinking**: looking for strengths and weaknesses, particularly in studies and theories
- **creative thinking**: designing studies and coming up with your own explanations for psychological phenomena
- **practical thinking**: applying psychological ideas to explain real-life phenomena.

Mastering these three ways of thinking should benefit you in two main ways. First, you will be able to do everything you are required to do for your exams, and you won't have to rote-learn a huge amount of material. You will also find that, having thought deeply about the things you are studying, you will tend to remember them well, and of course that won't do you any harm in exams! Second, thinking ahead to your future, you will have a set of skills that should be useful in a huge range of situations. Obviously, thinking like a psychologist will help if you go on to study psychology at university, but even if you never study psychology again you can benefit from advanced thinking. Once you have studied psychology you will probably never accept a 'fact' at face value again. You will respond quite differently to news stories for example.

KEY QUESTIONS FOR CRITICAL THINKING

To start you off thinking like a psychologist, we can offer you these critical thinking toolkits. One is for theories and one for studies. You will be asked to evaluate theories and studies in your exams. By using these key questions as thinking tools you will think more deeply about the material, making it easier to learn, and it will save you having to memorise evaluation points for every theory and every study you look at.

For theories

- **What sort of evidence is this theory based on?** If a theory is derived from a few unrepresentative cases, it might not apply well to everybody. If it is based on laboratory studies, then it may not explain people's behaviour in real-life situations.
- **Is this theory testable?** If it is difficult to test, then this is a weakness.
- **Is there supporting evidence?** Have you found studies that could be used to support the theory or does it seem to be based just on speculation?
- **Is there conflicting evidence?** Are there studies that suggest that the theory is incorrect, or at least limited in what it can explain?
- **Is the theory useful?** By that we mean, does it have applications in understanding or intervening in a real-life situation?
- **Is the theory socially sensitive?** By this we mean, is the theory likely to offend people, perhaps because it places blame on someone for a psychological phenomenon, or because it identifies something undesirable about human nature?
- **Is there something important that this theory cannot explain?** A common limitation of theories is the inability to explain all aspects of the phenomenon, for example why people vary so much individually.

For studies

- **Has this study been conducted ethically?** By that we mean, have participants been put at risk, taken advantage of, had their privacy invaded or in some other way had their rights violated? See p111 for a detailed account of the British Psychological Society code of ethics.
- **Are the findings socially sensitive?** Do the findings of the study risk giving offence to people because they place blame on particular people or justify discrimination against a vulnerable group?
- **Has the study involved a representative group of people?** If, as is often the case, the researcher used their own students as participants, how representative of the general population are students? Have both men and women, and people of a good range of ages, participated?
- **Has it been carried out in an artificial or a natural environment?** If the study was carried out in a laboratory, can we be sure that participants behaved as they would in their own surroundings?
- **Are the tasks given to participants like those they would encounter in real life?** A common limitation of research is to put participants in situations or give them things to do that bear little resemblance to their real lives.
- **How good are the measures used to record the results?** For example, if the study used a questionnaire, was it a standard one widely accepted by psychologists or did the researchers make it up for the study? If it is a standard measure, this is a strength of the study.
- **Do the findings of this study conflict with those of other studies?** If so, think about how the findings are different, and try to explain why they differ. You might be able to suggest which study was better designed and which results we should accord more importance to.
- **Are the findings of this study useful?** Results might have an important application to real life. Alternatively, they might be important to psychologists because they help us evaluate a theory or idea.

DEVELOPING YOUR RESEARCH SKILLS

There are two types of research, primary and secondary. Primary research involves conducting your own studies – gathering and analysing your own data. Secondary research involves finding information and explanations that are already published. You will develop your primary research skills throughout your course. We would also like you to think about your secondary research skills. Although we have put this book together with a lot of care, the last thing you should do is accept everything we say.

This may sound a little odd! However, it is important to realise that all writers in psychology see things slightly differently. If you read this and another text aimed at the same course, you won't find all the same theories and studies, nor all the same opinions or conclusions. To get the most out of your course, always read around and never rely on any one textbook. We will help by pointing you towards particular Internet sites and give you search tasks using free online databases like PubMed (http://www.pubmed.gov) and specialist search engines like Google Scholar (http://scholar.google.com).

USING THE LEARNING FEATURES OF THIS BOOK

In designing *Exploring Psychology* we have aimed to put together the most educationally advanced psychology textbook ever written. We provide everything you would expect to see in an AS-level textbook; we follow the AQA specification A very closely and give you regular practice questions closely based on the kinds of questions you will see in your exams. We also include a chapter specifically on preparing for and coping with the AS-level exams. However, we also aim to help you think and study more like a psychologist. This makes *Exploring Psychology* the first choice of textbook for anyone thinking about going on to study psychology at university, and for anyone who wants to get a significantly better grade in their AS level than they would expect from their GCSE grades. If either of those descriptions applies to you, then we strongly suggest that you make use of the following learning features, which have been designed on the basis of cutting-edge educational psychology:

- **Thinking critically about psychology**: this feature is designed to get you evaluating psychological material – in particular, theories and studies. For example, we ask you to use questions from our thinking skills toolkits to evaluate particular studies.
- **Thinking creatively about psychology**: this feature is designed to get you putting ideas together, for example designing a study to test an idea, suggesting your own explanations for a psychological phenomenon or putting together a leaflet to inform people about an area of psychological research.
- **Thinking practically about psychology**: this feature is designed to get you using psychological research and theory to explain the psychology behind real-life events.
- **Media watch**: similarly, this feature asks you to explain a news item using psychological theory or research, or both.
- **Problem solver**: this is also designed to develop your practical thinking. We give you the sort of problem you might be faced with solving as a psychologist. Your task is to use psychological theory or research, or both, to solve the problem.
- **Looking further**: this feature is designed to help you develop your secondary research skills by searching for good-quality information on the Internet using the same types of sources and search techniques that a professional researcher would use.
- **Over to you**: this is designed to help you develop your primary research skills, designing and carrying out small pieces of research.

A FINAL WORD

We hope that as you use this book you will work through these learning features. They are designed both to help you in your exams and to help you develop transferable skills of advanced thinking and research. Our most important advice, however, is to enjoy. Students choose psychology because it is fascinating, and most psychology students say it is their most interesting subject. We agree! If at the end of your AS course you would like to know more about taking psychology further, read the epilogue. This gives you a run-down of what to expect from A2 psychology and some advice about applying to study psychology at university.

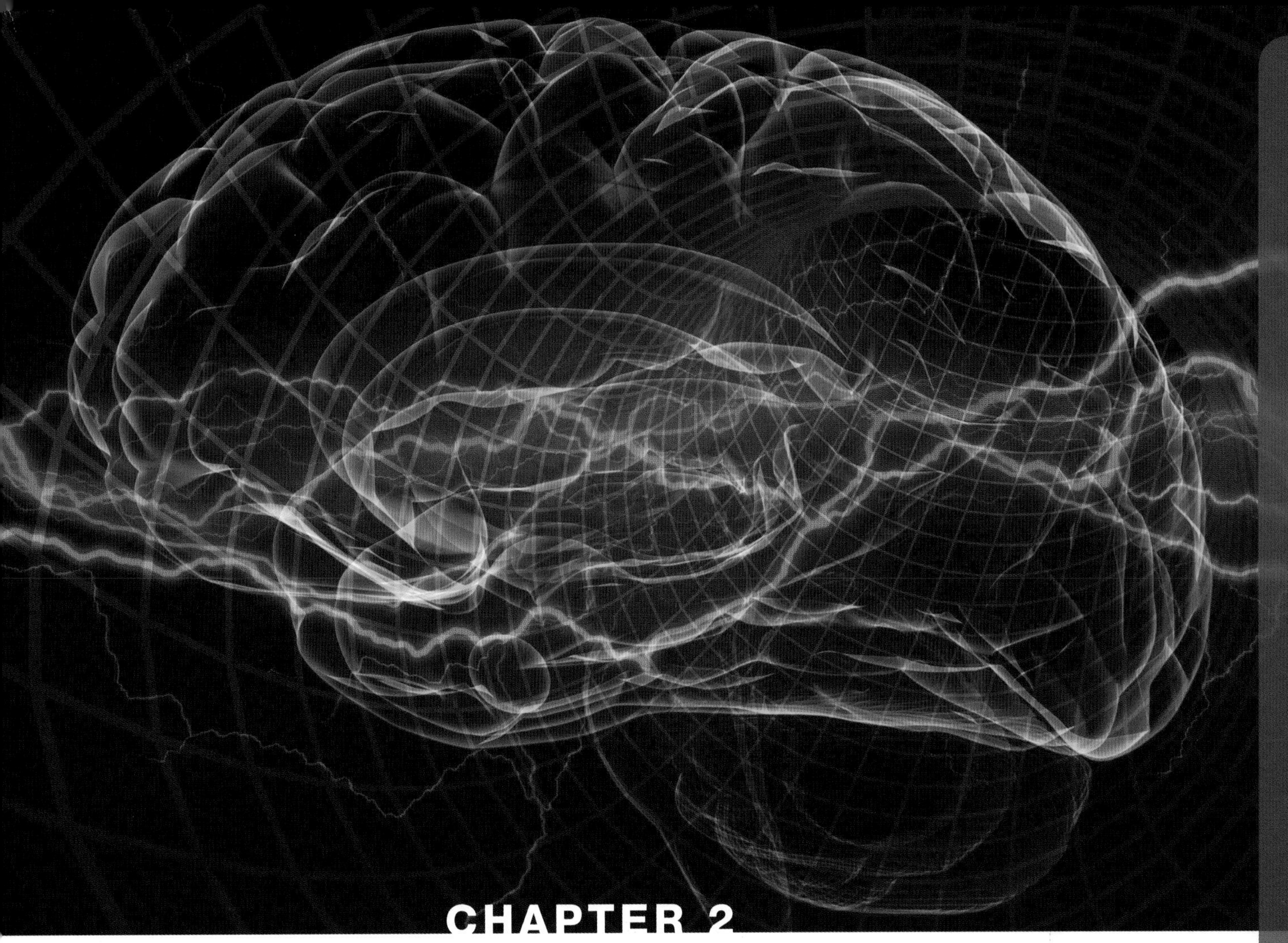

CHAPTER 2
Cognitive Psychology – Memory

Thinking ahead

By the end of this chapter you should be able to:

- **define and describe the concepts of encoding, capacity and duration**
- **describe and evaluate the multi-store model of memory**
- **describe and evaluate the working memory model**
- **outline techniques for improving memory**
- **apply your knowledge of memory to explain the use of these techniques**
- **understand some of the factors affecting eyewitness testimony**
- **apply your knowledge of memory to explain factors affecting eyewitness testimony**
- **describe the cognitive interview**
- **apply your knowledge of memory to explain the value of the cognitive interview**

COGNITIVE PSYCHOLOGY

KEY TERMS

cognition – the processes which allow us to change, store and use information. These include the processes of attention, perception, memory, decision-making and language.

Cognitive psychology studies the way we deal with information. Cognition can be defined as all the processes that we use to change, store, use and retrieve sensory information. Cognitive psychologists think of the mind as a system for handling information. We constantly receive information from the environment, interpret it in the light of existing information in our memory and think about it. We then respond to the information, for example with an opinion, an emotional response or with action. Cognitive processes thus include attention, perception, memory, decision-making and language. In this chapter we will focus on memory.

MODELS OF MEMORY

What is memory?

We often talk about 'remembering', but what do we really mean? According to psychologists, there are three distinct aspects to memory:

- encoding
- storage
- retrieval.

KEY TERMS

encoding – the cognitive way information is represented in memory, for example visual, acoustic (sound-based) or semantic (meaning-based)

memory – the encoding and storage of information that is later retrieved

free recall – the accessing of stored memories without, or with minimal, prompts

recognition – the accessing of memories by identifying things that have been encountered before

retrieval – the accessing of information held in memory

cued recall – the accessing of stored memories using prompts

Memories go through these three processes. Every memory needs to be encoded and stored. Although we do not successfully retrieve every memory – we forget things – for memory to be of any use there must be a system for finding stored material. First of all, anything to be remembered must be *encoded*. This means that the information must be represented in a form that can be used. This might, for example, be visual (iconic) or sound based (acoustic). Think about the way you remember a page number when you use the index of a book; you read it from a visual image but as you 'hold it in your head' it seems as though you can 'hear' yourself repeating it over and over again; this is an acoustic representation. Once encoded, the information must be *stored* – that is, kept for later use. So, even if we are interrupted after we have looked at our page number there is a good chance we will be able to remember it later.

Finally, we will want to use the stored information. In the case of our interrupted search for a page in a book, when we return to the task we can hopefully still call the page number to mind – that is, *retrieve* it. Sometimes retrieval is unprompted, as with the page number. This is called *free recall*. In *cued recall*, by contrast, there is some trigger to help us to locate the information. These triggers are called *cues*. An example of cued recall is answering short-answer questions in an exam. Having a number of questions, each requiring a short answer, provides us with memory cues. Recognition takes place when the memory task is to decide which item of information – such as a person in a police line-up – has been seen before. This is the sort of retrieval we use to answer multiple-choice questions in an exam. We will return to the role of cues later in the chapter.

The multi-store model

Atkinson & Shiffrin (1968) proposed a model of memory that explained two aspects of the memory system. These were the different 'stores' that hold information and the ways the information is handled, known as 'control processes'. The model describes three stores through which information passes (see Figure 2.1). At each of these stages information can be lost – that is, forgotten.

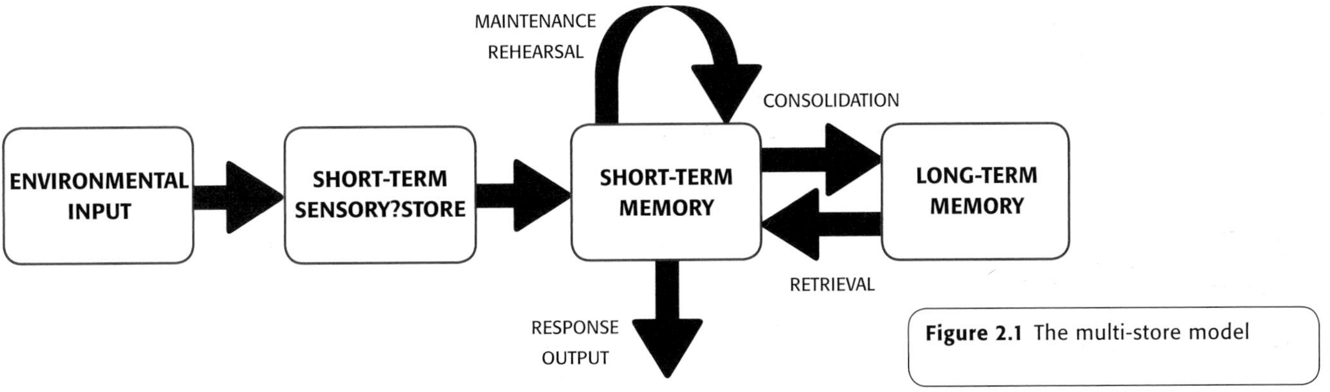

Figure 2.1 The multi-store model

Each of the stores is proposed as a separate system with properties distinct from those of the other stores. Distinctions between memory stores can be made in a number of ways:

- *encoding* – the form of representation that is used
- *duration* – how long an item lasts in the store
- *capacity* – the total amount of information that can be held in the store at one time.

These properties can be studied experimentally to find out whether the proposed stores do indeed have different characteristics. This forms the basis of the body of evidence supporting the multi-store model. We will now consider this evidence.

KEY TERMS

capacity – the maximum amount of information that can be held in a memory store before it is full

duration – how long information can be held in memory for, ie the length of storage over time

Short-term sensory store

Encoding

Information can enter the memory through any of the senses, for example via vision or touch. Each of these sources of incoming information enters its own short-term sensory store (STSS). There is a store for vision, one for sound, and so on. Because each of these stores is particular to the sense through which the information has come, they are described as being *modality specific*. The stores for vision and sound have been most thoroughly studied. These are called the *iconic* and *echoic stores* respectively.

STSS – the iconic store

Duration and capacity

The iconic store is the STSS for data entering the memory through the visual sense, so it holds visually encoded information. It appears to have a very limited duration but a moderately large capacity. Sperling (1960) used a laboratory experiment to test these two characteristics of the STSS. Participants were told that they would see a matrix of 12 letters arranged in three rows. This was presented very briefly (for 50 milliseconds).

A F Y I
Q H J M
G Z N U

Figure 2.2 A matrix of letters like that used by Sperling

Immediately after the matrix disappeared, the participants were cued to recall either all or part of the matrix. When trying to recall the whole matrix, they could remember, on average, only 4.32 letters. However, the results of partial recall, when they were asked to recall only the top, middle or bottom row, suggested that they could access much more than just four or five items. Regardless of which row they were asked to recall, participants were able to remember an average of 3.04 letters. This suggests that at the moment the matrix disappeared, participants had a very clear memory of the whole image, but in the time it took to report about four letters, the remainder of the memory had faded. So, Sperling's results indicate that the duration of the iconic store is in the

Figure 2.3 Testing eidetic memory

Conduct an investigation of eidetic memory using the interactive website http://www.ababasoft.com/games/find_pair.html. If you can, compare older and younger people. On the basis of the research discussed above, who would you expect to be best?

You can also consider whether younger children, who often play the game of pairs, might be better because of practice. If so, why is a test like Haber and Haber's better?

region of 0.5 seconds and that, while the capacity of STSS is small, it can hold at least 12 pieces of information.

The capacity of STSS has also been explored using children with a kind of photographic memory called an *eidetic memory*. In these children, the duration of the STSS seems to be much greater than normal, with the result (for researchers) that it can be studied more readily. Such children can be shown a complex picture and then asked questions about it. They can report in considerable detail specifics about the content of the image. For example, Haber & Haber (1964) showed children a picture of the Cheshire Cat from *Alice in Wonderland* for 30 seconds. Children were then given a blank card to look at and tested on their recall of the picture. They gave remarkably accurate answers to questions such as 'How many rings did the cat's tail have?', and while they were answering these questions, their eyes scanned the cardboard as if searching the picture itself, moving to the location that would have been occupied by the item in question.

The children answered the questions in the present tense, as if they were still looking at the original image. These findings suggest that a highly detailed representation of a picture can remain in the iconic store for longer than half a second – at least in those children with eidetic memory (about 8 per cent). This conclusion is supported by recent evidence showing that blinking during recall reduces accuracy. It seems that blinking disrupts the representation of information in iconic memory (Thomas & Irwin, 2006).

STSS – the echoic store

Duration and capacity

Like the iconic store, the echoic store is modality specific. It deals purely with incoming sound-based information and it is represented in this format – that is, acoustically. In terms of duration, the echoic store, again like the iconic store, is time-limited. Treisman (1964) tested the duration of the echoic store using a task in which participants heard a message playing in each ear. They were told to 'shadow' the message to one ear – that is, to listen to it and repeat it. The messages were identical, but one was slightly delayed. The participants only noticed that the messages were the same if the interval between them was 2 seconds or less. This suggests a maximum duration of 2 seconds for items in the echoic store – slightly longer than for the iconic store.

Thinking creatively about psychology

Sometimes, when a teacher asks you a question and you haven't really been listening, it feels as though it takes a while for the words to 'sink in'. You are rescued by the fact that you can 'replay' the last few words that were said – because they are still in your echoic store.

Design a way to observe this phenomenon in class.

Consider the answers to the following questions: What materials will you need? How can you accurately measure the delay between the teacher asking a question and a student replying? How might you find out whether they had to use the 'play-back' facility of their echoic store or were just slow to work out the answer? Is your procedure likely to be acceptable to students and staff?

We use the echoic store to retain sounds arriving at one ear until the matching sound has reached the other ear. This is what provides us with stereo hearing and enables us to localise sound. If a mobile phone rings immediately to our left, the sound reaches our left ear fractionally before it reaches our right (it is also slightly louder in the left ear). The difference between the sounds arriving at our two ears enables the brain to determine the position of the phone.

Figure 2.4 Your echoic memory helps when your teacher catches you daydreaming

You can demonstrate the role of your two ears and the echoic memory in sound localisation with a partner. One person (the 'participant') shuts their eyes and sits with their back to the 'experimenter'. The experimenter make a noise in different locations around the room, sometimes to the participant's left, sometimes to their right. The participant points to the source of the noise without opening their eyes. Once this has been repeated several times, with the accuracy being noted, the participant then blocks first one, then the other ear. Look at what happens to their directional accuracy.

Short-term memory

Duration

The short-term memory (STM) is that memory of which we are aware. It is a conscious store of information that is readily available. It is clearly a store with a short duration – but how short? An answer to this question was provided by Peterson & Peterson (1959) – see *Classic Research*.

CLASSIC RESEARCH

Peterson LR & Peterson MJ (1959) Short-term retention of individual verbal items. *Journal of Experimental Psychology* **58,** 193–8

AIM

To test the duration of short-term memory by measuring the retention of items in STM when rehearsal is prevented for differing lengths of time.

PROCEDURE

Twenty-four students were tested on their recall of test items presented one at a time. The items were trigrams, meaningless groups of three consonants such as CHJ. No two of the trigrams presented one after the other contained any of the same letters. Each participant was shown a trigram then given standard instructions to count backwards in threes or fours until a flashing light appeared in front of them. They then had to recall the trigram. There were various fixed durations between the experimenter saying the letters and the light signalling recall (3, 6, 9, 12, 15 and 18 seconds). Each participant was tested on each of these intervals once in each block of six trials.

FINDINGS

As the delay between hearing the trigram and reporting it increased, the ability to recall it decreased. This relationship can be seen in Figure 2.5. No participants could recall the letters after more than 18 seconds.

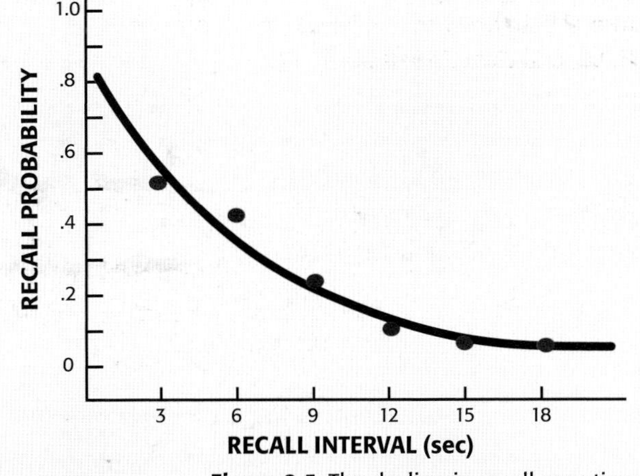

Figure 2.5 The decline in recall over time

CONCLUSION

When rehearsal is prevented items in short-term memory are lost quickly, lasting a maximum of approximately 18 seconds.

Thinking critically about psychology

1 Peterson & Peterson's study was a well-controlled laboratory experiment. Identify three of the controls and explain why each one was necessary.
2 Looking back at your key questions for evaluating studies (p5), identify two possible weaknesses with the experiment.

In this model, information is seen as being lost from short-term memory by *interference*. Interference takes place when new items in STM get confused with existing ones, just like when you try to remember an old phone number and find yourself thinking instead of your new one. Interference serves to prevent rehearsal, causing material in STM to decay and be lost. Without interference, this 'maintenance rehearsal' allows items to be held in STM for longer. One consequence of retention in the rehearsal buffer is the transfer of information to permanent storage – that is, to LTM. Thus rehearsal in STM helps to consolidate memories.

LOOKING FURTHER You can read Miller's paper in full at http://psychclassics.yorku.ca. You can also test your own digit span and demonstrate the effectiveness of chunking at http://www.youramazingbrain.org/yourmemory/default.htm.

Capacity

Another characteristic of STM is that it has a limited capacity – that is, it becomes 'full' even when it contains relatively little information. For example, it seems to hold fewer items than the iconic store. One way to measure the capacity of STM is by using the digit span technique. This simply requires a participant to hear or read a set of random digits and repeat them in the same order. The random list increases in length, and when the participant can no longer recite the list accurately, they have reached their maximum *digit span* – that is, the capacity of their short-term memory.

The basic digit span technique can be repeated for other stimuli, such as letters, words or pictures. Miller (1956) compared various such measures of the capacity of STM and concluded that it was limited to approximately 7 ± 2 items. These items Miller described as 'chunks'; the size of the chunk appeared not to matter, provided that it was a single unit of information. The capacity of STM can therefore be increased by '*chunking*' information – that is, by treating multiple items as one. For example, we would find it hard to recall this sequence of numbers: 1196661218180026601. Our short-term memory capacity would be exceeded, and some items would be forgotten. If, however, the same digits had been presented in reverse order, as 1066200818121666911, they would have been much easier to remember. This is because they could then be chunked into five items and thus would be within the capacity of STM (1066, 2008, 1812, 1666, 911).

KEY TERMS

digit span – the maximum number of digits (numbers) we can keep in short-term memory

chunking – the combining of to-be-remembered items into meaningful units that can be stored in STM as a single unit, i.e. a 'chunk'

Encoding

When information is passed from STSS to STM, it is encoded in a different way. Typically, information in STM seems to be held in an acoustic form. Evidence to support this suggestion comes from studies such as that Conrad (1964) (also Baddeley, 1966; see p14). Conrad presented participants with a visual series of six letters. When asked to report them from short-term memory (i.e. immediately) they tended to muddle up letters such as 'b' and 'p' or 'f' and 's'. The majority of errors related to similar-sounding letters. This tells us that the participants must have been using an *acoustic code* – converting the visual representation of the letters into their sounds – and it was this that led to confusion.

Long-term memory

Capacity

Marigold Linton conducted long-term diary-based investigations on her own memory. She studied recall for both everyday items, such as things she had done, and unfamiliar items, such as information about plants. Testing her own recollection of these items over long periods of time, she demonstrated considerable factual recall, illustrating the enormous capacity of long-term memory (LTM). Over many years, Linton kept a daily diary of events on cards, giving each day a key word. When she tried to recall any day's events, even up to seven years later, she could do so with an accuracy of 70 per cent with the minimal cue of the single key word (Linton, 1975). This illustrated the immense capacity of LTM, as an estimated 11,000 items were recorded in the diary.

More recently, Huang (1997), a university lecturer, has conducted a similar investigation on himself. He looked at his memory for 560 past students over more than two decades. He could accurately recognise whether or not an individual was a past student on more than 80 per cent of occasions. Although he found that his memory was best for the most recent classes, his accuracy levelled off and remained fairly constant for the more distant past. Like Linton, Huang has demonstrated that LTM can retain large numbers of individual pieces of information over long periods of time.

Figure 2.6 Some lecturers can recognise a remarkable number of ex-students years after they taught them

Figure 2.7 We are remarkably good at remembering street names from our childhood

Duration

Bahrick has conducted several studies into the length of long-term memory. For example, Bahrick (1984) investigated the recall of Spanish as a second language in participants who had ceased to learn the language up to 50 years prior to the study. He found that although recall fell sharply for the first three years or so, after that a significant amount continued to be available and subsequent decline was minimal (see Figure 2.8).

Another similar study (Schmidt *et al.*, 2000) investigated people's recall of incidentally learned material rather than information that had been specifically taught. They tested memory for recall of street names from each participant's childhood neighbourhood and their locations on a street map. The findings showed that, for retention intervals of 0–71 years, people showed a very similar pattern to that found in Bahrick's earlier study. Although details are lost at first, even decades later people still remember huge amounts of information.

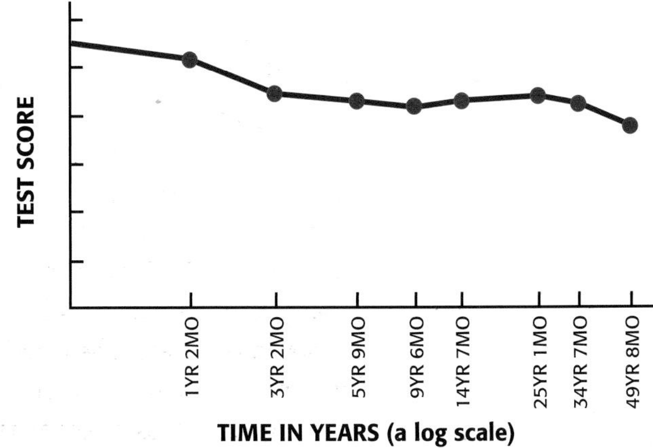

Figure 2.8 Recognition of Spanish as a second language over time by people who have ceased to learn the language

KEY TERMS

incidental learning – when memories are formed without any deliberate effort by the learner

Encoding

While memories in the STSS are encoded according to their sensory modality, and those in STM are encoded acoustically, information held in LTM seems to be different again. Here, memories are encoded according to their meaning – that is, using a *semantic code*. Baddeley (1966) provided evidence for this in an experiment that required participants to learn lists of words and recall them. The lists contained some items that were acoustically similar (such as mad, man, cad, can) and others that were semantically similar (such as big, long, broad, high). When asked for immediate recall, participants' errors were affected by the similar-sounding words, reflecting the use of an acoustic code in STM. When recall was delayed for 20 minutes, however, more errors were made on list items with similar meanings. This latter finding can be explained by the use of a semantic code in LTM; items were confused when they had similar meanings, so were less likely to be recalled accurately.

Problem solver

You have forgotten to revise for Monday's psychology test and it's Sunday morning. You know you have to do well or you'll be thrown off the course, so you decide to use all the ideas from the work you have done on the multi-store model to make your revision really work. You think about what you have learned about the characteristics of STM, and its role in laying down new LTM, to design an effective strategy. Think about:

- capacity (how much you should learn at once)
- duration and the serial position effect (how long to spend looking at an item before moving on to the next but avoiding displacing earlier items)
- encoding (how to present the material to make encoding and/or storage easy)
- the importance of chunking
- the role of rehearsal.

Suggest at least three things you could do and justify each one in terms of the characteristics of memory.

How do we know that STM and LTM are different?

From the findings of Baddeley (1966) we know that the STM and LTM can be easily distinguished by the types of errors we make when recalling from each store. Recent studies such as that by Smythe & Costall (see *Research Now*) also illustrate differences between the stores, as they can be affected independently. Another clear distinction between the two is demonstrated by the serial position effect.

Smythe JW & Costall B (2003) Mobile phone use helps memory in male subjects. *Neuroreport* **14,** 243–246

AIM

To investigate whether exposure to the electromagnetic field produced by a mobile phone affects memory.

PROCEDURE

Thirty-three male and 29 female student volunteers were each given three minutes to learn words that had been arranged in a pyramid. They were also given three minutes to recall the words, and this was done after a brief interference task of reading a newspaper (a short-term memory test) and one week later (a long-term memory test). For the word learning phase, each participant was randomly allocated to one of three conditions:

- holding an active mobile phone to their ear
- holding an inactive mobile phone to their ear
- no mobile phone.

FINDINGS

No differences in number of errors made were found in long-term memory between different conditions. On the short-term memory task, there were no differences for female participants, but the males made more errors when the phone was off (mean 23) than when it was on (mean 12.9).

CONCLUSION

Short-term but not long-term memory (in males but not females) is enhanced by the presence of an active mobile phone. This suggests that STM and LTM are different systems, as they can be affected independently, at least in males.

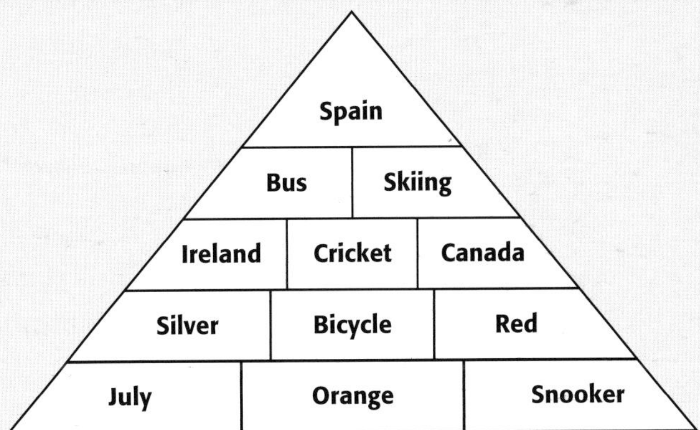

Figure 2.9 The word pyramid used by Smythe & Costall

Thinking creatively about psychology

Draw another word pyramid for Smythe & Costall's study. Think carefully about the things that you will control when choosing the words.

The serial position effect

In a serial position task, participants are presented with items in order and asked to recall them. If the short- and long-term memory stores are separate, this should affect how well items at the start and the end of the list are remembered. Specifically, provided recall is tested immediately, we would expect items at the beginning of a list to be recalled well, because they would have had time to be encoded and stored in long-term memory. Items at the end of the list should also be well remembered because they are still in short-term memory. We would, however, expect that items in the middle of a list would be poorly remembered, because whilst they are being encoded, more items are entering STM preventing rehearsal. This hypothesis was tested by Murdock (1962) – see *Classic Research*.

CLASSIC RESEARCH

Murdock BB (1962) The serial position effect of free recall. *Journal of Experimental Psychology* **64,** 482–88

AIM

To test whether items at the beginning and end of word-lists are better recalled than items in the middle, as we would expect if there are separate short- and long-term memory.

PROCEDURE

Groups of psychology students (103 in total) were read a list of words at a steady rate (in time with a metronome). The lists varied in length from 10 to 40 words. Immediately afterwards they were given 1 minute 30 seconds to write down as many words as they could, in any order.

FINDINGS

Recall for the early and late items in any list was much better than for the items in the middle. This happened for all lists, regardless of their length.

CONCLUSION

These findings support the existence of separate short- and long-term memory stores. The most obvious explanation for these findings was that items at the start of the list were well recalled because they had been properly encoded in LTM (called the primacy effect), while items at the end were still in STM (the recency effect).

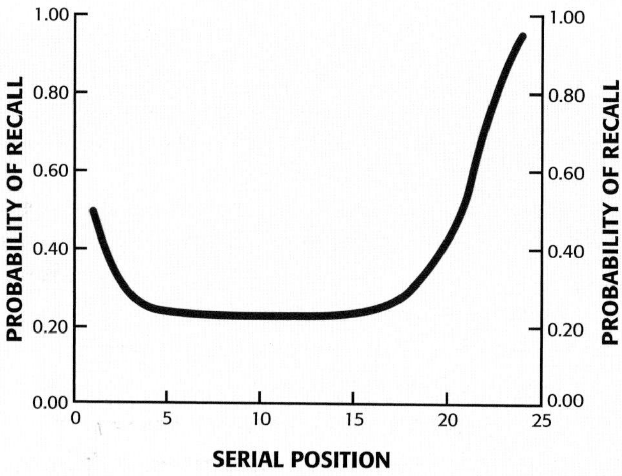

Figure 2.10 A serial position curve
From Murdoch (1962)

Thinking critically about psychology

Look back to your toolkit for evaluating studies (p5). Use this to consider the Murdock study. You may wish to think about whether the environment and the task given to participants are realistic and the extent to which the findings are useful.

A later study, by Glanzer and Cunitz (1966), also explored the serial position effect. They used different-length interference tasks between hearing the list and recalling the words (immediate recall or a 10- or 30-second delay). Fewer items were recalled from the end of the list with longer delays (see Figure 2.11). These results illustrate that interference prevents rehearsal and therefore affects the recency effect without changing the primacy effect. This supports the idea that STM and LTM are separate because it shows that one can be changed without affecting the other.

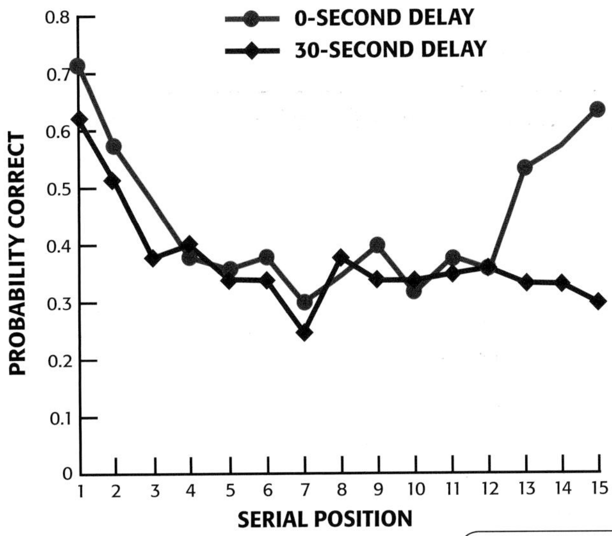

Figure 2.11 The serial position effect with a 30-second delay (after Glanzer & Cunitz (1966))

In common with much research into the function of memory, Murdock used a highly controlled laboratory experiment. This has obvious advantages in terms of the accuracy of the findings. However, in real life we often have to cope with information that is presented very quickly – perhaps in a lesson with a teacher who talks very fast – or with sources of interference such as the television or other people talking. Choose one of these effects and design an experiment that tests the primacy or recency effect in a more real-life situation. You might also want to think about using stimulus material that is more realistic than lists of numbers or one-syllable nouns.

Findings from people with amnesia

Amnesia refers to a severe loss of memory. In some cases, damage to very specific brain areas produces very specific memory deficits. Some such instances provide evidence that STM and LTM are independent facilities. Scoville & Milner (1957) described a famous case of a man referred to as HM (see *Classic Research*).

CLASSIC RESEARCH

Scoville WB & Milner B (1957) Loss of recent memory after brain lesions. *Journal of Neurology, Neurosurgery and Psychiatry* **20,** 11–21

Wicklegren WA (1968) Sparing of short-term memory in an amnesic patient

AIM

To describe the effects on memory of brain surgery for severe epilepsy on a male patient, HM, aged 27.

PROCEDURE

A detailed exploration and description of the effects of an operation to remove the inner parts of both temporal lobes of the brain (including the hippocampus). This case study used a variety of observations, interviews and tests to investigate the effects of the operation on HM's memory.

FINDINGS

After the operation, HM was virtually unable to form new memories for facts or events, although he could still learn new motor skills. He had only minor problems recalling events for the 11 years before the operation and no difficulty recalling events from earlier than that. Although he had severe problems with making new long-term memories, his short-term memory was relatively normal. He could hold the normal seven items in short-term memory but, unlike most people, he could not extend this by rehearsal.

CONCLUSION

HM had a severely damaged LTM but a largely unaffected STM. This suggests that short- and long-term memory are separate systems.

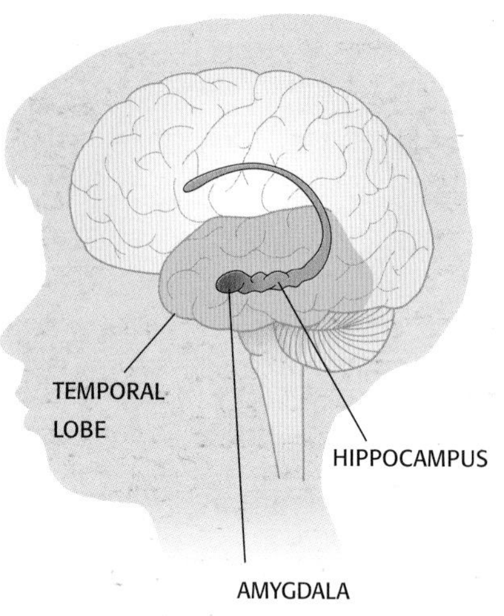

Figure 2.12 Cross-section of the brain showing temporal lobe and hippocampus

In a case similar to HM's, Wilson & Wearing (1995) and Wilson *et al.* (1995) studied a man called Clive Wearing whose brain was damaged by a virus. We can hear more about Clive Wearing from his wife in an article from the *Observer* (see *Media Watch*, p19).

As in the case of HM, Wilson's findings also suggested that STM could continue to function while the laying down of new LTM becomes impossible. In this case, however, there was also some impairment to the STM; it was even shorter in duration than normal. In both these cases there is clear impairment to LTM; no new long-term memories could be made although in both cases there was (at least some) STM capacity. This helps to confirm the conclusion that STM and LTM are separate stores.

You can read more about HM at the website http://www.brainconnection.com/topics/?main=fa/hm-memory. You can also read a recent publication by Suzanne Corkin, who has studied HM, at http://homepage.mac.com/sanagnos/corkin2002.pdf.

Type 'Clive Wearing' into www.youtube.com and look at one of the short video sections on Clive Wearing that illustrate his memory loss. Researchers, carers and his wife Deborah explain the limits of Clive's world. How long do you think Clive's memory lasts?

Thinking critically about psychology

The descriptions below are of investigations about memory. After reading each one, think carefully about your answers to the question(s) that follow.

1 Very little research has been conducted into the short-term sensory store for the sense of smell. Galan *et al.* (2006) found that bees have an STSS for odour and that it persists for approximately two minutes.
- Would you expect human STSS of odour to be similar and why or why not?

2 The amnesic HM (see p17) could not acquire new long-term memories such as how to walk home when he moved house. This type of fact learning is called declarative memory. He did, however, learn some new skills. For example, he learned to mirror-write (that is, write as if the letters were reflected in a mirror). Memories for movements are called procedural memories.
- What does this tell us about whether the LTM is a unitary (single) store?
- Does it contradict the conclusion that STM and LTM are separate? Explain your answer.

3 Smithson & Mollon (2006) investigated whether STSS was 'overwritten' by additional incoming information. They found that it was not.
- Is this a similarity or a difference between the STSS and STM?
- Why is it unlikely that STSS would be overwritten?

Strengths and weaknesses of the multi-store model

The multi-store model has stood the test of time and still remains an important overview of the human memory system. There is good evidence, from both experimental research and case studies, that we have separate memory stores with different properties – that is, they differ in terms of encoding, duration and capacity. For example, recent research using brain scanning has shown that different areas of brain activation are associated with the primacy and recency effects. This supports the idea that STM and LTM are different both in the way they operate and in their location in the brain (Wiswede *et al.*, 2007).

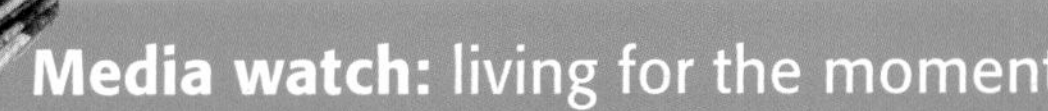

Media watch: living for the moment

source http://books.guardian.co.uk/departments/biography/story/0,,1396304,00.html

The death of yesterday

Deborah Wearing tenderly embraces her husband while he whispers sweet nothings. "You're beautiful", he tells his wife. "Absolutely gorgeous. I adore every thing about you. I could kiss you all day." Despite the chill January afternoon, the muddy garden, he twirls her around as though they're at a tea dance. They look and sound like they've just this moment fallen in love. Which, although they originally married 20 years ago, in a way they have.

In 1985 Clive was struck down with one of the most extreme cases of amnesia ever recorded. A virus destroyed a part of his brain essential for memory. It's not only most of the past from before the illness that he can't recall. It's practically everything since then. Every conscious moment is like waking up for the first time. New information, as Deborah describes it, "melts like snow, leaving not a trace". The one part of his previous life that he does remember – when he was a sought-after conductor and classical music producer for Radio 3 – is Deborah. Every time he sees her again, even if she's only been out of the room to make a cup of tea, he'll greet her with a rapturous hug.

Where once they used to share a smart, book-lined flat in Maida Vale, West London, now Clive lives in a care home and Deborah visits him from her new base in Reading, two hours' drive away. There's a laminated sign on his door: Clive's room. Inside, the drawers are labelled and a notice in big letters above the sink – 'Darling!' – reminds him to clean his teeth. On his piano, sideboard, bedside cabinet – so that they are the first things he sees every morning when he opens his eyes and tries to recall who and where he is – are pictures of Deborah …

It began with a headache and ended with Clive losing his mind. Fifty people a year are struck down with encephalitis or inflammation of the brain. Several viruses can cause it …

To begin with, following his physical recovery, he was manically euphoric. This could lighten the atmosphere: he'd jump out of wardrobes, waltz down the ward, play the hospital jester. On the whole this jocularity protected people from registering what had happened to his mind. Sometimes it was frightening. He'd be hard to control. He leapt out of the car on the dual carriageway. He was put on all kinds of tranquillisers – "liquid kosh", in Deborah's words.

Then his mood changed. "One day when I arrived from work, Clive's sobs were audible as soon as I was through the ward door", she recalls. "He was sitting on the edge of the bed, head bowed as though he were ashamed. He did not stop sobbing. I began to sob with him … He was inside himself, horrified, defeated by what he saw. All I could do was tell him that I loved him." He wept continually for over a month.

He became obsessed with finding out what had happened to him and yet what he didn't, couldn't, understand was that this knowledge was beyond his reach. His diaries show his desperation and also the articulate man he had so recently been. '7.46am: I wake for the first time. 7.47am: This illness has been like death till NOW. All senses work. 8.07am: I AM awake. 8.31am: Now I am really, completely awake. 9.06am: Now I am perfectly, overwhelmingly awake. 9.34am: Now I am superlatively, actually awake.'

Some fundamental facts he can remember. He knows that he is married but has no recollection of the wedding. He knows that he has children (from his first marriage) but cannot recall their names. When he was in hospital he knew his home phone number but had no memory of making calls …

Following the illness it's striking how they [Clive and Deborah] react in similar ways. Both are quick to laugh and cry, both find solace in music (the one thing Clive can still do is conduct and play the piano. The music miraculously seems to carry him along from one second to the next).

Interview with Deborah Wearing by Louise France, from the *Observer*, 23 January 2005

1 What ethical issues are raised by studying and publicising details of cases like Clive Wearing's?

2 What sort of memories does Clive Wearing still have undamaged?

Another line of evidence looks at the way that one part of the system (such as STM or LTM) can be affected independently of the other. Conners *et al.* (2000) compared the memory of individuals with Prader–Willi syndrome (a kind of inherited learning difficulty) to that of a group of participants without this condition who were matched in terms of age and intelligence. The participants with Prader–Willi syndrome were found to have relatively good LTM but poor STM compared to similar individuals without the condition. Like the evidence from amnesic patients, this suggests that STM and LTM are separate. However, continued research has shown that each of the stores is more complex than Atkinson and Shiffrin proposed.

One way in which the current understanding of the STM differs from the traditional ideas about STM is in the type of encoding used. Recent evidence suggests that, like LTM, the STM is capable of encoding material by meaning rather than just sound. Forde & Humphreys (2002) studied an amnesic whose errors illustrated that STM can make use of semantic encoding. The amnesic, FK, had difficulty learning information such as new words. He was compared on his recall of 'known' words (that is, those he had encountered before becoming amnesic) and newer, 'unknown' words. He made many more pronunciation errors when recalling unknown words. This suggests that the short-term memory relies not simply on an acoustic process of relaying words but on a degree of semantic processing too, which in the case of familiar words helped him to pronounce them correctly. The location of this error in STM was confirmed using serial recall. FK had a normal primacy effect for immediate recall but lacked a recency effect.

The short-term memory is often thought of as a single, limited-capacity acoustic store, but even as early as 1971 Atkinson & Shiffrin had identified that carrying out arithmetical calculations (a fairly similar task to their test of recalling of random five-letter consonants) did interfere with STM but other kinds of task, such as detecting a visual signal, did not. This suggested that the STM has separate systems for different kinds of information. Seitz & Schumann-Hengsteler (2000) demonstrated this distinction experimentally. Two different sources of interference were used to disrupt a mathematical task (doing multiplication sums): a visual source (tapping items on a map) and a sound-based source (listening to irrelevant speech). If the STM were a single store, either of these should disrupt recall but in fact only the speech did. This suggests that the STM separates visual and verbal information. In the next section we will consider an alternative explanation of the short-term memory that can account for these findings.

Our understanding of LTM has also changed. For example, distinctions are made between different kinds of long-term memories. Declarative memory (knowledge about general facts and events) is distinct from procedural memory (the learning of new physical skills). As we saw on p17, the amnesic HM was able to acquire skills (such as mirror drawing) but not new facts. Clive Wearing was still able to conduct and play the piano to a very high standard in spite of the terrible damage to his declarative memory. This is good evidence for the distinction between these two kinds of memory. Other amnesic patients have provided evidence for further distinctions, such as between semantic memory (declarative memory for general facts) and episodic memory (declarative memory for personal, autobiographical facts). Manes *et al.* (2001) studied an amnesic, RG, who, although able to recall and learn general facts and physical skills, was unable to recall episodic details about his own life. This finding supports the distinction between semantic and episodic memory.

Figure 2.13 Although the amnesic HM had no memory of having learned to, he acquired the new skill of drawing using a reflection in the mirror to guide him (Milner, 1970)

You are working on a neurological ward in a hospital. There are two patients with amnesia but they have different symptoms. One has normal long-term memories from the past but cannot make new long-term memories. The other has lost some LTM but has normal STM and can make new long-term memories. Which is which?

- Howie was knocked unconscious in a motorbike accident. He was brought to the hospital having been found wandering dazed along the roadside. He's been named 'Howie' because he was wearing a Howie's T-shirt when he was found. He doesn't remember his real name, where he lives or how he came to be on the road. You can, however, hold a normal conversation with him about what's in the news.
- Cheryl had a stroke a week ago and seems unable to grasp that she still needs to be in hospital. You keep explaining to her that she's not well but she keeps saying she's fine and wants to go home to feed her cat because it's teatime. She has no idea how long she's been on the ward. When visitors come to see her she recognises them, but once they've gone, she seems to forget that they have been to see her.

The working memory model

VISUO-SPATIAL SCRATCH PAD

CENTRAL EXECUTIVE

PHONOLOGICAL LOOP

Figure 2.14 The working memory model (Baddeley & Hitch 1974)

As we have seen, the idea of our STM being a single store appears to be too simple to account for our ability to carry out two different tasks that both require short-tem memory capacity without their interfering with each other. An alternative view, proposed by the working memory model (WMM), attempts to explain how we can do this. The WMM suggest that our 'temporary memory system' or primary memory is composed of several subunits. This model has been proposed in several different forms (e.g. Baddeley & Hitch, 1974; Baddeley, 1986, 2000).

The WMM suggests that primary memory is controlled by a 'central executive'. It is the job of the central executive to receive information in various sensory forms and to sort them before passing them on to the appropriate temporary store. Baddeley & Hitch (1974) proposed two of these temporary stores or 'slave units', each of which deals with a different kind of incoming information:

- *phonological loop* – this deals with linguistic and other sounds
- *visuo-spatial sketchpad*: visual information and data about three-dimensional space.

Phonological loop

The phonological loop is a sound-based store that holds items for 2-3 seconds, or longer if rehearsal is possible. This repetition does not have to be out loud, but without repetition the memory simply fades. Because each repetition of an item takes time, there is a limit to the amount that can be held in the phonological loop. If there is too much, it cannot all be rehearsed frequently enough to prevent decay. The capacity is therefore limited to the amount of information that can be repeated, and therefore refreshed, before it has faded away. This idea of the phonological loop explains two important things.

First, it explains why similar-sounding items tend to become muddled (see Conrad, 1964, p12). The phonological loop is essentially an acoustic store, so items with similar sounds, even if they have been presented visually, are likely to become confused. This is because there are few ways to tell them apart purely on the basis of their sound. For example, *p* and *v* may look very different, but as sounds they are very alike, so are hard to distinguish in the phonological loop.

Second, the limit to capacity is imposed by the time required for mental articulation. If items are 'long' – that is, if they take more time to 'say in your head' – fewer items will be processed before they start to decay. This accounts for the observation that a list of short words that are quick to say is remembered better than a list of long words. So, for example, 'helicopter, university, television, alligator, opportunity' would be harder to maintain in the phonological loop than 'sum, pay, wit, bar, hop' (Baddeley *et al.*, 1975). Furthermore, this difference disappears if sub-vocal rehearsal is prevented by having to repeat the word 'the', thus occupying the phonological loop. Baddeley (1996) suggests that the phonological loop is essentially limited to the amount that can be said in two seconds.

Visuo-spatial sketchpad

The visuo-spatial sketchpad (VSSP) provides a way to temporarily hold visual and spatial information and relationships between the two for example, remembering what two objects are and where they are in relation to each other. The fact that this system is separate from the phonological loop is shown by studies such as that by Seitz & Schumann-Hengsteler (2000) referred to on p20.

Baddeley (2003) reports an experience that illustrates how these aspects of working memory interact. While driving along a road listening to American football on the radio, he tried to visualise the game (as the sport was unfamiliar). As he did so, the car began drifting across the highway. He changed to a music channel! It appears that the spatial information that came from imagining the layout of the game interfered with his processing of the road layout, whereas the same did not happen when he was dealing with phonological information in the form of music. The involvement of both visual and spatial information in the sketchpad can be investigated experimentally by the creation of situations that cause interference between tasks requiring visual and spatial skills compared to verbal ones. Baddeley *et al.* (1973) required participants to remember a set of instructions. In one condition these could be memorised as a visual image (a spatial task); in another they had to be verbally rehearsed. Neither of these is difficult, but when the participant was also required to conduct a spatial task rather like Baddeley's driving (keeping a stylus on a moving spot of light), the spatial but not the verbal task interfered with performance. This finding shows how doing two things at once that both use the visuo-spatial sketchpad impairs performance but doing two things at once that use different systems does not. This work suggests that the two systems are separate.

RESEARCH NOW

McClelland A, Kemps E & Tiggemann M (2006) Practical applications of the working memory model. *Journal of Clinical Psychology*, **62**, 355–365

AIM	PROCEDURE	FINDINGS	CONCLUSION
To investigate the use of a working-memory-based technique for reducing food craving.	Fifty female undergraduates were asked to imagine their favourite foods. Each image was rated for vividness as well as their craving for it. A visuo-spatial task such as 'forehead tracking' was performed at the same time as the students were imagining the food images, and the change in craving was monitored. Forehead tracking involved the participant tapping an imaginary line across her forehead and following her finger with her eyes.	The visuo-spatial task of tracking reduced the vividness of images and the degree of craving.	The visuo-spatial task used up the resources of the sketchpad, leaving less opportunity for food visualisation. As forehead tracking can be done anywhere, not just in the lab, this may help to reduce food cravings at home.

How could you use the findings of this study to devise a technique for helping people who are trying to quit smoking?

Central executive

The central executive can use any form of encoding, and this part of the working memory model is seen as serving an organising function, to:

- attend selectively to a particular source of information
- achieve a balance between tasks when attention needs to be divided
- switch attention between different inputs.

The central executive directs information to the phonological loop or VSSP. Quite how it pays specific attention to different things, processes information or makes decisions about where to send that information processing is still unclear.

One way to investigate the action of the central executive is to study tasks that place demands on both processing and memory span. People with larger memory spans tend to find processing easier. Daneman & Carpenter (1980, 1983) devised a technique for testing working memory span. Participants were required to read several sentences and then recall the last word from each. Working memory span was indicated by the number of sentences that an individual could read and then accurately recall the final words. Daneman & Carpenter found that there was a strong relationship between working memory span and reading comprehension in university students.

Recent evidence looking at mathematical rather than language-related skills also supports the interaction of the phonological loop and the central executive. Imbo *et al.* (2007) investigated working memory by experimentally changing the difficulty of sums. When doing arithmetic in your head, you have to 'carry over' numbers (for example, from the 'units' to the 'tens' column). Think of how you would start to work out 17 × 17. You would start with 7 × 7, which is 49, so 9 goes in the units column and the 4 is carried over to the tens column. You need to hold the 4 in your head until you have done 7 × 1. This is where the phonological loop is used. The other functions – such as the calculation itself – involve the central executive. Imbo *et al.* varied the difficulty by altering the number of 'carries' over and the value of the carry. Both these factors increased the demand on working memory. Having more numbers to carry over and having bigger carry values made the sums more difficult. This suggests that the central executive plays a role in the processing associated with both 'holding' the number to be carried and storing its value.

Another role for the central executive is to interact with LTM. This is necessary in order to explain characteristics such as chunking (the increase in the capacity of STM if meaningful items are related). However, chunking cannot be explained if the central executive has no storage facility but is merely attentional. To overcome this difficulty, a more recent version of the working memory model (Baddeley, 2000) has proposed a third slave unit, the *episodic buffer* (Figure 2.15). This would enable the central executive to access information in LTM in order to integrate it with that in either of the other slave units.

CENTRAL EXECUTIVE

VISUO-SPATIAL SKETCHPAD | EPISODIC BUFFER | PHONOLOGICAL LOOP

VISUO-SPATIAL SEMANTICS | EPISODIC LTM | LANGUAGE

FLUID SYSTEMS

CRYSTALLIZED SYSTEMS

Figure 2.15 The current model of working memory, revised to incorporate links with long-term memory and the newly proposed episodic buffer (Baddeley 2000)

Strengths and weaknesses of the working memory model

The existence of the phonological loop and visuo-spatial sketchpad is well supported by experimental evidence, and they are clearly useful as explanations. For example, the observation that we are able to perform two different tasks (a visual and an auditory one) together but are unable to cope with two simultaneous inputs to the same slave system is easy to understand using this model. The model also has important practical applications, for example in clinical work (see the McClelland *et al.* study on p22). It also has important applications in education. Daneman and Carpenter's work on memory span for sentences has also helped us to understand one problem with reading skills in children. Oakhill *et al.* (1988) found that although some children could read quickly, their understanding of the text was poor. Those with a low working memory span found understanding links between information in the text more difficult than those whose working memory spans could hold more information. This shows that being able to retain and pay attention to more information at once helps in the task of processing for understanding.

Figure 2.16 Children with smaller memory spans have more problems with reading

However, not all evidence supports the idea of the phonological loop and the VSSP. According to the WMM, recall is affected by similarity of sounds and irrelevant speech because both are sources of interference for the phonological loop. If this were the case, measuring brain activity during such tasks should reveal activity located in the same areas, but it does not (Martin-Loeches *et al.*, 1997). Similarly with the VSSP: WMM suggests that this deals with both visual and spatial information. Therefore, if the VSSP were damaged, we would expect judgements about both vision and space to be impaired. Again, this is not so. Farah *et al.* (1988) describe a brain-damaged patient whose spatial processing was much better than his visual processing, suggesting that these are handled separately and are thus separate functional systems. In a review of studies using a range of techniques to relate brain activity to working memory function, D'Esposito (2007) concluded that working memory is not single system, nor does it have exclusive use of particular brain areas. He suggests that working memory is not localised to a specific area of the brain but is a property of the way that different areas of the brain, including an area at the front of the brain called the prefrontal cortex, interact.

Some recent evidence does, however, suggest that specific brain areas are associated with working memory function. Dolcos *et al.* (2007) compared activation in specific locations in the prefrontal cortex under three conditions of working memory rehearsal: these were memorising with distraction that was related to the task, memorising with distraction that was different from the task, and no memorising with distraction. The task-related distraction impaired performance compared to the other conditions, as predicted by WMM, and a corresponding difference in the pattern of brain activation was detected using a functional magnetic resonance imaging (fMRI) brain scan.

The central executive is still poorly understood and has tended to serve in part as a repository for any short-term memory functions that cannot otherwise be explained by the slave units of the working memory model. So, although it is described as a single system, it could well be composed of one or more independent or interacting components. Elsinger & Damasio (1985) describe a case study of a man with brain damage resulting from the removal of a brain tumour. His reasoning was good, his IQ was high and he coped well with interference during memory tasks – all of which indicated that his central executive was working well. However, his decision-making was very poor; for example, it took him hours to decide where to eat. If the central executive were a single system, we would expect all or none of these abilities to be affected, therefore this case suggests that it is not a single system.

In spite of these weaknesses, the WMM is able to explain many aspects of short-term memory function that the multi-store model cannot. For example, at a practical level it can help us to understand the effects of brain damage that leave some aspects of short-term memory unimpaired while others are severely affected. WMM also allows for rehearsal other than by verbal repetition, making the mechanisms for consolidating visual, spatial and other non-verbal items more understandable.

MEMORY IN EVERYDAY LIFE

We have already considered some studies of real-life memory, such as those of Linton (1975) and Huang (1997). Such studies help to illustrate that the findings of experimental research can generalise to remembering outside the laboratory. We have also looked at one example of the way that findings of psychological research can be usefully applied (McClelland *et al.*, 2006). In this section we will look at two more applications of research to improving memory and helping eyewitnesses.

Strategies for memory improvement

In this section you will need to learn about at least two strategies for improving memory.

Thinking creatively about psychology

Make a poster for Wrigley's chewing gum explaining how it can be beneficial to memory and justifying your claims.

The use of cues

How often do you go to find something, get distracted and forget all about it? The only thing that can then bring to mind the mission you were on is to go back to your original location. This is because the location acts as a prompt, reminding you of your intention. We call this trigger for recall a *cue*. In this example, the cue was the situation, so is called a context cue. The role of context cues has been demonstrated in many ways; for example, Abernethy (1940) found that students performed better in a test when it was conducted in the same classroom as they were taught in than if they were tested in a different location.

RESEARCH NOW

Baker JR, Bezance JB, Zellaby E & Aggleton JP (2004) Chewing gum can produce context-dependent effects upon memory. *Appetite* **43,** 207–10

AIM
To investigate whether the context of chewing gum would provide a sufficient cue to improve recall when the chewing cue was reinstated at recall.

PROCEDURE
Eighty-three students were randomly assigned to four learning groups offering each possible combination of learning and recalling with or without chewing gum. For two of these, the context for learning was the same as for recall; in the other two it was different (same context: gum–gum, no gum–no gum; different context: no gum–gum, gum–no gum). Each participant had two minutes to learn a list of 15 words. They then recalled them twice: once immediately after learning and again after a 24-hour delay. Those in chewing gum conditions were provided with Wrigley's Extra Spearmint Sugar Free Gum. They were given gum prior to the learning and/or recall opportunity and were asked to chew continuously through recall. Those in the gum–no gum group were warned in advance that they would have to remove the gum.

FINDINGS
Participants in the gum–gum group produced the best recall both immediately and after the delay. The recall of the other same-context group (no gum–no gum) was better than that of the different-context groups only in the delayed recall condition.

CONCLUSION
Chewing gum does produce a context-dependent effect, although this is more pronounced after a delay than following immediate recall.

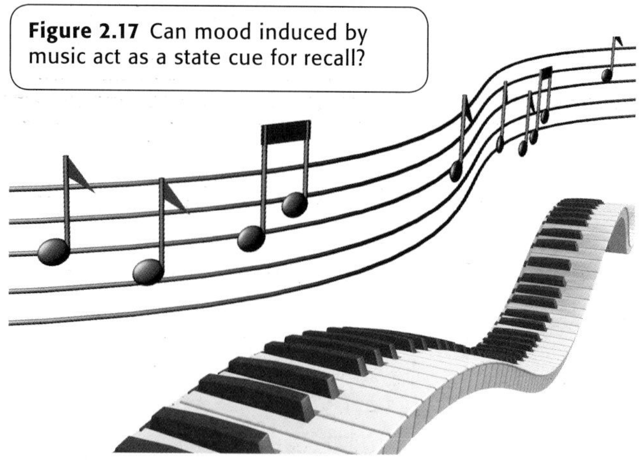

Figure 2.17 Can mood induced by music act as a state cue for recall?

Mead & Ball (2007) compared recall in contexts provided by different kinds of music. Music in a minor key is often perceived to be sad, whereas major keys sound happier. Mead and Ball compared recall for four learning/recall conditions: minor/minor, major/major, major/minor and minor/major. Conditions where the musical key at the time of learning was the same as at recall resulted in better recall. The researchers also measured mood and found that the music had altered the participants' feelings. It seems that the match in emotional state was responsible for the cueing of memories.

CLASSIC RESEARCH

Godden DR & Baddeley AD (1975) Context-dependent memory. *British Journal of Psychology* **66,** 325–331

AIM

To test the effect of context cues by investigating whether words learned in the same environment (either on land or under water) were recalled better than when the learning and recall environments were different.

PROCEDURE

Thirteen male and five female trained divers learned word lists presented on audiotape either on land or 20 feet under water. They then recalled the words in either the same or the other environment by recording them in pencil on a plastic-covered board. Each participant was tested in each of the four possible combinations of environments: land/land, land/water, water/water, water/land.

FINDINGS

Whether the words had initially been learned on land or under the water did not affect recall; accuracy was similar for the 'learn and recall on land' and 'learn and recall in the sea' participants, with a mean of 24.9 words. However, when recall took place in a different location as comparerd with learning, more words were forgotten (mean 17).

CONCLUSION

Context cues provided by the physical environment improved recall.

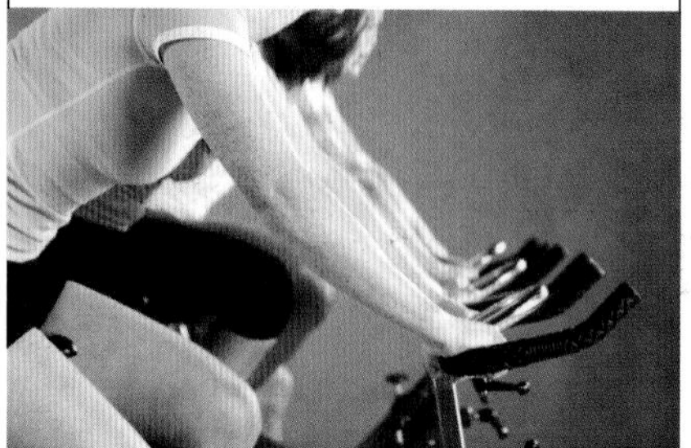

Figure 2.18 Exercise may act as a state cue for memory

An individual's mood or physical condition can act as a trigger for recall; these are called state cues. For example, a person who is calm when they learn new facts may find them difficult to recall if they are nervous; you may have experienced this in exams. Similarly, if you are afraid when you encode material – for example, as a witness to a murder might be – you may find it hard to recall when the fear has subsided. Such influences may be important in connection with the accuracy of eyewitnesses (see the next section). Evidence for state-dependent forgetting is provided by experiments such as that of Miles & Hardman (1998). They manipulated state using an exercise bicycle, with participants learning and/or recalling during rest or exercise. The findings showed that consistent resting or exercising states produced better recall than changes of state between learning and recall.

Media watch: smell of roses

source http://www.telegraph.co.uk/connected/main.jhtml?xml=/connected/2007/03/09/ecnore09.xml

Secret of exam success? Rosy memories

The fragrance of roses can be used to enhance memory, according to a remarkable study which heralds the day that smells are used to improve examination performance and other feats of recall.

Scientists have known for many years that sleep helps to consolidate newly-acquired memories, so powers of recall, from shopping lists to dance routines, are often improved after a good night's slumber.

In the journal *Science* a German team of neuroscientists reports a fascinating twist on the 'sleep on it' method of memory enhancement – the discovery that rose-scented recollections can further improve the ability to lay down memories …

During a memory game, the subjects received a puff of rose scented air through a nasal mask as they tried to remember the locations of pairs of cards. When the same smell was presented again during subsequent sleep, during a deep type of sleep called slow wave sleep, memory for the picture pairs was enhanced the next morning, and they were 15 per cent more successful in selecting correct pairs, compared to a control group that had not been exposed to rose scented memories during the night.

Although they didn't remember smelling roses in their sleep, the subjects who got the fragrant prompt remembered the matched pairs better the next day, getting 97 per cent correct compared to 86 per cent for subjects who'd received no odour during slumber. "The smell of the rose during sleep had reactivated the memories of the learned picture pairs, thereby enhancing the consolidation of these memories", said Prof Born. Follow up work revealed that the smell of roses alone during sleep was not enough to improve memory – it had to be present when subjects were trying to memorise the card pairs too. To probe deeper, the researchers also investigated brain activity when odours were used to revive memories. For this purpose, the participants had to sleep in a brain scanner at the University Clinic Hamburg-Eppendorf. Again, the odour was presented during learning and during subsequent slow-wave sleep.

The scanner revealed how a second exposure to the smell of roses during sleep activated the hippocampus, a brain structure that is critically involved in the storage of memories. What was fascinating was that the amount of activity was much greater in the hippocampus when the subject was exposed to the smell during deep sleep, as memories were being consolidated, than when awake. "It's the first study to really demonstrate that one can influence memory with stimuli that explicitly activate the hippocampus during sleep", comments Matthew Wilson of the Massachusetts Institute of Technology in Cambridge.

Roger Highfield, *Daily Telegraph*, 9 March 2007

1 What kind of cue do you think the smells are providing?

2 How does the information presented here help to explain Clive Wearing's memory problems?

In order to improve recall, context and state cues need to be as similar as possible to those of the original learning situation. In practical terms this means having an element of consistency between the classroom and examination hall. To provide context, you could revise with a mascot or a favourite pen – then carry it into the exam with you. To avoid a mismatch of state, you should aim to stay calm during the examination. This is clearly much better than trying to be scared while you are revising!

Figure 2.19 Does being in a familiar room or having a mascot help you to remember in exams?

Thinking creatively about psychology

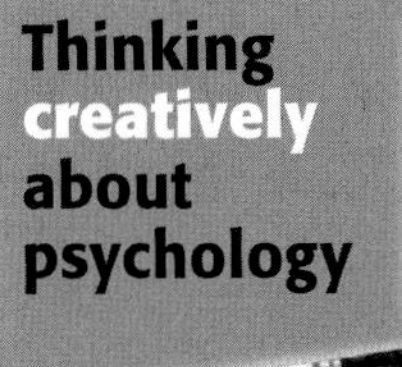

Different experiments have used exam halls, music, chewing, exercise and being underwater to test cue dependency. Think of another state or context cue and design an experiment to test whether it affects recall.

Cues can also be provided by meaningful items, such as category headings for lists of words. Tulving & Pearlstone (1966) played participants recorded lists of words to learn that included the category headings (although they were told not to try to remember these). They were then asked to recall the words either with or without the category headings as cues. If participants were given the headings for the categories to which the words belonged they recalled more than if these cues were not provided. We can be fairly certain that this effect was due to the category cues because if the participants who had been asked to recall without cues were subsequently given them, their recall immediately improved. This suggests that they had stored many more of the words than they were able to retrieve without cues. That is why you jot down brief notes in an exam before you start writing. These key words serve as cues for meaning.

Thinking creatively about psychology

Studies of memory cues suggest that in an exam situation you ought to be able to use cues to increase your recall of material. However, there has been very little research done into how students actually make use of cues in exams and how effective such strategies are. Put together a list of all the ways you might use state and context cues to improve your exam performance. Design an experiment to test the effectiveness of one of these cue-dependent strategies.

Using mnemonics

From our earlier discussion of cues, especially semantic ones, it may have already occurred to you that another way to improve memory would be to arrange information so that one item can act as a cue for another. This suggests that the organisation of material can affect how well it can be retrieved. Techniques for helping memory are sometimes called *mnemonics*. Many of these use an existing memory of a sequence to organise the to-be-remembered material. By imposing structure, you can recall the new items more easily. One way of imposing structure is the peg-word system. This uses numbers and rhyming words to provide a visual image on to which memories can be 'pegged'. By encoding them systematically, they are easier to retrieve, so more likely to be recalled. A common version of the rhyme goes:

One–bun
Two-shoe
Three–tree
Four–door
Five–hive
Six–sticks
Seven–heaven
Eight–gate
Nine–wine
Ten–hen

Ten to-be-remembered items can then be visualised, one with each noun. Let's say I want to remember five items I must pack for my holiday. I might visualise my passport inside a bun like a burger, my camera inside a shoe, my sunhat hanging from a tree, Euros flying out through a door and a beehive wearing my sunglasses. As I recite the rhyme, I am likely to be able to visualise the images complete with my holiday essentials. If it were important that I remember them in order, this would be possible too because I have imposed the list onto a sequential framework – the rhyme. Note that as well as being organised, the rhyme provides cues to assist with recall, which is why the system is so effective.

Figure 2.20 Using peg-word mnemonics can help recall

A similar mnemonic device involves using the changing visual scene associated with a familiar route. This can be a short journey, such as from your bedroom to the kitchen, or a long one, such as your journey to school or college. The important factor is that you must be able to recall clearly particular locations along the way. Items on the to-be-remembered list are then visualised at consecutive locations. Let's imagine I want to remember the things I need to take to school on Monday morning (exam paper, lunch, pencil case, DVD, teabags, purse, mobile, milk). I can then assign these to locations along my route from the front door to the back door. The exam paper is sticking through the letter box in shreds, my lunch is dangling from the lock like a bunch of keys, my pencil case is balanced on the end of the windowsill, the DVD is in the middle of the hall floor, there are teabags all over the stairs, my purse is resting on top of the lamp, my mobile is hanging on the door handle and there is milk flowing out of the back door. Because the route is familiar, I can imagine myself walking along seeing each of these objects in their unusual locations. The images are unique yet structured. The journey provides organised cues, and the images of the to-be-remembered items can be readily recalled.

However, both the peg-word and route methods only really work well when you are trying to remember lists of concrete nouns – that is, names of real things. If you were to try to apply them to more abstract ideas, like happiness or honesty, the visual imagery would be much more difficult and the systems less effective.

The importance of organisation cannot be overestimated. Our long-term memories are vast stores, and unless we store information in a structured way we are unlikely to be able to locate the information at a later date to retrieve it. The effectiveness of the two systems we have discussed rely on organisation in two ways. They provide links to existing memories, which ensures that the new information is encoded within a systematic framework, and they link information together so that retrieval of one item is likely to lead to the retrieval of another.

Problem solver

Your Gran is always complaining that she can't remember what she wants to buy when she gets to the shops. You've tried telling her to write a list but she says that makes her feel like a silly old woman and she wants to be able to learn the list before she goes. One day, you go to the supermarket with her and look around at the layout of the aisles and what is at the end of each one. There are things like the deli counter and the manager's desk that you know won't be moved around.

Your task is devise a way for your Gran to learn her shopping list using strategies such as cues or mnemonics to help her.

Eyewitness testimony

Eyewitnesses are individuals who have (knowingly or unknowingly) seen a crime or a situation that could contribute to the apprehension of criminals. They report evidence to the police and may also do so in court. The reliability of these testimonies is crucial to the criminal justice system. Psychologists are therefore concerned with the accuracy of eyewitness reports, factors that can reduce their accuracy, and procedures to improve their reliability.

Figure 2.21 The body of Jean Charles de Menezes lies in a train carriage after the shooting

LOOKING FURTHER

In 2005, Jean Charles de Menezes was mistaken for a terrorist by police officers and was shot dead at Stockwell Underground station in London. Many eyewitness reports of events are contradictory. Use the Internet to look up some examples of reports about this particular incident and identify some of the difference between testimonies.

You may wish to start with Wikipedia to find out a little more about the case. Some examples of sites offering news reports are:

- http://www.guardian.co.uk/attackonlondon/story/0,16132,1534138,00.html
- http://www.telegraph.co.uk/news/main.jhtml?xml=/news/2005/07/23/nshot23.xml
- http://observer.guardian.co.uk/focus/story/0,6903,1548808,00.html
- http://www.theage.com.au/articles/2005/08/17/1123958126875.html?from=top5

Factors affecting eyewitness testimony: anxiety

If you have ever witnessed a crime, think back to how you felt. Depending on the incident, you may have been very scared. How does fear affect recall? Research suggests that frightening situations may affect recall because attention is diverted away from the criminal. When a perpetrator is carrying a weapon, the witness focuses on that, rather than on their face (e.g. Loftus *et al.*, 1987). This means that witnesses who are frightened by criminals with guns or knives are less likely to be able to remember their faces. Recent evidence suggests that anxiety may shrink the witness' effective field of view. Oue *et al.* (2001) conducted an experimental study in which participants watched either an emotionally negative or a neutral event on a video screen. During the screenings, numbers appeared briefly in the four corners of the screen and participants were subsequently asked whether they had seen these numbers. Those who watched the emotionally negative event rated themselves as more tense and recalled fewer numbers than those who had seen the neutral event. This supports the idea that being anxious stops us from attending to details, so we cannot encode these into memory.

In the absence of weapons, more stressful crime scenes can sometimes produce higher levels of recall. Hosch and Cooper (1982) compared the accuracy with which participants could identify a thief from six photographs. The 'thief' had been seen entering the room while the participant was engaged in another task and had apparently stolen either the participant's own watch, another person's calculator, or nothing. The accuracy of participants' identification of the thief in the different conditions was 71 per cent, 67 per cent, and 33 per cent, respectively. Having something of their own stolen was most stressful for the participants but was also best recalled.

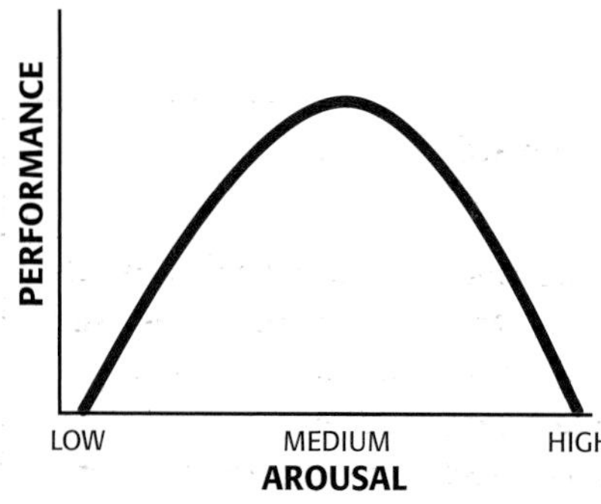

Figure 2.22 The Yerkes–Dodson law says that performance (e.g. recall) is best in moderately arousing conditions

Possible explanations for these varied results suggest that the relationship between anxiety (or arousal) and memory takes an inverted U shape, meaning that performance is poor in very high or very low arousal situations and best in conditions of moderate anxiety (this is known as the Yerkes–Dodson law). Ginet & Verkampt (2007) varied anxiety using pretend electrodes. They produced moderate arousal in one group of participants by telling them that the electrodes attached to their skin would administer electric shocks. A low-arousal group were told that the electrodes were just for recording. With the electrodes attached, all the participants watched a video of a road accident. One week later they were tested on their recall. The moderate-arousal group recalled more minor details than the lower-arousal group, supporting the inverted U relationship. Parker *et al.* (2006) investigated adult women's memory of a hurricane disaster. They also found an inverted U-shaped relationship between how badly an individual had suffered in the storm and their recall. Those women who had suffered most and least had the poorest memory (although recall by those with moderate and high anxiety did not differ significantly). This suggests that a measure of anxiety can improve memory in real situations.

Since it is unlikely that experimental situations can ever replicate the levels of anxiety experienced at real crime scenes, evidence from actual eyewitnesses is important. A study conducted by Yuille & Cutshall (1986) assessed the level of arousal and accuracy of testimonies from 13 witnesses to robberies or murders. One general finding was that witnesses reporting higher levels of arousal recalled fewer facts correctly than those with lower levels, although those with very high arousal levels were better than those with moderate levels. These findings do seem to support the Yerkes–Dodson law, but they could also be explained by the relationship with proximity to the crime: those who are closest will be most stressed but will also have the best view. This helps to explain why it is as important to study eyewitness testimony in the laboratory, where extraneous factors can be controlled, as it is to obtain real-world evidence.

An entirely different view suggests that anxiety could affect eyewitnesses by impairing retrieval of memories. One explanation of such effects is repression, an idea proposed by Freud (1894). In essence this is a theory of motivated forgetting – that is, it suggests that traumatic memories are made inaccessible to protect us from becoming upset by them. This idea would therefore suggest that in conditions of high anxiety, recall would be poor. Experimental evidence for this was provided by Köehler *et al.* (2002), who showed participants 50 words and recorded their galvanic skin resistance (GSR) to indicate the stress produced by each word. We would expect them to have repressed the words that induced the greatest change in GSR, as these would have been most stressful. This was what happened: the words that produced the biggest GSR changes were remembered worst. However, Hadley & MacKay (2006) presented 16 participants with stressful words such as *bitch* and *porn* and non-stressful words that were matched for length and frequency of use, such as *beer* and *pies*. The idea of repression would predict that the stressful words should be poorly recalled, but the opposite was found. The stressful words were more memorable! This finding does not show conclusively that repression does *not* occur, but it does suggest that under some circumstances the kind of memory we might expect to be repressed is in fact enhanced.

Thinking critically about psychology

Designing studies in this area is difficult for both practical and ethical reasons. Consider in particular the following:

1. **In the Hosch & Cooper study, results were interpreted as meaning that people were more stressed by having their own watch stolen than by someone else's calculator being stolen. What else other than stress might explain why they remembered a criminal better when the crime was against them?**
2. **In the Ginet & Verkamp study, why was it only possible to test people under conditions of low and moderate anxiety?**
3. **In the Hadley & MacKay study, results were interpreted as meaning that words like 'bitch' and 'porn' were more stressful than other words. However, in what other ways do they differ from more neutral words?**

Factors affecting eyewitness testimony: misleading information

Eyewitnesses' memories may be altered by encounters with misleading information. One line of research has been to investigate how the phrasing of questions can alter the way that a memory of an event is recalled. Early research, such as that by Carmichael *et al.* (1932), showed how verbal labels given at the time of encoding could alter subsequent memory. Their research demonstrated that identical figures presented with different words would be reproduced differently by participants (see Figure 2.23). Such evidence suggests that information is not recorded like a photograph but is 'rebuilt' from stored elements as it is retrieved – that is, that it is *reconstructed*. This reconstruction process can then be affected by misleading information. Much research into the effects of misleading information has been conducted by Elizabeth Loftus. From studies such as that by Loftus & Palmer (1974) and many other of her studies, it is clear that post-event information – that is, information provided after a memory has been encoded – can supplement or change existing memories. Recent research has shown that such misleading information can cause the loss of information from memory, too.

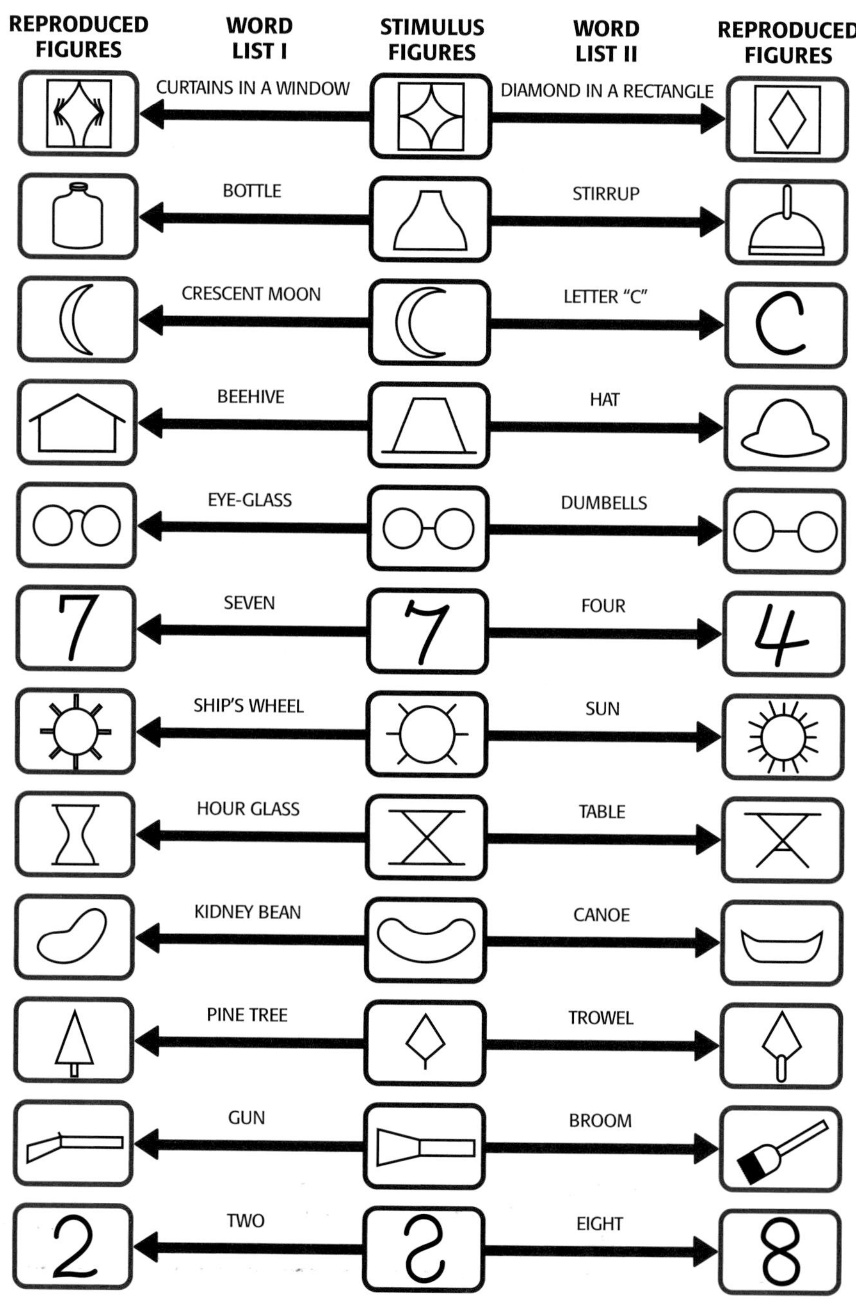

Figure 2.23 The figures used by Carmichael *et al.*

Loftus EF & Palmer JC (1974) Interaction between language and memory. *Journal of Verbal Learning and Verbal Behavior* **13** 585–9

AIM

To investigate the effect of a leading question about a car accident that implies damage on subsequent recall of speed and of damage caused.

PROCEDURE

Experiment 1 Forty-five students were shown clips of traffic accidents. They were then asked a series of questions about the film including one that read 'About how fast were the cars going when they … each other?' The missing verb was either *smashed, collided, bumped, hit* or *contacted.*

Experiment 2 One hundred and fifty students were shown a short film that included a four second scene of a car accident (which did not include any broken glass) and asked some questions. One-third of the participants were asked the critical question 'About how fast were the cars going when they smashed into each other?' A third were asked the same question but with the word 'hit', and the final third were not asked about speed. A week later the participants were given another questionnaire including the critical question 'Did you see any broken glass?'

FINDINGS

Experiment 1 Table 2.1 shows that more severe verbs resulted in higher estimations of speed.

Experiment 2 Table 2.2 shows that with a more severe verb, participants were more likely to report having seen (non-existent) broken glass.

Table 2.1 Speed estimates

verb	mean speed estimate (mph)
smashed	40.5
collided	39.3
bumped	38.1
hit	34.0
contacted	31.8

Table 2.2 Responses to 'Did you see any broken glass?'

verb condition	response	
	Yes	No
smashed	16	34
hit	7	43
control	6	44

CONCLUSION

The combined findings of the two experiments show that the leading information of the verb in the speed question affects the way in which the event was represented in memory. Over time, the misleading information from the question was integrated with the original memory so that, at retrieval, the memory was reconstructed to include this new information. This resulted in the inclusion of false memory of the presence of broken glass as well as speed.

RECONSTRUCTED MEMORIES

ABOUT HOW FAST WERE THESE CARS GOING WHEN THEY HIT EACH OTHER?

AVERAGE SPEED ESTIMATE 34 MILES PER HOUR 14% 'RECALLED' BROKEN GLASS.

ABOUT HOW FAST WERE THESE CARS GOING WHEN THEY SMASHED INTO EACH OTHER?

AVERAGE SPEED ESTIMATE 40.5 MILES PER HOUR 32% 'RECALLED' BROKEN GLASS.

Figure 2.24 People's recollections of car accidents are affected by how questions are worded

Thinking critically about psychology

Using your toolkit for evaluating studies (p5), critically consider the Loftus & Palmer study. In particular, you might like to consider the representativeness of the participants, the realism of the task and environment, the social sensitivity and the usefulness of the findings to real life.

To demonstrate how loss of details from memory can arise, Wright *et al.* (2001) used drawings of a restaurant scene, then asked participants to read descriptions from which critical elements (such as a guitar player or taking an order) had been omitted. Like the questions used by Loftus and Palmer (1974), the descriptions acted as misleading post-event information. When participants read descriptions that omitted critical scenes, they were less likely to recall these events.

Figure 2.25 One of the restaurant scenes used by Wright *et al.*

OVER TO YOU

Are you a good eyewitness? The website below will show you a film (you will need *Real Player*, *QuickTime* or *Windows Media Player* to view it). You will then be asked questions about the film and told whether you were correct: http://www.youramazingbrain.org/testyourself/eyewitness.htm. Have a go and find out!

It might seem possible that, rather than actually altering memory, post-event information simply provides participants with a way to answer questions to which they have (or believe they have) forgotten the answer. This explanation suggests that perhaps the participants are simply using the post-event information to please the experimenter. However, Lindsay (1990) has shown this is not the case. First, participants were shown slides of a maintenance man stealing money and a calculator from an office while listening to a woman's commentary. They then heard a misleading description of the events they had seen. This description was either immediate and in the same voice as the original commentary or delayed by two days and given by a male voice. They were finally told (truthfully) that any information in the description was wrong and were given a test of memory. Being told that the information in the description was wrong should have prevented errors. However, their results showed that the misleading description could affect memory but only if it was similar to the source (that is, in the same-day narrative/same-sex condition), suggesting that the effect of post-event information is genuine.

Thinking practically about psychology

Police officers have to interview witnesses who often can't seem to recall much about the perpetrators. Use the ideas in this chapter to explain why this might be so. How might the police use cues to elicit more information?

LOOKING FURTHER

You can find out more about the work of Elizabeth Loftus on eyewitness testimony from her websites. Try to explain the findings of other studies in terms of the effect of misleading information: http://faculty.washington.edu/eloftus/index.htm

Another source of information about criminal psychology is Gary Wells' website. This includes an interactive eyewitness testimony simulation:

http://www.psychology.iastate.edu/faculty/gwells/homepage.htm

Factors affecting eyewitness testimony: age of the witness

Children as witnesses

Children may be required to give evidence, either as witnesses or as victims, but how reliable are they? According to Brennan & Brennan (1988), six- to-fifteen-year-olds failed to understand one-third of questions asked by lawyers in court.

Carter *et al.* (1996) looked at the effect of the style of spoken language used in the courtroom ('legalese'). Children aged five to seven were more likely to answer incorrectly if asked a question in legalese (such as 'To the best of your knowledge, X, in fact, kissed you, didn't she?') than if they were asked a simpler question (such as 'X kissed you, didn't she?'). Note that the use of 'didn't she?' (a 'tag') in both these questions makes them leading, which, as we have seen, is likely to increase errors. Examples such as these would be possible questions in cases of alleged child sexual abuse in which young people are required to give evidence. The role of such tags in questions aimed at children in abuse cases was investigated by Krackow & Lynn (2003). Using a game of Twister, they set up two conditions in which children aged four years to five years ten months were either touched (on their hands, arms, calves or feet) or not touched by an assistant ('Amy'). One week later, the children were asked one of two questions. More children said "yes" to "Amy touched your bottom, didn't she?" than to "Did Amy touch your bottom?". Whether or not there had been any physical contact during play made no difference to the children's answers. Most who asked the direct question responded correctly (with "No") but those asked the question with the tag seemed to be responding randomly, with almost half giving an incorrect "Yes" answer.

Figure 2.26 Asking children misleading questions about a game of Twister produces incorrect answers

In experimental settings, children tend to change their answer if they are asked the same question twice (e.g. Samuel & Bryant, 1984). If this is the case in real life as well as in laboratory situations, it has important implications for the accuracy of child witnesses. Using transcripts of police interviews with children aged four to nine, Blades & Krähenbühl (2006) identified the repetition of questions that the child witness had been unable to answer. This suggested that inaccuracies may be introduced in the interviewing process. In order to investigate this possibility, Krähenbühl & Blades (2006) gave seven- to- nine-year-old children a 15-minute live presentation and then interviewed them using two kinds of questions: some they could answer and others that were unanswerable. When a question was repeated, the children often changed their answer, making their accuracy worse. They were more likely to change it in the case of unanswerable questions. They then generally stuck to this new answer, even if it was incorrect. This shows that both repetition of questions and persisting with questions that the child cannot answer result in less accurate testimonies.

Lewis *et al.* (1995) investigated the effect of leading questions on young witnesses. Children aged three to four years were shown photographs of adult males arranged like a line-up. One of these was labelled 'Daddy' (none was actually their father). When the children were subsequently asked, 'Is this man your daddy?' in a sequence of pictures, 29 per cent misidentified the previously labelled individual as 'daddy'. On one hand, this shows that young children are susceptible to the effects of leading questions. On the other hand, it also shows that the number affected by this manipulation is relatively small.

Memon A, Holliday R & Hill C (2006) Can stereotypes affect recall? ***Memory*****, 14,** 104–14

AIM

To see whether stereotypes affect children's recall of events.

PROCEDURE

Children aged five read one version of a story about a character called Jim by their class teacher. There were three different versions. They described Jim Step as either:

- careful (positive stereotype) – for example, pushing a chair in so he didn't trip
- clumsy (negative stereotype) – for example, dropping a teddy and getting it dirty
- neither careful nor clumsy (neutral).

A few days later 'Jim Step' visited their class, introduced himself and performed some neutral activities (such as showing them a picture of his dog and playing the flute). One and three days later the children were read a description about Jim's visit by an experimenter. This was the same for all groups and contained misleading details; some were positive and some negative. Three days after this, the children were tested on two sets of yes/no questions by a different experimenter. It was made clear to the children that one set related to what happened during Jim's visit, the other to what they were told about Jim's visit.

FINDINGS

Children who had heard the positive story about Jim gave answers that tended to fit the stereotype in the story; they were more likely to say 'yes' to positive statements about Jim. The negative stereotype did not bias the children's responses.

CONCLUSION

Positive (but not negative) stereotypes affect children's judgements about people. This suggests that people who have stereotypically positive features will be less likely to be considered guilty by children.

Figure 2.27 Even when behaviour is neutral, stereotypes can affect recall of events

Thinking practically about psychology

In 2003, Ian Huntley was convicted of the murder of two ten-year-old girls the previous year. He was the caretaker at their school and well liked by adults and children in the village. What light do the findings of Memon *et al.* (2006) shed on such situations?

Older adults as eyewitnesses

There is a common belief that our memories fail with age. Is this belief supported by evidence and, if so, does it affect the ability of older adults to offer reliable eyewitness accounts? Whether or not such differences exist, a related issue is whether such assumptions affect the way that testimonies from older adults are treated. Wright & Holliday (2005) assessed police beliefs about older adults (aged over 60 years) as witnesses. Their survey showed that the officers perceived older witnesses to be less reliable and less thorough than younger ones. Experimental evidence from tests such as recall of word lists and of sentences suggests that this perception is correct. The influence of this decline on eyewitness testimony has also been investigated.

Brimacombe *et al.* (1997) showed elderly and younger adults a video of a crime and then recorded their testimonies, also on video. The older adults were less accurate than the younger adults at reporting what they had seen. Also, when the recordings of their testimonies were viewed by other participants, they were rated as less credible. Their testimonies were then transcribed and judged by participants who were provided with false information about the witnesses' ages. The doubts about the older witnesses' statements remained even when the judges did not know their actual age. This suggests that the differences were not the result of negative stereotypes of the capacity of older adults as eyewitness. If such a difference exists, what can be done to improve the reliability of testimonies given by older adults?

Looking at the accuracy of testimonies from young (17–31), young-old (60–74 years) and old-old (75–95 years) adults, Wright & Holliday (2007) obtained similar results to those of Brimacombe *et al.*. Over the three age groups, recall became less complete and less accurate. However, when they used cognitive interviews (see below) in place of standard police interviews, both groups of older adults recalled significantly greater detail without giving any more pieces of false information. We can look now in more detail at cognitive interviewing.

Factors affecting eyewitness testimony: cognitive interviewing

Evidence such as that from Loftus' experiments has shown us that eyewitnesses are prey to the effects of leading questions, and our discussion of cues has shown that these can help to improve recall. The cognitive interview makes use of ideas such as these from cognitive psychology to improve the accuracy of eyewitness reports.

Geiselman *et al.* (1985) identified four key principles for the cognitive interview. It should aim to enable the witness to:

- recreate both the internal (state) and environmental (context) cues present at the time of the crime (for example, the how they felt and aspects of the surroundings such as smells and noises as well as what they could see)
- report everything they can remember about the incident even if the details seem irrelevant or fragmented (the inclusion of apparently trivial details can cue other memories)
- provide details of the incident in different orders, not just chronologically (e.g. from the time of the first gunshot or starting before they realised there was even a problem)
- provide details of the incident from different perspectives (e.g. what it would have looked like as seen from where the offender was standing or from outside).

Like Wright & Holliday (above), Geiselman *et al.* (1985) found that the cognitive interview allowed witnesses to recall more detail without loss of accuracy. These principles have been extended in the enhanced cognitive interview (Fisher *et al.*, 1987) which, additionally suggests that:

- distractions should be minimised (including the intrusion of police questions)
- the witness should be encouraged to speak slowly
- pauses between one question and the next should be tailored to suit the individual
- witness anxiety should be reduced.

Fisher *et al.* (1987) found that the enhanced cognitive interview was even more effective than the basic cognitive interview, with many more correct statements being recalled. However, this technique also tended to produce more 'false positives' – that is, recall of incorrect items. Ginet & Verkampt (2007) (see p30) found that cognitive interviewing improved recall for both low- and high-arousal participants in an experimental setting.

This technique has also been applied to real-world settings, such as in Miami in the Robbery Division of the Metro-Dade Police Department. Here,

Fisher *et al.* (1989) found that training police officers in the use of enhanced cognitive interview techniques produced an increase of 46 per cent in the number of statements that could be identified in tape recordings of interviews with witnesses. Where these statements could be checked against that of a second witness, they were found to be over 90 per cent accurate.

Two key problems with the cognitive interview relate to time delay and the effectiveness of context-reinstatement. First, witnesses often need to recall information that happened a relatively long time ago, but the cognitive interview is more effective when used closer to the time of the crime than after a long delay (Geiselman & Fisher, 1997). Second, the provision of cues has a greater effect on recall than on recognition. Therefore, although reinstating state and context might help witnesses to retrieve some information, it is likely to be unhelpful in enabling them accurately to identify the perpetrator in a line-up (Groeger, 1997).

Thinking creatively about psychology

Put together a leaflet or web page of information designed to help anyone, for example a police officer or barrister, who has to work with eyewitnesses. You will need to include information about the sort of things that affect the accuracy of eyewitness memory. Make some recommendations about what professionals can do and avoid doing in order to make the testimony of witnesses as accurate as possible.

CHAPTER SUMMARY

- Memories need to be encoded and stored. Remembering is successful retrieval; forgetting is when we cannot retrieve information.
- The multi-store model suggests that memories are moved through three different stores: the short-term sensory store, the short-term memory and the long-term memory. These stores differ in the way they encode information and in their duration and capacity.
- The short-term sensory store (STSS) uses a modality-specific code (information is held in the store corresponding to the sense through which it enters the memory), so there are different stores for different sensory systems: the iconic memory (vision), the echoic memory (sound) and the haptic memory (touch). Each store has a very short duration and a moderately large capacity.
- Information in short-term memory (STM) is encoded acoustically (that is, it uses a sound-based code). The capacity is small, only 7 ± 2 chunks of information, and the duration is short, about 18–30 seconds unless rehearsal is continuous.
- The long-term memory (LTM) uses a semantic code (based on meanings) and has a very large capacity and long duration; long-term memories last many years.
- The multi-store model is supported by evidence that illustrates these differences in encoding, duration and capacity.
- Other evidence also suggests that STM and LTM are separate stores. Murdock (1962) demonstrated the serial position effect. This shows that words at the beginning of a list are rehearsed more and transferred to LTM, the words in the middle are pushed out by new words, and those at the end, which stay in STM, are also recalled well.

- Some people with amnesia, such as HM, have brain damage that prevents them from making new long-term memories but they still have a short-term memory. As one store can be affected without the other, this suggests that STM and LTM are different.
- There is also evidence that contradicts the multi-store model. It has been shown that STM can use a semantic as well as an acoustic code and that it consists of more than one store. We can perform visual and acoustic tasks independently without them interfering with each other, which would not be possible in a single store.
- Long-term memory also exists in different forms, including declarative (fact) memory and procedural (skills) memory. Declarative memories can be further identified as either semantic (general facts) or episodic (personal facts), so LTM is much more complex than just a single store.
- An alternative explanation for STM is the working memory model. This suggests that a central executive directs two other stores, the visuo-spatial sketchpad (VSSP) and the phonological loop (PL).
- The PL is a sound-based store lasting two to three seconds, or longer with rehearsal. Its capacity is determined by both the number of items and how long they take to say; it can hold more 'short' words than long ones.
- The VSSP can hold both spatial and visual information but these both use up capacity. A spatial and visual task performed together will interfere, but an auditory one will not, as the PL is a separate store.
- The central executive directs information to and switches attention between the PL and VSSP. If the central executive is 'busy', performance falls.
- The central executive also interacts with the LTM and a new store, the episodic buffer, has been added to the working memory model to indicate this.
- The working memory model is supported by evidence that shows that two tasks requiring the same part of memory (e.g. two auditory tasks) cannot easily be performed together but two different ones (e.g. an auditory and a visual task) can. Evidence from brain scanning during matching distraction supports this distinction.
- The model also helps to explain real-world issues such as the problems some children have learning to read.
- Not all evidence supports the working memory model. If brain damage affects visual memory functions – that is, it has damaged the VSSP – spatial memory should be impaired too, but this is not always the case. Similarly with the central executive. It is possible to damage some of its functions, such as decision-making, without affecting others, such as coping with interference.
- Memory can be improved by using cues. Being in the same state or context during recall as you were during learning helps you to remember. States such as exercise/rest and contexts such as land/sea act as cues to recall. Meaningful items such as category headings can also help recall.
- Mnemonics are memory aids. They can assist recall by structuring information semantically or visually using familiar or easy-to-remember rhymes or patterns. These act as cues to help retrieval.
- Eyewitness testimonies are often unreliable. Factors affecting accuracy include the presence of weapons, the level of arousal or anxiety, leading questions and age of the witness. Witness accuracy can be improved by avoiding leading questions and by using cognitive interviewing.

Testimonies are more accurate if the witness is in a moderate state of anxiety than if their arousal level is very high or very low. High anxiety may prevent retrieval of memories through repression, but some kinds of stressful stimuli are well remembered.

- Leading questions cause memories to be reconstructed. By providing post-event information they can change memories, resulting in addition or loss of details.
- Child witnesses often misunderstand questions asked in court or by the police and so give inaccurate answers, and can be readily misled by stereotyped information and by leading questions. When questions are direct, however, they are very accurate.
- The police believe that older adults are less accurate, and this appears to be the case. Like children, older adults are better when the interview situation makes being accurate more possible, such as with cognitive interviewing.
- Cognitive interviews improve recall by making use of cues. Witnesses are asked to think about their state and context at the time to provide cues to trigger recall. They also use cues provided by the witness by asking them to describe even minor details, to report the events in different orders and to describe what could have been seen from different perspectives.
- During a cognitive interview, distractions are minimised, the witness is asked to speak slowly, there are pauses between the questions and the interviewer aims to reduce witness anxiety.
- Although cognitive interviewing produces an increase in 'false positives' (recall of additional false items), there is a bigger increase in the amount of correct information recalled compared to a standard interview.

What do I know?

1 (a) The working memory model is a model of short-term memory. Some of the following concepts relate to the working memory model. Use them to complete the table to describe the different parts of the model.

- all types of information
- central executive
- long-term memory
- images and shapes
- phonological loop
- sounds and speech
- holds 7 ± 2 chunks of information
- visuo-spatial sketchpad (3 marks)

Name of the component	The type of information it can process

(b) Peter is using a map to show Jane where he lives. Using the working memory model, outline how the information from the map would be processed by Peter. (4 marks)

2 (a) Outline key features of the multi-store model of memory. (6 marks)

(b) Explain **one** weakness of the multi-store model. (2 marks)

3 Derek's little brother Fred is nine years old and keeps coming home from school without his bag, coat, lunch box, PE bag or homework. Each day he can remember some of the things but not all of them. Derek has been studying psychology and has decided to help Fred to remember everything he needs to put in his bag before he leaves school.

(a) Outline **two** strategies that Derek might use to help Fred to remember all the items and explain why each of the strategies you suggest should work. (4 marks)

(b) Evaluate **one** of the strategies you have described in part (a). (4 marks)

4 (a) Explain one way in which anxiety may affect eyewitness testimony. (3 marks)

(b) Describe how the factor of age can affect eyewitness testimony. (4 marks)

(c) Evaluate research into eyewitness testimony. (12 marks)

5 The police service has asked a group of psychologists to test the use of the cognitive interview with six-year-old children. The psychologists decide to compare the children's recall of some pictures they are shown when being read a story at school. Each child is tested twice. The first week they are read a story and given a standard interview, the next week they hear a different story and are given a cognitive interview.

(a) What experimental design is being used in this investigation? Tick the correct box. (1 mark)

Independent groups ☐
Repeated measures ☐
Matched pairs ☐

(b) Outline one problem the psychologists might encounter in this situation because they are using this design. (2 marks)

(c) Describe how the problem you outlined in (b) could be avoided. (2 marks)

CHAPTER 3

Developmental Psychology – Early Social Development

Thinking ahead

By the end of this chapter you should be able to:

- **explain the origins of modern attachment theory**
- **outline and critically consider John Bowlby's theory of attachment**
- **describe and evaluate Mary Ainsworth's work on attachment types including the *Strange Situation* test and maternal sensitivity hypothesis**
- **outline some of the possible consequences of attachment type, for example quality of adult relationships, mental health and criminality**
- **explain cultural variations in attachment, including the work of Van Ijzendoorn and Kroonenberg**
- **understand the distinctions between deprivation, privation and institutionalisation**
- **describe and evaluate research into institutionalisation and privation**
- **consider critically research into the effects of day care on social development**
- **apply the findings of day care research to developing effective child care policies**

DEVELOPMENTAL PSYCHOLOGY

Developmental psychology is the branch of psychology that deals with how the human mind and behaviour develops throughout our lives. Much of the work developmental psychologists do is concerned with child development. This chapter is about the way young children form relationships with other people and what can go wrong with those relationships.

Many developmental psychologists believe that the quality of early emotional attachments has a huge effect on a child's later development. The first half of this chapter is concerned with explaining how attachments form and how variations in the quality of attachment can affect a person's development. The second half of the chapter is concerned with the sorts of events that may disrupt early attachments, such as severe abuse or being brought up in an institution. We also consider the debate over the possible effects on a child's development of spending time in day care.

Figure 3.1 The quality of our early relationships can affect the rest of our lives

ATTACHMENT

KEY TERMS

proximity seeking – staying close to an attachment figure

secure base behaviour – regularly returning to an attachment figure when exploring

separation anxiety – anxiety at being apart from an attachment figure

stranger anxiety – anxiety in the presence of strangers

An attachment is a close two-way emotional relationship between two people. We form attachments throughout our lives, but psychologists are particularly interested in our earliest attachments, formed in infancy with our main carer or carers. We tend to behave in particular ways towards our attachment figures, regardless of our age. We tend to want to be physically near them (psychologists call this proximity seeking). We get distressed when we are separated from them for long periods and we tend to use them as a 'secure base'. Secure base behaviour involves exploring the world but regularly coming back to our attachment figures, taking our sense of security from them. As young adults, for example, most of us like to spend time being independent of our parents, however, we also tend to enjoy coming home to them. Some attachment behaviours are age specific. Notably, young children show *stranger anxiety* (fear and distrust of unfamiliar adults) and *separation anxiety* (a dislike of being apart from the attachment figure).

Early approaches to explaining attachment

Psychology has existed since the late Nineteenth Century. Explanations for how and why babies and their carers (in particular their mothers) become attached to one another have been around almost as long. We can look at three early approaches to studying and understanding the form of mother–infant attachment.

Figure 3.2 This child is showing classic attachment behaviour

Learning theory

Learning theory dominated psychology for the first half of the Twentieth Century. Its basic idea is that our behaviour is acquired through experience. Two types of learning are especially important. First, we learn to respond to new events and people in the same way as we already respond to other events. This happens when the new event happens at the same time as the other. This type of learning is called classical conditioning. We also learn to repeat behaviours that lead to some sort of reward or, to use a technical term, *reinforcement*. This is called *operant conditioning*.

Figure 3.3 Babies love food, so learning theory says they will love their feeder too

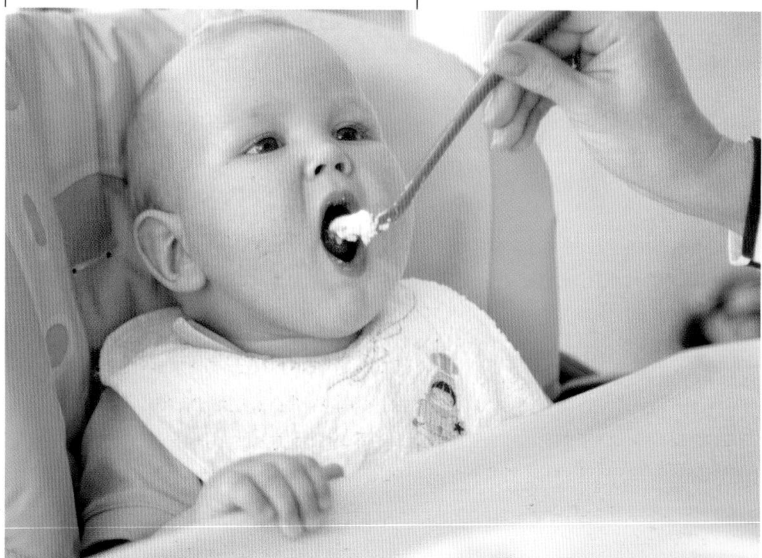

Figure 3.4 Our childhood relationships serve as prototypes for future ones

Learning theorists suggested that attachment develops between a baby and its main carer because the carer provides food. Dollard & Miller (1950) estimated that in a child's first year the child is fed around 2000 times, mostly by their primary carer. This allows for plenty of opportunity for conditioning to take place. A baby loves being fed! Once being fed takes place often enough in the presence of the same person, the baby will learn to respond to them as they would to their milk, therefore to love them. This is an example of classical conditioning. Operant conditioning can explain why adult carers learn to love babies. Whenever a baby cries and the carer responds by feeding or cuddling them, leading to the baby ceasing to cry, that loving behaviour is reinforced.

Although this sounds like a credible idea at first, there are some key reasons why very few psychologists believe nowadays that attachment can really be explained by conditioning. First, attachment is a very emotionally intense experience accompanied by complex behaviours. Conditioning best explains how we learn simple behaviours and simple emotional responses. Second, attachments of some sort generally develop between babies and those who meet them regularly, regardless of whether they are the people that feed them. Third, experiments by Harry Harlow (see p46) show that, when frightened, isolated baby monkeys ignore their feeding apparatus and seek comfort from a soft, cuddlable object. This shows that their attachment behaviour was directed towards something cuddly rather than food related, and so food alone does not lead to attachment.

Psychoanalytic theory

Psychoanalysis is an approach to psychology that sees adult experiences as rooted in childhood experiences and, in particular, early family relationships. Freud (1905) suggested that child development went through a series of stages. In the first year, known as the oral stage, the child is very focused on suckling as a source of both food and comfort. Because a single person, usually the mother, provides the bulk of both food and emotional nurture during the first year, the child invests a great deal of emotion in her and she becomes the 'primary love object'. Freud saw the infant–mother relationship as the prototype for future relationships.

If the oral stage is managed successfully, the child acquires the capacity to have emotionally close relationships. However, disruption to the oral stage could spoil the future relationships of the child.

Like the learning theorists, Freud was thinking very much in terms of a link between feeding and attachment. The two theories are sometimes collectively called the 'cupboard love' approach to attachment. However, rather than seeing love as a learned response, Freud saw it as an instinct, present from birth and waiting to be expressed towards a particular person. This is slightly closer to modern ideas of attachment. Freud's student Erik Erikson (1950) developed Freud's ideas about child development, saying that each stage of development has a task that has to be achieved in order for the child to continue to develop healthily. To Erikson, the child's task in their first year is to develop a sense of trust in the world through forming a good relationship with the mother.

Ethological theory

Ethology is the study of animal behaviour. In the early Twentieth Century a number of ethologists made observations about the relationships between infant animals and their mothers. Lorenz (1935) described the process of imprinting, in which newly hatched chicks attach themselves to the first moving object they see (most commonly their mother) and follow it wherever it goes. This allows them to keep relatively safe. Lorenz identified a critical period in which imprinting needs to take

KEY TERMS

critical period – a time during the development of a child or animal when an event must happen if normal development is to take place

instinct – an inborn tendency to behave in a particular way

place. If imprinting does not occur within the critical period, chicks will not attach themselves to a mother figure. He also investigated the relationship between the nature of the adults that young animals encountered and their preferences as adults. Most dramatically, Lorenz (1952) described the case of a peacock reared in the reptile house of a zoo. As an adult, this bird would only direct courtship behaviour towards giant tortoises!

Perhaps the most significant work in the area of infant attachment using animals was conducted by Harry Harlow (1958). Harlow and colleagues had reared Macaque monkeys and observed that when separated from adult monkeys and kept in a bare wire cage, newborn monkeys usually died within a few days. However, when given a cloth to cuddle they tended to survive. Harlow set out to test the idea that a soft object serves some of the psychological functions of a mother monkey. His original experiment is described here in *Classic Research*.

CLASSIC RESEARCH

Harlow H (1958) The nature of love. *American Psychologist* **13,** 673–85

AIM

To test cupboard love approaches to attachment by comparing attachment behaviour in baby monkeys given a surrogate mechanical mother that did or did not produce milk and was either hard or cuddly.

PROCEDURE

A baby-sized cloth-covered surrogate (substitute) mother was designed. A wire version was also built. Each of these devices (shown in Figure 3.5) dispensed milk. Sixteen baby Macaques took part in the experiment, four in each of four conditions. In two conditions the babies had both a cloth and a wire surrogate in their cage. In one of these conditions the wire monkey produced milk and in the other, milk was available from the cloth mother. In the two remaining conditions the monkeys each had a single surrogate, either wire or cloth. The eating patterns of the monkeys were compared. A stress test was conducted in which a noisy toy was presented to each monkey. The apparatus was also placed within a larger 'open-field' cage to test the monkeys' tendency to explore.

FINDINGS

Eating patterns did not vary between the conditions. However, the monkeys with only the wire 'mother' had significantly more watery faeces, a symptom of stress. When exposed to a frightening noise, the monkeys would retreat to their mother-figure. In the conditions with wire and cloth mothers they chose the cloth monkey irrespective of whether it produced milk. In the open-field test, monkeys with a cloth 'mother' explored more but returned more often to the surrogate.

CONCLUSION

Infant monkeys found a cloth surrogate preferable to a wire one, irrespective of which produced milk. They experienced less stress and showed more attachment to it than to the wire monkey. This suggests attachment has more to do with cuddling than with food.

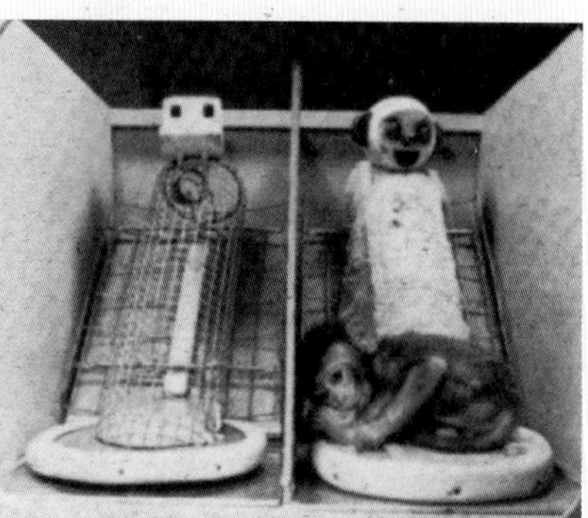

Figure 3.5 The wire and cloth surrogates

Figure 3.6 A frightened monkey cuddles a cloth mother

Figure 3.7 One of the toys used to frighten the monkeys

In later studies, Harlow demonstrated that when the cloth surrogate mother showed mother-like behaviours like rocking, the preference for the cuddly version increased. He and his colleagues also followed up monkeys into adulthood to see the long-term effects being deprived of a mother. Even the monkeys reared with a soft surrogate failed to develop normally. They were aggressive and unsociable, and bred less often than is normal for Macaques.

Thinking critically about psychology

Evaluate Harlow's work. You may wish to consider the following in particular:

1. Does it raise ethical issues?
2. Suggest two reasons why monkeys rather than human babies were chosen for this study.
3. How good were the sample size and sample characteristics in the 1958 study?
4. Why are the findings of studies like this socially sensitive?

LOOKING FURTHER

You can learn more about Harlow's research online. You can read the 1958 paper in full at http://psychclassics.yorku.ca. You can also watch footage of his procedures at http://www.violence.de/tv/rockabye.html. You can also check out some more recent research into attachment in monkeys by going to http://www.pubmed.gov and entering 'attachment' AND 'monkey' as your search terms. Note that you may have to scroll through a few pages of irrelevant studies to find what you are looking for.

Bowlby's theory of attachment

John Bowlby was a child psychiatrist and psychoanalyst who also had an interest in animal behaviour. Combining these interests, he put together ideas from psychoanalytic and ethological theories to create a theory of attachment. From Freud he took the idea that the mother or main carer has a unique role in a child's development and that the quality of the first relationship will affect future relationships. Bowlby called this special focus of attachment towards a particular person *monotropy*. From ethological theory he took the idea of a critical period in which attachment needs to develop and a role for attachment in keeping infants close to the main carer and therefore safe. On the basis of both psychoanalysis and ethological research like that by Harlow and Lorenz, Bowlby proposed that attachment behaviour is instinctive and that normal psychological development requires the development of a secure attachment between a baby and its main carer.

The evolutionary basis of attachment

Because attachment behaviour can be seen in a range of species, Bowlby (1957) proposed that it has developed through a process of evolution. The purpose of attachment behaviours is to keep the young person or animal safe. A million or so years ago, early humans lived in small settlements and faced real threats from predators such as wolves and big cats. By seeking proximity to a larger, stronger adult, signalling distress when left alone and returning from exploring for regular visits to its parents, Stone Age children would greatly increase their chances of survival. Attachment of adults towards children further increases the chances of the child's survival because attached adults are motivated to keep them close and defend them from predators.

Figure 3.8 These children are less at risk of being eaten if they seek proximity and display secure base behaviour

Social releasers

Bowlby suggested that babies are born programmed to behave in ways that encourage attention from adults. These 'cute' behaviours include smiling, cooing, gesturing, gripping and sucking. Bowlby called these behaviours *social releasers*, because their purpose is to release instinctive parenting behaviour in adults. He famously said: "Babies' smiles are powerful things, leaving mothers spellbound and enslaved. Who can doubt that the baby who most readily rewards his mother with a smile is the one who is best loved and best cared for?" (Bowlby, 1957, p237).

Figure 3.9 Babies' smiles have evolved to make adults care about them

The interplay between infant social releasers and instinctive parenting responses gradually builds the attachment between infant and carer. There is a sensitive period of around two years when the baby is particularly oriented towards trying to interact with adults. If the mother or main carer does not respond to social releasers during this sensitive period then the main opportunity is lost and it will be much harder for the child to form an attachment later. This means in practice that during a child's infancy a main carer has to be present and attentive much of the time.

Internal working models

Attachment has consequences for the later development of the child. Recall Freud's idea that a child's first relationship serves as a prototype for later relationships. Bowlby (1969) developed this idea, proposing that each child forms a mental representation of its first attachment, called an *internal working model*. This mental representation is called to mind in forming later relationships and particularly influences the child's own later parenting behaviour. If the child internalises a working model of attachment as attentive, loving and reliable, then this is what they will expect from and bring to future relationships. If, on the other hand, they are neglected or abused, there is an increased probability that they will seek out or display these behaviours themselves as an adult.

Discussion of Bowlby's theory

Bowlby's theory is thorough, explaining both *why* and *how* we form attachments. It also explains some of the consequences of the nature of individual attachments through internal working models. There is research to support the existence of social releasers and the importance of parenting responses. Brazleton *et al.* (1975) observed mothers and babies during their interactions. They noted that mothers and babies took turns to begin interactions and that they imitated each other's movements. Brazleton *et al.* called this process *interactional synchrony*. The researchers also undertook an experiment in which mothers were asked to ignore the babies' social releasers. They found that the babies quickly became distressed. Some even curled up and became motionless, exhibiting signs of depression. These findings support Bowlby's ideas about social releasers and the importance of responding to them.

Bowlby's idea of internal working models predicts that patterns of attachment will be passed on from one generation to the next. Bailey *et al.* (2007) tested this idea. They questioned 99 teenage mothers with one-year-old babies about their attachment to their own mothers. They also observed the attachment behaviours of their babies. Those mothers who reported insecure attachments to their own parents were much more likely to have children whose behaviour implied insecure attachments. This suggests that, as Bowlby proposed, a pattern of insecure attachment was being passed from one generation to the next. Van Ijzendoorn (1995) combined the results of 18 similar studies. (Combining studies in this way is called meta-analysis.) Results strongly supported the idea that secure parents tended to have secure children. This in turn means that security of attachment was being transmitted from one generation to the next.

KEY TERMS

monotropy – the tendency to direct infant attachment behaviours towards a single main attachment figure

social releasers – instinctive cute behaviours designed to stimulate interaction from adults

interactional synchrony – the synching of adult and baby actions so that they take turns and imitate each other's movements

meta-analysis – a statistical technique in which results of several studies are combined and analysed together

internal working model – a mental representation of the first relationship which acts as a prototype for future relationships

Thinking creatively about psychology

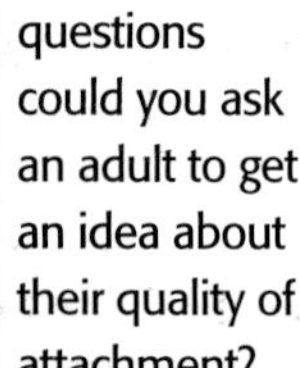

What sort of questions could you ask an adult to get an idea about their quality of attachment?

One approach is to ask about proximity to parents, distress at separation from them and secure base behaviour. Put together a short questionnaire containing five to ten questions that asks them about these attachment behaviours.

http:www.guardian.co.uk/technology/2007/nov/06/robots.sciencenews

Children bond with their robot playmates

Child-like robot playmates are being developed for nursery schools after researchers found that toddlers learn to regard them as human. The Japanese-built prototype silver robot Qrio possesses an 'impressive array' of mechanical and computational skills, according to the researchers. It can interact with humans, walk, sit down, stand up, move its arms, turn its head and even dance and giggle.

Scientists found that children's social contact with the robot increased over time and children found Qrio more interesting when it behaved in a 'human' interactive way than when it was programmed to dance randomly. At first, the toddlers touched the robot on its face and head, but later they touched only its hands and arms, mimicking the behaviour of children with other humans.

Care-taking behaviours were shown towards the robot but not towards a 'huggable' soft toy that was also placed with the children. The scientists wrote, 'Our results suggest that current robot technology is surprisingly close to achieving bonding and socialisation with human toddlers'.

Alexandra Topping, *Guardian*, 6 Nov 2007, p10

1 Using Bowlby's ideas about attachment formation, explain why the toddlers might have become attached to Qrio.

2 What parallels can you see between this research and Harlow's?

Although much of Bowlby's theory is supported by modern psychology, it has some limitations. The idea that we have evolved attachment behaviour to enhance children's safety has good *face validity* – that is, it seems to make sense. However, like many evolutionary ideas it is extremely difficult to test directly, so there is a lack of firm evidence. Another limitation concerns Bowlby's emphasis on the role of the mother. There is evidence from modern studies to suggest that in two-parent heterosexual families the quality of attachment with a father can also have an effect on children's development, for example in later criminality (see p56 for a discussion).

LOOKING FURTHER **Bowlby's ideas about internal working models have led many professionals who work with children to worry that adults who suffered abuse as children are at risk of being poor parents and even abusing their own children. Go to http://www.pubmed.gov and look for relevant studies. Try "internal working models" AND "abuse" as your search terms. What does the research suggest? The findings of Fitzgerald *et al.* (2005) are particularly interesting.**

ATTACHMENT TYPES

Bowlby distinguished between secure and insecure attachments and used the idea of internal working models to understand individual differences in attachment. However, it was his student – and later colleague – Mary Ainsworth who developed the system of attachment types most commonly used today. Ainsworth (1967) observed children's behaviour in their own homes as they interacted with their main carers and strangers. She proposed that babies and

Figure 3.10 The eight stages of the Strange Situation

toddlers divided fairly neatly into three attachment types, according to the degree of independence they showed when playing, the anxiety they displayed when left alone or with a stranger, and their response to being reunited with their primary carer. Ainsworth & Wittig (1969) developed a laboratory procedure designed to simulate these everyday events in order to classify attachment types. This is called the *Strange Situation*, and it is still the most popular procedure for classifying attachments.

Measuring attachment: the Strange Situation

The Strange Situation is a laboratory procedure designed to measure the security of attachment a child displays towards its primary carer. Secure base behaviour, proximity seeking, separation anxiety, stranger anxiety and response to being reunited with the primary carer are all assessed. The Strange Situation gets its name from the fact that the baby is placed in an unfamiliar – that is, strange – room. The procedure has eight episodes, the seven key stages of which last three minutes each. These are shown in Table 3.1 and Figure 3.10.

Table 3.1 The Strange Situation

Stage	Situation	Designed to measure
1	The child and carer are placed in an empty room	
2	The child is free to explore (encouraged if necessary)	Proximity-seeking and secure base behaviour
3	A stranger enters, greets the carer and attempts to play with the child	Stranger anxiety
4	The carer leaves the child with the stranger	Stranger anxiety plus separation distress
5	The carer re-enters and the stranger leaves	Reuniting response
6	The carer leaves the child alone	Separation distress
7	The stranger re-enters	Stranger anxiety
8	The stranger leaves and carer re-enters	Reuniting response

Ainsworth's attachment types

From observations made using the Strange Situation, Ainsworth proposed three types of attachment. Type B is secure attachment; types A and C are types of insecure attachment.

- *Type A*: **avoidant**. Type A children do not seek proximity with, or display secure base behaviour towards, their carer. They show no distress when she leaves nor do they make contact when she returns. 20 to 25 per cent per cent of British 12- to 18-month-olds are classified as type A.
- *Type B*: **secure**. Type B children play independently but seek proximity and regularly return to see the carer (secure base behaviour). They typically show moderate separation distress and stranger anxiety. They require and accept comfort from the carer in episode 8. 60 to 75 per cent of British 12- to 18-month-olds are classified as type B.

- *Type C*: **resistant (or ambivalent)**. Type C children explore less in episode 2 than others, intensely seeking proximity. They become very distressed on being left alone and with a stranger but they resist comfort when reunited with their carer. Around three per cent of British infants are classified as type C.

Thinking creatively about psychology

As well as forming attachments to their carers, children can also become attached to toys, especially cuddly ones such as teddy bears, just as Harlow's results suggest. Think about the Strange Situation and devise a test that a researcher could use to measure how attached a child was to a particular toy.

Figure 3.11 Children display attachment behaviour towards soft toys

Type D attachment

A minority of children do not fit into one of these three major attachment types. Particularly worrying are those who display a mixture of type A and type C behaviours. Mary Main and Judith Solomon (1986) have called this blend of avoidant and resistant behaviours the *type D* attachment, but some teams of attachment researchers prefer the term *type AC*. In the Strange Situation, type D children sometimes alternate between avoidant and resistant behaviour and sometimes they combine them, for example maintaining close proximity but resisting when cuddled. They may also freeze as if they have no idea how to cope with the Strange Situation. Often they appear to be afraid of the primary carer and prefer the company of the stranger.

Explaining attachment types: maternal sensitivity hypothesis

Mary Ainsworth proposed that variations in attachment type are chiefly the result of the behaviour of the mother or main carer towards the child. Most importantly, high levels of *sensitive responsiveness* are associated with secure attachment. Carers who are skilled at picking up and responding to the child's signals tend to have type B children. According to Ainsworth, attachment types A and C are the result of insensitive parenting. Type A and Type C patterns of behaviour in the Strange Situation represent different coping strategies for dealing with the anxiety of the situation. Type A children avoid contact with adults in order not to be disappointed by them. They are emotionally distanced from the situation. Type Cs on the other hand cope by using anger and control. They maintain very close proximity in order to keep their carer 'on a short leash' and display considerable anger when left alone and when reunited with her. A study by Stayton & Ainsworth (1973) demonstrates the link between sensitive responsiveness and attachment types.

Stayton DJ & Ainsworth MDS (1973) Individual differences in babies' responses to brief separations. *Developmental Psychology* **9,** 226–35

AIM

To see whether mothers' behaviour towards their babies in their own homes is associated with the attachment behaviour of the baby.

PROCEDURE

Twenty-six white, middle-class mothers and their babies were observed for four-hour periods every three weeks in their own homes. Infant attachment was measured by total time spent crying, crying when the mother left the room, following her and pleasure or otherwise on her return. Each mother's behaviour was rated on a scale of 1–9 according to four criteria: how sensitive she was to the baby's signals, how accepting she was of the needs of the baby, how co-operative she was (that is, the extent to which she arranged her routine around the activities of the child) and how accessible she was to the child (that is, how physically close she was and how much notice she took of the child).

FINDINGS

Strong relationships were found between maternal behaviours towards the babies and the babies' attachment-related behaviours. The maternal variable most consistently associated with attachment-related infant behaviour was sensitivity. Results came in the form of correlation coefficients (scores between 0 and 1, where the nearer the score is to 1, the stronger the relationship). There was a negative correlation of –0.4 between sensitivity and time spent crying (a sign of type C attachment) and +0.46 between sensitivity and being pleased to see the mother when she re-entered a room (a sign of type B attachment). (You will learn more about correlation coefficients in Chapter 4.)

CONCLUSION

A mother's sensitivity towards her baby is strongly associated with secure attachment of the baby towards her.

Modern research into the origins of attachment types

Modern research has supported the importance of sensitive responsiveness in developing secure attachments. In one study, Cantero & Cerezo (2001) observed 112 Spanish mothers interacting with their babies aged from five to 15 months, classifying attachment type at fifteen months using the Strange Situation. In line with Ainsworth's theory, they found that type B attachment at 15 months was associated with high levels of maternal sensitivity. Type A attachment was particularly associated with controlling or rejecting parenting, while type C was more associated with lack of responsiveness.

There seems to be little doubt that maternal sensitivity is important in affecting a child's attachment type. However, this is a very socially sensitive issue because mothers can be labelled as 'insensitive' and blamed for their baby's insecurity. The term 'insensitive' is normally used as an insult, so its use here implies that the mothers of insecure babies are of bad character. However, there are several reasons why a mother might not manage to pick up infant signals. In one recent study, Donovan *et al.* (2007) tested whether in fact so-called insensitive mothers may simply have difficulty processing the sort of information that would allow them to interpret their babies' signals correctly. The researchers looked at mothers' ability to judge emotion from pictures of babies' faces. They found that mothers who found this task hard

KEY TERMS

sensitive responsiveness – the ability of the adult carer to pick and respond to non-verbal signals from the baby

temperament – infant personality

when their babies were six months old were more likely to display insensitive behaviour and to have insecurely attached babies at two years. Thus, the research suggests that 'insensitive mothers' may simply have a cognitive disadvantage rather than a character flaw.

There are other reasons not to be too harsh in judging the main carers of insecure children. Most importantly, other factors as well as maternal sensitivity affect attachment type. Scher & Mayseless (2000) looked at lifestyle influences on the development of type C attachment in 98 Israeli mother–infant pairs. Mothers who were highly stressed, worked long hours and placed children in long hours of nursery care were more likely to have type C children. These observations show that the whole situation in which a main carer is parenting their child can affect attachment, as opposed to just the interactions between parent and child. Other studies have looked at the role of the child's temperament; see *Research Now*. It seems that some children are especially difficult to respond to and hence form a good attachment with.

RESEARCH NOW

Fuertes M, Santos PL, Beeghly M & Tronick E (2006) More than maternal sensitivity shapes attachment. *Annals of the New York Academy of Science* **1094,** 292–6

AIM

To investigate the role of both sensitive responsiveness and characteristics of the baby in the development of attachment.

PROCEDURE

Forty-eight premature babies and their mothers (who are at increased risk of insecure attachment) were followed up from birth to one year. At one and three months mothers rated them for how easy or difficult their temperament (personality) was. At nine months, observers using a standard observation measure assessed maternal sensitivity. At one year, infant attachment was assessed using the Strange Situation.

FINDINGS

Both difficult temperament and low levels of maternal sensitivity were associated with high risk of insecure attachment.

CONCLUSION

Although maternal sensitivity is important in affecting the quality of attachment, so is the nature of the baby. Not all babies are equally easy to form a secure attachment with.

Thinking critically about psychology

Evaluate the Fuertes study (above). You may wish to consider the following issues in particular:

1. Is the sample representative? Why might the researchers have chosen to look at this group?
2. Is there a potential problem with using mothers' ratings as a measure of temperament?
3. What is the advantage of using standard measures to assess temperament, sensitivity and attachment security?
4. Why is this study important in both theoretical and practical terms?

Figure 3.12 Stressed mothers with difficult babies may have a hard time forming a secure attachment

Findings like those of Scher & Mayseless (2000) and Fuertes *et al.* (2006) are important because they tell us that although maternal sensitivity is important, it is not the only factor affecting attachment, and that mothers do not have a level playing field. Not all babies are equally easy to build a secure attachment with, and not all families have an easy environment in which to do so. A mother of a baby with a highly irritable temperament, who also had to work long hours to make ends meet, might have a particularly difficult task to interact sensitively and build a secure attachment with her child.

Thinking creatively about psychology

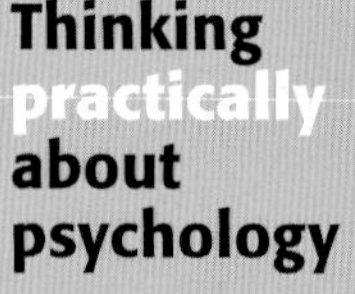

Design a study that eliminates the limitations of the Fuertes *et al.* study. Think about what sample you would like to study, what might be the most valid way of measuring temperament, and so on.

Thinking practically about psychology

Various psychologists and other professionals such as social workers offer attachment training for mothers and other main carers in order to help them form secure attachments with their babies. Use ideas from attachment theory, in particular sensitive responsiveness, to explain how attachment training might work.

ATTACHMENT TYPE AND LATER DEVELOPMENT

Ainsworth (1989) believed that attachment type as classified by the Strange Situation would remain fairly constant throughout the child's life and that it would lead to particular patterns of behaviour in adulthood. For example, as we have already seen (p48), securely attached people are advantaged in their ability to parent their own children. Ainsworth also believed that securely attached adults would find it easier to form successful friendships and romantic relationships. These advantages have been confirmed by modern research. In addition, securely attached people tend to have fewer mental health problems.

Figure 3.13 Ainsworth suggested that people with secure attachments have better friendships

Research has consistently shown that, as Ainsworth believed, securely attached adults are advantaged in their friendships and romantic relationships. McCarthy (1999) followed up 40 women aged 25 to 44 who had been assessed for attachment type as children during early attachment research. They were given a questionnaire designed to assess their current attachment type and an interview to assess the state of their adult friendships and romantic relationships. Type Bs were found to have the best friendships and romantic relationships. Type Cs had particular trouble holding down friendships, while Type As found the intimacy of romantic relationships particularly difficult. Type Ds fared worst in all relationships.

Figure 3.14 Research suggests that couples where one or both partners have an insecure attachment may have the most relationship problems

More recently, Banse (2004) looked at the relationship between attachment type and marital satisfaction in 333 German couples. Satisfaction of each partner was associated with type B attachment in themselves and their partner. In other words, where both partners were secure, satisfaction was greatest. Scores of secure attachment correlated strongly (coefficients of 0.43 for wives and 0.37 for husbands) with marital satisfaction. Scores for each of the insecure attachment types correlated negatively with satisfaction.

Attachment type also appears to influence our responses to losing loved ones. Wijngaards-de Meij *et al.* (2007) studied attachment type and psychological adjustment in 219 parents who had lost children. Type Bs emerged as coping best with their loss. Fascinatingly, it appears that responses to the loss of fictional characters are similarly affected by attachment type; see *Research Now*.

RESEARCH NOW

Cohen J (2004) Attachment type and loss of TV characters. *Journal of Social & Personal Relationships* **21,** 187–202

AIM

To test whether attachment type affects the emotional response to the loss of a television character. It was hypothesised that type Cs would be most affected and type As least affected.

PROCEDURE

A quota sample of 381 Israeli adults took part in the study. They each completed a measure of attachment (choosing which of three paragraphs best described their close relationships). They also named their favourite television character and completed a questionnaire to assess their attachment to that character (called parasocial attachment). They were then asked to imagine how they would feel if that character were taken off the air and to complete a short questionnaire.

FINDINGS

The hypothesis was partially supported. Type Cs reported significantly more emotional involvement with the character and significantly more distress than type As or Bs at their loss. However, there was very little difference in distress between types A and B.

CONCLUSION

Adults with an insecure-resistant attachment type get most intensely involved with fictional characters and most distressed at their loss.

Figure 3.15 Millions of fans have a strong parasocial attachment to Harry Potter. Research suggests a link between parasocial attachment type and response to the loss of such fictional characters

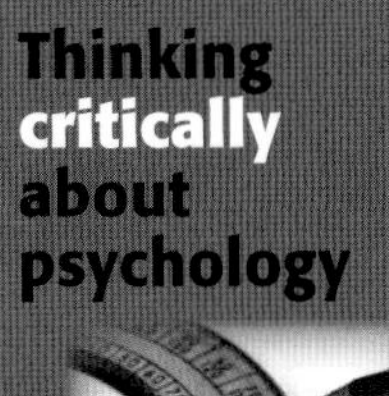

Thinking critically about psychology

The Banse (2004) study used a volunteer sampling in which 333 couples responded out of the 2000 that were contacted and asked to participate. Thus, only 16 per cent volunteered to take part in the study. The Cohen (2004) study used a quota sample of 381 people in an attempt to get a good balance of age, sex and light and heavy TV viewing.

1 Comment on the sample size in each of these studies.
2 Which sampling method is more likely to obtain a representative group of participants?

Design and carry out a study to find out whether there is a relationship between parasocial attachment to Harry Potter and anxiety at the idea of his death in the final book. You will need to think about how you will measure two variables: parasocial attachment type to Harry Potter and Potter death anxiety. For ethical reasons, you should *not* attempt to measure participants' *actual* adult attachment type. You may wish to present your results as a comparison of anxiety levels in parasocial types A, B and C (see p55). In this case, the easiest way of measuring parasocial attachment type is to produce three paragraphs representing what a type A, B or C Potter fan might feel towards Harry Potter and to ask participants to choose which best represents their feelings.

LOOKING FURTHER There is a large body of research linking insecure attachment to mental health problems. Go to http://www.pubmed.gov or http://scholar.google.com and search for studies linking insecure attachment to particular mental health problems. Use 'attachment' as a search term and try combining it with 'depression' or 'eating disorders'.

KEY TERMS

parasocial attachment – attachment to fictional characters

sexual coerciveness – willingness to put pressure on people, including physical force, in order to have sex with them

Adults with type B attachments also seem to fare better in terms of their mental health. Ward *et al.* (2006) gave 190 women a standard psychiatric assessment. Thirty of them who received a diagnosis and 30 who did not were selected and assessed for attachment type using a standard interview called the Adult Attachment Interview (AAI). Thirty-two per cent of women with secure attachments received a diagnosis, as compared to 63 per cent of type As, 100 per cent of type Cs and 65 per cent of type Ds. Actually, although type Cs and Ds consistently emerge as the experiencing the most mental health problems, most studies have found that type Ds are even worse off than type Cs (Zilbertstein, 2006).

Some research has also shown that attachment type is associated with criminality. Smallbone & Dadds (2000) assessed 162 male students for attachment to both parents and for aggression, antisocial behaviour and sexual coerciveness (likelihood of forcing someone into a sexual act against their will). Insecure attachment was associated with higher levels of aggression, antisocial behaviour and sexual coerciveness. Sexual coerciveness was most strongly associated with insecure attachment to the father than to the mother. This finding has important implications for the ideas of Bowlby and Ainsworth, who both placed their emphasis on the role of the mother.

Another aspect of criminal behaviour that may be associated with attachment is celebrity stalking. McCutcheon *et al.* (2006) assessed attachment type and attitudes to stalking celebrities in 299 college students. Those with insecure attachment were more likely to believe that it was all right to stalk a celebrity.

Thinking practically about psychology

Many celebrities suffer stalking. This can take the form of obsessive following, declaration of love and even murder. In Britain, recent celebrities to suffer the trauma of being stalked include Madonna and Robbie Williams. Using your knowledge of attachment theory, and in particular the research of McCutcheon *et al.*, Smallbone & Dadds, and Cohen, explain why stalking behaviour might come about.

Figure 3.16 Both David and Victoria Beckham have been stalked. Those who stalk celebrities appear to have attachment problems

CULTURAL VARIATIONS IN ATTACHMENT

Studies of infant attachment conducted in different cultures have revealed some variations in the proportions of securely and insecurely attached infants. In a classic study, Van Ijzendoorn & Kroonenberg (1988) carried out a meta-analysis of the combined results of published studies of attachment type in a range of studies.

CLASSIC RESEARCH

Van Ijzendoorn MH & Kroonenberg PM (1988) Cross-cultural patterns of attachment. *Child Development* **59,** 147–156

AIM

To investigate variations in the proportions of attachment types around the world.

PROCEDURE

Studies were selected on the basis that they used the Strange Situation to classify infant attachment type into types A, B and C (at that time, type D was only just being identified). Results were meta-analysed. This means that their results were combined and weighted for sample size. A total of 32 studies conducted in eight countries were included in the meta-analysis. The total number of children included was just over 2000.

FINDINGS

In all countries, secure attachment was the most common classification. In most countries (the exceptions were China, Japan and Israel), anxious-resistant (type C) was the least common. There were, however, some big variations in the percentages of types A, B and C. These are shown in Figure 3.17.

CONCLUSIONS

There are some similarities in patterns of attachment across the world. For example, each country had a majority of securely attached babies. However, the variations in percentages of types A, B and C suggest that child-rearing practices in different countries affect the attachment of their babies. Alternatively, it may be that the Strange Situation does not work well in different cultures.

Explaining cultural variations

There are a range of possible explanations for the sort of variations in attachment seen in studies like that of Van Ijzendoorn & Kroonenberg. Grossman and Grossman (1990) suggest that the idea of 'attachment' has subtly different meanings to different cultures. Take type A avoidant attachment. In Britain we are uncomfortable at the idea of emotionally disengaged children. However, what we call 'avoidant' in Britain and the United States might be called 'independent' in Germany, where independence is valued more highly. If that is the case, then we would expect there to be a higher proportion of type As in Germany than in Britain, an expectation that is confirmed by Figure 3.17.

An alternative explanation for apparent cultural variations in attachment is that the Strange Situation, which was developed in the United States, simply does not work in some cultures. For example, Takahashi (1990) suggests that the procedure is not appropriate for testing Japanese mothers. In Japan the cultural norm is for mothers and babies to be rarely separated, which means that we would expect to see very high levels of separation anxiety. Japanese mothers also tended to spoil the episodes of the Strange Situation assessing response to reuniting by rushing straight to the child and scooping them up. In the absence of a reuniting response to observe, it is quite likely that the severe separation anxiety of the Japanese children led to a falsely high number being labelled type C.

KEY TERMS

culture – the set of behaviours and beliefs that characterises a group of people, for example a nationality

cross-cultural study – a study that compares a psychological variable such as attachment in people from two or more countries

culture-bound – a criticism of a theory or procedure based on the idea that it works well only in certain cultures

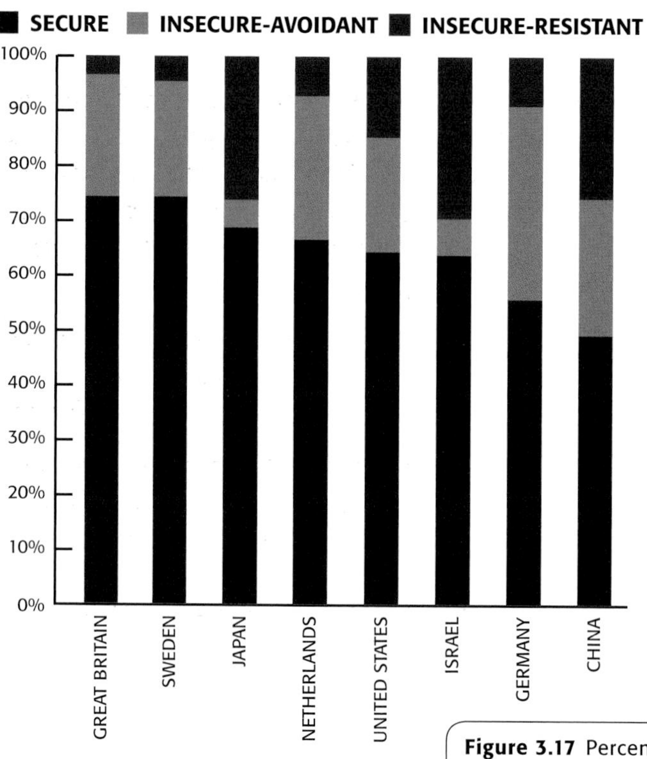

Figure 3.17 Percentages of attachment types in different cultures. Based on Van Ijzendoorn & Kroonenberg (1988)

A third possible explanation comes from Belsky (1999). Belsky developed Bowlby's ideas about the evolutionary origins of attachment further, suggesting that different attachment types are useful for people living in different environments. We know that insecure attachment is associated with early onset of sexual activity and a tendency to form less deep adult relationships. Belsky has proposed that parenting behaviours that lead to insecure attachments and so to early sexual activity and shallow adult relationships are actually *helpful* in environments where mortality rates are high and so people need to reproduce young and not invest too much emotion in relationships with partners who are likely to die young. Belsky also suggests that the stress of life in a high-mortality environment naturally leads to low levels of maternal sensitivity and hence high rates of insecure attachment.

Thinking creatively about psychology

All three of the explanations given above for apparent cultural variations in attachment can be tested scientifically. We could test the Grossmans' idea by seeing whether there is a correlation between the cultural acceptability of each set of attachment behaviours and how common it is in a range of countries. Similarly, we could investigate Belsky's idea by looking for correlations between mortality rates and percentages of insecure attachments. Design a study to test one of the three explanations.

The study of attachment security across different cultures poses a challenge to Bowlby and Ainsworth, who saw attachment as a universal factor in human development. If attachment has widely differing meanings in different cultures, and if our standard tests for attachment types do not work with people from different cultures, then we might have to accept that attachment theory and research is *culture-bound* – that is, it is applicable only in European and North American culture.

DISRUPTION TO THE FORMATION AND MAINTENANCE OF ATTACHMENT

Bowlby (1955) described the potential harm resulting from disruption to early relationships through separation of the baby from its main carer. However, at least in his early work, Bowlby did not distinguish clearly between the effects of different types of disruptive experience. Michael Rutter (1981) has developed Bowlby's ideas, making the important distinction between deprivation and privation:

- Deprivation involves temporary or permanent separation from the attachment figure.
- Privation involves the failure to form an attachment in the first place.

Deprivation (or separation) can be short-term, as happens when families use day care facilities, or long-term, as in hospitalisation of mother or child or in cases of family breakdown or the death of a parent.

Figure 3.18 Hospitalisation is one cause of separation of a mother and child

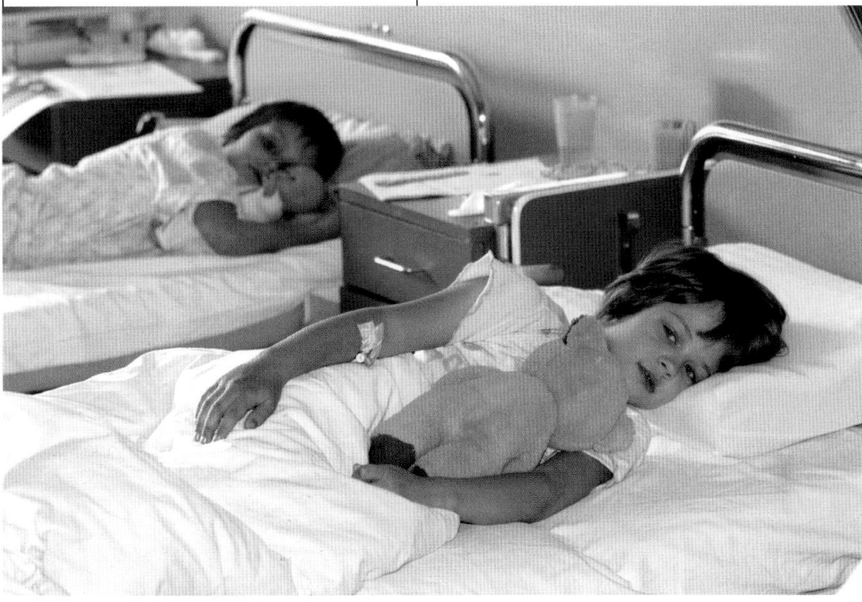

Privation can result when children are severely neglected or abused. It can also occur or when they grow up in a poor-quality institution in which there is no real opportunity to form attachments. Bowlby *et al.* (1952) proposed the *maternal deprivation hypothesis*, the idea that separation at any point in the first two years threatens and may destroy attachment, leading to severe problems for the child. As Rutter (1981) says, it is really *privation* that is generally associated with more severe effects rather than separation after attachment formation.

Privation

According to modern definitions, Harlow's experiments on infant monkeys could be said to be studies of privation. His findings showed severe long-term effects in monkeys, but what of humans? Researchers are interested in precisely what the effects of privation are and to what extent it can be reversed. However, studying privation in humans is methodologically tricky. Clearly, for ethical reasons we cannot deliberately cause privation to human children just to see how they turn out. This means that human privation has been largely studied by means of case studies. Case study research involves detailed recording of real-life instances. The problem is that real-life cases are each unique, and it is hard to draw conclusions. Consider the cases of the Czech twins and Genie.

- Koluchová (1972, 1991) described the case of two severely abused twin boys. The twins were born in 1960 in the former Czechoslovakia (hence they are commonly known as the 'Czech twins'). Their mother died shortly after they were born and they spent a year in an institution and were then fostered by an aunt for six months. Their father remarried and the twins were reared by their stepmother, who is believed to have had serious mental health problems. She kept them locked in a dark closet and regularly beat them severely. The boys were rescued at the age of seven years. They were severely retarded, had no speech and were very afraid of adults. They received two years of intensive hospital care including physiotherapy, speech therapy and psychotherapy, then a pair of sisters (said to be extremely sensitive and loving) fostered the boys. At 14 years they had normal speech, social behaviour and IQ. At 20 they had above-average IQ, were working and were experiencing successful romantic relationships. Both are reported (Clarke & Clarke, 1998) to have successful romantic relationships and careers.
- Curtiss (1977) has described the case of Genie, born in Los Angeles in 1957. When Genie was 20 months old a doctor told her family that she might have learning difficulties. In response to this, her unstable father kept her isolated in her bedroom. She was kept tied to a potty by day and tied into a sleeping bag at night. Genie was beaten whenever she tried to communicate, and she had only the most basic interactions with her father. Her mother and brother were not allowed to communicate with her or leave the house. Genie was rescued at the age of 13 when her mother ran away and took her to Social Services. When rescued, Genie had very little speech. She was fostered by a teacher and then by one of the psychologists studying her. At first she showed progress and developed limited language and attachments to her carers. However, when the research funding was terminated, psychologists returned her to Social Services and she was cared for in a succession of foster-homes. She was physically abused again, and she regressed to the state she had been in when first rescued. At this point Genie was briefly reunited with the psychologists, towards whom she showed great anger. Genie was then settled with an adult foster-carer with whom she still lives. Her carer (understandably) does not wish her to have anything more to do with psychologists. We therefore have no up-to-date information on her progress.

Thinking critically about psychology

The cases of Genie and the Czech twins are in some ways very similar. However, they had very different outcomes. Although our information is not complete, the twins are believed to have no long-term after-effects while Genie is believed to remain severely affected.

1 Identify three differences between the two cases that might have contributed to the different outcomes.
2 What do these studies tell us about the limitations of case studies?

To learn about further cases of children, visit http://www.feralchildren.com/. What sort of picture emerges overall from these cases about the effects of privation?

Institutionalisation

Institutionalisation occurs when children spend a substantial period living in an institution such as an orphanage or children's home. We can think of this sort of experience as privation if children do not have the chance to form attachments or deprivation if they do. Often institutions will contain a mixture of prived and deprived children. However, institutionalisation shows some distinctive patterns of attachment behaviour of its own, so it is worth thinking of institutionalisation as a phenomenon in its own right.

Most research has shown that children who enter full-time care institutions at a young age and who spend extended periods there are disadvantaged in particular aspects of their development. A classic study by Jill Hodges & Barbara Tizard running through the 1970s and 1980s teased out some of the effects of institutionalisation.

CLASSIC RESEARCH

Hodges J & Tizard B (1989) Relationships of ex-institutional adolescents. *Journal of Child Psychology and Psychiatry* **30,** 77–98

AIM

To compare the development of children who had been taken into institutional care at a very young age under three conditions: remaining in the institution, being adopted or being restored to their biological family.

PROCEDURE

Sixty-five children took part in the study. All had been in institutional care from before the age of four months. Twenty-four were adopted, 15 had been restored to their biological families and 26 remained in institutional care. They were assessed for social and emotional development at four, eight and 16 years by means of observations and interviews with teachers and carers.

FINDINGS

At four and eight years the adopted group had fewest behavioural problems. Adopted and restored children were more attention-seeking. They were clingier and less likely to have developed close relationships. The adopted group were now generally reported as having strong attachments to their carers, although they were generally slightly more physically affectionate than the norm. At school, all three groups were reported by teachers to be unpopular with peers, restless and aggressive. By 16 the adoptees had entirely normal relationships with adoptive families, but they still had some problems getting on with their peers.

CONCLUSION

Being institutionalised as a baby tended to have some long-term effects, regardless of whether infants were restored, adopted or stayed in institutions. However, the outcomes were considerably better following adoption than either of the alternatives. This suggests that the effects of institutionalisation are partially reversible.

Thinking critically about psychology

Evaluate the Hodges & Tizard (1989) study. In particular, you might like to consider the following: the sample size, given that the sample is divided into three conditions; the extent to which the three groups were alike before adoption or restoration; the range of measures of development; the practical applications of the research.

There is considerable research to support the idea put forward by Hodges & Tizard that children can be disadvantaged in their social development by early institutionalisation. Rutter (1981) has pointed out, however, that we need to be careful in suggesting a simple relationship between being in an institution and developmental problems. His own observations suggested that what happens to the child before being institutionalised is also important. Children who were institutionalised because of housing problems or parental illness were better adjusted than those who had suffered abuse or neglect within the family. A great strength of the Hodges & Tizard study is the early age at which the infants were institutionalised. This means that we can be reasonably sure that any problems experienced by the group were the result of institutionalisation rather than their prior experiences.

Figure 3.19 Images of the conditions in Romanian orphanages shocked the world

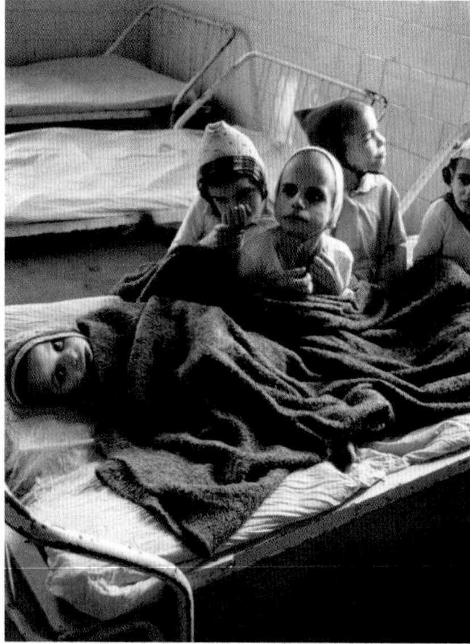

A large-scale if grim opportunity to study the effects of poor-quality institutional care came about in Eastern Europe in the early 1990s. In Romania under President Nicolae Ceauşescu it was a legal requirement for women to have five children. In many cases, parents could not afford to keep their children and they were handed over to the State, where they were kept in massive, very poor-quality orphanages. Following a revolution in 1989, conditions were improved and many of the children were adopted. This allowed psychologists to look in depth at the effects of institutionalisation and adoption. In an early study of the Romanian orphans, Rutter *et al.* (1998) followed up 111 children adopted in Britain. Their aim was to see the extent to which good care could make up for very poor early institutional experiences. The children were followed up to the age of four and periodically assessed with tests of physical and intellectual development. When they first arrived in Britain, the Romanian children were developmentally delayed. Around half showed signs of mental retardation and most were severely underweight. At four years, however, they had caught up with a control group of British children on both physical and intellectual development. A negative correlation was seen between age when adopted and development at four years – that is, the younger the child when adopted, the better they did.

Studies like those by Rutter and Hodges & Tizard, have tended to show some distinctive attachment behaviour particular to institutionalised children. This pattern of behaviour is called *disinhibited attachment*. Disinhibited attachment involves clingy, attention-seeking behaviour and indiscriminate social interaction with adults – that is, the children's social behaviour is directed towards all adults as opposed to a small number of attachment figures. One possible explanation for this sort of behaviour is the large number of carers young children typically see while in an institution (typically over 50 per week). Children in this situation may simply not see enough of any one carer for it to be possible for them to direct their attachment behaviour towards them in particular. There can also be considerable competition for adult attention in institutional care, so we can see how children might get into the habit of attention-seeking and indiscriminate sociability.

Rutter (2006) suggests that disinhibited attachment may be the result of the child adapting to multiple carers at a sensitive period of development. This sensitive period hypothesis was tested in a study by Rutter *et al.* (2007). They followed up 196 Romanian orphans who had been institutionalised then adopted, asking adoptive parents to rate their behaviour. At 11 years the institutionalised group still commonly showed signs of disinhibited attachment. The age at which they were adopted from an institution did not affect the amount of disinhibited attachment behaviour. This supports the idea of a sensitive period during which having multiple carers may lead to disinhibited attachment.

KEY TERMS

disinhibited attachment – a pattern of attachment behaviour typical of children who spend time in an institution

sensitive period – an age at which a child is sensitive to developing a pattern of behaviour if particular conditions occur

RESEARCH NOW

Zeanah CH, Smyke AT, Koga SF & Carlson E (2005) Attachment in institutionalised Romanian children. *Child Development* **76,** 1015–28

AIM

To compare rates of secure attachment and other measures of attachment behaviour in Romanian children in institutional care with children who had never experienced institutional care.

PROCEDURE

Ninety-five children who had spent most (on average, 90 per cent) of their lives in institutional care and a control group of 50 children who had never lived in an institution took part in the study. They were aged between 12 and 31 months. Their attachment type was measured using the Strange Situation, and carers were asked about signs of unusual attachment behaviour including *disinhibited attachment* – that is, clingy, attention-seeking behaviour directed inappropriately at all adults.

FINDINGS

Only 18.9 per cent of the institutionalised group as opposed to 74 per cent of the control group were classified as securely attached according to the Strange Situation. Very few in either group were classed as type A or C. However, 65.3 per cent of the institutional group as opposed to 22 per cent of the control were type Ds. Of the institutional group, 12.6 per cent behaved so oddly in the Strange Situation that they could not be classified at all. On a scale of 0–6 for disinhibited attachment, 44 per cent of the institutional group were rated as 3+, as opposed to less than 20 per cent of the control group.

CONCLUSION

Institutional care produces severe disturbances to attachment behaviour including type D attachment and disinhibited attachment.

Thinking practically about psychology

Based on research into disinhibited attachment, what recommendations would you make to those working in institutional care? Think about how they could reduce the incidence of disinhibited attachment.

DAY CARE

The most common circumstance in which babies and toddlers are separated for short periods from their main carers is day care. Economic and social factors mean that it has become the norm for both parents in British families to work, at least part-time. Consequently, many children spend a substantial part of the week apart from their main carer or carers. Recall Bowlby's maternal deprivation hypothesis (p59). This suggests that separation of child and main carer risks disruption to the attachment process. If we take this to include day care, then we might expect the use of day care to have negative effects on children's development. On the other hand, Bowlby's work was generally concerned with longer-term separations. Recall as well Rutter's conclusion that the most serious effects of separation identified by Bowlby were true of privation rather than deprivation. Day care is certainly not privation, nor is it long-term separation.

A bitter argument

The debate over the alleged effects of day care on children's development is one of the most bitter in psychology, so much so that Karen (1994) has called it the 'Child Care Wars'. On the one hand, opposing day care – or at least long hours in it – are psychologists and parents concerned about a potential risk to children's development. Also on this side of the argument are fundamentalist religious and politically right-wing groups. These groups are perhaps motivated more by the opportunity to discourage mothers from working than by concern for children's welfare. On the other hand, in the pro-day care camp are equally concerned psychologists and other professionals who see potential *positive* effects for children arising from day care. Allied to this point of view are feminists horrified by the thought of anyone putting pressure on mothers not to work. Also on this side of the debate are governments, which perhaps see an opportunity to reduce the money paid out in benefits to non-working mothers by encouraging them to return to work as early as possible. This is a complex picture where people with radically different views and priorities are seeking to claim the moral high ground.

LOOKING FURTHER

There is a huge volume of information about day care on the Internet. You need to develop good skills of information gathering, including spotting the biases in websites, particularly those that deal with highly political issues like day care. Go to http://www.fulltimemothers.org/index.htm and http://www.daycaretrust.org.uk and read their homepages and any links that grab your attention.

1. **Which of these is pro-day care and which is anti-?**
2. **What appears to be the main motivation underlying each organisation?**
3. **Identify at least one biased statement on each website.**
4. **Which site do you find in general to be a more credible source of information?**

Evidence for harmful effects

Jay Belsky (1986) sparked off the day care debate by suggesting that there was worrying evidence to suggest that babies placed in day care settings during their first year were at higher risk of developing insecure attachments and displaying aggressive behaviour than those cared for at home. This appeared to be especially the case where day care was full-time, or close to it. Since then a huge number of studies have been published in this area, and the majority have supported Belsky's view. In one study, Bates *et al.* (1994) examined teacher and peer ratings of social behaviour in 600 American five- and six-year-olds. Teachers rated the children who had spent a lot of time in day care during the first five years as significantly less socially skilled than others. Peers rated them as significantly less popular. In another American study, Hofferth (1999) sampled 519 children from a large national study and found that those spending long hours in day care typically showed higher levels of aggression.

Limitations of the evidence

Although the volume of research suggesting a risk of negative effects for children using day care is quite large, as with all things, size isn't everything! One serious problem is that comparisons between children who experience day care and those who do not are not necessarily comparing like with like. These studies are not true experiments because we can never randomly divide children into 'day care' and 'no day care' conditions. It therefore remains possible that some other difference between the groups accounts for differences in the social behaviour observed. One possible difference was explored in a study by Koren-Karie (2001). She compared 38 Israeli mothers who returned to work with a control group matched for age and income for their own attachment status. Far more mothers with insecure attachments to their own parents opted to return to work and use day care. Because patterns of secure and insecure attachment tend to be passed on from one generation to the next, any disadvantages in the social development of the day care group might well be due to having insecure mothers rather than to having day care.

Evidence for positive effects

A rather smaller but still respectable body of research has found that returning to work and using day care can have positive effects on children's social development. Andersson (1996) followed up 128 Swedish children who had been in day care from infancy to 13 years, when they were assessed for social skills and peer relations. As compared with a control group who had had full-time maternal care, the day care group were judged to be more popular and socially skilled. In another study, Harrison & Ungerer (2002) questioned 145 Australian mothers about their work behaviour and attitudes and assessed their babies for attachment at 12 months using the Strange Situation. Mothers who returned to work when their baby was less than five months old were the most likely to have babies classified as secure. Working mothers in general were more likely to have secure babies. Commitment to work and comfort with using day care also predicted secure attachment.

Another body of research supports the benefits of day care for children whose families are economically disadvantaged and so have a harder time providing optimal care. This is a very controversial idea (Kagan *et al.*, 1980) because it suggests that the middle classes make better parents and because it suggests a double standard: day care is good for one group of children but not for another. However, the evidence is strongly supportive: in a recent meta-analysis of day care studies, Ahnert *et al.* (2006) found a strong positive correlation between socio-economic status and attachment security in children who did not have day care. However, there was no such correlation in children who had day care. This suggests that day care was of benefit to poorer children.

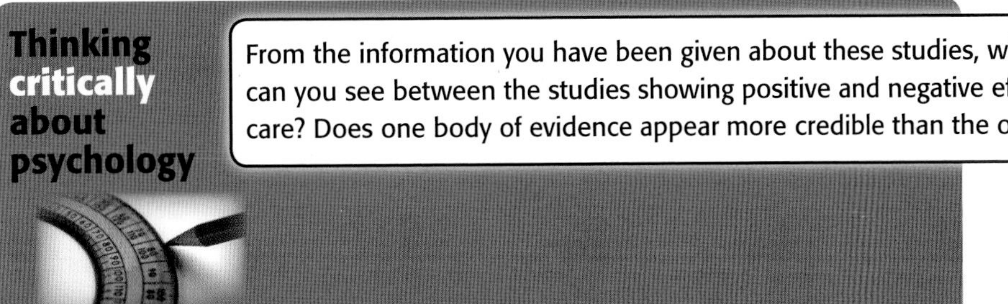

From the information you have been given about these studies, what differences can you see between the studies showing positive and negative effects for day care? Does one body of evidence appear more credible than the other?

Asking the right questions: what makes good and bad day care?

If we look at these conflicting findings, it is clear that in some cases day care appears to have harmful effects on children's social development. but in other cases it seems to have beneficial effects. We *could* unpick some methodological differences between studies, based on the quality of research and decide to

KEY TERMS

transition – the process whereby a child used to full time care at home is introduced to day care

dose effect – the idea that long hours in day care have more of an effect than just a few hours

stability – the extent to which a child keeps to the same day care arrangements

longitudinal study – a study in which people are followed up over long periods to study their development

Figure 3.20 Some research suggests that children who spend long hours in day care have a higher probability of behaving aggressively

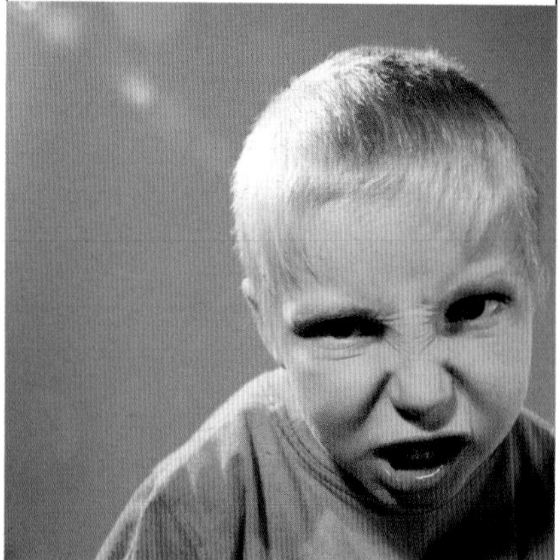

take sides in the debate. However, in the past few years there has been some valuable research into what factors affect the outcomes of day care. This has allowed us to say that asking whether day care is a good or bad thing in itself is simply the wrong question. It appears that day care *can* have harmful effects on social development, but probably only under particular circumstances. The age at which day care commences, the time spent in day care, the quality and stability of the day care, the management of the transition to day care and the pre-existing attachment type of the child may all mediate the effects of day care.

Starting age and dose effects

Virtually all the research into day care has involved children commencing day care prior to one year. Note that in his 1986 publication, Belsky himself only claimed that day care starting in the child's first year may have a harmful effect. There is no evidence and no serious suggestion that later day care, for example in the form of pre-school nursery sessions, is bad for children. The amount of time spent in day care may also be significant. Belsky (2002) explored this 'dose effect'. Looking at a national longitudinal study of the development of 1083 children across the United States, he noted that children who had averaged less than 10 hours of day care in their first 4.5 years were 5 per cent more likely to have higher than normal levels of aggression, whereas those averaging 30 hours or more showed a 16 per cent higher probability of increased aggression. This suggests strongly that the amount of time spent in day care is important.

The transition to day care

Some but not all parents introduce children to day care gradually, for example by staying with them in the day care setting and by leaving them at first only for short periods. The effect of this practice on attachment was tested in a recent German study. Ahnert *et al.* (2004) followed 70 German children in their first year as they entered day care, assessing attachment before and three months after day care began using the Strange Situation. A substantial number of children who started day care abruptly changed attachment type from secure to insecure. On the other hand, if mothers spent time introducing the child to day care, the secure babies maintained their attachment, and some insecure babies changed type, becoming securely attached. This study suggests that the stress of starting day care may affect children, but also that any harmful effect can be avoided by making the transition gradual. It may be that some children find the transition from full time maternal care to day care much more stressful than others. Belsky & Fearon (2002) assessed children's attachment type prior to starting day care and followed up after they had begun. They found that the negative effects of day care were associated only with children with type A attachments. Types B and C were unaffected.

Quality of day care

Leaving aside what we know about attachments, common sense suggests that the better a child is looked after, the better they will develop. Allhusen *et al.* (2003) carried out a sophisticated study of the effects of quality of day care. Nine hundred and eighty-five children and their professional carers were observed twice for half a day in their day care setting. Observers rated carers for sensitive responsiveness (p51), positive attitude towards the child and the amount of stimulation they provided. These combined quality measures correlated significantly with the child's social competence (+0.2), quality of interactions with a friend (+0.12) and behavioural problems (–0.16). This suggests that the quality of day care is important as well as the amount of time spent in it.

Figure 3.21 Child care professionals need to be sensitive and positive towards children

Stability of day care

We know that the formation of the attachment between a baby and its primary carer requires regular contact across a period of some months. We also know that if a child has too many carers during a sensitive period it is at serious risk of developing disinhibited attachment behaviour (p62). It seems logical, then, to propose that for a child to form secure attachments to one or more carers outside the family home, some stability is needed. Stability means the regularity of contact with the child's main substitute carer – this might be a childminder or a key worker at a nursery. High stability is associated both with the amount of time the child spends with a particular child care professional and the turnover of staff. Clearly, a child cannot form a secure attachment to a carer they rarely see, and it is disruptive if they form an attachment to a worker who then leaves. The impact of stability was studied by De Schipper *et al.* (2004).

RESEARCH NOW

De Schipper JC, Van Ijzendoorn M & Tavecchio LWC (2004) Stability in day care and children's well-being. *Social Development* **13,** 531–49

AIM

To investigate the relationship between stability of day care and social development.

PROCEDURE

Participants were 186 children in nursery care aged between six and thirty months. The stability of their care was measured using a scale called the LIDS (Leiden Inventory of Daily Stability). This measures the consistency of staffing, daily activities and contact with other children. Social development was assessed using a behaviour checklist, completed by nursery staff and a measure of emotional well-being completed by observers.

FINDINGS

Emotional well-being correlated with several aspects of stability. The strongest correlations were with consistent use of the same nursery (+0.25) and regular availability of a key worker (+0.21). Problem behaviour was associated with use of multiple day care settings.

CONCLUSIONS

Stability of day care arrangements is important for children's social-emotional development.

Thinking creatively about psychology

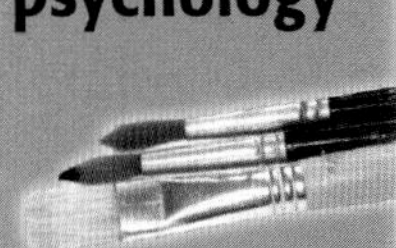

Design a study that will evaluate the care provided in your local nursery. You will need to think about the following:

- How will you measure outcome – that is, the social development of the children?
- Who will you use as a control group?
- What aspects of the care will you measure (e.g. quality, stability, transition) and how will you measure them?
- What ethical issues will you take into account?

Media watch: nursery tales

http://education.guardian.co.uk/earlyyears/story/0,,1367593,00.html

Nursery tales

Five beautiful, plump babies sit in their high chairs in a semi-circle, waiting for lunch. They are eerily quiet. Two nursery staff move around preparing bowls, bibs and spoons. As I stand there, I am fixed upon by 10 huge round eyes. Is it my imagination or does it seem that their eyes are begging for interaction, for an adult smile? Maybe it is just that they are hungry? Meanwhile, a little four-month-old baby, recently fed and changed, has been put in a bouncy chair on the floor where she is just out of sight, momentarily, of a carer; she begins to cry plaintively. After a little while, a member of staff comes to cuddle her and settle her in a cot. Did she get her reassurance quickly enough? As quickly as a mother or father would have given it?

I don't know the answers – nor do many thousands of other mothers and fathers who take the decision every day to place their babies, from as young as four months, in a nursery. Even here, in this nursery in leafy Caterham, Surrey, with its clearly dedicated staff, those eyes make me feel uncomfortable. Instinctively, it doesn't feel quite right. But I question my response: perhaps it is simply because I belong to a transition generation. For most mothers in their 30s and 40s, our earliest years were firmly tied to our mother's apron strings, but we are abandoning that model of motherhood in droves – more than half of us now hand over the care of our baby to others for many hours a day, before they reach their first birthday.

In the past two decades, we have revolutionised how we care for children in the first three years of life. In 1981, only 24% of women returned to work within a year of childbirth, while in 2001 it was 67%, and the proportion is expected to continue rising. Childcare has become a boom industry. The vast bulk of that expansion has been in private day nurseries; since 1997 alone, the number of places has doubled, and it has quadrupled in a decade. Just over 200,000 children under three now attend a day nursery. It comfortably outstrips all other forms of non-family care for under-threes ...

But the popularity of this revolution is at odds with what the experts are saying. Over exactly the time period that the sector has boomed, research on both sides of the Atlantic has reached remarkably similar conclusions; namely, that large quantities of care in a day nursery before the age of three increase the incidence of insecurity and aggression in children, and that these damaging effects are still evident years later.

What is extraordinary is how little impact this research has had, so far, on either public perception or government policy. This is partly because most of the experts have preferred to keep their heads below the parapet, well aware of the kind of panic headlines that their findings could produce. They are terrified of thousands of already anxious parents waking up to a Daily Mail splash – 'Day nurseries make children violent'. They have preferred to lobby government from the inside. Meanwhile, the private-sector day nurseries mushroom unchecked, and government ignores the negative findings ...

The Guardian, 8 July 2004

1 To what extent should we really worry at the increase in nursery care?

2 Using your knowledge of attachment (think back to Bowlby and Ainsworth), explain why the way the transition is managed, the sensitivity of workers and the stability of care might all be important to a child starting day care.

Implications of research for child care practice

The research we have looked at in this chapter can be applied to the making of decisions about day care, by both child care professionals and parents. For childminders and nursery staff, the major issues seem to be around providing consistent, good-quality care. For parents, there are difficult decisions to make about whether to use day care at all, what sort of care to choose, what age to begin and how many hours to leave their child. How parents feel about being separated from their child may also be important.

What day care providers can do

Figure 3.22 Childminders have the opportunity to provide highly consistent care

Consistency of care is important if children are to form secure attachments to professional carers. Childminders have an advantage here as they are the *only* carer, and some studies, including one by Melhuish *et al.* (1990), have found that children attending a childminder show higher rates of secure attachment, lower aggression and better peer relations than those in nurseries. In nurseries, consistency can be improved by having as high a staff–child ratio as possible and assigning each child a key worker who spends a significant amount of time with them. Recall the study by De Schipper *et al.* (p67) in which the availability of a child's key worker correlated significantly with their emotional well-being. Consistency is also achieved in a nursery by having a low turnover of staff. This can be addressed by providing good pay and working conditions.

Quality of care is also clearly important. Good quality is associated with sensitive responsiveness on the part of carers, a stimulating environment and positive attitudes among staff. Nursery managers have an important role here in employing sensitive and positive staff and providing necessary training. Howes *et al.* (1998) investigated the effectiveness of sensitive responsiveness training with nursery staff. Thirty-six children in an American nursery were followed up from 12 to 46 months. Observers rated the attachment security of the children and the sensitivity of staff at each point. Twenty hours of sensitivity training was given to staff after the initial assessment. Some staff improved in sensitivity following the training, and the children they were responsible for were more likely than others to maintain or achieve a secure attachment. This study suggests that sensitivity training is an effective strategy to improve the quality of nursery care.

Childminders and nursery staff can also help by having policies about how they and parents will manage the transition to day care. Recall the study by Ahnert *et al.* (2004) (p66). Having a gradual transition in which parents spend time with children in the day care setting and gradually increase the time spent in day care may be of great benefit for children, but parents may need to be made aware of this. Providing these initial settling visits free of charge is one way to encourage parents to opt for the kind of transition that will cause children the least anxiety.

Problem solver

Your local nursery has lost business after recent bad publicity about research showing negative effects of day care. They have asked you to put together a leaflet they can use to reassure potential parents. Put one together for them. You might want to explain why bad publicity might be unjustified, give evidence of the possible benefits of day care and offer a run-down of this particular nursery's policies and practices that ensure that children attending it get a good deal.

What parents can do

One important message from the research for parents-to-be is to know something about day care research but not to get too anxious. One reason not to worry too desperately is that the increased risks associated with day care are actually fairly modest. Recall the study by Belsky (2002) (p66). Even day care of over 30 hours per week was associated with only a 16 per cent greater risk of increased aggression. In the study by Allhusen *et al.* (2003), carer sensitiveness correlated only very slightly with social competence; it accounted for less than four per cent of the variance in children's social skills. These figures are large enough to be unlikely to be due to chance, and so they are of great interest to psychologists. However, they are nowhere near large enough to suggest that your child is doomed to poor social development just because you use day care. There is also evidence that the children of parents who are positive about returning to work are more likely to have secure attachments than those whose parents are very anxious about it (Harrison & Ungerer, 2002).

That said, every parent wants the best possible chances for their children, and where possible we want to avoid even small risks to their development. Parents can ask about the sort of factors that affect consistency of care, such as staff to child ratio, staff turnover and the policy on key workers. Parents can also observe the sensitivity of staff when interacting with children. Most importantly, according to the findings of De Schipper *et al.* (p67), parents should be consistent in using the same day care provider. To reduce risks still further, main carers may be able to consider returning to work part-time or delaying the return to work. Recall Belsky's research: risks to social development are reduced if the child spends fewer hours in day care, and in any case are only associated with day care beginning in the child's first year.

CHAPTER SUMMARY

- Attachment is a two-way emotional bond characterised by proximity-seeking, secure base behaviour and distress at separation.
- Early theories linked mother–infant attachment to provision of food, but this was challenged by Harlow's findings that baby monkeys separated from their mothers preferred a cuddly substitute mother to one that fed them.
- Bowlby proposed that attachment is an evolved system designed to maximise children's safety. He suggested that infants have instinctive behaviours called social releasers designed to elicit adult caring behaviour.
- Bowlby suggested that the child's first attachment serves as a prototype for later relationships, including relationships with their own children.
- Ainsworth developed Bowlby's ideas about secure attachment by proposing two insecure types, avoidant and resistant. Her Strange Situation test is the most popular way to assess infant attachment type.
- Research has largely supported Ainsworth's idea that the major factor affecting attachment security is maternal sensitivity, although other factors, such as stress and the temperament of the child, are also important.
- Research has shown that children with insecure attachments are more likely to have mental health problems and poor adult relationships.
- The rates of securely attached babies as measured by the Strange Situation vary from one country to another. This variation may reflect different child-rearing practices, or it may be that the Strange Situation does not work as a measure of attachment in some cultures.
- Privation occurs when children do not have the opportunity to form an attachment. Much of the research in this area is by means of case studies, which show severely disrupted social development. It is unclear to what extent this is reversible.
- Care in poor-quality institutions can also lead to privation. Even good-quality institutional care is associated with disinhibited attachment behaviour.
- The alleged effects of day care have led to one of the most bitter arguments in psychology. Evidence is mixed, but it seems that spending long hours in poor-quality or inconsistent day care from an early age leads to an increased risk of poor social development in at least some children.
- Research has revealed a number of factors that mitigate any ill effects of day care. Good day care thus involves high levels of stability, sensitive and positive workers, and a managed transition from maternal to day care.

What do I know?

1 (a) Identify the two **true** statements from the following. All are concerned with Bowlby's theory of attachment. (2 marks)

A Bowlby believed that babies become attached to adults who feed them. TRUE ☐ FALSE ☐

B Bowlby believed that being securely attached makes children safer. TRUE ☐ FALSE ☐

C Bowlby believed we form a working model of relationships from our first attachment. TRUE ☐ FALSE ☐

D Bowlby believed that fathers were as important as mothers. TRUE ☐ FALSE ☐

(b) Outline **one** criticism of Bowlby's evolutionary perspective on attachment. (3 marks)

2 (a) Outline **one** study of attachment by Mary Ainsworth. (4 marks)

(b) What is meant by a naturalistic observation? (4 marks)

3 (a) Describe what has been found out about one cultural variation in attachment. (3 marks)

(b) Outline **two** ethical issues that researchers working with young children should take account of. (4 marks)

4 (a) Explain what is meant by institutionalisation. (2 marks)

(b) Studies of institutionalisation are often natural experiments in which a group of institutionalised children are compared with non-institutionalised children. What are the features of a natural experiment? (3 marks)

(c) What has research shown us about the effects of institutionalisation on children's development? (5 marks)

5 The graph below shows a correlation between average hours spent in day care per week and aggression.

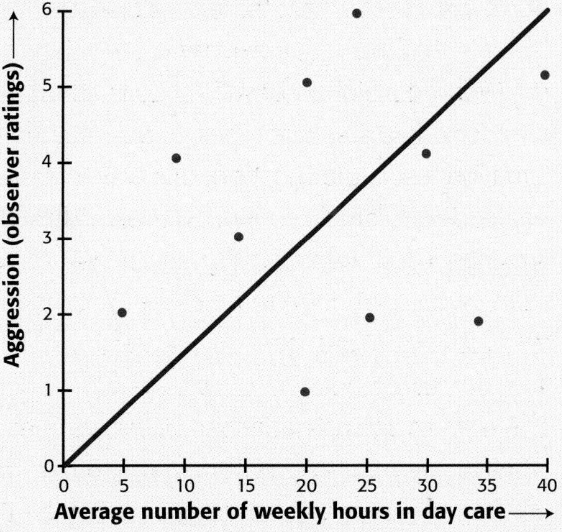

(a) Tick the box next to the term below that best describes what this graph shows.

A Strong positive correlation ☐

B Weak positive correlation ☐

C Strong negative correlation ☐

D Weak negative correlation ☐

(b) There has been a lot of recent bad publicity about nursery care. In particular, there have been claims that research has shown that children who experience day care are more aggressive. As a result, your local nursery is losing business.

They have approached you to ask you to write a report making a case in favour of day care. What would you say in your report? Refer to the information in this question in your answer. (5 marks)

6 Critically discuss the possible effects of day care on children's social development. (12 marks)

CHAPTER 4
Research Methods

Thinking ahead

By the end of this chapter you should be able to:

- **describe and evaluate a range of research methods (experiments, correlations, observations, questionnaires, interviews and case studies)**
- **design investigations (experimental, observational and self-report) and be able to understand aims, hypotheses, operationalisation, pilot studies, controls, reliability, validity, sampling, demand characteristics and investigator effects**
- **distinguish between and understand when and why different experimental methods are used (natural, field and laboratory)**
- **distinguish between and understand when and why different experimental designs are used (independent groups, repeated measures and matched pairs)**
- **show an awareness of ethical issues and of the BPS ethical guidelines and how these help psychologists to deal with ethical issues**
- **analyse and interpret quantitative data using measures of central tendency (mean, median, mode) and measures of spread (range and standard deviation)**
- **present and interpret quantitative data using graphs, scattergrams and tables**
- **analyse and interpret correlational data (positive and negative correlations and correlation coefficients)**
- **present and analyse qualitative data (including content analysis)**

METHODS AND TECHNIQUES

KEY TERMS

independent variable – the factor that the investigator manipulates in an experiment

dependent variable – the factor that the investigator measures in an experiment

operationalisation – defining variables so that they can be accurately manipulated, measured and replicated

experiment – a study in which an IV is manipulated and consequent changes in a DV are measured in order to establish a cause and effect relationship

Experimental methods

Independent and dependent variables

The general aim of an experiment is see how changes in one factor affect another factor. A situation is created in which the effects can be observed and measured. In a true experiment the variations in the first factor, called the *independent variable*, are deliberately created by the researcher. An experiment aims to show that the changes in the factor being measured, the *dependent variable*, are caused by the changes in the independent variable. So, an experimental investigation usually has two (or more) conditions or 'levels' of the independent variable (IV), and the dependent variable is measured in each of these situations. To be certain that any changes in the dependent variable (the 'DV') arise only because of changes in the IV, it is ideal to have controls that keep other factors that could affect the DV constant. This means it is possible to determine a 'cause and effect relationship' – that is, to be sure that changes in the independent variable (the IV) are responsible for changes in the DV.

Operationalising variables

In order to be certain about the findings of an experiment, we must be sure that we know exactly what has changed. For the IV this means knowing precisely how the variable was manipulated. For the DV this means being confident that the changes have been measured accurately. To achieve this, the researcher operationalises both variables. For example, in an experiment testing the effect of chunking on recall we can identify the two variables: the IV is chunking and the DV is recall. However, these are not sufficient as definitions; another researcher would not be able to tell what had been changed or how the effect had been observed, hence the need for operationalisation. To operationalise the IV we could state that there were two levels of the IV: one in which a word list could be chunked and one in which the list items were unrelated. This could be expanded to say the items on the chunked list were all items of furniture, stationery or fruit whereas on the non-chunked list every word was from a different category. Operationalisation of the DV would simply be the number of words recalled.

RESEARCH IN ACTION

Peterson & Peterson (1959) (p11)

In this study, participants were being tested for the duration of their short-term memory for nonsense syllables.

The **independent variable** was the length of the delay. It was operationalised as 3, 6, 9, 12, 15 or 18 seconds. This is an example of a study with more than two levels of the IV.

The **DV** was the probability of recalling the syllable. This was expressed as a percentage measured over several trials.

Thinking practically about psychology

1 **Conrad (1964)** (p12)
Identify the IV and the DV in this study.

2 **Baddeley (1966)** (p14)
How was the IV operationalised in this study?

3 **Peterson & Peterson (1959)** (p11)
How was the DV operationalised in this study?

Thinking creatively about psychology

Decide which is the IV and which is the DV in each of the following experiments. Then, for one or more of them, decide how you would operationalise the IV and the DV:

- In a test of memory, recall of long and short words was compared.
- An investigation aimed to measure whether there was a difference in ability to remember between young people and older people.
- Some students conducted an experiment to find out if it was easier to remember familiar things than unfamiliar ones by getting participants to play 'Kim's Game' (where the objects to be remembered are presented on a tray, then covered up).

Figure 4.1 Children playing a version of Kim's game using cards showing pictures of objects

KEY TERMS

experimental design – the way in which participation in an experiment is organised. Participants can perform in only one or all of the levels of the IV

independent groups design – an experimental design in which different groups of participants are used for each level of the IV

repeated measures design – an experimental design in which each participant performs in every level of the IV

matched pairs design – an experimental design in which participants are arranged into pairs. Each pair is similar in ways that are important to the study, and the members of each pair perform in the two different levels of the IV

Experimental design

In an experiment, participants may be tested in all, or only one, of the levels of the IV. The different arrangements are called experimental designs. There are three important ones to learn about.

Independent groups

In this experimental design, a separate group of participants is used for each level of the IV. This means that the set of data gained for each condition is 'independent' because it is not related to any other pieces of data, as it has come from different people. Note that this is not the same use of the word 'independent' as in the 'independent variable'. If we wanted to know whether age affected memory, we could test recall in a group of young people and then wait for them to grow old. However, it is much quicker to compare them to a group of older adults to look at the effect of age. This would be an independent groups design.

Figure 4.2 Randomly allocating participants to conditions can help to overcome bias caused by individual differences

Such a design has the advantage that the participants experience the experimental setting only once, which means that they are less likely to spot the aims of the experiment and respond to them. One disadvantage is that there may be individual differences between participants that could influence the findings. For example, in a study on the effect of repetition, all the people with good memories might end up in the 'no rehearsal' group. If that happened, it might look as though rehearsal was less important than it is in reality. This effect can be reduced by randomly allocating participants to different conditions. This should even out the differences between individuals across the levels of the IV. To randomly allocate participants, they are all given a number. The numbers are then randomly divided into two groups. This can be done by putting cards with numbers on into a hat and drawing out two sets or using a random number generator eg on a computer to do the same thing.

Peterson & Peterson (1959)
(p11)

This study was investigating the duration of STM. Each participant's recall was tested after six different length delays – **a repeated measures design**.

Baddeley (1966)
(p14)

This study tested the effect of similarity of the sound or meaning of words in a list on recall. Participants heard either the 'similar sound' list or the 'similar meaning' list – **an independent groups design**. This was important so that there would not be interference between the different word lists, as could have occurred if individuals had performed in both conditions.

Repeated measures

When the same group of people participate in each level of the IV, this is called a *repeated measures design*. You can think of this as the participants 'repeating' their performance under different conditions. For example, we could conduct a study like that of Conrad (1964) to investigate the effect of acoustic similarity on short-term memory. Each participant could learn two sets of nonsense syllables. One condition would consist of sound-alike syllables (e.g. jed, ved, det, ped, het, fet, ket, ged) and in the other each of the syllables would sound different (e.g. wug, rel, jun, vig, dac, hof, ker, gan).

A repeated measures design has the advantage that each person effectively acts as their own baseline. Any differences between participants that might influence their performance will affect both levels of the IV by the same amount, so this is unlikely to bias the findings. Supposing one person was very good at a memory task and another quite poor, this could be a problem if they happened to be in different groups in an independent groups design. In a repeated measures design, however, both participants are likely to show a difference in performance between conditions, doing better in one than another. So, in our nonsense syllable example, if some participants had very good memories and others bad, this wouldn't matter, as the difference between their scores in the sound-alike

KEY TERMS

participant variables – individual differences between participants (such as age, skills, personality) that could affect their responses in a study

order effects – changes in participants' performance due to their repeating the same or a similar test more than once. They can confuse the effect of the IV on the DV in a repeated measures design

practice effect – an improvement in performance on a task due to repetition, for example because of familiarity with or memory of the task

fatigue effect – an decrease in performance on a task due to repetition, for example because of boredom or tiredness

demand characteristics – aspects of an experimental setting that accidentally tell the participants the aim of the study. They can cause the participants' behaviour to change

and sound-different conditions would still indicate whether the acoustic similarity was affecting their recall. Individual differences between participants are called *participant variables*. These variables, such as age, gender or intelligence, can affect the participants' score on the DV. It is therefore important to make sure that such differences do not hide, or exaggerate, differences between levels of the IV.

There is, however, a disadvantage to a repeated measures design. As each individual participates in every level of the IV, they will perform the same or similar tasks two or more times. This repetition can lead to *order effects*. Specifically, repeated performance could cause the participants to improve because they have encountered the task before – a *practice effect*. This would matter because participants who were tested on one of the conditions first would perform worse than those who did it second. Alternatively, repetition may make performance worse, perhaps because the participants get bored or tired – a *fatigue effect*. Furthermore, the participants have more opportunity to work out what is being tested and are therefore more likely to respond to *demand characteristics*. These are features of the experimental setting that give away the aim of the study and lead the participants to respond differently, for example to do what they think the experimenter wants.

1 Bahrick (1984) (pp13–14)

If Bahrick compared people who had learned Spanish 10, 20, 30, 40 and 50 years prior to testing, these periods would be the levels of the IV. Why is it likely that an independent groups design would be used?

2 McClelland *et al.* (2006) (p22)

This study compared participants with and without an interference task designed to impair function of the visuo-spatial sketchpad. Which experimental design was this?

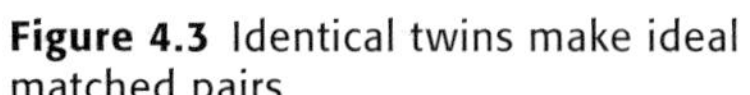

Figure 4.3 Identical twins make ideal matched pairs

Matched pairs

One way to overcome the problems associated with both independent groups and repeated measures designs is to use a *matched pairs design*. In this situation a different group of participants is used for each level of the IV. However, each participant in one group is matched to a corresponding participant in the other group(s). This matching is done on relevant variables. For example, in a study looking at the effect of amnesia by measuring recall of words, it would be ideal to compare each amnesic to an unaffected person who was similar in other respects (such as having the same age, intelligence or vocabulary). While some factors, such as age or gender, may be important characteristics for matching in many studies, others, such as vocabulary or attitudes may be very important in particular investigations but unimportant in others. When possible, identical twins make ideal matched pairs.

Conners *et al.* (2000)
(p20)

This study investigated the short-term and long-term memory of children with Prader–Willi syndrome (PWS). Each child with PWS was matched to one without PWS of similar age and intelligence. Each pair could then be compared directly in a **matched pairs design**.

Dykens (2002) conducted a study very similar to that of **Conners *et al.*** (p20), comparing children with PWS, other forms of mental retardation and normal children. They were tested in several ways, including their ability to carry out jigsaw puzzle and word tasks. The children were matched for age and intelligence. Suggest two other criteria upon which it would have been important to match the children.

Sources of error and how to control them

Order effects and counterbalancing

KEY TERMS

counterbalancing – a way to overcome order effects in a repeated measures design. Each possible order of levels of the IV is performed by a different sub-group of participants. This can be described as an ABBA design, as half the participants do condition A then B and half do B then A.

On p76 we described order effects. These arise in experiments with a repeated measures design because participation in one level of the IV can affect performance in the next. This can be overcome in two different ways: by randomisation or by counterbalancing. Let's assume there are two conditions in a memory experiment: 'delay' (D) and 'no delay' (N). In randomisation, participants are randomly allocated to do either condition D followed by N or vice versa. Since some will do each order, any advantage of doing one of the conditions first will probably be evened out in the results. To be more certain that possible effects are evened out, *counterbalancing* can be used. Here, the group of participants is divided into two, and one half will do D followed by N, the other half N followed by D. If on the second test there was a risk of participants muddling up items remembered from the first test, this would be a problem for exactly half the participants in the 'delay' condition and exactly half in the 'no delay' condition. Of course, an alternative would be to use a different design.

If you can, conduct a quick experiment in your class. It will be a repeated measures design that aims to test whether having auditory distraction affects a sound-based task more than a visual one. The tasks are:

- sound-based (S): learn a set of words such as are printed upside down at the bottom of p79
- visual task (V): learn a set of images such as are printed upside down at the bottom of p79

Divide the group in half and allocate everyone to perform either S then V or V then S. You need to give everyone a number and use the random allocator at http://www.assumption.edu/users/avadum/applets/applets.html. Click on 'Random assignment' and type in half the total number of people in your group as the 'n per group' and '2' as the number of groups. When you click on 'generate groups' you will be provided with two lists of random numbers. Use list number 1 for SV and list 2 as VS. Choose a source of auditory distraction such as having a radio talk show playing throughout both conditions.

Demand characteristics

Aspects of an experimental situation can make participants believe that they know how the researcher expects them to behave and can cause them to change their behaviour (to help or to hinder the experimenter). These cues from the experimental setting are called demand characteristics. In order to hide the purpose of the experiment, the researcher may deceive the participants about the aims of the study. For example, in a test of the effect of different kinds of musical interference on memory, the researcher might not want the participants to know it is a test of memory at all, because that would cause them to focus

KEY TERMS

single blind – an experimental procedure which ensures that the participants are unaware of the level of the IV in which they are performing. This helps to reduce the effect of demand characteristics.

investigator effects – any unwitting influence a researcher has on the participants. These include experimenter bias and the effects of researchers in non-experimental investigations such as in interviews.

experimenter bias – the effect of an experimenter's expectations on the results of a study, e.g. caused by differences in the way an experimenter behaves towards participants in different conditions.

double blind – an experimental procedure that protects against both demand characteristics and experimenter bias. It ensures that neither the researcher working with the participants nor the participants themselves are aware of which condition an individual is in.

on the task rather than the music. Instead, the participants might be told that it is a test of hearing or concentration and that they are to read the word list while listening. This would reduce the risk of demand characteristics affecting performance, but it also raises ethical issues (see pp110–13). There is clearly a dilemma for researchers between rigorous studies in which variables are effectively controlled and the need to keep participants informed about the aims and methods of a study.

If possible, only the researcher, and not the participants, should know which condition each individual has been allocated to. This is called a *single-blind* procedure and it helps reduce the risk that participants will try to produce the results they believe the experimenter wants.

In an independent groups design, demand characteristics should be less problematic than in a repeated measures design as the participants have only one opportunity to observe the experimental procedure. In a repeated measures design, not only are the participants exposed to the experimental setting twice but they see both levels of the IV, so it is more likely that they will correctly guess the purpose of the study.

Investigator effects

Investigators design investigations and experimenters conduct them. The investigator can accidentally affect the outcome of a study through the way it is designed. The experimenter can also affect the outcome by how they act when data are collected. In both cases the effect is ultimately on the way the experimenter interacts with the participant. For example, a design error might cause an experimenter to have much more contact with participants in one level of the IV than another. This could affect the results by making one group more nervous. A direct effect, however, comes from the experimenter's own behaviour. Both the indirect and direct influences are called *investigator effects*.

Like participants, experimenters too have expectations about what should happen in a study, and these can affect the way that they respond to participants. This is called *experimenter bias*. For example, if in one condition (such as one with a task designed to prevent rehearsal) participants are expected to perform less well, this might be unconsciously communicated by the experimenter. If so, this might cause the 'no rehearsal' group to do worse than the 'rehearsal' group.

Figure 4.4 STM in males is better when holding a phone – even if it is turned off

RESEARCH IN ACTION

Smythe and Costall (2003)

(p15)

This study aimed to find out whether mobile phones affect memory. Participants learned words with a phone turned on or off or with no phone. For males, STM was better with a phone that was switched on than off. It is likely that the difference in performance on the short-term memory task seen in the male participants was caused by **demand characteristics**. Although the participants were not told the aims of the study, it was necessary in terms of ethics to tell them it was about mobile phones. Those in the 'no phone' group would therefore have known they were the control group and may have paid less attention, creating the difference. However, in order to avoid demand characteristics producing a difference between the 'phone on' and 'phone off' groups, the participants were handed the phone but did not know whether it was switched on or off. This was a **single-blind procedure.**

Two aspects of the procedure can help to overcome experimenter bias. First, all experiments should have standardised instructions. These ensure that all participants are treated in exactly the same way. The experimenter may read the instructions from a script or they may be printed for participants to read to themselves. This reduces the risk that the experimenter will unwittingly give away their expectations about the results. Second, a *double-blind* procedure may be employed. This is where an experimenter sets up a situation but another researcher who is unaware of which participants are in which condition actually conducts the study. As in a single-blind procedure, the participants are also unaware of this. Although obviously more difficult to organise, a double-blind procedure has the advantage of reducing the risk of both demand characteristics and experimenter effects.

Thinking creatively about psychology

Choose a study such as that of **Peterson & Peterson (1959)** (p11) or **Baddeley *et al.* (1973)** (p22). Write a possible set of standardised instructions that might have been used in the study. Try to provide as much information to the participants as you can about what will happen without giving away the aims of the experiment. Decide whether you can arrange the experiment as a single or double-blind procedure.

Figure 4.5 Chewing gum at learning and recall improves performance

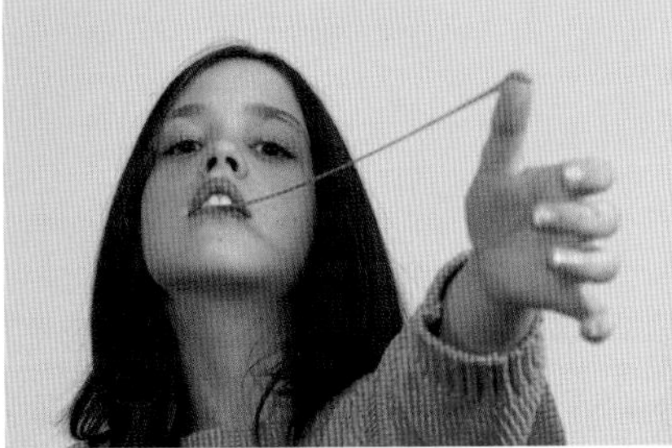

RESEARCH IN ACTION

Baker *et al.* (2004)

(p25)

This was a **laboratory experiment** into the effects of chewing gum on memory. In the laboratory, the experimenters could **control** factors such as how much chewing gum the subjects were given, the length of time available for learning and recall of the words, and the length of the delay before recalling. They could also ensure that there were no distractions during the learning or recall phases and that other factors such as light levels that might affect the ease with which participants could see the words were kept constant.

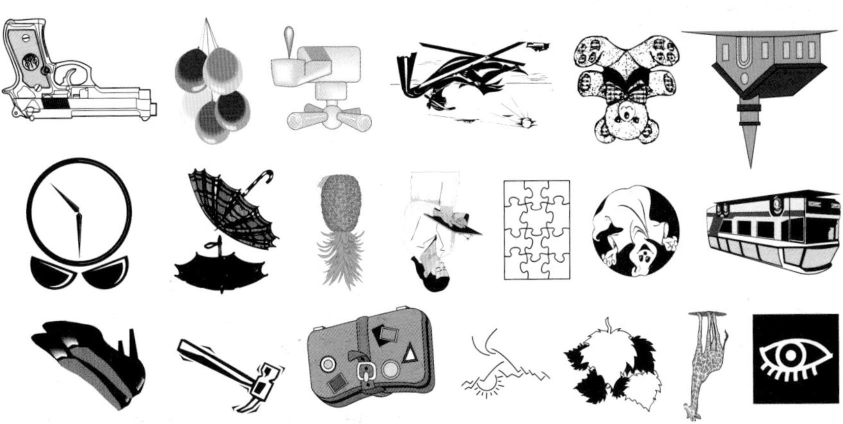

sound-based task list: *cloth, dog, lamp, bucket, flower, toaster, scarf, curtains, cloud, shop, book, ball, coffee, steps, snout, television, fence, dollar, portrait, button.*

visual task list:

Laboratory experiments

The examples of experiments we have looked at so far in this chapter have all been laboratory experiments. This means that the experiment is conducted in a contrived environment such as a laboratory. The participants come into this setting in order to be part of the study; they would not be there normally. By setting up the situation artificially, the experimenter can control many variables that might influence the participants' behaviour. This control of extraneous variables is central to a laboratory experiment. It is one of the main reasons that the researchers choose to conduct laboratory experiments: they can be confident that if the IV does appear to affect the DV, the relationship is a causal one (see p73). One important variable to control in memory experiments is distractions. We know that rehearsal is important and that it can be prevented by interference so, in laboratory experiments, factors such as noise and the presence of other people are regulated. Factors in the surroundings such as noise or light that can disrupt an experiment are called *situational variables*.

As we have seen, using a laboratory experiment generally also makes it easy to allocate participants to conditions, to counterbalance or to use standardised instructions. One final advantage is that because the procedure is so rigorously controlled, laboratory experiments are easy to replicate – that is, to repeat exactly. Doing this allows researchers to be more confident about their findings.

There are also some disadvantages to conducting experiments in a laboratory. As the participants know they are involved in a study, they are likely to try to work out the purpose of tasks they are given, so tend to respond to demand characteristics. Also, because the participants are not in their normal environment they may respond in a different way from the way they would usually. For example, participants in a study into the effects of auditory interference on recall may also be distracted by the new sights or smells in the lab. These uncontrolled variables might make their performance uncharacteristic of their normal memory capacity. Demand characteristics and investigator effects may also be problematic in laboratory experiments. These are some of the reasons why an experimenter might choose a different technique such as a field or natural experiment.

RESEARCH IN ACTION

Godden & Baddeley (1975) (p26)

This study tested how context cues help recall. Words were recalled better when the learning and the recall environment (land or water) were the same than when they were different. In this **field experiment** the divers knew they were participating in a study. Remember also that the participants *were* familiar with diving, making the study ethical in terms of the risk participants experienced.

Situational variables caused problems in this study because it was a field experiment. These included having to use different dive sites for different participants (including two in fresh water rather than the sea), participants being tested at different times of day and using slightly different diving apparatus. During an experimental session, one participant was nearly run over by an amphibious truck!

Field experiments

An alternative approach to using a laboratory is to conduct a *field experiment*. In this case, there is still an IV that is manipulated by the experimenter and a DV that is measured. The setting, however, is the participants' normal environment in relation to the behaviour being investigated. For example, the effect of different revision methods on memory might be tested in a classroom environment. The investigator could set up a situation in which a teacher uses revision diagrams for one topic and revision songs for another. The IV would be the memory strategy, either visual (diagrams) or auditory (songs). The DV would be measured using tests of each topic. As the situation would be familiar to the students, they should be far less affected by being in an experiment than they would be for a similar test in a lab. They might not even know that they are in an experiment at all. This is sometimes, but not always, the case in field experiments. When the participants are unaware of the experiment, their behaviour is more likely to be representative of real life, which is an advantage of field experiments. However, although they are less likely to respond to demand characteristics, carrying out field experiments does, however, raise ethical issues.

One clear disadvantage of the field experiment is that it is difficult to maintain control over situational variables. This means that changes in the DV may be caused by factors other than the IV. In the case of the classroom example, the different topics could have been more difficult or interesting or have been taught at different times in the term when the students were more or less tired. Any of these variables could have caused differences between conditions which would look as though there was an effect on the DV caused by the IV.

Thinking critically about psychology

Look up each of the following studies and decide whether they were laboratory or field experiments. In each case, decide why that approach was taken.

Sperling (1966) (p9)
McClelland *et al.* (2006) (p22)
Krackow & Lynn (2003) (p35)
Memon *et al.* (2006) (p36)

RESEARCH IN ACTION

Hodges & Tizard (1989)
(p61)

This study was a **natural experiment** investigating the effects of different kinds of subsequent care on children who had been in institutional care from under four months of age. It was essential that this study was conducted as a natural experiment as it would not have been ethical to have manipulated the children's care for the purposes of an investigation. There were three levels of the IV:

- adoption
- returning to the biological family
- remaining in institutional care.

Comparisons between the groups were made at ages 4, 8 and 16 years. The measures of the DV of social and emotional development taken at these times included indicators of:

- how clingy the children were
- the extent to which they sought attention
- the closeness of their relationships
- how physically affectionate they were
- their popularity with other children
- how aggressive they were.

KEY TERMS

laboratory experiment – a study conducted in an artificial environment in which the experimenter manipulates an IV and measures the consequent changes in a DV while carefully controlling extraneous variables

field experiment – a study in which the researcher manipulates an IV and measures a DV in the natural setting of the participants

natural experiment – a study in which an experimenter makes use of an existing change or difference in situations to create levels of an IV and then measures the DV in each condition

Natural experiments

A *natural experiment* differs from a true experiment in that the experimenter does not set up the levels of the IV. Natural experiments make use of natural – that is, not artificially produced – changes or differences in circumstances to provide the experimental conditions. They can be conducted in laboratory or field settings. Researchers use natural experiments when it would be impractical or unethical to generate the conditions necessary for the different levels of the IV. For example, when comparing men and women, we cannot randomly allocate people to the 'male' and female' levels of the IV, and if we wanted to investigate the effects of maternal deprivation in humans we could not, as Harlow did with monkeys, randomly allocate babies to deprived and non-deprived conditions.

As we described on p64–65, experiments comparing children who are in day care with those who are not are not true experiments as the children cannot be randomly allocated to conditions. There may be important differences, such as in attachment type of the mother herself, family stability or wealth, between those who do choose day care and those who do not. It is then difficult to identify whether any differences in the DV of the children's development are caused by the IV of day care or one of the extraneous variables.

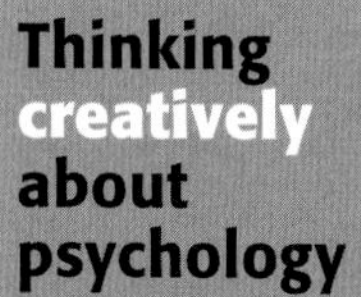

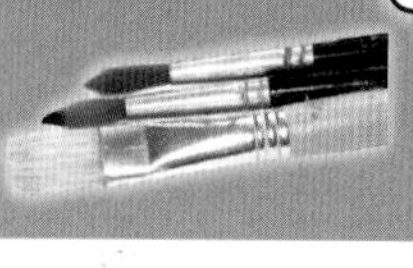

Make a poster that illustrates two real experiments using pictures. One of the studies must have an independent groups design, the other a repeated measures design. Incorporate into the poster some advantages and disadvantages of these designs.

Where natural experiments are conducted in the field, they have the benefit that the participants are in their usual environment so their behaviour is more likely to be representative of real life. Since the participants are not actively allocated to conditions, it is more possible that the existence of the experiment can be hidden from them. This reduces the risk of demand characteristics affecting behaviour. Of course, because participants are not randomly allocated to different levels of the IV it is difficult to distinguish between the effects of any existing differences between groups of participants and those differences that are due to the experiment. For example, if we were to investigate the effects of organisation on revision using a natural experiment, we might compare people who revise using cue cards and mind maps (high-organisation) and those who revise using a highlighter pen to go through their class notes (low-organisation). Although the people who used the high-organisation techniques might get better results (that is, there may be an effect on the DV), we wouldn't know whether the superior results were brought about by the revision method (the IV) or whether the participants in the high-organisation group were simply more intelligent, or spent more time working, than those in the low-organisation group.

You can conduct a natural experiment on your class. Ask everyone to write down whether they generally work with music playing, the TV on or neither. Once everyone has done this, turn over and continue following the instructions on p84.

Figure 4.6

Thinking critically about psychology

Zeanah *et al.* (2005) carried out a natural experiment (p63).

- What were the two levels of the IV?
- Why was it necessary to conduct this investigation as a natural experiment?
- What was the DV and how was it measured?
- Would the mothers have known that they were participating in an experiment?
- Is this an advantage or a disadvantage and why?

The children in this study were not selected for adoption on the basis of how well adjusted they were, unlike in Hodges & Tizard's study (p61) in which this was a possibility. Why is the design of Zeanah *et al.*'s study better in this respect?

Table 4.1 Strengths and weaknesses of the experimental method

Experimental method	Strengths	Weaknesses
Laboratory experiments	• Good control of extraneous variables • Causal relationships can be determined • Strict procedures allow them to be replicated so researchers can be more confident about their findings	• The artificial situation may make participants' behaviour unrepresentative • Participants may respond to demand characteristics and alter their behaviour • Investigator effects may lead to biased results
Field experiments	• As participants are in their normal situation, their behaviour is likely to be representative • Participants may be unaware that they are in a study, so demand characteristics are less problematic than in laboratory experiments	• Control over extraneous variables is more difficult than in a laboratory • The researcher cannot be sure that changes in the DV have been caused by changes in the IV • There are fewer controls, so they are more difficult to replicate than laboratory experiments • If participants are unaware that they are in a study, this raises ethical issues
Natural experiments	• They can be used to study real-world issues • If participants are in their normal situation, their behaviour is likely to be representative • If participants are unaware that they are in a study, demand characteristics will be less problematic • They enable researchers to investigate variables that could not practically or ethically be manipulated	• They are only possible when naturally occurring differences arise • Control over extraneous variables is more difficult than in a laboratory experiment • As the researcher is not manipulating the IV they can be less sure of the cause of changes in the DV so a causal relationship cannot be extablished • They generally cannot be replicated

Thinking critically about psychology

Identify the experimental method (laboratory, field or natural) and the design (repeated measures or independent groups) being used in each of these studies:

Abernethy (1940) (p25)
Baddeley (1966) (p14)
Harrison & Ungerer (2002) (p65)
Koren-Karie (2001) (p65)
Wright and Holliday (2005) (p36)

KEY TERMS

correlational analysis – a technique used to investigate a link between two measured variables

causal relationship – a relationship between two variables such that a change in one is responsible for a change in the other

positive correlation – a relationship between two variables such that an increase in one accompanies an increase in the other

negative correlation – a relationship between two variables such that an increase in one accompanies a decrease in the other

scattergram – a graph used to display the data from a correlational study. Each point represents the participant's score on scales for each of the two measured variables

Decide what you would like to investigate – for example, the effect of distraction during revision or the effect of auditory versus visual distraction. Using the information about work habits, you can divide the people in you class up into groups: those who listen to music (auditory distraction), those who have the TV on (auditory and visual distraction) and those who have no distraction. These are the levels of the IV. Finally, ask your teacher to provide a list of recent test or homework grades. This can be done anonymously if you give your teacher the class list divided into groups and you receive in return a list of grades under each level of the IV. Is there a difference in achievement? If so, which work habit produces the best average grade?

Correlational analysis

A correlational analysis aims to investigate whether two variables are related. In order to do this, each variable is measured on a scale. Although the scales for each variable may be different, they both need to be numerical (or it must be possible to convert them to numbers). For example, variables such as 'brain weight' or IQ are numerical and could be used in a correlation. However, responses to the question 'What's your favourite colour?' or 'What's your employment status?' could not; the possible responses are not on a scale. If we obtained answers of 'employed', 'self-employed', 'student', 'retired' and 'at-home mum', we could not put them in order. (For more about kinds of data, see pp116–18).

The findings of a correlational analysis are used to assess the nature of the relationship between the two variables. This can be described in two ways: by the direction and by the strength of the link. In a positive correlation both variables increase in the same direction – that is, higher scores on one variable correspond with higher scores on the other. When two variables are negatively correlated, higher scores on one variable correspond with low scores on the other. There may alternatively be no relationship at all between two variables, in which case there is a zero correlation. The different relationships can be illustrated visually on a scattergram (see Figure 4.7). For example, if we were to collect data for a correlational analysis on the variables of brain volume and braininess, we might expect both to increase together. This would be a positive correlation. Alternatively, we could measure brain volume and reaction time. Now we would expect faster speeds (i.e. smaller reaction times) with bigger brains. This would be a negative correlation.

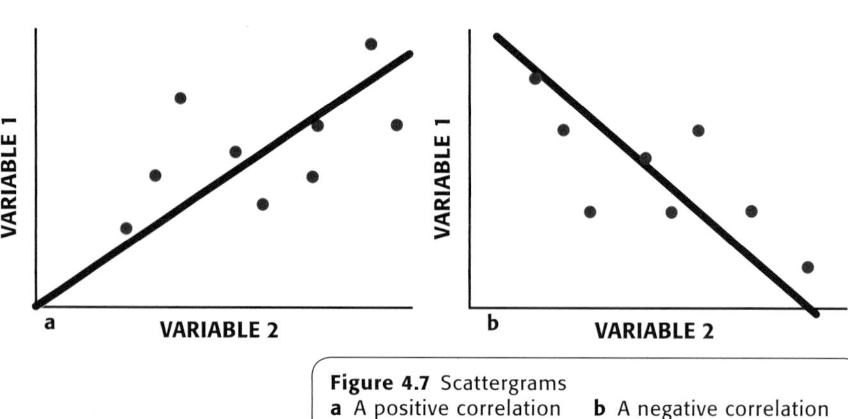

Figure 4.7 Scattergrams
a A positive correlation **b** A negative correlation

Another aspect of the findings of a correlation is the strength of the relationship. If a correlation is very strong, the two variables are closely linked. This can be readily seen on a scattergram – a graph on which each point represents one pair

Figure 4.8 What looks like a causal relationship between two factors may actually result from a third

My goldfish lives in a tank on my desk. The more fizzy drinks I consume, the more active my fish is. It's tempting to assume there is a causal relationship – seeing the bubbles in my glass makes her excited. In reality, there is no causal relationship; both variables are affected by a third factor – temperature. The hotter the weather, the more I drink and fish are more active in warmer water.

of scores. These two scores usually relate to one participant, although in some situations they may not, for example when comparing data from pairs of twins. On p123–24 we will see how we can use graphs and numbers to describe the strength of a correlation.

Note that we cannot say from one correlation that an increase in one variable has *caused* an increase (or decrease) in the other. This is because it is possible that the changes in both variables could have been caused by some other factor. Suppose we measure the two variables, short-term memory span and number of GCSEs, and find they are positively correlated. It might be tempting to say that a bigger memory span is responsible for getting better grades, but we cannot be sure that is the case. It is possible that both of these factors depend on another variable such as the amount of practice at learning and recall the individual has had in their lifetime. All we can conclude is that the two factors we have measured vary together, not that there is a causal relationship between them. If we want to make judgements about causality, we need to conduct an experiment where we can be sure that it is the manipulation of one variable that is responsible for the changes in the other. Of course, if we conduct a correlational analysis and find there is no link between two variables, then we can conclude that there is *no* causal relationship.

RESEARCH IN ACTION

Stayton and Ainsworth (1973)
(p52)

In this study two **correlations** were investigated. In one, the two variables measured were maternal sensitivity and how pleased the infant was to see the mother after a period of absence. The researchers found that the more sensitive the mother was, the more pleased the infant was on her return. This is a **positive correlation.**

In the other correlational analysis the two variables measured were maternal sensitivity and the amount of time the infant spent crying. They found that the more sensitive the mother was, the less the infant cried. This is a **negative correlation.**

There are some other advantages to correlational analyses. If a variable can neither be actively changed nor exists in different forms, it is not possible to use it as an IV in an experiment. The correlational method allows us to study variables such as intelligence or aspects of personality that cannot be manipulated. Furthermore, because there is no need to manipulate the variables, only measure them, correlational studies can also be used when it would be impractical or unethical to create changes artificially – for example, in investigating the effects of different degrees of intellectual impairment in people with learning difficulties. This is an important reason why researchers use correlational techniques.

Thinking critically about psychology

Rutter *et al.* (1998) (p62) studied Romanian orphans and found that the younger the age at which they were adopted, the more successfully they developed once adopted. **Ahnert *et al.* (2006)** (p65) investigated the effects of day care and found that for children in day care there was no link between socio-economic status and security of attachment. For children who did not have day care, those from families of higher economic status were more securely attached.

From these two studies, identify three situations: a positive correlation, a negative correlation and a zero correlation.

Thinking practically about psychology

De Schipper et al. (2004) (p67) measured several variables relating to children's day care in order to find factors that related to emotional well-being and problem behaviour. These included consistent attendance at the same nursery, consistency of staffing, daily activities, contact with other children and regularity of contact with a key worker.

Select two of these variables and decide how you would expect them to be related. Operationalise each variable so that they could be measured in a day care setting.

Thinking creatively about psychology

Scher & Mayseless (2000) (p53) correlated factors relating to the development of resistant (type C) attachments. They measured maternal variables such as being stressed and working long hours as well as the length of time the child spent each day in a nursery. They found that each of these variables was linked to a higher likelihood of the child being type C. These findings suggest that there is a relationship between the mother's lifestyle and the infant's attachment, but they are only correlational.

Why is it not possible to draw causal conclusions about the influence of maternal lifestyle on the child's attachment type?

On the basic of these findings, design a natural experiment to test this issue further.

Table 4.2 Strengths and weaknesses of correlational analysis

Strengths	Weaknesses
• A correlational study can be conducted on variables which can be measured but not manipulated – that is, when experimentation would be impractical or unethical • A correlation can demonstrate the presence or absence of a relationship so is useful for indicating areas for subsequent experimental research	• A single correlational analysis cannot indicate whether a relationship is causal so when a relationship is found this may be due to one of the measured variables. Alternatively another, unknown, variable may be responsible • Correlational analysis can only be used with variables that can be measured on a scale

KEY TERMS

disclosed observation – watching and recording the behaviour of participants who are aware that they are being observed

non-disclosed observation – watching and recording the behaviour of participants who are unaware that they are being observed

participant observation – the observer is a member of the group or activity being observed

non-participant observation – the observer is hidden from the participant(s) being observed, for example by using a video camera

Observational techniques

Observations are used when psychologists want to record the behaviour of participants (including animals and children as well as adults). One reason why researchers choose to use observations is that they measure actual responses – what people do – rather than what they think or say they would do. Another reason for conducting an observation is in cases when the participants are unable to follow instructions or give verbal responses, for example when babies or animals are being investigated. Clearly, the only way to gain information about infants' attachment from the infants themselves is to watch them.

In common with correlational analyses, observations can be used when experimentation is not possible. Observational techniques may be used as a research method in their own right or as a means to measure the DV in an experiment. In either case, records may be taken in the form of a checklist, with each occurrence of a behaviour being tallied. This is called event sampling.

RESEARCH IN ACTION

Cantero and Cerezo (2001) (p52) observed Spanish mothers interacting with their babies using the Strange Situation. Since the observer is not one of the participants in the Strange Situation, this is a **non-participant observation**. The role of the observer was also known to the participants, so this was also a **disclosed observation**.

Koluchová (1972, 1991) (p60) studied the development of twin boys who had been isolated for much of their early life over many years. Some of this work included conducting a **participant observation** in which Koluchová engaged with the boys in activities.

Alternatively, records may be taken at fixed time intervals such as every 10 seconds. The events may also be recorded so that a more detailed analysis can be performed at a later date.

The observer's role

Observations may be useful if the behaviour being investigated might be strongly affected by participants' expectations or beliefs. For example, we are more likely to obtain representative information about carers' responses to an infant's persistent crying by seeing how parents behave than by asking them. This is simply because people might not know how they would respond or might choose to lie because they want to give a socially desirable impression.

However, this advantage may be lost if they are aware that they are being observed. In a *non-disclosed observation* the participants do not know that they are being watched whereas in a *disclosed observation* the participants are aware, at least to an extent, that they are being observed. Clearly, non-disclosed observations raise both ethical and practical issues.

In general, a non-disclosed observer is physically hidden, for example by observing from far away. However, it is also possible to include them as part of the group being observed so that their role is disguised. The latter arrangement is described as a *participant observation* because the observer is a member of the group and the real participants believe them to be so. In a *non-participant* observation the observer is not included within the activities being studied. Non-participant disclosed observations are readily achieved using a video recorder or one-way screen.

Non-participant observations are easier to conduct as the observer can concentrate exclusively on the behaviours of interest. This would be more difficult in a participant observation as focusing on one individual or behaviour might draw attention to the role of the observer within the social group. It is also easier for the observer to remain objective if they are non-participant, that is, to avoid becoming biased by their own personal viewpoint. In contrast, a participant observer may benefit from precisely the opposite: by becoming involved in the social situation, they may gain greater insight into the participants' feelings or motives than a non-participant observer. Using non-disclosed observation is especially important in situations when the participants may change their behaviour to conform to what they think the researcher wants to see or what is socially acceptable. These are examples of participant reactivity. For example, a carer may respond more quickly to a child's needs because they know they are being observed.

Thinking critically about psychology

Ainsworth & Wittig (1969) (p50) used the Strange Situation to simulate real-life events so that they could classify infants' attachment types.

Were they participant or non-participant observers? Were they disclosed or non-disclosed?

Curtiss (1977) (p60) studied Genie, a child who had suffered severe privation.

One of the ways in which Curtiss observed Genie's development was to engage in activities with her. What kind of observational technique is this?

KEY TERMS

naturalistic observation – the participant is watched in their own environment – that is, in the normal place for the activity being observed

controlled observation – the participant is observed in a situation that has been set up by the researcher for the purpose of observing specific behaviours that have been decided in advance

Naturalistic and controlled observations

In *naturalistic observations* the participants are watched in their normal environment without input from the researcher. This allows the observer to gain information about the normal behaviour of the individuals in real life. For example, we might observe the parenting behaviour of wild animals in their natural habitat or the behaviour of children at home or in their usual nursery.

It is also possible to conduct observations of situations that have been artificially contrived. These are called *controlled observations*, and enable researchers to observe the same situations repeatedly without having to wait for them to happen spontaneously. This would be very time-consuming and each event would potentially be slightly different. If we wanted to observe infants' responses to particular behaviours by their carers (such as smiling at them or ignoring them), this would be much quicker and systematic in a controlled observation than a naturalistic one.

Naturalistic observations are highly representative of real behaviour because they are records of the way people behave in actual situations. However, they are harder to control and may present more ethical issues than controlled observations as participants are less likely to be aware that they are being observed.

Ainsworth (1967)
(pp49–51)

Ainsworth observed children in their own homes interacting with their main carers and strangers. This was a **naturalistic observation**.

Harlow (1958)
(p46)

Harlow observed rhesus monkeys in artificial situations with different kinds of surrogate mothers. This was a **controlled observation**.

Thinking critically about psychology

Lorenz (1935) (pp4–5) observed imprinting in chicks – the way that hatchlings follow their mother because she is the first moving thing they see. Is this a naturalistic or controlled observation?

Lorenz went on to conduct further observations using ducklings and goslings in which he manipulated aspects of the environment, for example showing they would imprint on him but only if he was crouching down when they first encountered him! (Lorenz, 1952). What kind of observation was this?

Fuertes *et al.* (2006) (p53) observed both maternal sensitivity and attachment. Were these measured using naturalistic or controlled observations?

Brazleton *et al.* (1975) (p48) observed mothers and babies turn-taking during interactions. They then asked the mothers to ignore the babies' signals so that they could observe whether this caused them distress. Which aspects of the observations in this study were naturalistic and which were controlled?

Bailey *et al.* (2007) (p48) used controlled observations to measure maternal sensitivity in teenage mothers and the attachment behaviours of their babies. What advantages are there for this technique over naturalistic observations?

Figure 4.9 Lorenz with his goslings

Stayton & Ainsworth (1973) (p53)

This study observed mothers and babies in their own homes. Observation sessions lasted for four hours and were repeated every three weeks. The **behavioural categories** used to measure infant attachment were:

- total time spent crying
- crying when the mother left the room
- following the mother
- pleasure or otherwise on her return.

A rating from 1 to 9 was given in each of the following behavioural categories to measure maternal behaviour:

- how sensitive she was to the baby's signals
- how accepting she was of the needs of the baby
- how cooperative she was – that is, the extent to which she arranged her routine around the activities of the child
- how accessible she was to the child – that is, how physically close she was and how much notice she took of the child.

Figure 4.10 Direct involvement in the social situation allows the participant observer to gain insights into the group's feeling and motives but they may lose objectivity

Using behavioural categories

In a non-focused observation, the observer tries to keep a continuous record of all the behaviours they see. Although this may be useful at a preliminary stage of an investigation, it is too difficult to record everything that is going on. As a consequence, it is usual for the researcher to decide which behaviours will be the focus of observations. As in an experiment these behavioural categories must be operationalised, ie clearly defined. This is particularly important when there is more than one observer as it is essential that they record the same information when observing the same events.

When a large number of behavioural categories are being recorded they may be given codes such as letters or numbers to assist in recording. Later, in analysing the data, clusters of related categories can be grouped into themes. This is one way in which information from the continuous stream of events can be converted into numerical data.

Ainsworth and Wittig (1969) developed the Strange Situation as a protocol for measuring attachment in infants (see p50). The observer watches the behaviour of the infant in response to different situations and people in a controlled observation. The behavioural categories used to record the infant's behaviour during the different stages of the Strange Situation are as follows:

- seeking proximity
- exploring
- playing independently
- displaying secure base behaviour to the carer (e.g. returning to the carer during play)
- showing distress when the carer leaves
- making contact with carer when she returns
- showing distress and anxiety in the presence of a stranger
- requiring comfort from the carer
- accepting or resisting comfort from the carer.

Main & Solomon (1986) have added some further behavioural categories to observations of behaviour in the Strange Situation:

- alternating between avoidant and resistant behaviour
- combining avoidant and resistant behaviour (for example, maintaining close proximity but resisting being cuddled)
- freezing.

Note that Main and Solomon recorded 'freezing', and, although it can be observed, it is not possible to establish from this alone whether or not this is because the infant has 'no idea how to cope with the Strange Situation' (see p51). Similarly, although behaviours such as cowering or crying can be observed, 'being afraid' cannot be. In an observation we can only record visible behaviours, not states of mind. This appears to be a disadvantage of observations but it can also be seen as a strength; observations can be highly objective. Since all that is being recorded is directly observable behaviour there is no need for interpretation, and, especially when the observer is non-disclosed and non-participant, data collection should have limited investigator effects. A related strength of observations is that they allow information to be collected from all kinds of participants – including those who cannot speak, read or follow the instructions for an experiment, such as infants and animals.

In contrast to the objectivity of some observational settings, an observer may choose to be participant, which offers the advantage of gaining information about the emotional components of the experiences of the participants. When, however, this is unintentional, there is the disadvantage of investigator bias. The observer's judgements may be affected by their participation, making their recordings less objective. Such situations are also problematic in terms of ethics. If the participants are unaware that they are being watched in a non-disclosed, participant observation – particularly in a naturalistic setting – this raises issues of consent (see pp110–111).

Thinking creatively about psychology

Donovan *et al.* (2007) (pp52–53) classified mothers' maternal sensitivity using a controlled observation to measure their ability to detect specific facial expressions in infants aged six months. Suggest two behavioural categories you would record as indicators of sensitive responsiveness. The researchers also conducted naturalistic observations of free play between mothers and their infants at 24 months. Suggest two behavioural categories that could be observed that would indicate the quality of the interactions between the toddlers and their mothers.

De Schipper *et al.* (2004) (p67) measured the social development of children in day care using a behavioural checklist which was completed by nursery staff. Why do you think it was useful to have the nursery staff conducting this observation? Suggest four behavioural categories that could have been used to indicate social development in children aged between six and thirty-six months.

Figure 4.11 Why might it be important to use familiar individuals as observers?

Hodges & Tizard (1989) (p61) also used observations to record indicators of social development but their participants were aged 4, 8 and 16 years. Suggest four additional behavioural categories that could be used to observe social development in older children in interactions with peers, carers or teachers.

Another weakness of the observational method arises when more than one observer is used. It is difficult to ensure that they are each making the same record when they see the same behaviours. This issue is called *inter-observer reliability* (see p107). This can be improved by agreeing operational definitions and by practising recording data together.

Table 4.3 Strengths and weaknesses of observational techniques

Strengths	Weaknesses
• In naturalistic settings and with non-disclosed observers, behaviour is likely to be highly representative of real life, unlike questionnaires or interviews, in which people may report behaviours different from what would be their actual behaviour • The technique allows for data collection from participants who are unable to contribute to interviews, questionnaires or experimental testing • Observational techniques can be used to collect data when manipulation of a situation would be unethical or impractical	• Participant observers may be biased if they become involved in the social situation they are observing • If multiple observers are used, inter-observer reliability may be low • Ethical issues arise when participants are unaware that they are being observed • It is harder to control extraneous variables, even in a controlled observation, than in a laboratory experiment

Self-report techniques

Self-report techniques are so called because the participant is reporting to the researcher their beliefs, thoughts or feelings about themselves rather than these being recorded directly. These methods include questionnaires and interviews. In both techniques the researcher presents the participant with questions. In a questionnaire, these are on paper (or on a computer) and the participant fills them in. In an interview the questions are asked by the interviewer, usually face to face or by telephone. The methods share some basic question types although there are some differences too. As participants are in the company of a researcher in an interview but not in a questionnaire, they may be more likely to be truthful about socially sensitive issues in a questionnaire. However, face to face, an interviewer can respond to the answers a participant gives, making it a more flexible method and more likely to yield useful, detailed information when this is difficult to obtain.

KEY TERMS

self-report methods – ways to obtain data by asking participants to provide information about themselves

questionnaire – a self-report method using written questions

interview – a self-report method in which participants reply verbally to questions asked by an interviewer

closed questions – questions offering few alternative responses and no opportunity to expand on answers

open questions – questions allowing participants to give full and detailed answers in their own words

quantitative data – numerical data collected as totals in named categories or on numerical scales (see also levels of measurement, pp116–17)

qualitative data – descriptive data providing depth and detail

Open and closed questions

Both open and closed questions can be used in either questionnaires or interviews. A closed question gives the participant little choice and often requires just one of a small number of alternative answers. In a questionnaire these may be presented as boxes to cross or tick. For example:

Do you frequently find that you forget things you have deliberately tried to remember?

yes ☐ no ☐

Which of the following memory aids do you use?
(Tick all that apply)

lists ☐
notes to yourself ☐
repeating things over and over again ☐
tying a knot in your handkerchief ☐

What is your main occupation? ________________

One advantage of using closed questions is that the results they generate are easy to analyse because they are simple numbers. For example, we could ask a group of mothers and fathers whether they cuddled, smacked or played with their children using a yes/no format. This would allow us to say that X% of mothers and X% of fathers reported particular parenting behaviours. Results that are numerical are called *quantitative data*.

An open question does not require a fixed response and should, instead, elicit an extended answer if the participant has one to offer. For example, an open question 'How do you express your affection to your child?' will supply much more information than ticking boxes about cuddling or play. Unlike the numbers produced by closed questions, the results generated by open questions are *qualitative* – that is, they are detailed and descriptive. Such data are more difficult to analyse, the aim being to look for common themes across different participants' responses. For example, if carers from different cultures were interviewed about their child care strategies and similar themes emerged, this would suggest that cultural differences were small. If different themes could be identified, it would suggest that cultural differences in parenting styles were greater.

Both qualitative and quantitative data can be collected using either questionnaires or interviews. In practice, researchers mainly use questionnaires to gather specific, quantitative information and interviews to gather more in-depth, qualitative data.

RESEARCH IN ACTION

In a study related to Parker *et al.*, (2006), p31, **Bahrick *et al.* (1998)** investigated children's recall of a hurricane. They asked one **open question** followed by open prompts to encourage the children to elaborate without leading their responses. They asked, "Remember the really big hurricane we had here? I'm really interested in what kids can remember about that hurricane. I've already talked to some kids about what happened and they told me all kinds of interesting things. I bet you can remember a lot about the hurricane, too. Can you think really hard about the hurricane and tell me everything that you can remember about it?" (They followed up with non-directive prompts: "What else?", "Anything more?", "Anything else?", "What?" and "Any other things?".)

Figure 4.12 Open questions encourage detailed responses from interviewees

Questionnaires

In a questionnaire the questions are generally strictly ordered, so it is 'structured'. It is possible, especially using computers, to tailor the questions somewhat to each participant (for example, when a questionnaire says, 'Leave out this section if ...'). However, in general, questionnaires are necessarily more structured than interviews.

A greater variety of closed questions can be used in a questionnaire than an interview as in written form it is possible to offer a variety of choices for responses. One form of forced-choice question used in questionnaires is the Likert scale, used to elicit opinions. It allows the participant to offer one of a range of responses:

strongly agree ☐, agree ☐, don't know ☐, disagree ☐, strongly disagree ☐.

Questions like this can be used to find out people's views for example in relation to day care. Participants would indicate their response on the scale above to statements such as:

- I think that day care is good for children
- I believe that a child should spend his or her early years with the mother
- It is wrong to separate children from their parents during the working day
- All parents ought to have the opportunity for a fulfilling working life
- I feel that my child benefits from spending time with other children
- Families need quality time together

Banse (2004)
(p55)

Banse used a questionnaire called the 'Relationship Assessment Scale' to assess marital satisfaction and found that the more insecure an individual's attachment type was, the less satisfied they were in their partnership – a negative correlation. The questionnaire included **closed questions** such as this one.

Note that in the last question the responses are reversed – the 'good' answer is on the left, not the right.

1 How well does your partner meet your needs?

A	B	C	D	E
Poorly		Average		Extremely well

2 How much do you love your partner?

A	B	C	D	E
Not much		Average		Very much

3 How often do you wish you hadn't gotten into this relationship?

A	B	C	D	E
Never		Average		Very often

When Likert scales are used it is important to 'reverse' some statements so that the 'positive' or socially acceptable response is not always at the same side of the page.

Other kinds of questions that generate quantitative data can be used in questionnaires, for example the semantic differential. This is designed to elicit people's feelings about a topic or situation. For example, in relation to an eyewitness the following questions could be posed:

Does the prospect of giving a statement in court make you feel:

powerful	______________________	weak
confident	______________________	doubtful
tense	______________________	calm
sad	______________________	excited

Again it is important to ensure that some of the scales have the positive emotion on the left, others on the right.

Questionnaires often end with an invitation that reads, 'Please tell us anything else you would like to about this topic.' This is an open question that allows the researchers to collect some qualitative data. However, it is likely to be much less effective that the qualitative research conducted through interviewing as, in the absence of prompts from the interviewer, the participant may give very little information.

Thinking creatively about psychology

Cohen (2004) (p55) asked participants to complete two questionnaires about a favourite television character. One assessed their attachment to the character and the other measured how they would feel if the character were taken off the air. Devise two short questionnaires using different kinds of questions that could have been used by Cohen.

Fuertes *et al.* (2006) (p53) found out about infants' temperament by giving the mothers a questionnaire. Consider what advantage there might have been to avoiding assessing temperament by observation. Devise about five questions that could have been used by Fuertes *et al.* to investigate infant temperament.

Thinking critically about psychology

Smallbone & Dadds (2004) (p56) used questionnaires to assess variables such as aggression, antisocial behaviour and sexual coerciveness in males. Why do you think they chose to use a questionnaire rather than an interview?

Interviews

The interview as a research method uses questions spoken by the interviewer to the participant. These may be structured but can be much less so than a questionnaire. In an *unstructured interview*, new questions can be incorporated in response to the participant's answers, which cannot be done in a questionnaire. This makes interviews particularly useful for gaining in-depth information about individuals and for new topics of investigation. The advantage in both cases is that if new themes arise that have not been encountered before, these can be explored thoroughly. In such situations a questionnaire would be unable to delve further. For example, a questionnaire or structured interview about a child's attachment may ask the carer, 'Does the child display resistant behaviours?', followed by another saying, 'If yes, indicate which of the following' with a list such as 'turning face away', 'avoiding being held', 'moving away'. The answers are fairly limited, whereas an unstructured interview could pursue lines such as when the child resists, what the carer is doing prior to the behaviour, how the carer responds, etc. This would give a much fuller picture of the carer–infant relationship.

Structured interviews generally employ closed questions that are asked in the same order. These are the kinds of interviews you may have encountered in surveys being conducted outside supermarkets or in town centres. Everyone is treated in the same way and numerical data are generated – that is, the findings are quantitative. In semi-structured and unstructured interviews more open questions are used. These generate detailed, descriptive responses – that is, qualitative data. These are the type of interview you probably have with your doctor. This will generally begin with "How are you feeling?" The questions that follow depend on the symptoms the patient describes. The quantitative data produced by questionnaires and structured interviews is relatively easy to analyse because it is numerical. The findings of unstructured interviews, in contrast, are qualitative. There may be a great deal of information in the form of continuous speech. This has to be analysed by identifying themes – that is, ideas within the respondent's comments that can be classified or interpreted. This kind of analysis is much more difficult and time-consuming. It is also potentially open to investigator bias, as the interviewer's beliefs about the findings in general or particular participants may bias the way they extract or interpret information.

KEY TERMS

structured interview – closed questions are asked in a fixed order

semi-structured interview – fixed schedule of questions including open ones allowing respondents to give detail when they want to

unstructured interview – generally, the investigator will begin with the same question but from there, questions depend on the respondent's answers

Thinking creatively about psychology

Ward *et al.* (2006) (p56) used the Adult Attachment Interview (AAI) to measure attachment type in adult women. This interview is semi-structured; it is standard for all participants but includes open questions. It begins with a request for a general description of the relationship between the interviewee and her parents during childhood. This is an open question. From the woman's reply the interviewer extracts the adjectives the woman used to describe the relationships. Next there are a series of questions asking for recall of specific episodes that illustrate why she chose each adjective. There are then specific questions about what the interviewee did when she was upset, hurt or ill and how her parents responded.

Then follow questions about separations, rejection, discipline, abuse and loss of a parent through death. Finally, the interviewee is asked about whether she thinks the experiences affected her, why she believes her parents behaved as they did and about current relationships with the parents and children.

Design three questions that could be used in the AAI: the very first question, one relating to an adjective (imagine one that might be used to describe a parent) and one other.

There are some potential problems with interviews as a research method. People may be less likely to be honest in interviews than in questionnaires. Imagine how a respondent in a questionnaire study compared to an interview study might feel towards questions about punishing their child. There is likely to be a greater effect of social desirability when the respondent is face to face with the investigator. Conversely, participants in questionnaire studies may develop a different sort of response bias, one in which they tend to always give the same kind of answer. Have you ever done a quiz in a magazine that asks you questions with answers 'a', 'b' or 'c'? After a few responses you have decided which 'type' you are and this will colour the way you answer the rest of the quiz. Have a go at the quiz from Sugar magazine in Figure 4.13.

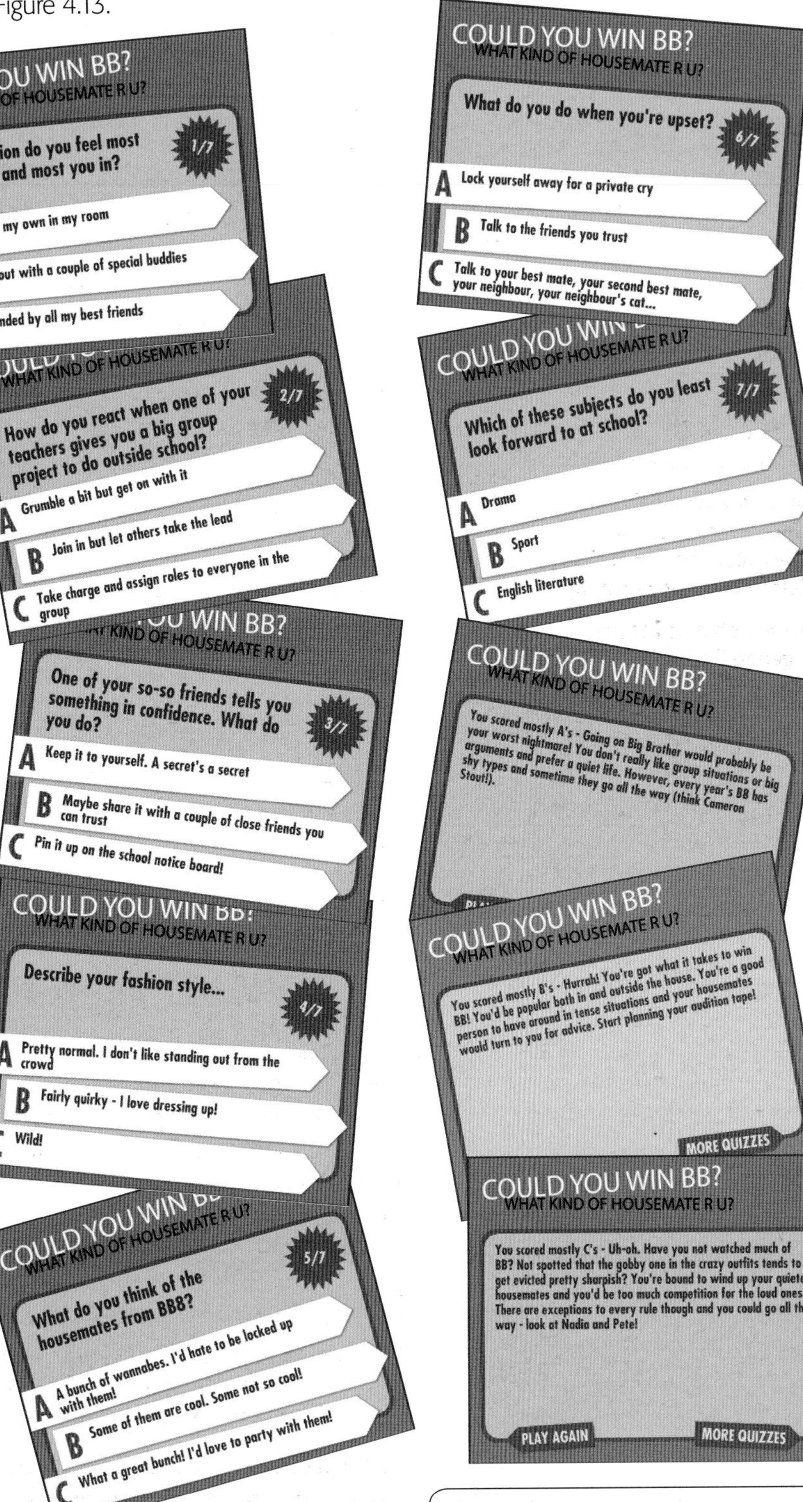

Figure 4.13 A structured questionnaire using closed questions

RESEARCH IN ACTION

Bahrick *et al.* (1998) (p93) used three **semi-structured interviews** to elicit children's memories for events leading up to, during and after a hurricane. The interview about pre-hurricane preparations began with an open question followed by a standardised set of increasingly more specific questions: "Can you tell me what your family did to get ready before the hurricane came? Think about all the things that you and your mommy and daddy did to get ready for the hurricane. Tell me everything you can. What was the first thing that your family did?"

If the child did not mention the following items, the specific questions were asked and followed by non-directive prompts.

"What did your mommy and daddy do outside the house? Did they bring anything inside? Plants? Lawn furniture? What did your mommy and daddy do inside the house? What about the rugs? Furniture? Water?"

Thinking critically about psychology

Harrison & Ungerer (2002) (p65) used an interview to find out about mothers' working lives and their attitudes to work. Their answers were then related to their children's attachment type. Why do you think they chose to use an interview rather than a questionnaire to assess this variable?

McCarthy (1999) (p54) used a questionnaire to assess adult women's own attachment type but an interview to assess their adult friendships and romantic relationships. Identify one advantage and one disadvantage of using an interview in this context.

Hodges & Tizard (1989) (p61) used interviews with teachers and carers in addition to observations to find out about attachments and behaviour in previously institutionalised children. What additional kinds of information would be available through interviewing that could not be gained by observation?

Participating in a questionnaire or interview study requires time and effort from participants and a willingness to divulge things about themselves. Especially when some of the questions might invade their privacy or bring back painful memories, some people would be reluctant to participate – think about participants asked about losing a parent when they were young, or those in studies about crimes or disasters. This means that the people who do volunteer are probably not very representative of the whole population. In a questionnaire study the participants also have to return the completed form. Even when they are provided with a postage-paid envelope, many potential participants do not return the questionnaire. This adds an additional bias to the sample. We will consider this problem in more detail on p115. The strengths and weaknesses of self-report techniques are summarised in Table 4.4.

Table 4.4 Strengths and weaknesses of self-report techniques

	Strengths	Weaknesses
Questionnaires	• They are relatively easy to administer and can be sent or emailed to participants, making them time- and cost-efficient • Respondents may be more truthful than in an interview as they are not face to face with someone, especially if their answers are personal • Data is relatively easy to analyse as it is quantitative	• Response biases such as tending always to answer 'no' or always tick the box on the left can lead to biased results if the questionnaire is not well designed • Limited because, unlike unstructured interviews, there is no flexibility to allow for collection of useful but unexpected data as new questions cannot be added
Interviews	• Structured interview data is relatively easy to analyse as it is quantitative • Semi-structured or unstructured interviews enable the researcher to gain specific and detailed information from the respondent that may be missed in structured techniques	• Structured interviews are limited by fixed questions • Investigator bias may be a problem, as the expectations of the interviewer can alter the way they ask questions, so unconsciously affecting the respondents' answers, or can affect the way their responses are interpreted
Both questionnaires and interviews	• Structured questionnaires and interviews can be easily repeated, allowing researchers to generate more data or check their findings • They can be used to generate quantitative or qualitative data	• Participants may be affected by biases such as social desirability and may be influenced by leading questions • As only some people are willing to fill in questionnaires or be interviewed, the participants may not be representative of the majority of the population

Figure 4.14 Single individuals with rare conditions allow us to provide evidence for specific ideas, such as Wilson & Wearing's (1995) and Wilson *et al.*'s (1995) investigation into the effect of Clive Wearing's brain damage on his memory

Case studies

Case studies differ in several fundamental ways from other methods used by psychologists. First, they focus on a single instance – usually one person, although it is sometimes a family or an institution. This is explored in detail, with other methods often being employed in order to gain a range of information. For example, a case study of an infant might include observations, giving the parents questionnaires and interviewing them.

Second, there are several reasons for conducting case studies. In general, experiments and other methods are used to gather evidence; they are planned with the aim of discovering new information. In contrast, case studies are typically conducted as a consequence of an event or situation that has already happened. For example, the subject of a case study might be a person with amnesia due to brain damage or a child who has suffered deprivation. The intention here is to record the details of an interesting and often rare situation to share the findings with others. In addition, the primary aim of many case studies, especially in areas such as psychodynamic or clinical psychology, is to help a client or patient who is distressed by their condition. This illustrates one further difference: case studies allow us to investigate situations that would be unethical to generate, such as brain damage or isolation. They thus provide us with an invaluable source of information about unusual events.

Figure 4.15 Curtiss (1977) says of this drawing, produced by Genie aged about 19, that it "... is testimony to the importance and strength of the mother–child relationship ... At first she drew only the picture of her mother and then labeled it 'I miss Mama.' She then suddenly began to draw more. The moment she finished she took my hand, placed it next to what she had just drawn, motioning me to write, and said 'Baby Genie.' Then she pointed under the drawing and said, 'Mama hand.' I dictated all the letters. Satisfied, she sat back and stared at the picture. There she was, a baby in her mother's arms. She had created her own reality."

RESEARCH IN ACTION

Curtiss (1977)

(p60)

Curtiss conducted a **case study** on Genie to investigate the effects of her privation. This included testing, observations and face-to-face contact like an interview. The tests used were initially non-verbal ones such as tests of memory for sequences and visual recall. Later, verbal tests were used. Observations were often participant. For example, when Genie was 14 her teacher observed her response when he asked another child, who was holding two balloons, how many he had. When the child said, 'Three', Genie looked shocked and gave him another balloon.

The observations were also generally naturalistic. Curtiss observed and recorded Genie's behaviour in a wide range of situations such as at mealtimes, out shopping, in therapy settings, with other children, etc. Genie's understanding was assessed in conversation using an unstructured interview approach. For example, she was asked, "How many sides does a triangle have?" and answered "Three". When then asked "How many sides does a circle have?", she answered "Round". Simple questions like these could illustrate her understanding of concepts.

A case study typically involves a single researcher and a single participant. A history of the participant is obtained – ideally directly, although this is not always possible, for instance if they are very young, cannot talk, are very psychologically disturbed or have severe amnesia. The nature of the questions asked will depend on the reason for interest in the participant, their condition and the theoretical perspective of the researcher. The latter will also have a bearing on the way that the findings of these interviews are interpreted. In case studies about privation, for example, the researcher will focus on the child's experiences prior to and during their isolation and relate these to their subsequent development. Case studies of people with brain damage will focus instead on the abilities that the individual does and does not demonstrate.

The aim of a case study may be to report on, investigate or help someone, so the outcomes are also varied. It is possible to use the findings of such cases as evidence. So, although we could not for ethical reasons give people brain damage, people who have suffered brain injuries can provide useful tests of ideas that could not be investigated using experimental methods. In such case studies the context in which information is gained is a real one. This means that the findings are likely to be representative, at least of that one individual's experience, because the situation includes all the complex interactions that exist in real life. For example, in a case study of a victim's recall of a crime, many more variables could be considered than would be explored in a single experiment that might test just leading questions or the role of anxiety. In real life, many other factors such as prior experiences of crimes as a witness or victim, the extent of injuries or the familiarity of the perpetrator could be important. Only in a case study would it be possible to explore these variables together.

The obvious advantage of the case study method is the depth and detail of the data collected. By using several different techniques, a researcher can produce a large amount of information about the case and can explore those findings that seem most interesting or useful in more depth. Also, using several techniques enables the researcher to be more sure about the value of their findings. For example, in a case study of a child who has experienced privation, indicators from tests, interviews and observations might all suggest the same problems with language, attachment or cognition. Similarly, a case study of a patient with amnesia might use tests to assess the effect on short- and long-term memory, interviews with the family to find out whether the patient had a good memory before, and observations to see if the same problems arise in everyday life. When researchers use several techniques to check their findings, this is called triangulation. So although case studies are not a traditionally 'scientific' approach to research, the findings can be validated in this way.

One disadvantage of case studies is that they are impossible to replicate because no two cases are the same. As they cannot be repeated, it is both impossible for researchers to replicate the data collection themselves to be sure that the results are correct, and difficult for any findings to be checked by others. Another consequence of the uniqueness of a case study is that we cannot generalise the findings to other people.

Thinking critically about psychology

Scoville & Milner (1957) (p17) studied the case of the amnesic HM whose STM was unaffected but LTM was severely impaired. Many different sources of information were used to investigate the extent of HM's memory loss. Why would it be difficult to rely purely on interviewing in this instance?

Forde & Humphreys (2002) (p20) conducted a case study on an amnesic, FK, whose errors provided evidence that STM can use semantic as well as auditory encoding. This investigation used a single-participant experimental design. What were the two levels of the IV?

Koluchová (1972, 1991) (p60) described the case of the 'Czech twins'. Unlike the two case studies just mentioned, which aimed to provide evidence relating to the multi-store model, Koluchová's purpose was somewhat different. How?

Figure 4.16 Having a 'pet theory' can lead to biased results

There are also potential problems with conducting a case study. As a researcher would usually spend many hours interviewing their participant, they are likely to get to know them well. On the one hand, this is good, as the individual will learn to trust them and may reveal more about themselves. However, the researcher's relationship with the participant is also likely to make them biased, as they will become less objective.

Another source of bias is the researcher's psychological beliefs. If the researcher has a particular view, a 'pet theory', they are likely to be biased towards finding examples and interpreting evidence so that it fits with their thinking. This is another way in which they can become less objective. The setting itself makes these biases more of a problem than they would be in an experimental setting, as variables cannot be controlled. For example, interviews are likely to be unstructured and observations participant and disclosed. These situations mean there is more opportunity for uncontrolled variables to affect both the participant and the investigator.

Table 4.5 Strengths and weaknesses of case studies

Strengths	Weaknesses
• Case studies provide rich, in-depth data that provide more detailed information than can be obtained through methods such as experimentation • Rare cases offer opportunities to study situations that could not – ethically or practically – be artificially contrived • The realistic context of an individual's life or other unique instance allows for the investigation of the complex interaction of many factors • Using many different sources of information from a range of techniques allows researchers to verify findings and be more certain about them	• Each case study is a unique investigation of a single situation or individual, so the findings cannot be generalised to others • The evidence obtained from an individual that relates to the past may be hard to verify • When an investigator studies an individual in depth, they may get to know them well and begin to lose objectivity • In a case study, variables cannot be controlled, so the method cannot be used to investigate causal relationships • The theoretical perspective of the investigator may cause them to interpret their findings in a biased way

DESIGNING INVESTIGATIONS

Many aspects of the design of an investigation are shared by several of the research methods we have explored so far in this chapter. These include the identification of aims, writing of hypotheses, the defining of variables and the need to obtain accurate data. When an investigator plans their research, they make a series of design decisions about these and other issues that are discussed below.

Aims

Each piece of psychological research is conducted for a specific purpose, which is expressed in the aim of the investigation. The aim is stated in general terms, identifying only the intention of the study, not how this will be achieved. However, establishing a clear aim helps a researcher to make subsequent decisions such as which variables should be measured, manipulated or controlled. For example, in a study that aimed to find out whether distraction affected LTM, it would be important to manipulate levels of distraction, measure memory and control other factors such as repetition

RESEARCH IN ACTION

Sperling (1960)
(p9)
Sperling tested how many letters participants could recall from a matrix presented for only one-twentieth of a second. His **aim** was to find the capacity of the iconic store.

Conrad (1964)
(p12)
Conrad measured the accuracy of immediate recall for letters that sounded alike or different. His **aim** was to show that STM uses a sound-based code.

Linton (1975)
(p12)
Linton kept a daily diary for many years and tested her recall of past events. Her **aim** was to demonstrate the vast capacity of long-term memory.

RESEARCH IN ACTION

Ginet and Verkampt (2007)
(pp30–31)
Ginet and Verkampt investigated whether fear about receiving an electric shock affected recall. Their hypothesis could have been 'Anxiety level affects the recall of words'. This is a **non-directional hypothesis.**

Ward *et al.* (2006)
(p56)
Ward *et al.* compared the mental health of women with different attachment types. Their hypothesis could have been 'Women with secure attachments are less likely to be diagnosed with mental health problems than women with insecure attachments'. This is a **directional hypothesis.**

that could also affect recall. Conversely, if the aim were to test the effect of repetition on memory, repetition would be manipulated and possible distractions controlled.

Hypotheses

A *hypothesis* is a testable statement of the investigator's predictions about the results of their study. In most published research the hypotheses are not stated, so you are unlikely to have encountered them even if you have read original journal articles. However, they are useful to the process of drawing conclusions from research, and you need to understand this process.

Figure 4.17 An experimental hypothesis for this situation might predict that: 'There is a difference between the number of words recalled when listening to loud or quiet music' or 'Testimonies from eyewitnesses who have discussed events with others are less accurate than those of witnesses who have not discussed events'

The experimental hypothesis

Most studies have a hypothesis as well as an aim, but some, for example some case studies, are not testing a particular idea, so do not. The aim in an experiment, by contrast, is very specific. If you conduct an experiment to find out whether increasing arousal with loud music makes recall of words better or worse, your aim would be to test this effect. You would need a corresponding hypothesis, for example *There is a difference between the number of words recalled when listening to loud or quiet music*. This would be your experimental hypothesis. An *experimental hypothesis* states the difference you expect to find between levels of the IV.

Directional and non-directional hypotheses

The experimental hypothesis (H_E) above is a non-directional hypothesis. When we are expecting that the IV will change the DV but we are not sure whether the effect will be an increase or a decrease, we use a non-directional hypothesis. We would choose this type of hypothesis if we tested the effect of a variable that had not been investigated before – for example, if we were investigating the effect of eating jelly babies on recall. They might help memory, as chewing gum does, or distract us and cause displacement. If most previous research suggests that we can be confident about the nature of an effect, we can use a directional hypothesis. In a test of how post-event information from talking to other witnesses affects testimonies, we could be confident that talking would make them less accurate. This is a directional prediction, so a hypothesis might be: *Testimonies from eyewitnesses who have discussed events with others are less accurate than those of witnesses who have not discussed events.* The corresponding non-directional hypothesis would have been: *There is a difference in accuracy of testimonies from witnesses who have and have not discussed events.*

Thinking critically about psychology

What do you think the aims were for these two studies?

- **Baddeley (1966)** (p14)
- **Seitz & Schumann-Hengsteler (2000)** (p20)

Write a non-directional hypothesis for Ward *et al.* (2006) (see p56). Also write a directional hypothesis for Ginet and Verkampt (2007) (see pp30–31).

Suggest a suitable aim and a directional experimental hypothesis for **Hadley & MacKay (2006)** (p31).

The null hypothesis

As well as the experimental hypothesis, you also need to be clear about the *null hypothesis*. This states that any difference in the DV between levels of the IV is so small that there is a high probability that it has arisen by chance. This is an important idea because it is used in statistical testing. These tests, which you will study in A2, help you to decide whether it is likely that the null hypothesis is correct. A typical null hypothesis (H_0) would be: *Any difference in the accuracy of testimonies from witnesses who have and have not discussed events is due to chance.* The null hypothesis basically says that 'Any difference in the DV between *condition X* and *condition Y* is due to chance.' If we were investigating the effect of rehearsal on memory, a suitable null hypothesis would be: *Any difference in recall between older and younger witnesses is due to chance.* So that the sentence makes sense it is sometimes better to swap the order around, but always make sure that you state both of the levels of the IV. So, a slightly different way to write a null hypothesis would be: *Any difference between older and younger witnesses' recall is due to chance*. It is generally easier, however, to use the first layout.

Tulving & Pearlstone (1966)
(p28)

These researchers looked at the effect of cues from category headings on recall. A suitable **null hypothesis** for this experiment could have been: *Any difference in recall with or without category headings is due to chance.*

Memon *et al.* (2006)
(p36)

These researchers investigated the effect of presenting stereotyped information about a visitor to a classroom on children's memory. Their **null hypothesis** could have been: *Any difference between stereotyping in children's recall when exposed to positive or negative descriptions is due to chance.*

Hypotheses in correlational studies

RESEARCH IN ACTION

Ahnert *et al.* (2006)

(p65)

Ahnert *et al.* investigated the relationship between economic status and attachment. Their hypothesis could have been: *There is a relationship between family economic status and security of attachment.* This would be a **non-directional correlational hypothesis**. The corresponding **null hypothesis** would be: *Any relationship between family economic status and security of attachment is due to chance.*

Rutter *et al.* (1998)

(p62)

Rutter *et al.* found that the younger an orphan was adopted, the better they developed. Their hypothesis could have been: *There is a negative correlation between age at adoption and developmental success.* This is a **directional correlational hypothesis**. The corresponding null hypothesis would be: *Any correlation between age at adoption and developmental success is due to chance.*

Another term for the 'experimental' hypothesis is the 'alternative hypothesis', as it is the 'alternative' to the null. This is a more appropriate term for correlational studies. A non-directional hypothesis in a correlational study simply predicts that there will be a relationship between the two measured variables. A directional hypothesis states whether this relationship will be a positive or a negative correlation. For example, in a study looking for a relationship between brain volume and braininess, we might say: *There will be a relationship between brain volume and braininess*. This would be a non-directional hypothesis. Alternatively, we could suggest a directional hypothesis such as *There will be a positive correlation between brain volume and braininess*. We could also say *As brain volume increases, braininess increases*. This would also be a directional hypothesis. Remember that we cannot say that one factor *causes* the change in the other.

It is also possible to write directional hypotheses for negative correlations, for example *As brain size increases reaction time decreases*. This could alternatively be written as *There will be a negative correlation between brain size and reaction time*.

As with experimental studies, correlational studies need to have a null hypothesis. This predicts that any relationship could have occurred by chance. A typical null hypothesis for a correlational study reads: Any relationship between *variable X* and *variable Y* is due to chance. For example, *Any relationship between brain volume and braininess is due to chance.*

Figure 4.18 Is brain size related to braininess?

Thinking critically about psychology

Write a null hypothesis for each of the following studies:

- **Ward *et al.* (2006)** (see p56)
- **Ginet & Verkampt (2007)** (see pp30–31)
- **Hadley & MacKay (2006)** (see p31)

The hypothesis in **Cohen (2004)** (p55) was: *A positive association will be found between parasocial relationships and the intensity of expected distress following the loss of a relationship with a favourite media character.* Is this:

- an alternative or a null hypothesis?
- for an experimental or correlational design?
- a directional or non-directional hypothesis?

Thinking critically about psychology

Write a non-directional hypothesis for **Rutter *et al.* (1998)** (pp62 & 102).

Write a directional hypothesis for each of the correlations in **Stayton & Ainsworth (1973)** (pp52 & 85).

Look at **De Schipper *et al.* (2004)** (p67). Write a non-directional alternative hypothesis and null hypothesis for any one of the possible correlations.

Naturalistic observations

In naturalistic observations, behavioural recording takes place in the participant's usual environment. This might be the home for infants and their carers, a nursery for young children or a classroom for students. When a researcher conducts a naturalistic observation, they have to make design decisions similar to those made in an experiment. Whereas an experimenter makes choices such as lab versus field and repeated measures versus independent groups, a researcher planning an observation has to decide whether to be disclosed or non-disclosed and participant or non-participant. Decisions must also be made about what to record.

The development and use of behavioural categories

Instead of choosing the levels of the IV and how to measure the DV as in an experiment, an observer has to decide which behaviours to record. The process often begins with non-focused observations in which the observer develops a list of behaviours they might record. Imagine a naturalistic observation of an infant and its mother. You might observe that a baby makes a range of movements and noises: sitting up, smiling, frowning, dribbling, playing, moving their arms and legs, cooing, babbling, crying, giggling, screaming, blowing bubbles, etc. An observer can rarely record everything that is happening, so careful selection takes place. The chosen behavioural categories must be distinct from one another, reasonably easy to see, and definable.

Figure 4.19 Each behavioural category in an observation needs to be operationally defined

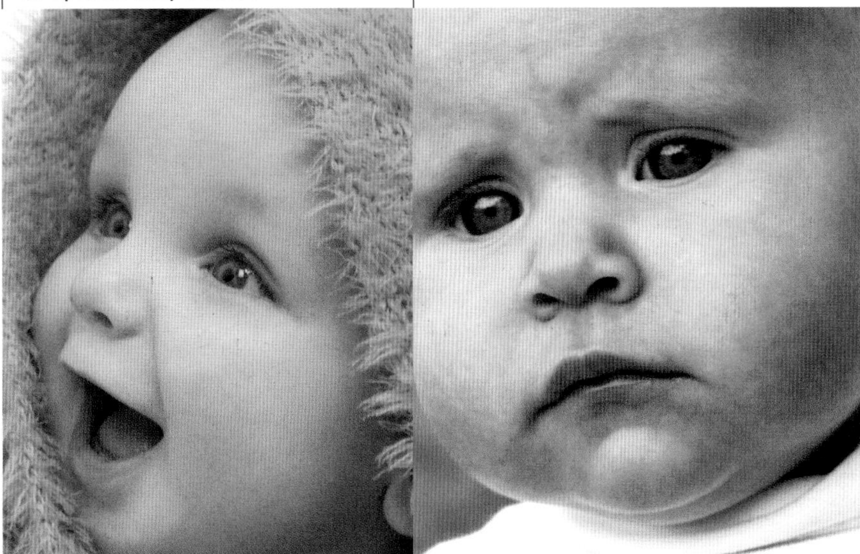

First it must be possible to separate the behaviours. When does dribbling become blowing bubbles? A researcher needs to be confident that they know when to stop recording one behaviour and start to record another. Then they need to decide which behaviours are important to the research they are doing. If an observer is investigating communication between the mother and infant, then behaviours such as smiling and crying are more likely to be of interest than blowing bubbles. Once the behavioural categories have been decided, each one must be operationalised (see also p89). It is important that the definitions are based on what can be seen, not on assumptions about states. For example, an observer could record 'screaming' or 'frowning' but not 'being upset'. Finally, it may be possible to combine some categories; for example, cooing and giggling are 'happy noises', crying and screaming are unhappy ones.

Designing questionnaires and interviews

Questionnaires and interviews may be used as techniques to measure a DV in an experiment or as research methods in their own right. In either case the researcher must choose the topic areas for questions, the style of the questions and, in the case of an interview, whether it will be structured or unstructured. The topic area is decided by the aims. For example, if the aim is to find out about adults' attachments, there are likely to be questions about relationships with parents and with romantic partners, and about commitment, trust and intimacy, and anxiety in relationships. There is likely to be a mix of question styles, but the choices will be determined by what the researcher plans to do with the data that they collect. If the information will be used to produce a detailed, descriptive account of the nature or variety of a characteristic such as adult attachment, then there are likely to be more open questions. These would be described as qualitative data. If the information is going to be used to make generalisations of predictions about the frequency of different patterns of attachment in the population, then quantitative data would be more useful. To obtain numerical results, more closed questions would be used. When the intention is to gain detailed information relating specifically to the individual, unstructured interviews will be used. When it is important to gain the same information from each participant, more structured interviews or questionnaires would be better.

Thinking creatively about psychology

Imagine conducting a naturalistic observation of the problems experienced by people in a day care centre for amnesics. Suggest four behavioural categories that could be recorded and give operational definitions for each one.

In the same environment you might conduct a questionnaire to ask the care staff about the patients' memory problems and how they affect them. Write a short questionnaire designed to gather qualitative data.

Pilot studies

In a naturalistic observation (see p88) an observer is likely to 'test the water' by conducting a non-focused observation. For most other methods a good starting point is to do a small-scale trial run so that, if necessary, the subject area and/or the procedure can be improved. In controlled observations with several observers, pilot studies provide an opportunity to make sure that they agree on operational definitions of behavioural categories so that they record accurately.

Figure 4.20 Pilot studies help to identify problems in a study

When a researcher is using questionnaires or interviews, a pilot run will show up any questions that participants do not understand or tend to refuse to answer, so that they can be changed.

In an experiment, a pilot study allows the researcher to be certain that:

- participants can follow the standardised instructions
- the measure of the DV covers a wide range of possible scores – ensuring that the task is not too difficult or too easy
- there are sufficient control measures to keep extraneous variables from affecting the participants' responses.

Potential problems in an investigation cannot always be predicted, so pilot studies are very useful. Imagine a memory study in which participants have to remember their way around a virtual maze on a computer when this has 'landmarks' on the maze and when it does not. A pilot study might tell you that the maze you have chosen is too difficult, or that it is so easy for people who are used to playing computer games that differences caused by the IV cannot be seen. You might also discover that it is useful to count the number of times each participant 'turns round and goes back' as well as the total time it takes them to find the end of the maze. The instructions you had written might need to be modified, perhaps giving them a picture of which keys to use to go left, right, backwards and forwards, rather than just telling them. Finally, you might change the lighting so that they can see the screen more clearly or use a computer with a bigger monitor. All of these will help improve the investigation.

Thinking creatively about psychology

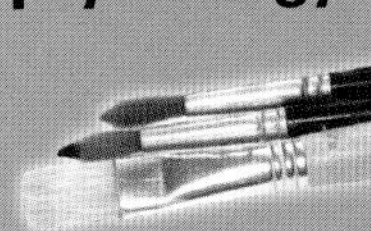

A group of students plan to conduct a field experiment on eyewitness testimony. Their aim is to see how well people remember a fight breaking out between two shoppers over a sale item. They decide to stage a fight. In one condition nobody is hurt and the shoppers apologise and carry on shopping. In the other, one shopper pretends to have been knocked out and is carried away by a friend. As people leave the store they are asked what they can remember about the incident if they saw it.

Plan a pilot study for this experiment. Describe in detail at least four things that might need to be changed about your plan as a result of the pilot study.

Controlling variables

To be sure that changes in the DV in an experiment have definitely been caused by the IV, an experimenter must be sure that all other variables – called extraneous variables – are kept constant between conditions. We have already seen some ways to do this. We can control:

- participant variables by using a repeated measures design (p75)
- order effects by using randomisation or counterbalancing of the order in which participants do different conditions (p77)
- for demand characteristics using a single-blind procedure (p78)
- experimenter bias using a double-blind procedure and standardised instructions (p79)
- situational variables by choosing a laboratory experiment so that factors such as noise, onlookers, light levels and other distractions can be minimised (p80)

RESEARCH IN ACTION

Hadley and MacKay (2006)

(p31)

Hadley & MacKay measured participants' recall of stressful (taboo) and non-stressful (neutral) words. The taboo words were insults, sexual words and swearwords, such as 'suck' and 'porn'. The neutral words were food- and cooking-related words such as 'stew' and 'pies'. The words in the two groups were matched for length and frequency of use. This was an important **control**, as shorter or more common words could have been easier to remember.

The words in the lists were ordered so that they did not form familiar pairs such as 'bake'– 'cake', 'wheat'–'flour' or 'soup'–'dish'. This helped to control for sequences that might aid recall.

The participants were also warned that they might see obscene words. Apart from being necessary from an ethical point of view, this was a control to ensure that any effect was due to the nature of the words, not the shock of seeing them unexpectedly.

Reliability and validity

Psychologists need to be able to measure variables accurately. When we talk about accuracy in everyday life we mean how well something is measured. When we buy 1kg of apples we need to be confident that the shop's scales are going to give us our money's worth. Many variables that we study in psychology cannot be judged so effectively, because there are generally no absolute measures of things like 'arousal', 'attachment' or 'temperament'. As we cannot measure exactly, we can only estimate the accuracy of these scales or tests. We use two estimates of accuracy: reliability and validity.

RESEARCH IN ACTION

Loftus and Palmer (1974)

(p33)

Loftus & Palmer conducted two experiments on misleading questions. In one, they just asked about a car's speed using different verbs, and in the other, they asked about the speed of cars and later about whether there had been any broken glass. Different participants were used in each experiment but in both tests they found that speed estimates were higher when the word 'smashed' was used than when the word 'hit' was used. Hence, this finding was **reliable**.

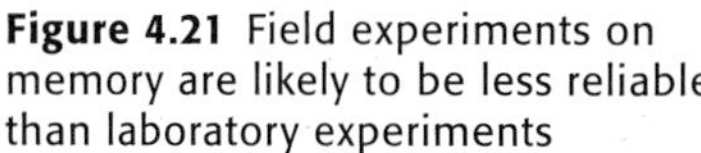

Figure 4.21 Field experiments on memory are likely to be less reliable than laboratory experiments

Reliability

Reliability refers to how consistent something is. If you are a reliable student, you regularly turn up to your lessons or hand in your homework. A reliable psychological test or measure has consistency as it will always produce the same results in the same situation. Laboratory experiments are likely to be reliable because they are highly controlled, so the situation can be reproduced exactly. When we repeat – or replicate – a study, we expect to get the same results. If we do, it is reliable. We are less likely to be able to replicate a field experiment, as real situations change, making the results less reliable. For example, in a memory study where people are required to learn lists of 20 five-letter common words, we can expect similar scores if we replicate the study. If, however, we conduct a field experiment in which people are asked to part with their shopping lists on the way into a supermarket so that we can see whether they remember everything, we are likely to get more variable results if we repeat the experiment. We are likely to find that the shopping lists are of different lengths, have different items on them and are laid out differently. All these factors will reduce reliability.

Assessing reliability

Researchers need to be able to find out whether the tests, interviews or questionnaires they are using are reliable. If they are, then any person should always give similar answers to similar questions. Here are two ways to test this:

- *Test–retest procedure*: give the test or questions to the same people on two separate occasions. A positive correlation between the first and second set of scores indicates good reliability.
- *Split-half procedure*: give the test to a group of people. Split the test or questions into two halves (for example, the even-numbered questions and the odd-numbered questions). If there is a positive correlation between the two half-sets of scores, then the reliability is good.

Wijngaards-de Meij *et al.* (2007) (p55) measured depression and grief in parents who had lost a child. The **test–retest reliability** for both measures was good at approximately 0.8, indicating a strong positive correlation between scores on testing and retesting.

Another kind of reliability is the consistency between researchers. This is important in methods such as observations and interviews. If two researchers observe the same behaviours or interview the same person, they should collect the same data. If they do, then they have high *inter-observer reliability* or high *inter-interviewer (inter-rater) reliability*.

Parker *et al.* (2006) (p31) investigated mothers' memories of a hurricane. Seven interviewers were used, and **inter-rater reliability** was high at over 90 per cent.

Validity

Validity is about a researcher being sure that they are measuring what they set out to measure. We would hope that if we interview people about lapses of memory they would report them accurately – but would they? Older adults might lie if they think they forget too much because they are getting old. Students might say they are very forgetful because they frequently 'forget' to do their homework. We cannot even be sure that people genuinely remember every time that they forgot something! This means that in the case of older adults we might be accidentally measuring the frequency with which the respondents *believe* they should forget things. For the students we might be measuring a different sort of social expectation. And even if people are responding truthfully, they may not be very accurate. All these factors would reduce the validity of our measure. There are many different kinds of validity; some are more relevant to methods such as questionnaires and interviews, others relate only to experiments.

In relation to self-report methods, we are interested in *internal validity* – that is, whether we are sure that they measure what we intended them to.

We can judge the internal validity of a measure such as a questionnaire or interview in the following ways:

- *Face validity*: a simple judgement about whether a measure looks as though it will assess what it set out to assess. For example, are the questions in a structured interview about day care related to relevant factors?
- *Content validity*: the opinion of a panel of experts is used to judge whether a measure is appropriate for investigating the aims. For example, a group of child psychologists could read and comment on a structured interview about day care.
- *Concurrent validity*: a comparison between results obtained with a new measure and those from an existing one. If they show the same thing, then they have concurrent validity. For example, if we interview people about how often they forget and send a questionnaire to their families asking the same thing, we should find that the two produce the same results. If they do, then they are valid.
- *Predictive validity*: a comparison between a current measure and later performance. If the current measure accurately predicts people's subsequent behaviour, it is valid. Using the example from above about interview data on people's forgetting, we would expect their results to predict how many times they would forget to attend appointments. If interview results suggest someone will forget appointments often, and they do, then the interview has predictive validity.

In experiments, we are concerned with internal validity and with another aspect: external validity. In an experiment, internal validity is about how sure we can be that changes in the DV have only been caused by the IV. Controls can therefore increase internal validity. Experimenter bias and demand characteristics also threaten internal validity, which is why we use standardised instructions and blind procedures, and limit the information we give to participants about a study. There are different threats to internal validity in different experimental designs. In repeated measures designs, order effects can lower internal validity, so are avoided by randomisation or counterbalancing. In an independent groups design, individual differences between participants are a problem. To minimise these, participants are randomly allocated to conditions (or a matched pairs design can be used).

Figure 4.22 Would studies of parenting from the 1940s have historical validity today?

The *external validity* of an experiment relates to whether our results would generalise beyond the experiment itself. It is about whether they are relevant to other times, groups of people or settings. For example, a questionnaire study about attitudes to the mother's role in child care would produce very different results now than in the 1940s; an old study would lack *historical validity* now. Similarly, a study about sensitive mothering might produce somewhat different results if conducted in different cultures. If so, the findings would not be representative of all cultures, so would lack *population validity* in this respect.

The results of an experiment should also generalise to other situations. This is called *ecological validity* and is important in a laboratory experiment as it means the findings must apply beyond the experimental setting. It is likely, though not guaranteed, that field experiments will be more ecologically valid as they are conducted in real-world environments; but this may not be enough. Experiments also have to use tasks that are like those we would encounter in real life. A study that uses tasks that are like real life has *mundane realism*. This is important if the findings are going to represent the real world. For example, if you wanted to test memory, you could ask people to remember lists of nonsense syllables or shopping lists. The shopping list task would have higher mundane realism as this is a memory task we do actually perform.

Godden & Baddeley (1975)

(p26)

Godden & Baddeley compared divers' performance in two genuine contexts (on land and under water) so the experiment was realistic in terms of its setting. Although the task of learning word lists seems artificial and lacking in **mundane realism**, the study was based on real observations about North Sea divers in the early years of oil exploration. The divers kept forgetting what they had seen once they were out of the water. This study therefore has higher mundane realism than you might expect.

Figure 4.23 North Sea divers forgot what they had seen under water when they returned to the oil rig

Loftus and Palmer (1974)

(p33)

Loftus & Palmer conducted a well-controlled laboratory experiment. Although they were testing a real-world problem concerned with eyewitness testimony, neither the task nor the setting was really like the experiences of an eyewitness. Being in a lab watching short film clips is unlikely to represent fairly the motivation or emotions of a witness to a real car accident. The study therefore had low **ecological validity**, as the findings might not generalise to other settings.

Thinking critically about psychology

How do these studies differ in terms mundane realism and why?

- **Wright *et al.* (2001)** (p34)
- **Peterson & Peterson (1959)** (p11)
- **Krackow & Lynn (2003)** (p35)
- **Smythe & Costall (2003)** (p15)

You may have noticed that increasing mundane realism presents the experimenter with problems. The same things that improve mundane realism and make experiments better can also make them worse because they tend to create uncontrolled variables. This presents a dilemma for researchers. Good experiments need both to be representative of the real world and to manipulate and measure variables accurately. This is not always possible, so in any area of research there are likely to be some studies that are highly controlled and others that have high generalisability.

Thinking creatively about psychology

Design a study that has high mundane realism that aims to test the effect of leading questions on children. Think about the balance between mundane realism and controls as you plan.

Ethical issues and how psychologists deal with them

If you have read the earlier chapters, you will have encountered some of the ethical dilemmas that psychologists face. Here we will look at these in more detail.

Consent

As we saw on p77, it is important in experiments to hide the aims from participants. This stops them from guessing how they are 'supposed' to respond. However, potential participants also have the right to know what is going on; they need to give their informed consent. These two opposing needs mean that it may be hard to get genuine consent. In some studies it may even be necessary to deceive the participants to ensure that the experiment produces meaningful results. Similarly, in observations, participants should be given the chance to give their informed consent. In reality, this may be impractical in some naturalistic settings when participants are unaware that they are being watched.

When the participants are children, there are further issues of consent. Not only should the children themselves be asked whether they are happy to participate – and in a way that they understand – but their parents or guardians must be asked too. This means that researchers would need permission from schools to test students, for example.

In some situations a researcher cannot ask the participants for their consent. This is often (but not always) the case in naturalistic observations and field experiments. In these situations, a researcher can attempt to decide whether the research is likely to be acceptable to the participants by asking other people. Using a group of people similar to those who will become participants, the researcher can ask whether they would find the study acceptable if they were involved. This is called presumptive consent because it allows the researcher to *presume* that the actual participants would also be happy to participate.

In some experimental designs it is essential that the participants are *mis*informed about the aims of the study. This may be necessary to avoid demand characteristics or to produce necessary differences between conditions. For example, in studies about leading questions, the purpose of the experiment would be lost if the participants knew they were going to be given misleading

RESEARCH IN ACTION

Lindsay (1990)

(p34)

Participants were told that the study involved memory for detail in a slide sequence when, in fact, the aim was to test the influence of verbal suggestions. This is an illustration of the way that **deception** may be necessary in experimental studies.

information. Deception should only be used when there is no alternative, and even then, participants should be informed about the real purpose as soon as possible. This is one of the functions of the debrief, but debriefing should not be used as an alternative to designing ethical experiments. When deception has been used, participants should also be given the opportunity to remove their results from the study.

RESEARCH IN ACTION

Banse (2004)

(p55)

Banse investigated attachment type and marital satisfaction. A group of 2000 women who fitted criteria such as age were selected from a civil register and sent questionnaires. Of these, 16.7 per cent were returned, providing 333 couples to study. Each partner had consented to participate separately and provided this consent in writing. This ensured that they were fully aware of the study so had given their **informed consent.**

Hadley & MacKay (2006)

(p31)

Hadley & MacKay told the participants that during the study they might see offensive or taboo words and that they could swap to a different study without taboo words if they wanted. This allowed the participants to give their **informed consent** without giving away the aims of the study. No participants chose to exercise their **right to withdraw**.

Wijngaards-de Meij *et al.* (2007)

(p55)

Wijngaards-de Meji *et al* were collecting data from adults who were distressed by the loss of a child. Even though data were lost as a consequence, it was important that the participants could exercise their **right to withdraw**, and 17.8 per cent did so.

Figure 4.24 Children may express their right to withdraw from a study in different ways from adults

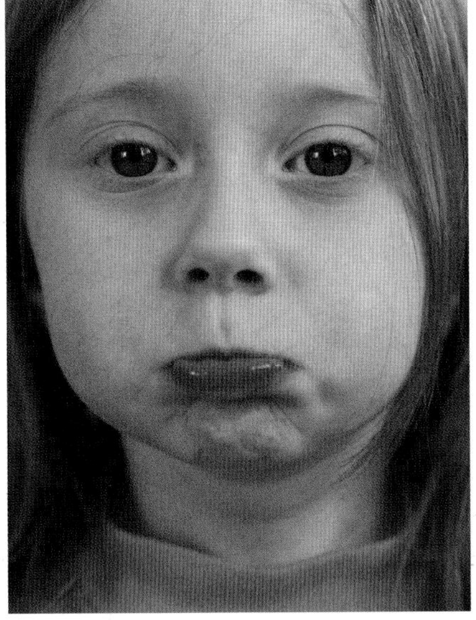

The right to withdraw

All participants have the right to leave a study at any time if they want to. This is their right to withdraw, and it must be made clear to them at the start of the study. The right to withdraw must be observed even if it means data are lost. For example, if a participant leaves an experiment with a repeated measures design between the first and second conditions, the results that have been collected become useless.

Participants can be offered incentives to join a study but these cannot be taken back if they leave. This is to ensure that they do not feel compelled to continue if they do not want to. Nor should researchers use their position of authority to encourage participants to continue beyond the point where they want to stop.

Children, like adults, should also be given the chance to leave a study if they want to. Adults can simply be told that they can leave at any time but it is important to remember that children may express their desire to withdraw from a study in different ways from adults. For example, a child might not want join in or may walk away. Such signals should be recognised and responded to.

Thinking creatively about psychology

Plan a study to investigate how well children remember visitors who come to their nursery school and either stand in the classroom and talk only to the staff or talk to the children too. Include in your design variables that you will control and steps you will take to make sure that the study is ethical.

Protection from harm

Many studies have the potential to cause participants harm. This could be psychological, such as the distress of knowing there are other participants who might have performed 'better' or answering stressful questions about bereavement or unpleasant childhood experiences. Alternatively, there might be risks of physical harm, such as dangerous activities like diving or painful experiences such as electric shocks. In any of these cases, participants have the right to be protected from harm. They should not be exposed to any greater risk than they would be in their normal life. If participants have been negatively affected by a study, such as worried by a procedure, the researcher should be prepared to talk to them until they are returned to their previous condition. This is one of the functions of the debrief: the opportunity for the participant to ask questions about the study and to be reassured. It is important, however, that debriefing is not used as an alternative to designing ethical studies.

RESEARCH IN ACTION

Godden and Baddeley (1975)
(p26)

The issue here was the need to use two very different environments versus the **right of participants to be protected from physical harm**. This dilemma was solved by choosing land and water as the contexts and using trained divers who were going on a dive anyway as participants. This meant they were not at any greater risk than they would have been in their normal life.

Wijngaards-de Meij *et al.* (2007)
(p55)

The issue in this study was the need to collect data from parents who had suffered the death of a child versus the **right of participants to be protected from psychological harm**. One step taken to resolve this dilemma was to exclude people who were grandparents as well as parents. This was because they would be suffering additional stress coping with their grandchildren who had lost a parent as well as having lost their own child.

Privacy and confidentiality

Observations present other ethical issues such as the risk of invading privacy. To ensure that an observation is ethically acceptable, psychologists should only watch people in situations where they would expect to be on public display. Such environments may also raise privacy issues relating to the location itself. Places like shops, which are essentially 'public' in that we should expect to be seen by others, are nevertheless privately owned, and researchers must obtain permission to avoid infringing customers' rights to privacy. For example, an observation of attachment behaviours between mothers and their children at a toddler group would need the permission of the group organisers.

Another way in which participants' privacy must be respected is in the completion of questionnaires. In studies such as those asking about criminality or personal issues such as adult romantic relationships, it is common for participants who complete the questionnaire in a lab to be given an individual space. They are also assured of complete confidentiality and security of the data.

Figure 4.25 To ensure privacy, participants may complete a questionnaire in isolation

RESEARCH IN ACTION

Scoville and Milner (1957)
(p17)

The issue in this study was **confidentiality**, the need to protect the participant's identity versus the need to be able to describe the individual in detail. This was resolved by referring to the participant, HM, by his initials.

In all studies it is essential to respect the participants' right to confidentiality. When records are made that could identify individuals, such as scores in experiments and responses to questionnaires or interviews, it is essential to protect the participants' identities. This is usually done by allocating each person a number and using this to identify them. In experiments with an independent groups design, this helps to identify and keep a record of which condition each participant was in. In repeated measures designs, participant numbers are essential to pairing up an individual's scores in each condition. In case studies, including those of larger groups such as institutions, confidentiality is still important and identities must be hidden. For example, one reason that doctors give for failing to follow hospital hygiene rules (e.g. washing hands and wearing gloves) is 'I forgot'. A questionnaire study of doctors' behaviour would have to protect the identities of both the staff and institutions where the research was conducted.

Ethical guidelines

In order to guide psychologists on how to deal with such ethical issues, the British Psychological Society (BPS) regularly updates its ethical guidelines. Since psychologists are concerned with people's welfare, it is important that these guidelines are followed. They are summarised in Box 4.1. When research is conducted at institutions such as universities, the planned study must be approved by an ethical committee. This ensures that these guidelines are being followed.

Box 4.1 *British Psychological Society Code of Ethics (2006) in summary*

1 **Introduction:** the public need to have confidence in psychology, so the way that researchers treat participants is important as it affects public perception of all psychologists.
2 **General:** psychologists must always consider the ethical implications of their research. Foreseeable threats to the well-being, dignity, health and values of participants should be eliminated. They should only conduct research in areas where they are competent.
3 **Consent:** researchers must take reasonable steps to obtain *real* consent from participants. Real consent can only be given by participants who fully understand what they are agreeing to. Researchers should not use payment or their position of power over participants to persuade them to consent to activities.
4 **Deception:** deceiving participants should be avoided whenever possible. Participants should be told about the aim of the investigation as soon as possible. Deception should not be used when it is likely that participants will object or become distressed when debriefed.
5 **Debriefing:** whenever participants are aware that they have taken part in a study, they should be given a full explanation of the research as soon as possible. Researchers should also ensure that the participants' experiences were not distressing and that they leave the study in at least as positive a mood as they entered it.
6 **Withdrawal:** participants should be made aware of their right to withdraw from a study at any point and that payment does not affect this right. When debriefed, participants have the right to withdraw their data.
7 **Confidentiality:** unless agreed with participants in advance, their individual results and any personal information about them should be completely confidential.
8 **Protection:** participants should be protected from physical and psychological harm, including stress. They should not be exposed to any more risk than they would encounter in their usual lifestyle.
9 **Observation:** observational studies risk invading privacy. If participants are unaware they are being observed, this should only be done in places and situations where they would expect people to watch them.
10 **Advice:** If a researcher sees signs of a physical or psychological problem that the participant is unaware of, but which might be a threat, they should inform them about it. Where participants seek professional advice, the researcher should be cautious.
11 **Colleagues:** If colleagues are seen to break any of these principles, it is important to tell them and to try to persuade them to alter their conduct.

Krakow & Lynn (2003) (p35) carried out a study of children's testimonies, and the findings led to useful conclusions about evidence in child abuse cases. The parents were told what would happen in the study, including the questions that would be asked (such as about whether the child had been touched on the bottom or kissed, although neither of these things actually happened). It was made clear to the parents that they could cross out any questions they didn't want asked and could opt not to continue with the study. Some parents decided not to continue. Those who stayed in the study were asked not to tell the children that they would be asked about what they could remember. The general source of participants, such as from adverts in preschools, is stated. The names of the preschools, families and children, however, are not reported in the paper. The study had been approved by the Institutional Review Board, the researchers' university ethical committee.

What ethical dilemmas were being faced and how were they dealt with in this study?

Populations and samples

The group of participants in a study is called the *sample*. They are selected from the target population and should represent that population. However, not all samples are in fact representative of the population. Researchers often choose a sample simply by using those people who are around at the time. This is called *opportunity sampling* and is unlikely to represent the population fairly. Think about any studies you have done. You probably conducted them on your classmates, friends, family or students in the canteen. These people will all tend to be very alike; they won't include the variety that exists in the population from which they come. For example, your classmates are probably all in the same year, doing the same subjects and may be predominantly of one gender. This means your results may not reflect the scores that people of different ages and interests at your school or college might produce. Despite this potential problem, opportunity sampling is the most common method, even for professional psychologists, many of whom rely on university students for participants. This is acceptable where the results are unlikely to be affected by age, education or socio-economic status.

KEY TERMS

sample – the group of people selected from a population to represent that population in a study

target population – the group from which a sample is drawn

opportunity sampling – selecting participants according to availability. It is non-representative

volunteer sampling – this is a way to recruit people through advertising. The participants respond to a request rather than being approached by the experimenter. It is non-representative

random sampling – selecting participants such that each member of a population has an equal chance of being chosen. It is representative of the population

Figure 4.26 If unusual participants are needed for a study, such as for measuring attachment in premature babies, volunteer sampling is helpful

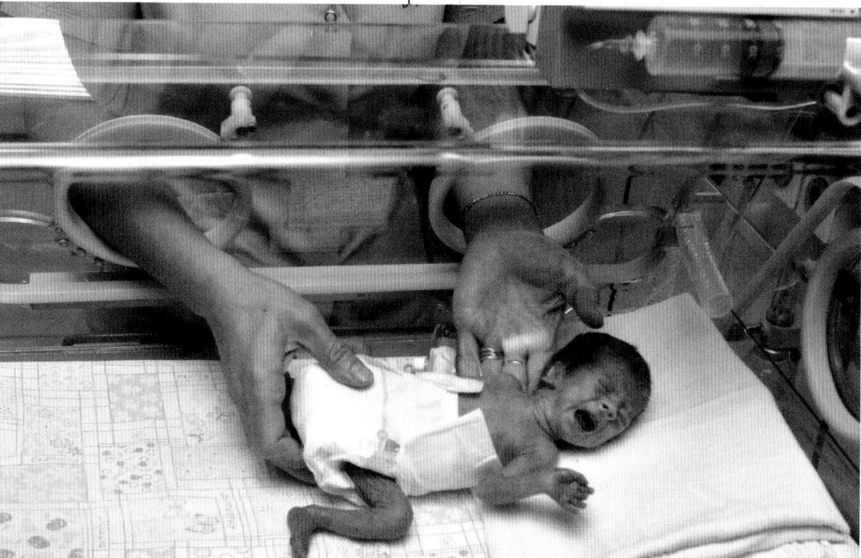

Rather than asking people directly, you might request volunteers. This might be done by putting up a notice, making an announcement or posting a request on the Internet. The people who respond and become participants are a *volunteer sample*. This sampling technique is also unrepresentative of the population. Volunteers are likely to have more free time than average and, apart from being willing, tend to have other characteristics in common, such as being better educated. However, it is a very useful technique when looking for participants who are unusual in some way. For example, in a study looking at attachment in 'incubator babies', volunteers could be requested from among the mothers at a hospital maternity department.

RESEARCH IN ACTION

Baker *et al.* (2004)

(p25)

Baker *et al* investigated context-dependent memory using chewing gum. Their participants were an **opportunity sample** of undergraduate students from Cardiff University.

Krakow & Lynn (2003)

(p35)

Krakow & Lynn found participants by putting advertisements in paediatricians' offices, preschools and the birth announcement pages of newspapers. This was **volunteer sampling**.

De Schipper *et al.* (2004)

(p67)

De Schipper *et al* obtained a list of all 1004 day care centres in three areas of the Netherlands. From these, 140 were **randomly selected** for inclusion in the study (although mothers and professional carers from only 119 eventually participated).

Figure 4.27 De Schipper *et al*. randomly selected 140 Dutch day care centres to participate. This sample is likely to be representative of the target population.

So, both opportunity and volunteer samples run the risk of being biased; they will probably contain very similar people and are unlikely to represent the spread characteristics in the population. A better way to obtain participants is by *random sampling*, which ensures that each person in the population has an equal chance of being chosen and means that the sample is much more likely to be representative. This is quite different from an opportunity or volunteer sample. If you place an advert for volunteers on the library notice board, students who never go to the library cannot be selected. If you find people by opportunity at the start of the day, the students who are always late cannot be selected. If, however, you start with a numbered list of all students and use a random number generator to choose the sample, any individual is equally likely to be chosen. For a small population this can be done by allocating each person a number, putting pieces of paper with each number on in a hat, and drawing out numbers until there are enough for the sample.

Thinking critically about psychology

What sampling method was used in each of these studies?

- **Banse (2004)** (p55) contacted participants from their postal addresses provided by the Civil Register Office in Berlin to invite them to participate in a study about attachment and adult relationships.
- **Loftus & Palmer (1975)** (p33) used university undergraduates as participants in their study into eyewitness testimony.
- **Lindsay (1990)** (p34) also investigated eyewitness testimony, using college students from two American colleges. They participated either as part of an optional classroom demonstration or as a scheduled extra-credit lab session.

DATA ANALYSIS AND PRESENTATION

The findings of research need to be presented so that other people can readily understand what has been found. To do this, the results are often summarised and presented using tables and charts. This is only possible when the results are numerical – that is, for quantitative data. Quantitative data can also be analysed mathematically, for example by using averages or correlations. If the results are descriptive – that is, qualitative data – different methods are used. One technique, called *content analysis*, allows qualitative data to be converted to quantitative data so that they can be analysed and interpreted.

Presenting, analysing and interpreting quantitative data

When quantitative data is collected, there will be one or more 'scores' or numerical values for each participant. These need to be summarised in order to be interpreted. Typically, averages and measures of spread are used, and these figures are tabulated (put into tables) and represented on graphs. There are several different ways to do this in each case. One key factor that will help you to decide how to analyse data is the level of measurement.

Levels of measurement

Quantitative data can be recorded in many different ways. Although they are usually numerical, sometimes this is not obvious. For example, when a researcher uses Likert scales (see p92) the results are points on a scale from, say, 'strongly agree' to 'strongly disagree'. However, these scores can still be counted up, making the data quantitative.

There are four different types of numerical data, referred to as different levels of measurement. These are:

- Nominal
- Ordinal
- Interval
- Ratio.

Note that their initial letters spell 'NOIR', a helpful way to remember them.

Nominal data

Results that are just totals in two or more named categories that are unrelated are called nominal data. Nominal data include answers to simple questions, such as saying 'yes' or 'no'. There can be more than two categories, for example if attachment is classified into types A, B and C. The important idea is that these groups are not related in a way that would allow them to lie along the same scale. Closed questions in interviews or on questionnaires often generate nominal data. To help you remember that nominal data are in named categories, think *nom*, the French for 'name'.

Ordinal data

In ordinal data the results are points from a scale. The results themselves may be numbers or words but the points relate to one another, so they could be put in order, for example from smallest to biggest or worst to best. There needs to be a clear increase in the value of points along the scale but the size of each increase does not have to be equal – that is, the gaps between the points on the scale do not have to be the same.

For example, we could ask participants to rate how good they think their memory is on a scale that read: 'very poor', 'poor', 'average', 'quite good', 'very good'. We would know that people who rated themselves as 'very good' were much better than average, but we would not know for sure whether they were twice as good as people who said they were 'quite good'.

Numerical scales can also produce ordinal data, for example if an eyewitness indicates how certain they are that their recall is accurate on a scale of 1 to 10. Because the participants are only estimating, we cannot be sure that one person's interpretation of the scale is the same as another's, so the absolute value of each point may not be the same.

To help you to remember that **ord**inal data means points in **ord**er along a scale, look at the first three letters.

Interval data

Like ordinal data, interval data has scores on a linear scale; the points increase in value. However, on an interval scale the divisions between the points are equal. For example, if participants in a memory test have to recall trigrams, like FZC, DMP, WBR, HTG, LXV, SQJ, each one is equally memorable as they are all unfamiliar three-letter nonsense consonant syllables. The same may be true for some word lists such as ant, cat, dog, hen, fox, pig, as they are all familiar three-letter, one-syllable animal names. These would be interval scales. However, on a word list that included 'rhinoceros' or 'porcupine' it is unlikely that each item would be equally memorable, so the gaps between the points on the scale of 'the number of words recalled' would not all be equal. This would mean that the scale could not be described as an interval level of measurement.

In psychology, commonly used interval scales include measures of intelligence and personality. To help you to remember interval scales, remember that there are equal *intervals* between the points.

Figure 4.28 Measures such as pulse rate and blood pressure are ratio scales

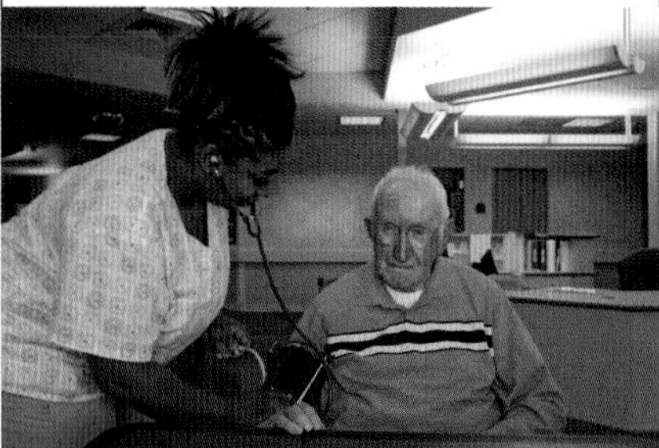

Ratio data

Ratio data, like interval data, have equal intervals between the points. They differ because ratio scales also have a real zero. Although it might not be possible for a participant to score zero, that is where the measurements on the scale start. For example, in an experiment on anxiety in eyewitnesses we might measure pulse rate to indicate how anxious the participants were. Even the most relaxed people would not score zero for their pulse rate, but the scale of 'beats per minute' would be measured from this baseline.

Think back to the example of remembering a word list. If a person scored zero for recall of words it would not necessarily mean they had no memory (they might just be poor at remembering animal names). However, if a participant had a pulse rate of zero, it *would* mean that they had no pulse at all.

All physical measures, such as centimetres, kilograms and degrees Celsius, are ratio scales. To help you remember that ratio scales are often mathematical units, think of working out ratios in maths.

Measures of central tendency

One way to analyse quantitative data is to work out the measure of central tendency or 'average'. This is a single number that indicates the 'middle' or typical point in a set of data. There are different measures of central tendency to use with different levels of measurement: the mode, median and mean.

Mode

The mode is the most frequent score in a set of results. If two (or more) scores are equally common, there will be two (or more) modes. For example, if the Strange Situation is used to assess attachment and the researcher finds that out of 50 children, 12 are type A, 36 are type B and 2 are type C, the modal attachment type would be type A.

The mode can be used with any kind of data, but it is the *only* measure of central tendency that can be used with nominal data.

Median

The median is found by putting all the scores in a set into order from smallest to largest and finding the one in the middle of the list. When the scores in a group with an even number of participants are put in order (i.e. 'ranked'), there will be two numbers in the middle. These should be added together and divided by two to find the median (see p119). The median cannot be used with nominal data but can be used with data of any other level of measurement. For example, if a researcher has used a Likert scale, the median response can be calculated.

Mean

The mean is the measure of central tendency we usually call the 'average'. It is worked out by adding up all the scores in the data set and dividing by the total number of scores (including any that were zeros). The mean is the most informative measure of central tendency because it takes every score into account, but it should only be used with interval or ratio data.

Since many memory studies use carefully controlled lists of stimuli, such as numbers, nonsense syllables or words of equal frequency and length, the mean is often used as the measure of central tendency.

Smythe and Costall (2003) (p15)

These researchers looked at the effect of mobile phones on memory. Participants with active mobiles made a **mean** average of 12.9 errors, but 23 errors were made by those with inactive mobiles.

Measures of dispersion

Whereas measures of central tendency describe the 'middle' of a set or scores, measures of dispersion describe how spread out the scores are. There are three ways to illustrate this: the range, the interquartile range and the standard deviation.

Range

The range is the difference between the smallest and the largest score. For example, if a memory test produces scores of: 11, 12, 13, 15, 20, 20, 25, 26, 28, 30, the range is between 11 and 30. 30 – 11 is 19, so the answer is written as range = 19 (11 to 30). Compare this to another data set: 1, 4, 9, 15, 20, 20, 25, 30, 37, 39. The range is 38 (1 to 39) which tells us that the data in this group are much more spread out. This is useful as if you compare the mean, median and mode of these sets they are exactly the same (20). The range tells us how the data sets are different.

Interquartile range

The interquartile range is worked out in a similar way to the median. When the set of scores is ranked, the median is the halfway point. The upper and lower quartiles are the quarter and three-quarter points along the list. In other words, the lower quartile is halfway from the lowest score to the median and the upper quartile is halfway from the median to the highest score. Working out the medians for the sets of scores above would give:

Set 1:	11,	12,	**13,**	15,	**20,**	**20,**	25,	**26,**	28,	30
			lower quartile		**median**			**upper quartile**		
Set 2:	1,	4,	**9,**	15,	**20,**	**20,**	25,	**30,**	37,	39
			lower quartile		**median**			**upper quartile**		

The interquartile range is then the range between the upper and lower quartiles. For Set 1 this is 13 (13 to 26) and for Set 2 it is 21 (9 to 30). Again we can see that measures of dispersion tell us about differences between the sets of scores that were not indicated by measures of central tendency.

Standard deviation

The standard deviation (sd) is a calculation that works out the average amount of spread around the mean. A larger value for standard deviation indicates that the scores are spread out a long way from the mean; a smaller value shows that the scores are generally clustered close to the mean. The standard deviation is calculated from the formula:

x = each score
$\bar{x}$ = the mean
Σ = 'sum of'
n = the number of scores in the set
$\surd$ = square root

$$\text{standard deviation (sd)} = \sqrt{\frac{\Sigma(x-\bar{x})^2}{n-1}}$$

To work out the standard deviation of a set of scores, you need to follow this set of instructions:

a Work out the mean ($\bar{x}$)
b Set up a table with each score in the set (x) down the left-hand column.
c Find the difference between each score and the mean (it doesn't matter if it is a negative number) $(x - \bar{x})$
d Square each of these differences $(x - \bar{x})^2$
e Add up all the squared differences $\Sigma(x - x)^2$
f Subtract one from the number of scores in the set $(n - 1)$
g Divide the total of the squared differences $\Sigma(x - \bar{x})^2$ by $(n - 1)$.
h Find the square root.

Here is an example using Set 1 above:

a) $\text{Mean} = \dfrac{11+12+13+15+20+20+25+26+28+30}{10} = \dfrac{200}{10} = 20$

b) score (x)	c) $(x - \bar{x})$	d) $(x - \bar{x})^2$
11	9	81
12	8	64
13	7	49
15	5	25
20	0	0
20	0	0
25	5	25
26	6	36
28	8	64
30	10	100
		e) $\Sigma(x - \bar{x})^2 = 444$

f) $n - 1 = 10 - 1 = 9$

g) $$\frac{\Sigma(x - \bar{x})^2}{n - 1} = \frac{444}{9} = 49.3$$

h) standard deviation $$= \sqrt{\frac{\Sigma(x - \bar{x})^2}{n - 1}} = 7.02$$

You could calculate the standard deviation for Set 2 in the same way. Would you expect this to be bigger or smaller than the standard deviation for Set 1? Why?

RESEARCH IN ACTION

Godden and Baddeley (1975)

(p26)

The results of this study were as follows:

	recall environment				
	dry		wet		
learning environment	mean recall score	SD	mean recall score	SD	TOTAL
dry	13.5	5.8	8.6	3.0	22.1
wet	8.4	3.3	11.4	5.0	19.8
TOTAL	21.9		20.0		

From these results we can see that recall in the same environment (dry–dry or wet–wet) was better than in a different environment from learning (dry–wet or wet–dry). We can also see that the standard deviations were smaller in the 'different environment' conditions, showing that the scores were not so widely spread. The participants produced more varied scores when the recall and learning environments were the same.

Tables

So that other people can clearly see the outcome of a study, a summary of the findings is usually presented in a table. Tables should always have an informative title and clear headings for each row and column that include units of measurement if appropriate. Results such as totals or frequencies, percentages, means, medians, modes, ranges, interquartile ranges and standard deviations can all be tabulated.

Godden & Baddeley (1975)

(p26)

The results of this study can be illustrated using a bar chart (Figure 4.29). This shows that recall was better in both of the 'same environment' conditions that in either of the 'different environment' conditions.

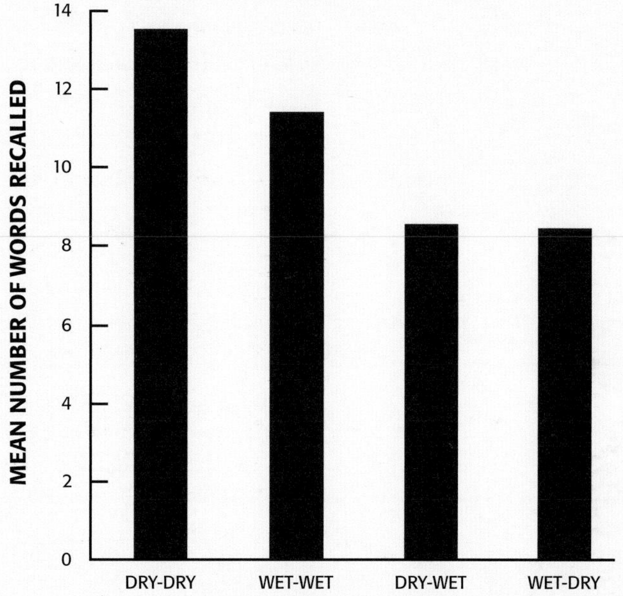

Figure 4.29 Mean recall of words in 'same environment' and 'different environment' conditions

Thinking critically about psychology

Krakow & Lynn (2003) (p35) tested children's memories using leading and non-leading questions about being touched by an adult in a game of Twister. For non-leading questions such as 'Did Amy hug you?' the mean percentage of correct answers was 93 per cent. For leading questions such as 'Amy hugged you, didn't she?' the mean percentage of correct answers was only 51 per cent. The standard deviations were lower for the non-leading questions than for the leading questions.

Which set of scores was therefore more spread out?

Abernethy (1940) (p25) tested first-year students' recall with either the same or a different invigilator and in the same or a different room from where the learning had taken place. She found the following results: same invigilator and same room, mean = 86.13, SD = 7.00; same invigilator and different room, mean = 83.97, SD = 10.80; different invigilator and same room, mean = 84.66, SD = 9.95; different invigilator and different room, mean = 83.30, SD = 10.01.

- In which condition did the students achieve the best and the worst test scores?
- In which condition were their scores most spread out?
- In which condition were their scores closest to the mean?
- Draw a table of these results

Graphs

Graphs are used to illustrate the findings of studies. Like tables, they may illustrate totals or frequencies, percentages and any of the measures of central tendency or spread. However, different graphs are used for different types of data.

Bar charts

A bar chart is used when the data are in discrete categories – that is, when the groups or sets of scores are not on a continuous scale. For example, bar charts would be used for the totals of nominal data and for all measures of central tendency (modes, medians or means). The bars on a bar chart must be separate; this is because the *x*-axis represents distinct groups, not a linear scale. If you are plotting the results of an experiment, the levels of the IV go along the bottom (on the *x*-axis) and the DV goes on the *y*-axis.

A special kind of bar chart is the bar and whiskers plot. The height of the bar is the median, and the upper and lower quartiles are drawn as short horizontal lines with a vertical line between them. This forms a pair of 'whiskers' sticking out above and below the top of the bar to indicate the spread of scores. For example, a researcher might collect scores on a scale measuring maternal sensitivity that produced an ordinal score from 1 to 15. If data were gathered in two conditions, from those with infants having an 'easy' or 'difficult' temperament, two sets of scores would be gathered.

Participant number	1	2	3	4	5	6	7	8	9	10
'Easy' temperament	9	14	10	2	12	13	13	7	8	11
'Difficult' temperament	3	7	9	8	12	4	8	5	6	10

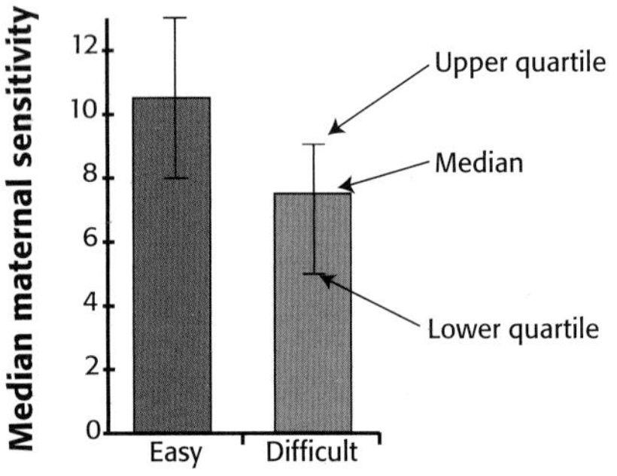

Figure 4.30 Bar and whiskers chart

To draw a bar and whiskers chart (Figure 4.30) we need to work out the medians and interquartiles for each set:

'Easy' temperament: 2, 7, **8**, 9, **10**, **11**, 12, **13**, 13, 14
Median = $10 + 11/2 = 10.5$, lower quartile=8, upper quartile=13

'Difficult' temperament: 3, 4, **5**, 6, **7**, **8**, 8, **9**, 10, 12
Median = $7 + 8/2 = 7.5$, lower quartile=5, upper quartile=9

From Figure 4.30 we can see several things. Mothers with infants with easier temperaments are more sensitive. These mothers show greater sensitivity than mothers with 'difficult' babies, but there is quite a lot of overlap between the sensitivity of mothers in the two groups.

This type of graph can be drawn in a number of different ways. For example, the whiskers can represent the standard deviation or the range.

Histograms and frequency distributions

Histograms are used to illustrate continuous data – for example, to show the distribution of a set of scores. The scale of the DV is plotted along the *x*-axis and the frequency of each score is plotted up the *y*-axis. The scores along the *x*-axis may be grouped into categories. Because the scale being represented is continuous, the bars are drawn next to each other.

An alternative way to present the same frequency data is as a line graph. This is constructed on similar axes, but instead of drawing bars, a point is marked at the height of frequency of each score. These points are then joined to form a line. This type of graph is a frequency distribution curve. A serial position curve is like this (see p17). The *y*-axis represents the frequency of recall and the *x*-axis corresponds to the position of each item on a list, from the first to the last.

Murdock (1962) (p16) produced a graph from his results. What type of graph is it?

Van Ijzendoorn & Kroonenberg (1988) (p57) produced data that was presented graphically. What kind of graph is illustrated?

Loftus & Palmer (1974) tested eyewitness recall. There are two tables of their data on (p33). Which kind of graph would be best for these results?

Draw graphs using data from the following studies:

- **Godden & Baddeley (1975)** (p26)
- **Krakow & Lynn (2003)** (p35)
- **Abernethy (1940)** (p25).

Analysis and interpretation of correlational data

We briefly described how to deal with data from correlational studies on pp84–85. Now we are going to look at analysing this sort of data in more detail.

Scattergrams

Scattergrams are used to display the findings of correlational studies. To construct a scattergram, a dot is plotted at the point where the individual's score on each variable crosses. A line of best fit is then drawn at an angle so that it comes close to as many points as possible. In a strong correlation, all the data points lie close to the line; in a weak correlation they are more spread out. Where there is no correlation, the points do not form a clear line at all (Figure 4.31).

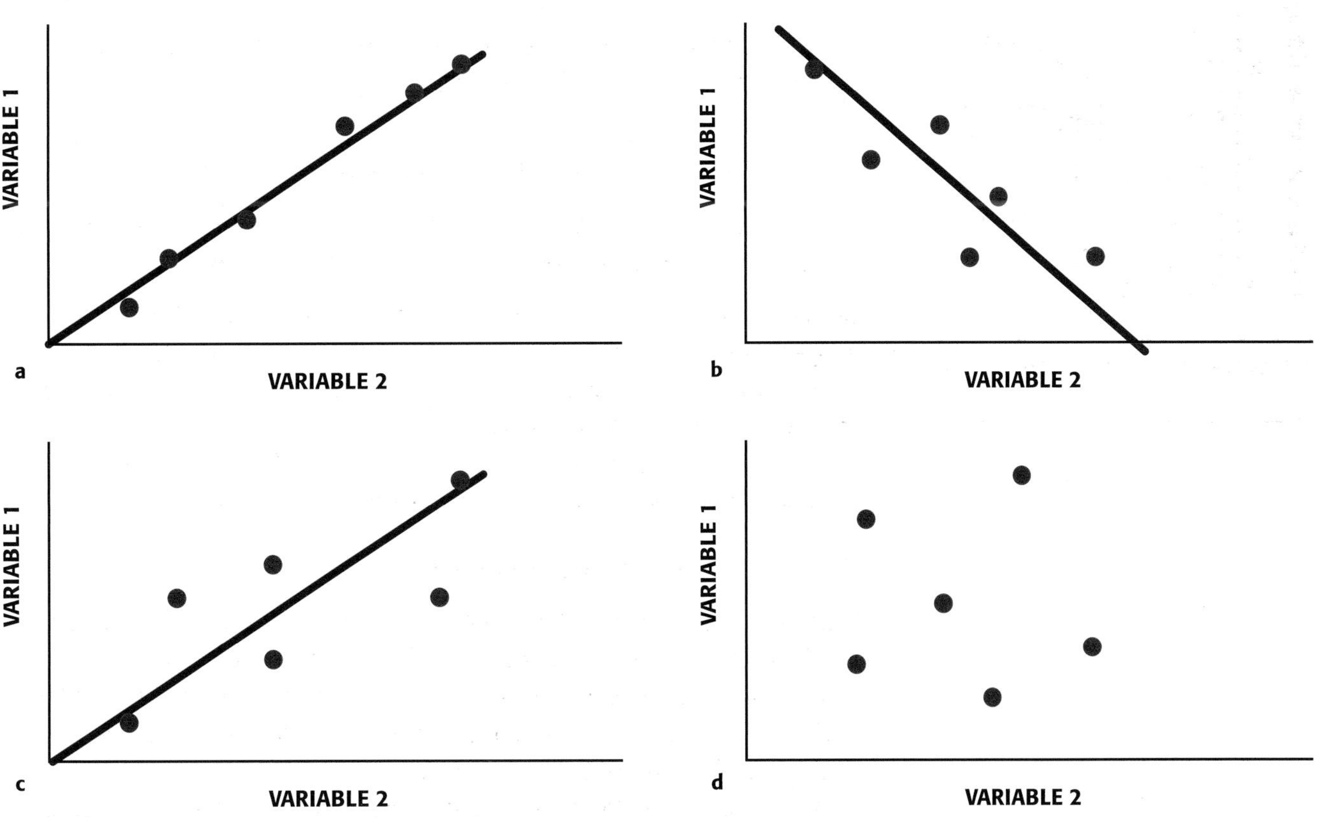

Figure 4.31 Scattergrams and the strength of correlations
a A strong positive correlation
b A weak negative correlation
c A very weak positive correlation
d A zero correlation

Correlational coefficients

One way to see the strength of a correlation is to look at how close the points are to the line of best fit. A more accurate way to describe this is using a correlational coefficient. This is a single number calculated from all the scores and is given the symbol r. A zero correlation has $r = 0$. A perfect positive correlation is $r = +1$ and a perfect negative correlation is $r = -1$. The closer the correlation coefficient is to plus 1 or minus 1, the stronger the correlation. For example, a strong positive correlation between the number of times an item is rehearsed and how well it is recalled might give a value of $r = 0.85$. A weak positive correlation between how attached a mother was to her own parents and the strength of her child's attachment might be $r = 0.4$. A very strong negative correlation between the number of lessons students miss and their exam results would be $r = -0.95$.

RESEARCH IN ACTION

Stayton & Ainsworth (1973)
(pp52 & 85)

Stayton & Ainsworth found a **negative correlation** of $r = -0.4$ between maternal sensitivity and time spent crying and a **positive correlation** of $r = +0.46$ between sensitivity and how pleased the infant was to see the mother.

You can calculate correlational coefficients for yourself using a statistical test called the Spearman rank correlation. You will need access to the Internet and two sets of scores to correlate.

1 Go to http://faculty.vassar.edu/lowry/VassarStats.html.
2 Follow the link to 'Correlation and regression' on the navigation bar, scroll down to 'Rank Order Correlation' and click on it.
3 Fill in the number of participants in your data set.
4 Scroll down the page to 'Data Entry' and key in your scores.
5 Click on 'Calculate From Raw Data' and look for the r_s box. This will be the value of your correlation coefficient.

Thinking critically about psychology

Allhusen *et al.* (2003) (p66) found that better quality day care correlated with children's social competence (+0.2), the quality of their interactions with a friend (+0.12) and their behavioural problems (–0.16). Describe these correlations in terms of whether they are positive or negative and how strong they are.

Analysis and presentation of qualitative data

In contrast to quantitative data, qualitative data is descriptive. Findings from open-ended questions in interviews and questionnaires and from some observations can produce qualitative data. This data can be simplified and changed into numerical data and analysed as we have described in the previous section. Alternatively, the detail can be preserved and it can be analysed in ways that allow researchers to explore information such as the connections between ideas. One technique for collecting data that we have not yet met is content analysis, which can be used to generate qualitative or quantitative data. We will consider this first.

Figure 4.32 Content analysis can be used to find out about the way that the media present concepts of interest to psychologists

Content analysis

Content analysis is a way to study the media, such as television programmes and books. It allows researchers to look at psychological variables and extract both qualitative and quantitative data. For example, newspaper articles might be explored to see whether they represent day care positively or negatively. Information extracted from a media source can include a variety of different data such as actual words, general meanings (such as stereotypes) or tones of voice.

The design of a study using content analysis needs planning in a similar way to other designs. The first stage is to decide on the material to be sampled, such as which TV programmes, the number of episodes and the length of viewing sample. For example a study looking at the way mothers and babies are presented in popular magazines might choose two magazines, over six monthly issues, looking at every page.

The next step is to choose coding units. These are the items to be recorded. They might be images, words or general themes. For the example of mothers and babies, coding units might include 'physical contact', 'facial expressions' or 'positive feelings'. Written comments can then be coded. For example, 'I hold my baby close to me' and 'When my baby screams I put her down' would be coded under 'physical contact'. The coding units can be categorised into groups. For example, 'I hold my baby close to me' would be coded as a positive example of physical contact and 'When my baby screams I put her down' as a negative example.

Design a content analysis to test how fairly day care is represented in media such as films.

A researcher can also extract qualitative data from the magazines, providing context to the comments. For example, a mother may choose to provide physical comfort for an infant in distress but ignore their cries when it is time for the baby to sleep. This information would be lost if the data were coded purely into simple categories. However, it is usual for the results of a content analysis to be presented as quantitative data. This is easy to do as the number in each coding unit or category can be counted up, providing totals. For example, if two magazines were compared for how positive they were towards parents using day care facilities, the number of positive and negative comments in each could be counted up. These could then be used in as numerical data in a quantitative analysis.

Figure 4.33 Films such as *Daddy Day Care* provide interesting material for content analysis

Qualitative data from interviews, questionnaires and observations

Answers to open questions and non-focused observations can produce detailed descriptive data that can be analysed using qualitative methods. The aim in analysing this type of data is to summarise the findings without losing the meanings. One technique is to identify repeated themes. For example, if in many interviews with amnesics there are reports of feeling lost, these can be represented as a concept, and specific examples can be chosen and reported in full. This is called *thematic analysis*. The total amount of data is still reduced, but the richness of the information is preserved.

Another technique for ensuring that appropriate detail is preserved in qualitative data is to involve the participant. In a case study the participant may read the researcher's report of their findings and comment on whether this fairly reflects their experiences or feelings. This is called collaborative research. It allows the researcher to refine the detail of their findings in order to improve validity. For example, in a study of an adult who experienced privation as a child, the transcript of an interview may be interpreted by the researcher. When the participant reads the report, they can correct any misinterpretations and add insights into the analysis.

Thinking critically about psychology

Curtiss (1977) (p60) conducted a case study of Genie that collected a great deal of qualitative data. Some of this information is presented as short transcripts of conversations with Genie that illustrate a frequent problem that she experienced. Is this a case of reducing qualitative data to quantitative data or the use of thematic analysis?

CHAPTER SUMMARY

Methods and techniques

- A true experiment has an IV that is changed by the experimenter and causes an effect on a DV. This change is measured. These variables are operationalised to increase validity and reliability.
- There are three experimental designs. Independent groups uses different participants in each condition and repeated measures uses the same participants in each condition. In matched pairs, participants who are similar on key variables are paired up and one member of each pair is put in each condition.
- Independent groups designs avoid order effects and reduce the effect of demand characteristics but participant variables are a problem. These can be minimised by random allocation of participants to conditions and a single-blind design. In repeated measures designs, order effects are avoided using counterbalancing. Using a matched pairs design solves most of these problems but finding similar pairs of people can be difficult.
- Investigator effects can cause bias, for example when an experimenter has expectations about the effect of the IV and so influences the participants' behaviour. This problem can be avoided by using a double-blind procedure.
- Laboratory experiments are highly controlled, which helps to limit situational variables and increase experimental validity. However, tasks may be unrealistic (low mundane realism), and the findings from the false situation may not generalise to the real world (low ecological validity), although this is not *always* the case in laboratory experiments. Field experiments are conducted in the participants' normal environment so they are likely to act more naturally, although ecological validity is not *necessarily* higher than in a lab.
- A natural experiment is not a true experiment because the IV is not manipulated by the experimenter. Instead they take advantage of a naturally occurring difference to provide experimental conditions. Participants cannot therefore be randomly allocated to levels of the IV, which lowers validity.
- In a correlational analysis, two variables are measured to look for a link between them. The relationship can be a positive correlation (both variables increase together) or a negative correlation (as one variable increases, the other decreases). A researcher cannot be sure from a single correlation whether this relationship is causal; changes in both variables could be being caused by another factor. Correlations allow researchers to investigate variables that could not be manipulated for practical or ethical reasons.
- Observational techniques can be used either as a research method used to record behaviours or as a measure of a DV in an experiment. An observer may be disclosed or non-disclosed and participant or non-participant. Non-disclosed observers cannot affect the behaviour of the participants, and non-participant observers are less likely to become subjective because of their involvement. The observation can take place in an artificial situation or can be naturalistic. Observations of the latter kind are harder to control but produce valid data as the situation is real.
- When conducting an observation, the researcher decides on behavioural categories to record, which must be operationalised. When more than one observer is used, these definitions should be agreed and recording practised so that they have high inter-observer reliability.

- Questionnaire and interview studies can use closed or open questions. Questionnaires are written whereas interviews are conducted verbally. Questionnaires also tend to be highly structured whereas interviews can be unstructured. The order and nature of the questions in an unstructured interview can be adapted, which allows for a wider range of information to be collected, although this can differ between participants, making them hard to compare. Closed questions have a limited number of possible answers and produce numerical data that is easy to analyse using quantitative techniques. Open questions produce longer, descriptive answers that take longer to analyse. This can be done with qualitative techniques or the answers can be reduced to quantitative data.
- A case study investigates one person in detail using techniques such as interviewing, observation and conducting tests. A case study can be done in rare instances, such as of children who have experienced privation or people with brain damage, that could not be created artificially but can provide useful information. The findings are very thorough and come directly from real situations, which increases validity, but the results may not generalise to other people as each case is unique. The researcher may begin to lose objectivity as they get to know the participant, and unstructured interviewing can reduce objectivity further.

Designing investigations

- Having a clear aim for a study helps a researcher to choose an appropriate research method and to make decisions about variables and controls.
- A hypothesis is a testable statement about the expected outcome of a study. There are several different types of hypothesis.
- The experimental hypothesis states the difference in the DV expected between levels of the IV. This can be a non-directional hypothesis, which just predicts that there will be a difference, or a directional hypothesis, which predicts which condition will be 'better' or 'bigger'.
- The null hypothesis states that any difference found is due to chance.
- In a correlation the hypotheses refer to relationships or correlations rather than differences, and a directional hypothesis predicts whether the correlation will be positive or negative.
- In experimental studies, design decisions must be made about whether to conduct a lab, field or natural experiment; how to operationalise the IV and DV; which experimental design to use; and what controls to implement.
- In observational studies, design decisions must be made about where to conduct the observation (in a controlled or naturalistic environment), about the role of the observer(s) and about operationalising behavioural categories.
- When designing a self-report study a choice has to be made between a questionnaire or an interview. Then the type, number and wording of questions must be decided (although this is much more flexible in an unstructured interview).
- A pilot study is a small-scale test run. It is useful before any investigation to find out whether the intended method works, for example if the DV can be measured accurately or whether people understand the questions in a questionnaire or the standardised instructions in an experiment. Improvements can be made to the design as a result of the findings of a pilot study.

- It is important to control variables in experiments. Ways to do this include using a repeated measures design to remove participant variables; counterbalancing to reduce order effects; using an independent groups design and single-blind procedures to reduce the effect of demand characteristics; using a double-blind procedure and standardised instructions to reduce the effects of experimenter bias; and controlling situational variables in a laboratory.
- Reliability refers to the consistency of a measure. Controlled situations such as in a laboratory help to improve reliability. The reliability of a task such as a questionnaire can be measured using a test-retest or split-half procedure. Reliability between observers or interviewers can be increased through practice.
- Validity refers to being sure that you are measuring what you set out to and whether your results apply outside the population your sample was taken from. Internal validity is about being certain you are measuring what you claim to and that your research can be judged as having face, content, concurrent or predictive validity.
- External validity is about being sure that your findings will generalise, and can be judged as having historical, population and ecological validity. Ecological validity presents experimenters with a problem because experiments need to be well controlled, but this need for control conflicts with the need to make them realistic in terms of the task and setting.
- Ethical issues are important to psychologists and they are guided by a Code of Ethics which, in the United Kingdom, is published by the British Psychological Society. This identifies some important ethical issues: consent, the right to withdraw, protection from physical and psychological harm, privacy and confidentiality.
- Issues of consent are resolved by providing participants with enough information to allow them to decide whether they want to participate and, if this is not possible, by debriefing them and allow them to withdraw their data, or by the investigator having obtained presumptive consent from a different group of people.
- The right to withdraw must be explained to participants and should not be affected by payment or the authority of the researcher.
- As studies could cause psychological or physical harm, psychologists must ensure that participants leave their studies in at least as good a condition as the one in which they entered them. Effective debriefing is important in this.
- Participants must be certain that their information is safe. They should not be identified by name and the data should be kept secure. Observations should not be carried out in situations that people would expect to be private.
- The sample of participants used in a study should be representative of the population they came from. An opportunity sample is taken on the basis of availability, so is the most commonly used, although it is unrepresentative as it only includes the people who are easiest to find. In volunteer sampling the participants offer themselves, for example in response to an advertisement. This is a good way to get an unusual group, for example mothers of premature babies, but the sample is likely to be biased. Random sampling is more representative as every member of the population has an equal chance of being chosen.

Data analysis and presentation

- Quantitative data are numerical and can be scored on a nominal, ordinal, interval or ratio level. These levels of measurement refer respectively to data in named categories, points in order, points on a scale with equal intervals and points on a scale that has a real zero.
- Measures of central tendency are ways to describe the middle or average of a set of data. They are the mode, median and mean. They are a way to summarise whole data sets.
- Measures of dispersion are ways to describe the spread of a set of data. They include the range and standard deviation. They are another way to summarise whole data sets.
- Tables are used to present summary data. It is important that they have a clear title and column and row headings.
- Graphs are another way to present data. Bar charts are used for data in discrete categories such as nominal data or averages. A histogram is used for continuous data, for example for showing frequency distributions.
- Scattergrams are used to show the findings of a correlational study. In a positive correlation the line of best fit runs diagonally from the origin; in a negative correlation it runs downwards from left to right. The closer the points are to the line of best fit, the stronger the correlation. This closeness of fit can also be expressed as the correlation coefficient. The closer the number is to 1 (or –1 for a negative correlation), the stronger the correlation.
- Content analysis is a method used to investigate media such as books and TV programmes. It takes samples of the chosen media source and records information in pre-decided coding units. These can be words, images or general themes such as 'expressing anger'. These can be grouped into categories or can be kept as detailed examples. When detailed examples are used to represent general themes that can be found throughout the chosen media, this is an example of qualitative data.
- Qualitative data can also be obtained from interviews, questionnaires or observations. In each case, detailed data, for example as answers to open questions or descriptions of behaviour, is used to illustrate important, repeating themes. This is thematic analysis.
- Qualitative research may also be collaborative, with input from the participant themselves guiding the interpretation to improve validity.

CHAPTER 5
Biological Psychology

Thinking ahead

By the end of this chapter you should be able to:

- outline the role of the sympatheticomedullary pathway in the body's response to stress
- outline the role of the pituitary adrenal system in the body's response to stress
- explain the relationship between stress and illness
- describe how life changes affect stress
- describe how daily hassles affect stress
- describe and evaluate the relationship between personality and stress
- outline issues relating to workplace stress
- distinguish between emotion- and problem-focused strategies for coping with stress
- evaluate emotion- and problem-focused strategies for coping with stress
- describe and evaluate psychological ways to cope with stress, including cognitive behavioural therapy
- describe and evaluate physiological ways to cope with stress, including the use of drugs

BIOLOGICAL PSYCHOLOGY

KEY TERMS

endocrine system – all the hormones and the glands that produce them

neurone – a nerve cell

neurotransmitter – a chemical that passes a message from one neurone to the next or to another organ, such as a gland

central nervous system (CNS) – the 'control centre' of the nervous system, consisting of the brain and spinal cord

The biological approach looks at psychology from the physical perspective of the body. Understanding physiological processes can help us to see how our thinking, emotions and behaviour are controlled. One area in which the biological processes involved are well understood is stress – that is, our response to threatening situations. In this chapter we will explore the biological events that cause the feelings and behaviours that we associate with stress and its negative consequences. We will also consider various factors that affect the severity of the response to stress, which illustrate how biological factors interact with psychological ones.

There are two key biological systems investigated by biological psychologists. The nervous system consists of many nerve cells called *neurones*. These cells send electrical messages along their length and communicate from one to the next by means of chemicals called *neurotransmitters*. The *endocrine system* uses the bloodstream to move chemicals called hormones around the body. There are many different types of hormone released from glands and each has an effect on one or more target organs in the body.

WHAT IS STRESS?

KEY TERMS

stress – the biological and psychological responses experienced on encountering a threat that we feel we do not have the resources to deal with

stressor – internal or external factors that are threatening and have the potential to cause a stress response

Stress is the biological and psychological response that we experience when we encounter a threat that we feel we cannot overcome. These threats, called *stressors*, may be internal or external, for example being too hot or feeling that you have too much work to do. The same situations may be acceptable if we feel able to cope with them, but become stressors when we do not have the resources to manage them. For example, being baking hot might be perfectly okay if you're on the beach with nothing to do, but will be judged less positively if you are in a boiling-hot exam room and can't concentrate. The difference is that in one situation we judge that we can cope (by sleeping, swimming or having an ice cream). In the other, however, we are likely to assess our ability to cope differently. We cannot move or change the situation – so we experience stress.

THE BODY'S RESPONSE TO STRESS

The sympatheticomedullary pathway

Think about what happens to your body when you encounter a stressor such as a big, barking dog. The immediate changes that occur are things like breathing faster, your heart beating faster and your pupils dilating (getting wider). These are all changes that would help you to run away or defend yourself, hence this response is sometimes referred to as 'flight or fight'. The changes are all caused by the nervous system. Messages from the senses that detect the threat (for example, your eyes seeing the dog or ears hearing it bark) are rapidly transmitted to the brain, and the *sympathetic pathway* of the *autonomic nervous system* (ANS) is activated (see Figure 5.1). The ANS consists of two approximately antagonistic (opposite) halves:

- the *sympathetic pathway* (sANS) – this activates the body when arousal is high
- the *parasympathetic pathway* (pANS) – this is active during relaxation (such as when we are resting or have eaten a big meal).

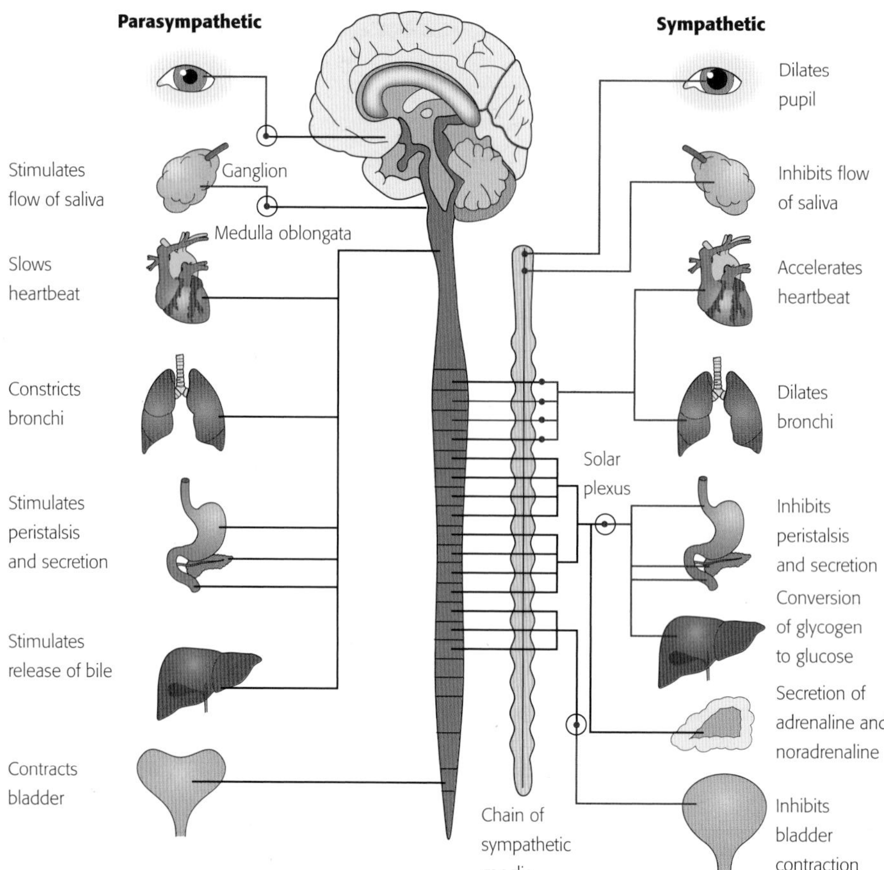

Figure 5.1 The sympathetic pathway of the autonomic nervous system links to the adrenal gland to stimulate the release of adrenaline

The effects of sympathetic activation prepare us for action. Glucose is released from the liver and we breathe faster. Together with a faster heart rate, these changes ensure that blood travelling to the muscles provides energy and oxygen, so we are more likely to be able to fight or run away. The sympathetic part of the ANS is organised in a 'chain' alongside the spinal cord, so all the changes associated with sympathetic activation tend to occur together. In contrast, activation of the different parts of the parasympathetic system can occur independently.

KEY TERMS

autonomic nervous system (ANS) – this is part of the peripheral nervous system, ie it lies outside the CNS. The neurones of the ANS transmit messages around the body to all the vital organs

sympathetic pathway – the part of the ANS activated during arousal that produces changes such as increased heart rate

adrenal glands – a pair of endocrine glands lying above the kidneys. Each is like two glands: the **adrenal medulla** produces adrenaline and the **adrenal cortex** produces cortisol

adrenaline – a hormone produced by the adrenal medulla in response to a stressor. It has effects such as increasing heart rate

Figure 5.2 The sympatheticomedullary helps us to cope with sudden stressors such as slipping and falling over

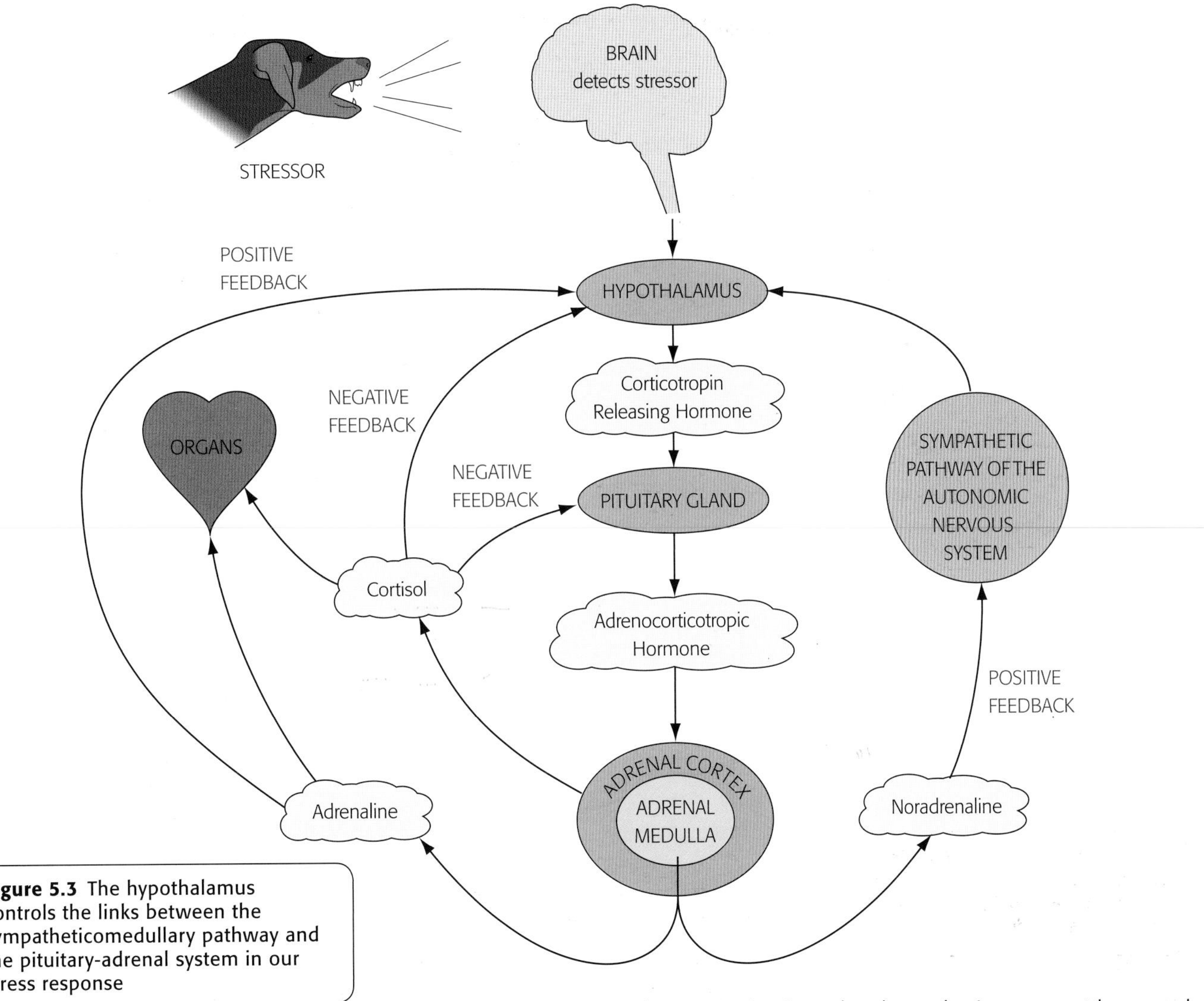

Figure 5.3 The hypothalamus controls the links between the sympatheticomedullary pathway and the pituitary-adrenal system in our stress response

One other effect of sympathetic activation is to alert the endocrine system. The central region of the adrenal glands, called the *adrenal medulla*, releases the hormone *adrenaline*. The effects of adrenaline are like those of the sANS itself. However, the sANS, being part of the nervous system, sends rapid electrical messages so has a fast but short-lived effect. Hormones, in contrast, travel in the blood so are slower to have an effect but are longer-lasting. This means that the bodily changes that could protect us from the stressor are maintained in the face of the danger.

As well as stimulating the release of adrenaline, the sANS also triggers the release of a small amount of noradrenaline from the adrenal medulla into the bloodstream. Noradrenaline is not a hormone but a neurotransmitter, and is the one used by the sANS. The effect of this noradrenaline release is therefore to maintain sympathetic activation. This is called positive feedback; the more noradrenaline is released, the more the sANS is activated and the more it stimulates the release of noradrenaline. Think about how you feel when you knock over a pint of milk – for a while after you have caught it and the stressor has gone, your heart continues to beat furiously. This is the effect of positive feedback (see Figure 5.3). To break this cycle, the pANS eventually returns the body to normal when the threat is not longer there.

The link between the sympathetic nervous system and the adrenal medulla is called the *sympatheticomedullary pathway* (SMP). The SMP is therefore responsible for the body's reaction to acute (short-term) stressors, such as emergencies like falling over or getting lost. The whole SMP is under the control of the hypothalamus, a complex area of the brain that can function both as part of the nervous system and as part of the endocrine system. It can trigger the action of the sANS and pANS and monitors levels of hormones in the blood.

KEY TERMS

sympatheticomedullary pathway (SMP) – the system that responds to acute stressors consisting of the sANS and adrenaline.

hypothalamus – a small, complex part of the brain which interacts with both the nervous system and the endocrine system

The pituitary-adrenal system

Figure 5.4 The pituitary-adrenal system controls the response to long-term stressors such as living in a crowded place

If the stressor persists, the body's active state is not maintained by adrenaline. Other hormones take over. Two of these are from the *adrenal cortex*, the outer region of the adrenal glands. They are:

- *cortisol* – which makes more energy available through the breakdown of fats and release of glucose from the liver
- *aldosterone* – which keeps the blood pressure high.

As the hypothalamus monitors both the nervous system and the endocrine system, it has an 'overview' of the body's response to stress. In the face of continued danger, the hypothalamus triggers a sequence of changes in the response to stress. Acting as an endocrine gland, the hypothalamus releases *corticotrophin-releasing hormone* (CRH). The target organ of CRH is the pituitary gland and in response it releases *adrenocorticotropic hormone* (ACTH). Finally, ACTH acts on the cortex of the adrenal glands causing the release of a hormone, *cortisol* (a corticosteroid). One consequence of this is to reduce sympathetic activation and the release of adrenaline, so cortisol replaces adrenaline as the main hormone in the response when the stressor is chronic (i.e. long-term). The release of cortisol, unlike that of adrenaline, is controlled by a negative feedback loop. The presence of cortisol in the blood is detected by the hypothalamus, and this reduces the release of CRH. The stressor must continue to be present for cortisol release to be maintained. The link between the pituitary and adrenal glands is called the *pituitary-adrenal system* (PAS). The PAS is therefore responsible for maintaining the body's response to persistent threats such as having a stressful job or living in a crowded place.

Stress-related illness and the immune system

When a long-term stressor persists, the body loses the ability to cope. As cortisol increases blood pressure, this puts strain on the heart, and one health risk associated with stress is cardiovascular disease. Another system that begins to

Cohen S, Tyrell D & Smith A (1993) Stress and susceptibility to the common cold. *Journal of Personality and Social Psychology*, **64** 131–40

AIM

To investigate the effect of stress on resistance to disease as an indicator of immune functioning.

PROCEDURE

Three hundred and ninety-four healthy participants completed a questionnaire about stress levels. A nasal drip was then used to administer either a cold virus (experimental group) or saline solution (control). Participants were quarantined, and the progress of their illness was assessed in two ways: as *infection* (the amount of cold virus) and *clinical disease* (symptoms of a cold).

FINDINGS

The participants with high stress ratings were significantly more likely to become infected and to develop symptoms.

CONCLUSION

Stress increases the risk of infection and disease.

Figure 5.5 Being stressed puts you at risk from colds

KEY TERMS

immune system – the body structures and mechanisms used to fight disease, including lymphocytes

lymphocyte – a type of white blood cell that defends the body against disease. Some lymphocytes fight infection, others target cancerous cells

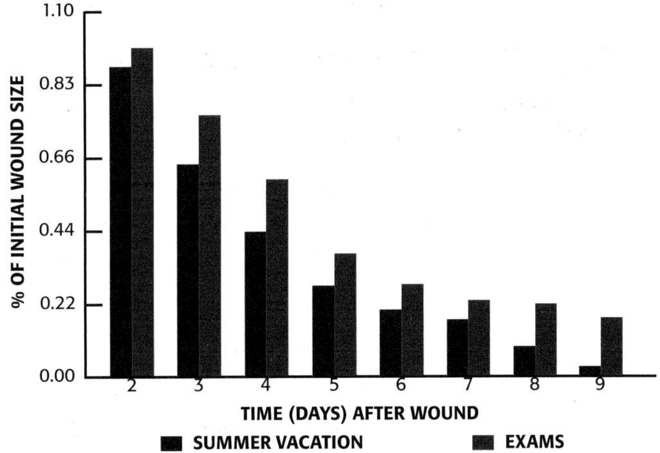

Figure 5.6 The chronic stressor of preparing for exams impairs recovery

fail is the immune system – that is, the body's mechanisms for fighting disease. High levels of hormones such as cortisol change the activity of cells that are important in the immune response, such as lymphocytes. This leads to an increased risk of disease. Some special types of lymphocytes, called killer T cells, become less effective, and because their job is to remove cancerous cells from the body, the incidence of cancer increases (see also pp136–138 & 144). Evidence also shows that our capacity to recover from injury is impaired during periods of prolonged stress. Marucha *et al.* (1998) tested the effect of stress on healing in 11 dental students. They volunteered to have a small, deliberate cut to the roof of their mouth. This was done during their summer holidays, and recovery was measured daily, using a video image of the injury. The procedure was repeated six weeks later just before their exams. The rate of reduction in wound size when stressed and not stressed can be seen in Figure 5.6. The students were 40 per cent slower to recover during exam time than during vacations!

STRESS AND EVERYDAY LIFE

Things that happen to us, such as getting stuck in traffic or losing a loved one, can act as sources of stress. The impact these have on us can be measured, and their effect on our ability to cope can be predicted from these experiences. Two measures of stressful experiences are life changes and daily hassles.

In addition to looking at the causes of stress in our lives, psychologists have considered how people cope with stress. You will have noticed that not everyone deals with stressful situations in the same way. We will look at two different strategies that people use to help themselves. Sometimes people need extra assistance to overcome the effects of stress. Psychological and physiological psychology offer different approaches to helping people to cope with stress. We will look at two techniques from each of these perspectives.

Stress and life events

As we have seen, stress can make people ill. What sorts of stressful things that happen to people are most likely to cause ill health? It might seem that big crises, such as someone dying or being ill, would be most stressful. On the other hand, the niggling things that get you down every day, like being stuck in traffic or losing things, might be more important. Both these have been considered by psychologists using scales that allow participants to report the stressful things that have happened to them.

Life changes

Holmes & Rahe (1967) developed a questionnaire for identifying major life events. Each one of 43 events was awarded a value for 'Life Change Units' depending on how traumatic it was felt to be by a big group of participants. Using this information, Holmes & Rahe were able to produce the Social Readjustment Rating Scale (SRRS), which allocates a mean 'stress score' to each event (see Table 5.1). A total value for stressful life events over a period of time (e.g. the previous six months) can be worked out by adding up the score for each event that has been experienced. The higher the total, the more stressors an individual has had to cope with, and the greater their chances of being ill. Note that this scale measures events that disrupt our lives, including both bad and good things. Christmas, holidays and weddings, for example, are positive occasions but also cause us to cope with changes. This need for readjustment is a cause of stress.

Table 5.1 The Social Readjustment Rating Scale (SRRS)

Rank	Life event	Mean value	Rank	Life event	Mean value
1	Death of spouse	100	23	Son or daughter leaving home	29
2	Divorce	73	24	Trouble with in-laws	29
3	Marital separation	65	25	Outstanding personal achievement	28
4	Jail term	63	26	Wife begins or stops work	26
5	Death of close family member	63	27	Begin or end school	26
6	Personal injury or illness	53	28	Change in living conditions	25
7	Marriage	50	29	Revision of personal habits	24
8	Fired at work	47	30	Trouble with boss	23
9	Marital reconciliation	45	31	Change to working hours or conditions	20
10	Retirement	45	32	Change in residence	20
11	Change in health of a family member	44	33	Change in schools	20
12	Pregnancy	40	34	Change in recreation	19
13	Sex difficulties	39	35	Change in church activities	19
14	Gain of new family member	39	36	Change in social activities	18
15	Business readjustment	39	37	Mortgage or loan under $10,000	17
16	Change in financial state	38	38	Change in sleeping habits	16
17	Death of close friend	37	39	Change in number of family get togethers	15
18	Change to different line of work	36	40	Change in eating habits	15
19	Change in number of arguments with spouse	35	41	Vacation	13
20	Mortgage over $10,000	31	42	Christmas	12
21	Foreclosure of mortgage or loan	30	43	Minor violations of the law	11
22	Change in responsibilities at work	29			

Source: Holmes & Rahe (1967, p216)

One of the most consistent findings in relation to life events is the relationship to ill health, for example as demonstrated by Rahe *et al.* (1970) – see *Classic Research* opposite. More recently, Yamada *et al.* (2003) have found a relationship between score on the SRRS and the development of a disease called sarcoidosis (in which organs develop lumps). The higher the score, the more likely sarcoidosis was to develop. Similarly, Palesh *et al.* (2007) found that women who had had breast cancer were more likely to relapse if they had experienced more stressful life events.

Rahe RH, Mahan JL & Arthur R (1970) Prediction of health change from subjects' life changes. *Journal of Psychosomatic Research*, **14** 401–6

AIM

To conduct a prospective study into the effect of stress on illness.

PROCEDURE

The crew of three naval ships (2684 men) were assessed for life change units (LCUs) in the preceding two years. They then spent six to eight months onboard ship and the naval medical staff kept a record of their illnesses.

FINDINGS

A positive correlation was found between life events in the six months prior to departure and subsequent illness. When there were few pre-departure life events, on-board illness rates were low. The results were divided into different LCU bands and this was plotted against illness score (see Figure 5.7). Various factors affected this pattern, such as the overall stress level of the crew (e.g. how dangerous their mission was) and their age and marital status.

CONCLUSION

Higher LCUs are associated with higher illness rates, although the link is more apparent in older and married men than in younger, single ones.

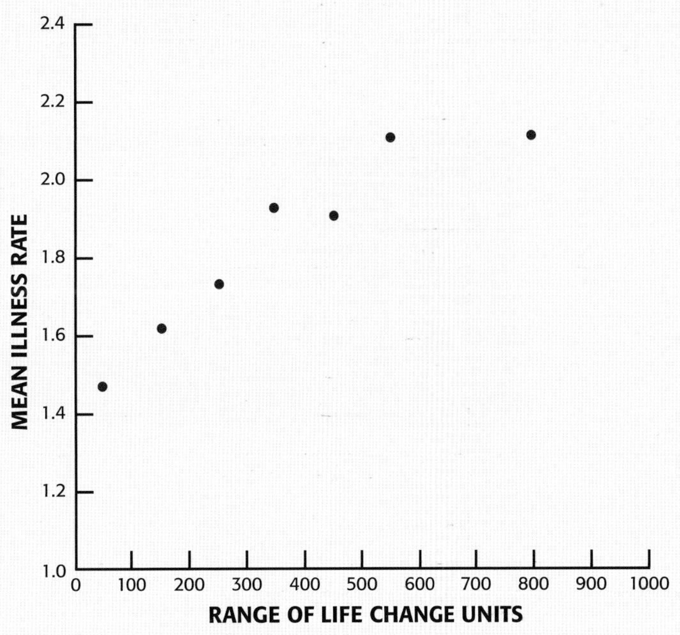

Figure 5.7 The effects of stress on illness from Rahe *et al.*

Much of the research on life events and health has been conducted on samples of patients who are already suffering from a health problem. However, Gupta & Gupta (2004) investigated the presence of skin disorders in a sample of healthy people. The participants were asked to complete an SRRS for the previous six months and to rate the severity and frequency of skin problems such as itching, burning sensations, pain, numbness and pins-and-needles. They found that the severity of symptoms correlated with the score for life events. The more stressed people were, the worse their skin conditions.

An updated, online stress test can be found at http://www.geocities.com/beyond_stretched/holmes.htm. Why do you think it has been necessary to update the test since it was used by Holmes & Rahe?

Menéndez Villalva *et al.* (2002) investigated the effect of stressful life events on blood pressure in 236 older participants (mean age 64 years) already suffering hypertension. Initially a reading was taken of their blood pressure and pulse. In a follow-up they were asked to complete an SRRS, and almost half the participants reported some life changes since the previous test, with a mean score of 47.65 life change units (LCUs). Those participants with an LCU of more than 150 showed a significant increase in blood pressure of 10.91 mmHg and heart rate (up 9.48 beats per minute). This shows that stressful life events have a damaging effect on blood pressure in patients with cardiovascular problems.

However, not all evidence demonstrates a link between life events and ill health. Vidal *et al.* (2006) followed up 163 patients with inflammatory bowel disease (IBD). They were asked to complete a version of the SRRS in Spanish, as this was their native language. At the time of testing, all the patients were in remission – that is, their IBD was inactive – although all had relapsed before. Over the next 11 months the patients' health was monitored. Although 51 patients relapsed (and eight dropped out of the study), there was no relationship between relapse and their reporting of stressful life events. This finding suggests that, at least for some disorders, high levels of stressful life events are not associated with health problems.

Thinking critically about psychology

Studies such as that by Vidal *et al.* (2006) are described as prospective because they measure stress levels before the onset of (new) health problems. Other studies (e.g. Gupta and Gupta, 2004) are retrospective, asking people to look back on previous stressful events once health issues have been identified. Decide which procedure is better and justify your decision.

The SRRS has also been used to show how stress impacts on other aspects of our lives. For example, De Meuse (1985) found that students who had higher stress ratings performed less well in their examinations. Simantov *et al.* (2000) recorded four important life events in a group of adolescents (death of a close friend, parental divorce or separation, a parent losing their job or a parent getting in trouble with the law). They found that these adolescents were more likely to smoke and to drink alcohol if they had experienced higher levels of stressful life events. These findings also show that different life events may have more or less significance for different people. The SRRS is not the only measure of life changes; there are others that include more life events and that are specific to a particular age group, such as children.

Finally, our experience of life events may also make us less able to cope with new sources of stress. This was explored by Bonanno *et al.* (2007) in relation to the attacks on the World Trade Center on 11th September 2001 (see *Research Now* on the next page).

Bonanno GA, Galea S, Bucciarelli A & Vlahov D (2007) What predicts psychological resilience after disaster? *Journal of Consulting and Clinical Psychology*, **75 (5)** 671–82

AIM

To investigate factors that help people to resist the effect of post-traumatic stress disorder, including the importance of recent and previous life stressors.

PROCEDURE

Participants from New York City and nearby areas were telephoned using a random-digit dial system to obtain a sample. They were interviewed in English, Spanish, Mandarin or Cantonese. One set of questions related to their experience of recent life events such as death of a spouse or close family member. Others related to how directly they had been affected by the events of 11th September and measures of whether they were suffering from post-traumatic stress disorder.

FINDINGS

There were many patterns in the data, one of which was a relationship between the number of stressful life events and resilience. People who had experienced fewer recent life events were better able to cope with the effects of the disaster. Those with only one recent life event were about twice as likely to be resilient to the effects of 11th September as those who had experienced two or three recent life events.

CONCLUSION

These findings suggest that the effects of stressful life events are cumulative. The more bad things happen, the worse people become at coping.

Figure 5.8 People with more prior life events were less resilient to the effects of the attacks on the Twin Towers

Daily hassles

If the effects of stress build up, then we might expect that the little things that irritate us all the time would also have a negative effect. How often do you say, "That's driving me nuts", "He gets on my nerves" or "Argh! That bugs me"? Those are the kinds of frustrating things that Lazarus and his colleagues wanted to measure. They developed a scale of 117 events that could annoy people on a daily basis – the Hassles Scale (Kanner *et al.*, 1981). This includes minor problems such as queuing or having an argument.

They measured hassles in a sample of 100 people over nine months and found that those who reported the most hassles also suffered more psychological symptoms of stress such as depression and anxiety. In fact, the hassles score predicted their experience of symptoms better than their life events score. Kanner *et al.* also produced a scale for measuring the daily positives that we experience, called the Uplifts Scale. This consisted of 138 good things that can happen on a daily basis, such as getting enough sleep or eating out.

Box 5.1 *The ten most frequent hassles and uplifts*

Hassles:

1 concerns about weight
2 health of a family member
3 rising prices of common goods
4 home maintenance
5 too many things to do
6 misplacing or losing things
7 yard (garden) work or outside home maintenance
8 property, investment or taxes
9 crime
10 physical appearance.

Uplifts:

1 relating well with your spouse or lover
2 relating well with friends
3 completing a task
4 feeling healthy
5 getting enough sleep
6 eating out
7 meeting your responsibilities
8 visiting, phoning or writing to someone
9 spending time with family
10 home (inside) pleasing to you.

Figure 5.9 Daily hassles are an important stresser

Although a measure of uplifts alone does not seem to be related to health, using the two together is important, as our experience of stress depends on how we view a situation. If we see it as more negative, it will have a more damaging effect on us. Having some 'uplifts' can therefore help us to help us to cope better.

Research has also shown that, like life events, daily hassles are related to health. DeLongis *et al.* (1988) revised the hassles scale to make it easier to use. Instead of rating each of the 255 items on a three-point scale, participants only had to rate 53 things (such as 'the weather') as a hassle or an uplift on a four-point scale. Using this version, they found that people experiencing more stressors had more symptoms of stress such as getting flu, a sore throat, headaches and backache. This scale is also more useful as it measures how stressful the participant sees the situation as being. It measures their *perception* of stress, which is more important than the actual amount of stressors they are exposed to. This is because stress is the extent to which an individual feels that they can or cannot cope with a threat.

There are many ethical and practical issues to consider when investigating stress-related issues. You can, however, conduct this exercise on your class. Each individual should first make a record of illnesses (e.g. how many times they have had a cold this term or how many days they've had off sick). Everyone should then complete a test similar to the Daily Hassles Scale.

Printable versions of tests can be found at http://www.atkinson.yorku.ca/~psyctest/hassles.doc or http://www.quantifyingconnections.com/images/NEScaleadultfreq-sever.pdf.

Compile the class data anonymously, for example by getting each individual to type their two scores into a table on a computer. Look at the two sets of data. Does there seem to be a relationship?

Newman E, O'Connor DB & Conner M (2007) Daily hassles and eating behaviour. *Psychoneuroendocrinology*, **32 (2)** 125–32

AIM

To investigate a link between daily hassles, cortisol level and unhealthy behaviour. The hormone cortisol is linked to stress (see p134). People whose cortisol level responds to a stressor tend to eat more snack foods. They would therefore also be expected to respond more strongly to real-life stressors such as daily hassles.

PROCEDURE

Fifty women (who were not on the contraceptive pill or menopausal) were initially tested for cortisol reactivity. They provided saliva samples (for cortisol testing) eight times. First they gave a baseline sample, then another after reading magazines and listening to a relaxing CD. They were then stressed. They were told to prepare a five-minute presentation on a controversial topic (e.g. abortion and sexual equality) that would be recorded and judged by a body language expert. They gave their presentation to the experimenter. There was a video camera, although it was not filming. The participants were, however, prompted to complete the whole five minutes. They were then asked to count backwards quickly and accurately in 13s from 1022. If they made a mistake they had to start again. Another saliva sample was then taken. Four more samples were taken at intervals over 40 minutes and a final one after the participants had been relaxing for 20 minutes in a separate room. The participants were then given a daily hassles questionnaire to complete and kept a 'snack diary' for 14 days.

FINDINGS

The women were divided into those with high cortisol reactivity, whose salivary cortisol was higher after the stressor, and those with low reactivity. In women with high cortisol reactivity only, there was a link between the number of daily hassles and snacking. Women who reported more hassles also ate more snacks.

CONCLUSION

It looks as though women who have a strong hormonal response to stress are likely to engage in stress-induced eating. This means that, in addition to the direct effects of stress on illness, stressors may also have indirect effects that are bad for health, such as snacking.

Figure 5.10 Daily hassles cause behaviours that are bad for health, such as snacking

Thinking critically about psychology

Identify the potential ethical issues in this study. What would the researchers have had to do to ensure that the study was conducted in an ethical way?

Courtois *et al.* (2007) looked at the influence of both life events and daily hassles on adolescent drinking and smoking. Although there was a relationship between these problems and life events, the link to daily hassles was stronger.

Important hassles related to family problems, issues at school and their self-perception. Having more daily hassles affected drug use in two ways: stressed adolescents started using alcohol and tobacco earlier and became more dependent on them. Recent evidence suggests that daily hassles are also important to adults. Erlandsson & Eklund (2003) looked at stress and health in Swedish women. They found that women's well-being was lower if they had higher levels of hassles. Well-educated women and those who worked had the most hassles and those with more than two children and fewer leisure pursuits had fewest uplifts. The findings of Newman *et al.* (2007) would suggest that the high-risk women Erlandsson & Eklund described would be more likely to engage in health-damaging behaviours too. Indeed, Waldrop *et al.* (2007) found that female cocaine users who were most sensitive to daily hassles were most likely to relapse in negative situations. Also, both males and females who had many current hassles also had more emotional difficulty dealing with previous stressors such as childhood abuse. These findings indicate that hassles make coping even more difficult and are closely linked to health-impairing behaviours.

LOOKING FURTHER You can look at a hassles and uplifts scale at the site http://www.drstephanie.org/dailyhassles.htm. You can use an interactive social readjustment rating scale at the site http://www.stresstips.com/lifeevents.htm.

Figure 5.11 The type A personality is associated with drive but also with ill health

Stress and personality

As we have seen, external factors such as life events and daily hassles increase our experience of stress. However, some of this evidence (such as that of Waldrop *et al.* above) also suggests that some people may be more sensitive to the effects of stressors than others. One reason for this may be differences in personality.

The type A personality

Two doctors, Rosenman and Friedman, found a link between stress and coronary heart disease. This finding was based on an observation of the patients with heart conditions in their waiting room. Unlike most patients, who wait patiently, these individuals seemed unable to sit in their seats for long and wore out the chairs. Rosenman & Friedman (1958) concluded that these people (whom they called type A personalities) experienced higher levels of stress and were more likely to suffer from heart disease. They went on to investigate whether they were more likely to be ill because they found life more stressful or because their personality tended to expose them to more stressful experiences.

The type A personality is competitive, aggressive and goal directed. A person of this type is likely to know what they want out of life and be determined to get

Figure 5.12 People with type A personalities may suffer more coronary heart disease because their hearts are more sensitive to activity in the sympathetic nervous system.

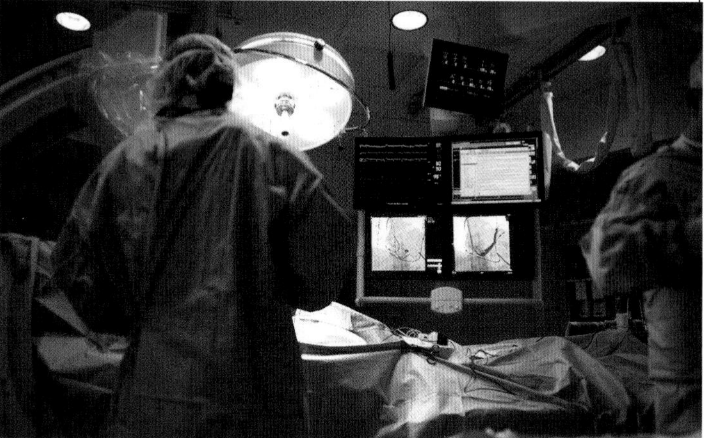

it. They may have high-powered jobs, engage in competitive sport and always be in a hurry. Type A differs from other personalities such as the more laid-back type B, type X who are not clearly in either category, or type C who repress their emotions. Forgays *et al.* (2001) compared the levels of stress experienced by mothers, both those at home with their children and those in employment outside the home. Regardless of whether they were at-home mums or not, those with type A personalities found motherhood more stressful. This suggests that individuals with type A personalities find equivalent situations more stressful than other people. However, not all evidence suggests this is the case.

Thinking creatively about psychology

Identify the kinds of parenting-related stressors that type A mothers might respond to if they are:

- at-home mothers
- mothers who work outside the home.

Figure 5.13 Road rage can make life more stressful for type A personalities

Perry & Baldwin (2000) investigated driver behaviour in relation to personality type. They found that type A personality was linked to aggressive behaviour on the road. One interpretation of this finding is that people with type A personalities are more likely to engage in activities such as tail-gating (driving on people's bumpers). This would suggest that their personality causes them to engage in behaviours that increase exposure to stress. Bettencourt *et al.* (2006) reviewed evidence relating to behaviour in situations that would or would not be likely to provoke aggression. They found that type A personalities were only more likely to become aggressive when provoked, not in general. This suggests that their personality causes them to respond differently from others to potentially stressful conditions, possibly making the situation even more stressful.

RESEARCH NOW

Lee JM & Watanuki S (2007) Cardiovascular responses of type A and type B behaviour patterns. *Journal of Physiological Anthropology*, **26 (1)** 1–8

AIM

To test the effect of stressful visual images on the cardiac activity of people with type A compared to type B personalities.

PROCEDURE

Fourteen type A and 16 type B personality students were given a daily life questionnaire and were monitored six times to see how the electrical pattern of their heartbeat (ECG) and blood pressure changed during resting, stress and post-stress recovery. They faced a screen that was grey during rest, showed video clips of forests or the grey screen during recovery, and unpleasant images during the stressor episode.

RESULTS

The type A participants had a greater level of sympathetic nervous system activity controlling the heart rate than type B participants both during rest and when under stress. They also had a higher cardiac output – that is, their hearts pumped more blood per minute than type Bs. In both type A and type B participants, parasympathetic activity reduced the heart rate but the decrease was smaller in type As.

CONCLUSION

The heart function of people with a type A personality is different from that of type Bs. They are more reactive to sympathetic nervous system activity and less reactive to parasympathetic activity. As a result, their hearts work harder at rest and under stress.

Thinking creatively about psychology

Suggest a list of visual images that could be used as stressors in a study such as that of Lee & Watanuki.

LOOKING FURTHER You can read more about the type A personality at the site http://www.msnbc.com/onair/nbc/nightlynews/stress/default.asp?cp1=1. It also has a link to an online type A personality test.

However, not all evidence suggests that people with type A personalities suffer the most stress or ill health. Mitaishvili & Danelia (2006) found no relationship between type A personality and the rate of coronary heart disease. Instead, they found that factors such as high job strain and having little social support, such as from friends or family, were both associated with increased risk. In addition, the type C personality has also been linked to stress, especially as these individuals repress their emotions, tend to have little social support and experience strong feelings of hopelessness and helplessness. For example, Shaffer *et al.* (1987) found that over a 30-year period, doctors with type C personalities were more likely to suffer from cancer. These findings suggest that personalities other than type A may also experience high stress levels and be at risk from associated ill health. Furthermore, links have also been found between type D personality – typified by distress, pessimism and anxiety – and ill health. Denollet (1998) found that of 246 men being treated for coronary heart disease, 12 patients were additionally diagnosed with cancer, of whom 8 were type D but 4 were not type D. As a percentage of the personality types in the sample, these were 13 per cent (8 out of 60) and 2 per cent (4 out of 186) respectively. So, although type D was not the most common personality for patients with heart disease, they were more likely to suffer the additional complication of cancer. They were also more likely to die from their cancer (10 per cent died, compared to 2 per cent of non-type D patients).

Workplace stress

Some jobs are more stressful than others, and one source of stressors identified by both the Life Events scale and the Hassles Scale relates to employment. Having a job can clearly be stressful, more so if you have less control over the demands of your work. Marmot *et al.* (1997) reported that higher-grade employees were less stressed than lower-grade ones, and were less likely to die from coronary heart disease-related illnesses. Findings such as this suggest that having some say in when, where, how or how much work you do helps to limit the effects of stress. For example, Sparks *et al.* (1997) conducted a meta-analysis and found a relationship between the length of the working day and health: people who worked long hours were at greater risk. A similar pattern was found by Kageyama *et al.* (1998), who also reported greater sympathetic nervous system activity in participants working long hours (doing more than 60 hours of overtime per week). Furthermore, they found that those people who had a long journey to work, commuting for more than three hours daily, had the same sign of chronic stress.

One recent source of workplace stress is email. Hair *et al.* (2007) found that some workers experience considerable stress from emails. Of their sample of 137 participants 34 per cent checked their inbox at least every 15 minutes.

One contributory factor to the experience of work stress may be personality. Jepson & Forrest (2006) investigated factors affecting stress in teachers. They found a positive relationship between type A behaviour and perceived stress, showing that personality is one of the influences on stress in the workplace. Similarly, Hallberg *et al.* (2007) identified a relationship between type A personality and work stress. They found that 'burnout', where an employee works so hard that they become physically and emotionally exhausted, is positively correlated with type A behaviour. They suggested that this arose because people with this personality type tended to strive harder to achieve and were more impatient and irritable. These negative effects of mood seemed to be more problematic than their perception of stress at work.

Figure 5.14 *You've Got M@il*: emails are a potential source of stress

Whilst there is clearly evidence that too much work is stressful, too little work can also be a source of stress. 'Underwork' can reflect either not having enough to do or feeling that your skills are underused. This can lead to low job satisfaction – another source of stress. Having no job at all is also stressful. Hammarstrom & Janlert (1997) followed a group of 1060 school leavers over five years and found that unemployment was linked to greater signs of stress, including anxiety and depression.

Coping with stress

Emotion- and problem-focused strategies

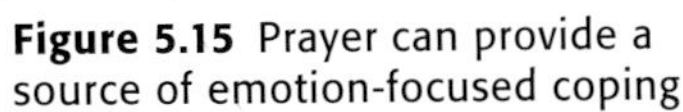

Figure 5.15 Prayer can provide a source of emotion-focused coping

If you think about the way your friends deal with stressors like exams, you will see a range of different coping responses. Some people will pace around or tell you how worried they are, others will revise, or pester their teachers for clues about the questions. The first group are managing their fears; they are making themselves feel better about the situation. This is called emotion-focused coping. It aims to reduce the negative effects of the stressor. Some emotion-focused strategies include:

- keeping yourself busy to take your mind off the issue
- letting off steam to other people
- praying for guidance and strength
- ignoring the problem in the hope that it will go away
- distracting yourself, for example by eating
- building yourself up to expect the worst.

The second group are doing something about the problem itself; they are coping using problem-focused strategies. These aim to remove or reduce the cause of the stressor. Some problem-focused strategies include:

- seeking advice from friends or professionals
- investigating alternative plans
- getting information, for example from the Internet
- taking positive action against the stressor
- using your past experience to solve the problem.

Thinking creatively about psychology

What emotion- and problem-focused strategies could be used by people experiencing stressors such as noisy neighbours or industrial pollution?

In reality, people tend to use a mixture of emotion- and problem-focused strategies in any situation, although there are some situations where one or other approach is better. In general, problem-focused coping is best, as it removes the stressor, so deals with the root of the problem. This approach also seems to be more healthy. Epping-Jordan *et al.* (1994) found that patients with cancer who employed avoidance strategies, such as denying that they were very ill, deteriorated more quickly than those who faced up to the problems. Similarly, Genco *et al.* (1999) found the same pattern in relation to dental health. For patients who were facing the stressor of financial problems, those who dealt with them in practical ways with problem-focused strategies suffered fewer problems with their teeth than those who used emotion-focused coping strategies. This suggests a more general relationship between coping style and health. Desmond (2007) studied men dealing with the stress of an upper arm amputation. The results showed that those relying on emotion-focused strategies were less effective at coping and that promoting the use of problem-focused strategies was important to helping people to cope in this situation. Many studies therefore suggest that a problem-focused style can improve coping.

However, it is not always best, or even possible, to use problem-focused strategies. When somebody dies, problem-focused strategies are not very helpful for the bereaved. Dealing with the feelings of loss requires emotion-focused coping. This

Figure 5.16 Residents around Three Mile Island at the time of the nuclear accident coped best using emotion-focused strategies

is the case in any situation where it is beyond the ability of the individual to remove the source of stress. The consequences of industrial accidents fall into this category. Once a disaster has happened, there is little that one can do to reduce the problem, but it is still important to manage the negative feelings, such as fear, in order to cope. Collins *et al.* (1983) studied the people living near to the Three Mile Island nuclear power plant. In March 1979 this was the site of a very serious nuclear accident, and residents feared that radiation from the meltdown would be extremely hazardous (although this appears not to have been the case). Those people using emotion-focused strategies coped better than those employing problem-focused strategies who were trying to take direct action. In situations of ill health where patients need to rely on health care for practical support and use inner resources to help them to cope with their feelings, emotion-focused strategies are important. For example, Aldridge & Roesch (2007) found that children with cancer were more stressed if they attempted to use problem-focused strategies to cope.

Emotion-focused strategies can be effective in other contexts too. Toda *et al.* (2006) found that an eight-day stay at a spa resort helped to alleviate stress in women who reported stressful life events. This experience would have provided a range of different opportunities for emotion-focused coping but little chance for problem-focused approaches. A similar pattern was seen in an experiment that manipulated sources of emotion-focused distraction. Toda *et al.* (2007) reported that subjective measures of stress (report by the participants on a scale) decreased after watching comic but not non-humorous films. They concluded that laughter helps to relieve the effects of stress by producing feelings of being uplifted or fulfilled.

RESEARCH NOW

Lee T, Toshiaki S, Megumi I, O Kaoru, Yuichiro Y & N Shingo (2006) Evaluation of psychosomatic stress in children. *Acta Paediatrica,* **95 (8)** 935–9

AIM
To test the effectiveness of distraction in reducing stress in children when they have to have venipuncture (puncturing of a vein, e.g. for a blood test).

PROCEDURE
Measures of chromogranin A (an indicator of stress, present in saliva) were taken immediately before and after venipuncture and after 60 minutes. This was done with or without the distraction of a kaleidoscope for the child.

FINDINGS
In the children tested without the kaleidoscope, chromogranin A increased immediately after the medical procedure and decreased over time. No increase was seen in the children who were distracted from the procedure with a kaleidoscope.

CONCLUSION
Distraction acts as an effective emotion-focused strategy for reducing stress in children during unpleasant medical procedures.

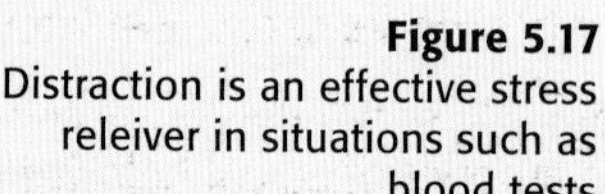

Figure 5.17
Distraction is an effective stress releiver in situations such as blood tests

Thinking creatively about psychology

Dental procedures are a common source of stress for adults. Design a study to test the effectiveness of distractions such as music or a ceiling-mounted TV for reducing stress through emotion-focused coping.

There are individual differences in the way people cope. For example, in general, women tend to use more emotion-focused strategies than men (Billings & Moos, 1981). However, Nicholls *et al.* (2007) asked 749 undergraduate athletes about stressors relating to the demands of playing in a team situation. Unlike previous researchers, they showed that women used problem-focused strategies more often than men. There are also cultural differences. Frydenberg *et al.* (2003) compared how students from several countries coped with stress. Although all the adolescents coped by working hard – either to remove the stressor of work or to take their mind off the problem – there were also differences in the typical ways that they managed stressful situations. German and Australian adolescents tended to use physical recreation as a distraction, an emotion-focused strategy. Palestinian and Colombian students also used emotion-focused strategies, but they tended to seek spiritual support, to worry and rely on others for social support. These findings also show that various aspects of our social environment can help us to manage stress through both emotional and problem-focused strategies. In *Classic Research* we look at the importance of another aspect of our surroundings, the physical environment, as a source of stress reduction.

CLASSIC RESEARCH

Parsons R, Tassinary LG, Ulrich RS, Hebl MR & Grossmann-Alexander M (1998) The natural environment and stress recovery. *Journal of Environmental Psychology*, **18** 113–140

AIM

To test whether the natural environment is better at assisting stress recovery and immunising against the effects of stressful situations than artificial environments.

PROCEDURE

One hundred and sixty students, males and females, were mildly stressed and then viewed one of four different videotaped simulated drives through an outdoor environment consisting of artificial and natural scenes. Immediately after the video they were mildly stressed again. The effects of watching the video was measured as changes in blood pressure and GSR (galvanic skin resistance, a measure of 'sweatiness' indicating activity in the ANS and therefore raised stress) and changes in facial expression (frowning and smiling).

RESULTS

Participants viewing natural scenes recovered from viewing the pre-video stressor more quickly and became less stressed by the post-viewing stressor than those viewing artificial scenes.

CONCLUSION

Natural scenes help to reduce the effects of a stressor and can provide immunisation against stress.

Figure 5.18 The natural environment helps to reduce stress

Our social environment provides us with social support. This can be important to both emotional- and problem-focused strategies. We may use other people in a practical way, for example as a source of information, or to listen to us and bolster our feelings – that is, for emotional reasons. Interestingly, we do not even need to *use* their support to feel better when under stress. Just knowing that there are people who could help us if we needed them is enough. This *perceived support* is more important than the amount of actual help we receive. Remember also that other people can be a source of stress; they appear on the Daily Hassles scales.

Media watch: canine coping

http://www.telegraph.co.uk/news/main.jhtml?xml=/news/2007/01/22/ndog22.xml

Improve your health, become a dog owner

Owning a dog is good for your mental and physical health, more so even than cats, researchers claim today.

Dr Deborah Wells, a senior lecturer at the Canine Behaviour Centre of Queens University, Belfast, found that dog owners have lower cholesterol and blood pressure, fewer minor physical ailments, and are less likely to develop serious medical problems.

In a paper published today by the British Psychological Society, she said 'It is possible that dogs can directly promote our well-being by buffering us from stress, one of the major risk factors associated with ill health. The ownership of a dog can also lead to increases in physical activity and facilitate the development of social contact, which may enhance both physiological and psychological human health in a more indirect manner.'

She found that people who took cats and dogs from animal rescue shelters noticed a decrease in minor ailments such as headaches, colds and dizziness a month after the rescue visit. But only dog owners maintained the improvements ten months later – cat owners did not.

The research, published in the Health Psychology Journal, found that dogs could also act as 'early-warning systems' for more serious illnesses including cancer and epilepsy.

Figure 5.19 Dogs but not cats help to reduce stress

Lynne Wallis, *Daily Telegraph*, 22 January 2007

1 Using your understanding of the causes of stress and ways to minimise its effects, explain why pets might be useful to people.

If you want to know more about the links between stress and health, you can read about how cancer is linked to stress at http://www.cancerproject.org/survival/cancer_facts/exercise.php.

Stress management

Psychological stress management strategies

Psychological therapies are used to help people with a range of different psychological disorders. The theory behind the cognitive approach, discussed here, is described in detail in Chapter 7. Basically, the cognitive approach to helping people with stress suggests that faulty thinking or beliefs are the cause of our inability to cope. The aim of cognitive therapy is therefore to change the individual's cognitions (which may also cause a change in their behaviour) to enable them to deal effectively with the stressor. To do this, negative and dysfunctional beliefs are challenged and behavioural tasks are used to help the individual to overcome their irrational thinking. These techniques are therefore sometimes called cognitive *behavioural* therapies. Most therapists now use a mixture of approaches which were developed as many separate therapies, including rational emotive behaviour therapy and cognitive behavioural therapy, which will now be discussed.

Rational Emotive Behaviour Therapy (REBT)

Ellis (1977b) suggested that activating events (A), such as stressors, trigger beliefs (B), such as about our ability to cope. If these beliefs are negative, ie that we cannot cope, the consequence (C) will also be negative – we will feel stressed. This can be represented as an 'ABC' model (see Figure 5.20).

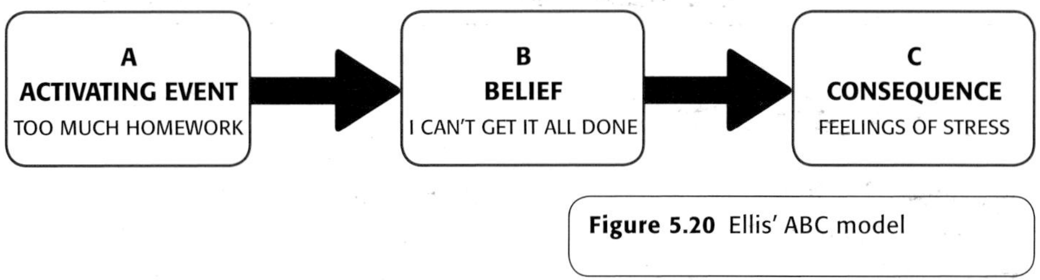

Figure 5.20 Ellis' ABC model

According to Ellis, we sustain irrational beliefs in this way. He proposed that if an individual could control their beliefs, they would be able to control their emotions and, hence reduce the negative effects of stress. Since the consequences of activating events are controlled by beliefs, these false beliefs must be changed to improve coping. This is the aim of REBT. The ABC model is extended to include the two stages of REBT:

- **D** – ***d****isrupting* irrational beliefs
- **E** – the ***e****ffects* of this disruption. These effects may be:
  - *cognitive* – changing irrational beliefs to rational ones so that the individual evaluates experiences constructively
  - *emotional* – changing feelings from negative to positive
  - *behavioural* – changing behaviour to improve coping.

These aim to make individuals more stoic in their approach to experiences – that is, more able to withstand stressors. Changes could include rejecting the belief that a situation is intolerable or avoiding over-reacting to minor problems.

In support of REBT, evidence suggests that the experience of stress is linked to negative thinking. Balevre (2001) investigated burn-out in nurses. The results suggested that those individuals with maladaptive thinking, such as perfectionism and creating unrealistic demands, were more likely to experience burn-out thoughts and behaviours. In this situation the nurses would have benefited from REBT to change their unrealistic expectations. In some situations, REBT is effective. Engels *et al.* (1993) found that it was a more successful treatment for anxiety than behavioural therapies alone or behaviour therapy and REBT combined. However, studies on REBT tend to demonstrate effectiveness only in the short-term. There are also clear ethical issues in the aggressive nature of the challenges to the individual, especially when they are under stress. Ultimately, the therapy suggests that the problem lies within the individual and their ability to cope. In fact, the blame may lie elsewhere – that is, the stressor itself, such as an employer, may be at fault. REBT therefore has the potential to be abused.

Cognitive behavioural therapy

Beck (1976) suggested that an individual's emotional responses to a negative event such as a stressor depend on their cognitive processing. As people's cognitions differ, so does their ability to cope with stress, because their thinking will have different consequences in terms of emotions. When people have dysfunctional beliefs, these will cause negative automatic thoughts – such as feelings of hopelessness and self-doubt. This relationship between thoughts is circular; negative thinking generates more negative thinking. Beck illustrated this in his *cognitive triad* of automatic thought (see Figure 7.19). This can lead the individual to identify things as threatening when they are not, or to interpret situations in a distorted way, such as by concluding that they cannot cope when in fact they could.

Cognitive behavioural therapy (CBT) aims to reduce the symptoms of emotional disorders by changing dysfunctional cognition. This is achieved by the therapist teaching the client to identify and monitor the automatic thoughts they experience when they are stressed, by asking questions such as 'what are you thinking about yourself/your future?'. Their answers, such as 'I never do well in my homework, I'll get chucked off the course', are challenged. The client might be asked to keep a record of what they have done and identify examples of finished tasks at work and of positives elsewhere in their life. This will counter the individual's negative belief in their failure. Tasks that demonstrate the irrationality of the client's beliefs are also used. For example, a stressed client may be set 'homework' to identify examples in their life where they have dealt with a difficult situation at work to challenge their belief that they are unable to cope when the pressure rises. The client is encouraged to plan ways to test out their new, healthier and more flexible beliefs in everyday life.

In support of the idea that distorted thinking is important, Gallards *et al.* (1999) tested depressed and non-depressed people on a word task. The participants were put into a sad mood (by playing them sad music and asking them to recall unhappy memories). The depressed participants paid more attention to the unhappy stimuli, suggesting their attention was indeed biased. In practice, CBT is also effective. Butler & Beck (2000) conducted a meta-analysis and found that CBT was very useful for anxious and depressed clients. The relapse rate for depression was only 29.5 per cent after CBT, compared to 60 per cent with antidepressant treatment.

Physiological stress management strategies

Physiological therapies, like psychological ones, are used with many different psychological disorders. Most physiological therapies rely on drugs, and some of these approaches are discussed in detail in Chapter 7. Another physiological technique is biofeedback. Both drug therapy and biofeedback are described here in relation to stress.

Drugs

Stress can lead to anxiety, panic attacks and depression. Symptoms such as these may be treated with medication. At the beginning of this chapter we describe the role of neurones and explain that they communicate chemically using neurotransmitters (see p131). This chemical stage in the transmission of messages in the nervous system makes it possible for other chemicals to affect brain function. Drug molecules resemble neurotransmitters. They can enter the gaps between neurones (the synapses – see Figure 7.7) and affect the activity of neurones. By doing this they can artificially influence emotions, cognitions or behaviour, so can alter the symptoms of stress. There are several different ways that drugs can act, each related to the action of neurotransmitters. They can:

- *mimic neurotransmitters* – by attaching to neurones and having the same effect as the normal neurotransmitter, such as causing stimulation of neurones
- *block receptors* – prevent neurotransmitters from attaching to neurones, so reducing their activity
- *prevent the recycling of neurotransmitters* – this effectively causes an increase in the amount of the neurotransmitter that normally affects neurones.

In depression, the levels of a neurotransmitter called serotonin are lower than normal. A group of drugs called selective serotonin reuptake inhibitors (SSRIs) counteract these reduced levels. These drugs, such as Prozac, prevent the recycling of serotonin. This causes there to be relatively more of the neurotransmitter in the synapses, and so increases the chance for serotonin molecules to attach to neurones.

Evidence suggests that these drugs are effective at reducing the symptoms of depression. Trivedi *et al.* (2006) studied an SSRI called Citalopram. Almost 3000 out-patients with depression were tested before and after a treatment lasting up to 14 weeks. For 47 per cent of the patients their depression score was halved, in many cases within eight weeks. The effectiveness of the drug depended on the type of person, however. It was most effective for well-educated, employed white women who were not suffering from other psychological or physical disorders.

Although drugs can be effective at reducing symptoms, the treatment of stress-related disorders with drugs can be criticised. They can treat only the symptoms, not the cause of the problem. However, it is possible that being able to cope using medication in the short-term would allow someone to overcome a stressful situation in a constructive way that would not be possible if they were feeling very anxious or depressed.

Thinking critically about psychology

Think about the findings of Trivedi *et al.* (2006). Using the ideas that you have learned about earlier in the chapter, consider how the differences between different types of participants might be explained.

Biofeedback

In biofeedback the client is given information about the current state of their biological functions, for example their pulse rate, blood pressure or muscle tension measured using instruments such as blood pressure monitors and electromyograms (which detect muscle contraction). When reliable physiological information about levels of tension or relaxation is provided in this way, a client can learn to become more relaxed. The information about the biological measure may be presented as a changing tone or a visual display. Initially, the client will be unable to change their state at will, but over time the feedback allows them to become aware of the things they can do that have an effect. For example, a stressed person may discover by trial and error that shutting their eyes and imagining a nice scene causes the tone to indicate that their blood pressure is falling. It is not essential, however, that the client is conscious of how the change takes place.

The process may also be assisted externally, for example by placing a person on a tilt-table to help their blood pressure to fall or by supplying relaxing video images.

One of the earliest studies into the effectiveness of biofeedback is described in *Classic Research* (see p152).

CLASSIC RESEARCH

Budzynski TH, Stoyva JM, Adler CS and Mullaney DJ (1973) Biofeedback and tension headache. *Psychosomatic Medicine*, **35 (6)** 484–96

PROCEDURE

Eighteen participants were chosen because they experienced frequent tension-related headaches. Each participant charted the frequency and intensity of their headaches before training began. The biofeedback procedure provided information about the contraction of scalp and neck muscles that causes these headaches. This was measured using an electromyogram (EMG). The participants were divided into three groups receiving either real feedback about muscle tension, false feedback (a tape recording of the first group's feedback) or no training. Muscle contraction produced a high click rate through headphones for the real-feedback group and they were told to try to find out what they could do to reduce the rate. The false-feedback group also heard the clicks but were told they would help them to relax. The control group heard no clicks but were regularly exposed to the instrumentation to keep them encouraged so that they did not drop out of the study. The feedback groups received two sessions a week for eight weeks. After this, all groups continued to monitor their headaches for a further three months.

FINDINGS

There was a large decline in EMG tension in the experimental group and a small decline in the false-feedback group. The EMG levels for the real- and false-feedback groups were significantly different at the end of the 16 training sessions and after three months. The groups also differed in their headaches. Only the real-feedback group had significantly fewer symptoms at the end of training, and this improvement was maintained after three months. The real-feedback group also reported reduced use of medication.

CONCLUSIONS

Biofeedback makes a lasting difference to the physiological cause of the tension headaches and to the experience of symptoms. This is because the patients learn to use feedback rather than because of hearing clicks or because of the attention given to participants in experiments (although both of these have small effects).

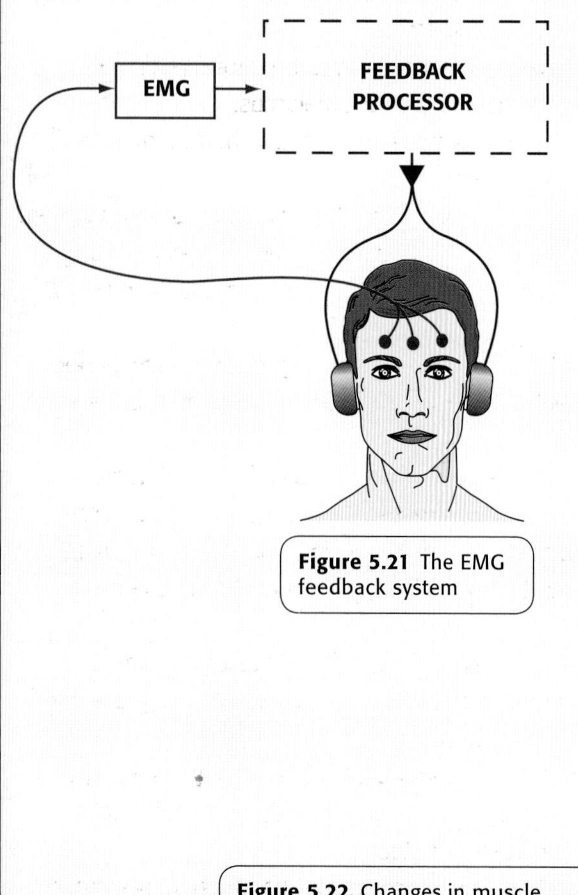

Figure 5.21 The EMG feedback system

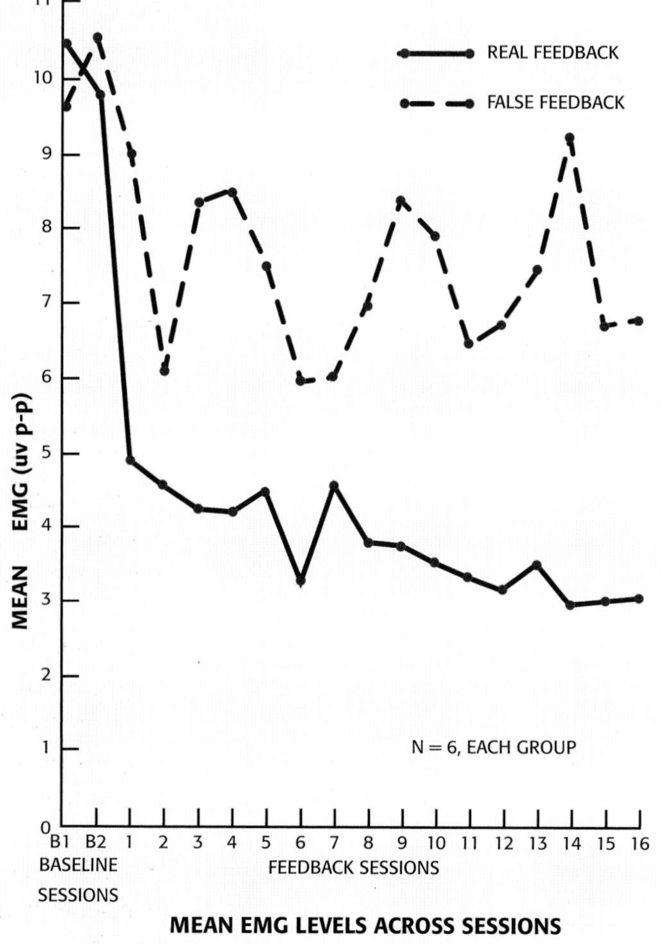

Figure 5.22 Changes in muscle tension with and without biofeedback

Recent evidence has shown that biofeedback is effective for a range of symptoms of stress such as headaches and muscle tension. For example, Tsai *et al.* (2007) found that biofeedback based on real information about changes in blood pressure produced a greater reduction in blood pressure in patients with mild hypertension than those given sham feedback. Nakao *et al.* (1997) used biofeedback to help people with hypertension. They were taught to control their blood pressure and were able to reduce it even when confronted with a deliberately stressful laboratory situation.

CHAPTER SUMMARY

- The biological approach explains thinking, emotion and cognition in terms of biological systems, for example the nervous system and hormones.
- The nervous system sends fast electrical messages via neurones connected by chemicals across synapses.
- The endocrine system sends slower, longer-lasting messages via hormones from glands. These travel in the blood stream to target organs.
- Stress is a biological and psychological response to threats (stressors) we perceive to be unmanageable.
- The sympatheticomedullary pathway responds quickly to stress by activating the sympathetic part of the autonomic nervous system and causing the release of adrenaline from the adrenal medulla. Both of these have effects such as raising the pulse and blood pressure, preparing us for 'fight or flight'.
- The pituitary-adrenal system maintains the response to chronic stressors through the release of cortisol from the adrenal cortex. This is triggered by adrenocorticotropic hormone from the pituitary gland. This maintains high glucose levels and raised blood pressure.
- Both the sympatheticomedullary pathway and the pituitary-adrenal system are ultimately governed by the hypothalamus.
- Bodily changes associated with stress are harmful to health, for example by impairing the immune response.
- Life events such as death of a partner or getting fired are assigned values on the Social Readjustment Rating Scale, which can be added up to give a total stress score. People with higher SRRS scores tend to have poorer health.
- High SRRS scores are also associated with other problems such as poor exam performance, greater drug use and reduced ability to deal with other sources of stress.
- The Daily Hassles scale measures the day-to-day irritations that are stressful, such as traffic jams and arguments. People with more hassles have worse symptoms of stress, such as anxiety and depression, than those with fewer hassles. Having uplifts (good things) to counteract hassles reduces stress.
- Having a higher Daily Hassles score is linked to ill health, for example headaches and backache, and to social problems such as drug use, family problems and difficulties at school.
- People vary in their ability to deal with stress. The type A personality is associated with experiencing more stress and suffering poorer health, although this pattern has been disputed.
- The type A person may find experiences more stressful or may expose themselves to more stress. Types C and D have also both been linked to ill health.

- In support of the link between type A and stress, this personality type is associated with aggression (on the road and when provoked) and with becoming more stressed at work and with parenting.
- In addition, the type A personality is linked to a biological sensitivity to increased heart rate and blood pressure when under stress and when at rest.
- People can cope with stressors by dealing with the negative feelings using emotional strategies, or deal with the stressor itself using problem-focused strategies. The latter are generally better but not always possible.
- Early evidence suggested that women used more emotion-focused strategies than men but recent research has shown that women frequently use problem-focused coping too.
- Psychological stress management techniques are based on the idea that stress is caused by faulty thinking that prevents us from coping. Rational emotive behaviour therapy and cognitive behavioural therapy therefore try to alter thinking so that feelings and behaviour become more adaptive. This is done by challenging the client's false beliefs.
- Physiological stress management techniques attempt to control the symptoms of stress. Drugs can be used to reduce anxiety and depression. They act by affecting the neurotransmitters that communicate between neurones. Biofeedback gives the client information about their own body functions. This awareness leads to the client being able to control symptoms such as high blood pressure. This enables them to reduce the damaging effects of the stress response.

What do I know?

1 **The list of terms below relate to stress. Write the correct term from the list alongside each definition on the right.** (4 marks)

- endocrine system
- pituitary-adrenal system
- immune system
- neurotransmitters
- sympatheticomedullary pathway

Term	definition
	A biological system that maintains a long-term response to stress
	A biological system that responds quickly to a short-term source of stress
	A system of glands that release hormones into the bloodstream
	The body's defences against disease, such as lymphocytes

2 **On the left-hand side below are examples of different coping strategies that someone might use in the stressful situation of a burst water pipe. Put an E in the box beside each emotion-focused example and a P in the box beside each problem-focused example.** (3 marks)

crying ☐
looking up a phone number for a plumber ☐
asking a practical friend what to do ☐
going out shopping ☐
putting down lots of absorbent paper and cloths ☐
deciding that you wanted a new carpet anyway ☐

3 Charlotte is having a bad time. She set off to work this morning and got stuck in a traffic jam. When she arrived at the building, she found she had lost her office keys. When she finally sat down at her desk with a cup of coffee, she spilt it down herself. Derek isn't having a good time either. He has been fired from work and, as a result, has had to move out of the house he owned and into a rented flat, as his new job isn't so well paid. It's January and he went away on holiday just after Christmas.

The concepts of life events and daily hassles help to explain how stress can affect us. There is evidence to suggest that both of these factors are important.

(a) **(i)** Which concept best explains Charlotte's stressors? (1 mark)

(ii) Outline the concept you have named using examples in Charlotte's life in your answer. (2 marks)

(iii) Explain how the stressors she is experiencing might affect her. Use some psychological evidence in your answer. (6 marks)

(b) Explain how the stressors Derek is experiencing might affect him. Use some psychological evidence in your answer. (6 marks)

(c) **(i)** For **either** Charlotte **or** Derek, describe a psychological or physiological approach to managing stress and outline how it might help them to cope. (2+2 marks)

(i) Evaluate the stress management strategy you have described in (c) (i). (6 marks)

4 Some people cope really well under pressure and others just crumble at the slightest hint of stress. Discuss how differences in personality factors can affect an individual's ability to cope with stress and the damage that having a stressful life could do to them. (12 marks)

5 Dr Bright is investigating the effect of stress on health. She is comparing the time it takes for a scratch on the back of her participants' hand to heal. The student participants are given a standard 2cm-long scratch on their left hand. This is done once during the holidays and once in the time before examinations. The time taken for the scratch to heal is measured by the students.

(a) Use ticks to fill in the correct research method and design in the table below. Tick each column only **once**.

Term	Research method (put only one tick in this column)	Design (put only one tick in this column)
Repeated measures		
Experiment		
Observation		
Correlation		
Matched pairs		
Independent groups		

(b) The participants are all right-handed, so one reason to put the scratch on the left hand is so that they can still write. Outline why else it was important for Dr Bright to always make the cut on the participant's left hand. (2 marks)

(c) What is the independent variable in this investigation? (1 mark)

(d) What is the dependent variable in this investigation? (1 mark)

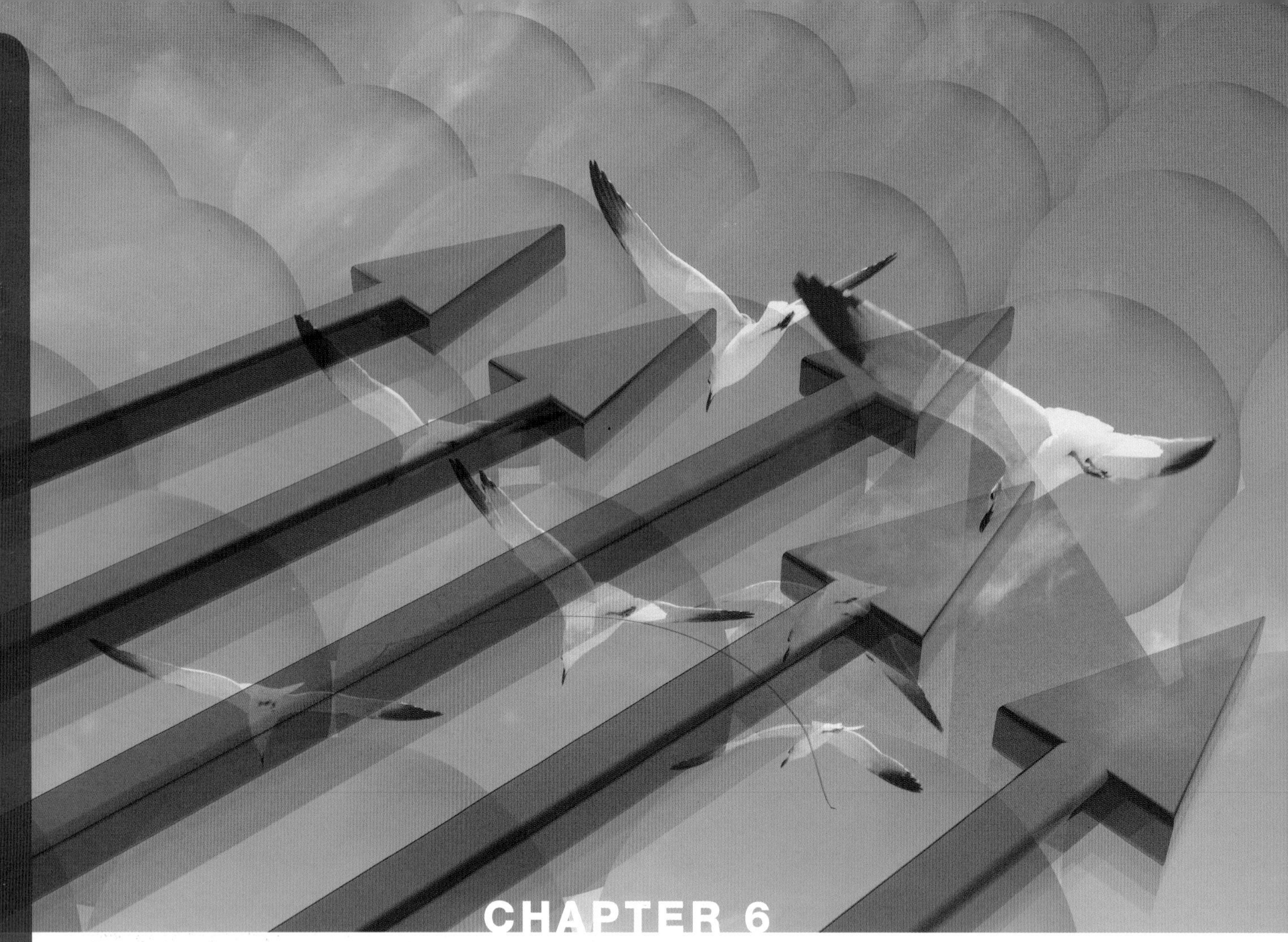

CHAPTER 6
Social Psychology

Thinking ahead

By the end of this chapter you should be able to:

- **define conformity and distinguish between compliance, identification and internalisation**
- **describe and evaluate studies of conformity, for example by Solomon Asch**
- **understand explanations of conformity, including normative and informational influence**
- **define obedience and discuss studies of destructive obedience including by Stanley Milgram**
- **outline and critically consider explanations for obedience, including agency and transformational leadership**
- **explain the role of minority influence, reactance and attributions in resisting social pressure**
- **be aware of individual differences in conformity and obedience, with particular regard to the authoritarian and compliant personalities and locus of control**
- **apply your understanding of social influence to explain how social change takes place**

Social psychology is the branch of psychology that deals with how people interact and affect one another. This chapter is particularly concerned with social influence. We all influence other people and are influenced by them all the time. Two of the ways other people influence us are conformity and obedience. We conform when we adopt the behaviours, opinions and so on of a group and we obey when we follow orders from someone in authority over us. The first part of this chapter is concerned with types of conformity and some of the factors that influence conformity. In the second part of the chapter we look at studies and explanations of obedience. Finally, we look at how people can resist social pressure to conform and obey, and discuss ways in which this resistance can lead to social change.

CONFORMITY

Conformity is an example of *majority influence* – that is, it takes place when a larger group of people influence a smaller number. We adjust our behaviour or opinions to fit in with those of the majority of people around us, irrespective of whether we actually agree that the majority are correct. Kelman (1958) distinguished between three types of conformity:

- *Compliance* takes place when we change our behaviour to be more like the majority but we do not privately change our minds about what we believe or how we would like to act.
- *Internalisation* takes place when we change our minds about something because the majority have convinced us they are right, and so we adjust our behaviour.
- *Identification* takes place when we adjust our behaviour or beliefs in order to become like an individual or group we admire and would like to be like – or, to use the technical term, *identify* with.

Early studies of conformity

Muzafer Sherif (1935) carried out an early study of conformity. He asked participants individually to watch a stationary light in a dark room. Because we constantly make small eye movements called saccades, lights in a dark room appear to move. Sherif's participants all agreed that the light moved, but varied in their beliefs about how often and in what direction it moved. When, however, they were placed in groups of three and asked to repeat the task, there was considerable agreement between them about when and where the light moved. In other words, the view of each participant conformed to those of the others in their group.

Solomon Asch also demonstrated this conformity effect in a classic study. In fact, Asch took the study of conformity a stage further than Sherif. Sherif demonstrated conformity in a situation where there was considerable doubt about what the appropriate response was. Asch, however, was interested in situations where people conform even when the majority are blatantly incorrect – as George Orwell, and more recently the rock band Radiohead put it, when 2+2=5.

Asch SE (1955) Opinions and social pressure. *Scientific American*, **193** 31–5

AIM

To investigate to what extent people will conform to a majority opinion even when it appears obviously incorrect.

PROCEDURE

Participants were 123 American male students. Each participant joined a group of seven to nine young men sitting around a table. They were told only that they were taking part in a psychology experiment and were unaware that the other young men were stooges working for Asch. The group was given the task of matching the length of a target line to one of three alternatives (Figure 6.1). Each group member in turn named line A, B or C as the correct match, the real participant naming last. In the first two trials the stooges named the line correctly. However, they named the same wrong line in 12 of the 18 trials each participant went through. In a control condition the stooges always named the correct line.

FINDINGS

In the control condition, participants named the correct line 98 per cent of the time. However, when the stooges all named the wrong line the participant named the correct line only 63.2 per cent of the time. In nearly 37 per cent of trials they conformed to the majority answer even though it was blatantly wrong.

CONCLUSION

People tend to conform to majority behaviour even when the majority are obviously wrong.

Figure 6.1 Lines like those used by Asch (1955)

Thinking critically about psychology

Evaluate Asch's study. You might like to think in particular about the following:

1. To what extent was his sample representative?
2. What ethical issues are raised by his design? See p113 for a summary of the British Psychological Society's ethical guidelines.
3. Are the results socially sensitive? If so, why?
4. Was the environment controlled?
5. How natural was the environment and how realistic were the tasks given to participants?

LOOKING FURTHER

You can hear a sound file featuring some top psychologists discussing the Asch study at http://www.bbc.co.uk/radio4/science/mindchangers1.shtml. If, on the other hand, you like information in written form, you can read the full text of Asch's 1955 paper at http://www.wadsworth.com/psychology_d/templates/student_resources/0155060678_rathus/ps/ps18.html.

Figure 6.2 Anti-abortion protesters tend to internalise rather than comply with Christian values

Later interviews revealed that Asch's participants had not believed the wrong answers given by their group – that is, they *complied* with their group rather than having internalised the group answer. Of course in the Asch study the correct answers were clear. But what would have happened if the answers had been ambiguous? Would people have still just complied or would they be more likely to internalise their opinion?

This was tested by Holzhausen & Glyn (2001). They investigated compliance and internalisation further in a situation similar to the Asch experiment. Three hundred and twenty-one American students were given answers to mathematical problems and told they were the majority view. They were asked publicly (a test of compliance) and privately (a test of internalisation) whether they agreed with the majority answers. They found that when the problems were easy and the credibility of answers good, the majority of participants publicly complied and privately agreed – that is, they internalised the response. When the credibility of the answers was poor, they complied but did not internalise. However, when the problems were difficult, they would internalise as well as comply, regardless of the credibility of the answer. This suggests that when the correct answer is unclear, we tend to internalise the norms of our group.

We can see this sort of internalisation in ambiguous real-life situations. People tend to take on passionately the majority opinion of their own group regarding difficult issues. Take, for example, the abortion debate. This is morally ambiguous because people arguing on both sides of the debate are motivated by their concern for human rights. However, people tend to commit strongly to one side of the debate or the other, and more often than not in line with their group membership. Thus, feminists do not merely comply with their group norm by emphasising a woman's right to choose, they internalise this belief. Similarly, Christians who oppose abortion are not merely complying with their group norm but have internalised it. This tendency to internalise group norms over controversial issues is what makes moral debates like this so passionate and sometimes bitter.

Thinking creatively about psychology

Design a study to investigate conformity in pro- and anti-abortion protesters. Do members of these groups really internalise their opinion or are they are just complying? You will need a measure of compliance and a measure of internalised opinion. Look back to the Holzhausen & Glyn study for ideas about these.

EXPLANATIONS FOR CONFORMITY

There are a number of reasons why we might conform to the behaviour or opinions of the majority, and a number of factors affect how much we conform. Deutsch & Gerard (1955) made the important distinction between normative influence and informational influence.

Normative influence

Normative influence occurs when we conform because we wish to be liked or accepted by other group members, and to avoid being rejected by them. It seems likely that this is the major explanation for Asch's findings. Participants

KEY TERMS

compliance – going along with majority behaviour without agreeing with it

internalisation – going along with majority behaviour and believing it is correct

normative influence – conforming to majority behaviour in order to fit in with the group

informational influence – conforming to majority behaviour in the belief that the majority is likely to be correct

found themselves in a new social situation where they were working alongside people very much like themselves. In that sort of situation, rather like entering a new class at college, most of us would be anxious to get along with other people and avoid being rejected by them. We can tease out a bit further exactly what we mean by being liked and rejected. For example, we might wish to appear attractive to potential mates in the group. We might even wish to protect ourselves from potential danger from the group. A study by Griskevicius *et al.* investigated both self-protection and mate attraction as motives for conformity.

Figure 6.3 One reason people conform to dress codes is to avoid rejection

RESEARCH NOW

Griskvicius V, Goldstein NJ, Mortensen CR, Cialdini R & Kenrick D (2006) When fundamental motives influence conformity. *Journal of Personality & Social Psychology,* **91** 281–94

AIM

To investigate whether the need for self-protection or wish to attract a mate makes people more or less conformist.

PROCEDURE

One hundred and thirteen male and 124 female American undergraduate psychology students took part in the study. They were primed to think either about protecting themselves or about attracting a member of their target sex. This was done by giving them an 850-word story to read, about either a stranger breaking into a house in the night (to prime self-protection) or about someone falling in love on holiday (to prime mate attraction). They then sat on computers and went into a chat-room in which they were given the task of evaluating paintings alone and in groups of four. In a control condition there was no priming. The extent to which they conformed to their group's evaluation of the paintings was measured.

FINDINGS

In the self-protection condition, both men and women conformed to the group opinions about the paintings to a greater extent than in the control condition. In the mate attraction condition, women conformed more than in the control condition but men conformed less.

CONCLUSION

Desire for self-protection leads to conformity in men and women. Desire for a mate, however, affects the sexes differently, making women more conformist but men less so.

Evaluate the study by Griskevicius *et al.*. You might like to consider the following in particular:

1. How valid do you think the measure of conformity is?
2. Is the environment controlled?
3. Is the environment realistic?
4. Are the tasks like those we encounter in real life?
5. Do the results have any real-life applications?

Figure 6.4 Members of subcultures tend to conform to norms of alcohol, tobacco and cannabis use

Normative influence is important in understanding a number of real-life issues, for example in health-related behaviour. Verkooijen *et al.* (2007) investigated the role of membership of youth subcultures in drug and alcohol use. Six thousand 16 to 20-year-olds from Denmark were sent a survey asking about their subcultural affiliations and use of alcohol, tobacco and cannabis. Those who identified themselves as part of skater, hip-hop, techno and hippie groups were particularly likely to use drugs, while those identifying with nerdy, sporty and religious groups were least likely to do so. The more strongly individuals identified themselves as part of their group, the more they conformed to its norms of alcohol, tobacco and cannabis use. It seems, then, that the subculture members conformed to their group norms mostly for normative reasons.

Normative influence also affects our conformity to the prejudices of our peers. Crandall *et al.* (2002) found an almost perfect correlation (+0.96) between the extent of prejudice shown towards 105 minority groups and how socially acceptable participants judged this particular prejudice to be. The minority groups ranged from sex offenders (who attracted most prejudice and were judged most acceptable to be prejudiced towards) to visually impaired people, who attracted least prejudice and were felt to be the least acceptable targets of prejudice. The correlation is shown in Figure 6.5.

For ethical reasons, you should generally avoid carrying out experiments in which people conform. You won't be able to obtain real consent, and participants may be stressed or embarrassed by their behaviour. However, you could replicate the work of Crandall *et al.* (2002). This is a demonstration of normative influence on behaviour: the more socially acceptable a prejudice, the more you will find people hold that prejudice. You will need a range of groups who are targets of prejudice and you need scales to measure strength of prejudice and social acceptability of prejudice towards each group. To avoid causing distress, avoid using minority groups who suffer real prejudice in your own community and groups who are represented in the population you are researching. Draw a scatterplot like the one in Figure 6.5. How do your results compare?

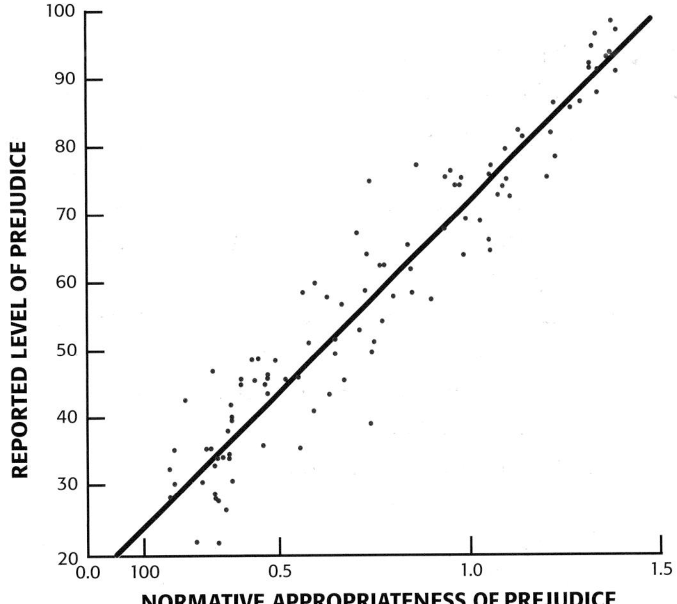

Figure 6.5 The correlation between prejudices and their social acceptability (from Crandall *et al.* 2002)

Problem solver

The producers of *The X-Factor* have approached you, concerned that the panel of judges might be conforming to each other's judgements of contestants rather than judging contestants independently. Explain why this might happen (refer to normative and informational influence) and, second, suggest a way to avoid these conformity effects.

Figure 6.6 Judges in talent shows like this may be affected by conformity

On a lighter note, think about the current popularity of British television shows such as *The X-Factor* and *Strictly Come Dancing*, which feature panels of judges assessing performance together. Is it possible that each judge in the panel conforms to the decisions the others have made? This phenomenon was studied by Boen *et al.* (2006). They divided twenty-seven judges into panels of up to five and asked them to judge 30 videotaped performances of skipping. In one condition the judges could hear each other's judgements and in the other they could not. There was more agreement when they heard each other's feedback. This suggests that judges do conform to the judgement of the panel.

Informational influence

Another important factor affecting conformity is informational influence. This occurs when we believe that the majority has better information than us or is more competent to make a decision based on that information. Think back to Sherif's study (p157). In this case, unlike in the Asch study, the participants appeared to really believe that the others in their groups had a better idea when and where the light was moving. The conformity they showed was thus at least partially informational in nature. In this sort of study we cannot separate out normative and informational influence because participants are in the physical presence of the group and interact with them. However, we can separate out informational influence from normative influence by providing people with information about other people's behaviour or opinions without any giving them contact with those people.

One such study involving only information in the absence of contact with a group, by Eyssel *et al.* (2006), investigated the role of informational influence in men's conformity to belief in rape myths (inaccurate stories surrounding rape, for example that women enjoy being raped) and their likelihood of committing rape. One hundred and seventeen male German participants rated their acceptance of rape myths. They were then presented with fictional responses from fellow participants showing either a high or a low group acceptance of rape myths. They then rated again their likelihood of committing rape. Those exposed to a group informational norm of high rape myth acceptance tended to conform to this and rated themselves more likely to commit rape.

Thinking creatively about psychology

People have very strong views about music, and groups of friends tend to agree about what sort of music they like. Design a study to find out whether groups of friends who listen to the same music are influenced by normative or informational factors. Remember that when groups are together when making judgements about music, they will be exposed to normative influence and informational influence. When they know how the other group members have rated music but are not together, then any conformity will be informational.

Cognitive dissonance

KEY TERMS

cognitive dissonance – an unpleasant sensation resulting from holding in mind two ideas that should not both be true

Another way of explaining conformity is cognitive dissonance. Cognitive dissonance has been studied since the 1950s but has only recently been applied to explaining conformity. Festinger (1957) suggested that we experience the unpleasant sensation of dissonance when we hold in mind two ideas that are unlikely both to be true. Our arousal levels increase and we experience anxiety. Festinger was also interested in how attitudes change. He proposed that when we encounter new information that is incompatible with an existing attitude, we experience dissonance and may change our attitude in order to escape the anxiety. Matz & Wood (2005) have applied the idea of cognitive dissonance to explaining conformity. When we have a particular belief and we find that we are surrounded by people who have a different belief we can experience dissonance. Similarly, when we realise that some aspect of our behaviour is not in line with that of people around us, we may experience dissonance. As this is an unpleasant sensation, we may change our behaviour or belief in order to restore our comfort.

Figure 6.7 Conformity is a potential problem for juries

Matz & Wood set up an experiment to investigate whether cognitive dissonance resulted from disagreement with a group. One hundred and ninety American psychology undergraduates were invited in groups of four to six to complete attitude surveys. They were then told that they either agreed or disagreed with the rest of their group and either that they would or would not be taking part in a group discussion on the issue. They rated their anxiety. In the condition where students expected to have a face-to-face discussion with people who disagreed with them we would expect anxiety. However, the students also experienced significant anxiety when told they disagreed with their group in the absence of any face-to-face interaction with other group members. This suggests that they were experiencing cognitive dissonance. In a follow-up, another group of students took part in a mock jury. When they were told that their opinion concerning the defendant's guilt or otherwise differed from that of the majority of their group, they similarly experienced anxiety; however, this declined if they changed their mind. This suggests that cognitive dissonance is reduced by conformity.

Thinking practically about psychology

A very important situation in which people are at risk of conforming to majority views is when serving on a jury. Explain how normative influence, informational influence and cognitive dissonance might make a person who initially believed a defendant to be innocent change their mind and go along with a majority who believed they were guilty.

OBEDIENCE

Figure 6.8 Sixty years on, the world is still shocked by images of the Holocaust

Obedience means to follow direct orders from a person who is in a position of authority over us. This is quite different from conformity, which means to adopt the attitudes, behaviours, and so on of the majority of people around us. We all like to think of ourselves as free and independent, but much of the time a degree of obedience and conformity is no bad thing. Imagine the carnage on the roads if we didn't usually obey road signs and conform to driving rules. Obeying your psychology teacher is probably also a good idea if you want to do well in your AS level! However, there is a serious downside to our tendency for obedience. When an authority figure orders us to do something immoral, such as hurting someone, we are very likely to obey, even though doing so will cause us distress. This phenomenon is known as *destructive obedience*.

The attention of psychologists turned to destructive obedience after the Holocaust. In the 1940s under the Nazis, ordinary Germans obeyed unquestioningly when they were ordered to exterminate several million Jews, Romanies, communists, people with disabilities and trade unionists. Stanley

Figure 6.9 Milgram's apparatus

Milgram, a student of Solomon Asch, was part of a network of researchers committed to investigating the psychology underlying the Holocaust in order to help prevent similar events in the future. Early attempts to apply psychology to explaining the Holocaust focused on German culture, in the belief that the Holocaust could not have taken place anywhere else simply because other people would not have displayed the conformity and obedience necessary. Milgram initially set out to test the idea that the German people were unusually obedient, but he soon found that people in general are much more obedient than anyone had realised. Milgram's original experiment is described in detail in *Classic Research*.

CLASSIC RESEARCH

Milgram S (1963) Study of obedience. *Journal of Abnormal and Social Psychology*, **67** 371–8

AIM

To see how obedient people would be in a situation where obeying orders would mean breaking their moral code and hurting an innocent person.

PROCEDURE

Forty American men aged 20–50 were recruited by advertisement. They were told they were taking part in a memory experiment and introduced to 'Mr Wallace', apparently a fellow participant but actually a stooge working for Milgram. By fiddling an apparently random procedure Milgram ensured that the real participant was always a teacher and the stooge the learner. Mr Wallace was then strapped into a chair behind a screen and connected to a shock generator (see Figure 6.9). The participant tested him on his memory for word pairs. The experimenter ordered him to flick a switch to give Mr Wallace a shock whenever he got an answer wrong. In fact there were no real shocks, but there was no way for the participant to realise this. The shocks increased by 15 volts each time, up to a maximum of 450 volts. As the level of shocks increased, Mr Wallace cried out and begged to be released. At 300 volts he went silent apart from occasional weak knocking on the screen. When participants protested at having to continue shocking him, the experimenter gave them a series of verbal prods (see Table 6.1). Obedience was measured by the percentage of participants giving different voltages and the average maximum voltage given by participants. Qualitative data were also gathered by observing the reactions of participants during the procedure.

FINDINGS

Every participant gave at least 300 volts, and 65 per cent gave the full 450 volts. The distribution of maximum voltages is shown in Table 6.2. The mean average maximum voltage given was 368.25 volts. Observers noted that most participants became highly distressed, sweating and pacing around the room. Several cried. These signs of stress disappeared, however, once they decided not to obey any more.

CONCLUSION

People have a strong tendency to obey orders even when these go against their morals. This effect is so powerful that most people will injure or kill a stranger when ordered to by a figure in authority. However, people become very distressed when obeying orders that breach their moral codes.

Table 6.1 The verbal prods given in the Milgram procedure

	Prod
1	'Please continue' or 'please go on'
2	'The experiment requires that you continue'
3	'It is absolutely essential that you continue'
4	'You have no choice, you *must* go on'

Table 6.2 The distribution of maximum voltages given by participants

Voltage	Number of participants giving this as a maximum
15–60	0
75–120	0
135–180	0
195–240	0
255–300	5 (at 300V)
315–360	8
375–420	1
420+	26

Variations in the procedure

Over the next few years following the original study, Milgram conducted a number of variations on the original procedure. These included varying the location of the study, the directness of the participants' involvement in harming Mr Wallace and the appearance of the experimenter and the learner. Some of Milgram's findings are summarised in Table 6.3.

Table 6.3 Variations in the Milgram procedure and results

Rank order of obedience	Condition	Percentage giving 450V
1	Victim is silent throughout	100
2	Standard procedure	65
3	Procedure in run-down office block	48
4	Victim in same room	40
5	Orders phoned in	20.5
6	Experimenter has no lab coat	20
7	Fellow participants disobey	10
8	Teacher has choice of voltage	2.5

Over the past four decades these variations have been replicated many times by other psychologists. Lüttke (2004) has reviewed these studies, however, and concluded that only some of Milgram's findings have proved reliable. In particular, two variations have very significant effects on obedience rates; the proximity of the victim (obedience falls when the victim is near and visible) and the presence of obedient or disobedient co-participants. We can look in detail at Milgram's study of the latter later in this chapter.

Discussion of the Milgram studies

Milgram's studies were of great practical value, as they showed that we have a surprising tendency towards destructive obedience. This in turn helps us understand historical events, such as the Holocaust, in which large numbers of people obeyed orders that required them to breach the moral codes by which they normally lived. Milgram's procedure was easy to replicate, and, by and large, replications have reproduced similar results. The exceptions to this are in variations in which the experimenter changed his appearance and in which the location was moved to a less respectable setting. Most replications have not found that these variations made much difference to obedience rates (Lüttke, 2004).

There have been other methodological criticisms of Milgram's work. He carried out his studies under laboratory conditions and gave participants a task that they do not normally come across in everyday life. Thus, the situation in which participants found themselves was in some ways quite artificial. However, many features of the experiment reproduced quite accurately the features of destructive obedience in real life. As a scientist running an experiment, the experimenter was in a position of legitimate authority and, dressed as scientist and based in a university laboratory, he had the trappings of authority. In some ways this made him comparable to a military commander with a title and uniform. On the other hand, some features of Milgram's procedure differed from the situations in which destructive obedience takes place in real life. For example, the experimenter assured participants that, although the shocks were painful, Mr Wallace would come to no real harm. That is very different from, say, the position of a Nazi concentration camp guard, who could have had no doubt that his charges would die as a result of his actions.

Remind yourself of the British Psychological Society ethical guidelines (p110). Of course, such guidance did not exist in Milgram's time, but see how many ethical principles he would have risked breaching had he run the study today.

LOOKING FURTHER

Go to http://home.swbell.net/revscat/perilsOfObedience.html. This site contains some of the records of Milgram's original conversations with participants. Look at the transcripts. Do any participants buck the trend and act less obediently, as Milgram expected most people to? How obedient are they? Look at Mr Batta's transcript in particular. What do you notice that is unusual about his behaviour and how could this be explained?

Later studies of obedience

Several other studies, including some carried out in real-life settings, have confirmed that people have a tendency to obey those in authority. In a field experiment, Hofling *et al.* (1966) tested whether nurses would obey orders from doctors even when they had reason to believe that doing so might endanger their patients.

Hofling KC, Brotzman E, Dalrymple S, Graves N & Pierce CM (1966) An experimental study in the nurse–physician relationship. *Journal of Nervous and Mental Disorders*, **143** 171–180

AIM

To test whether nurses would obey orders from an unfamiliar doctor when doing so would risk harm to patients. A secondary aim was to see whether nurses knew how obedient they tended to be.

PROCEDURE

Boxes of capsules labelled 'Astroten' were placed in medicine cabinets of 22 hospital wards of American hospitals. The capsules contained sugar, harmless to most patients, but the label said that the maximum safe daily dose was 10mg. A male researcher identifying himself just as 'Dr Smith from the psychiatric department' called the nurses on duty on each ward and ordered them to give a particular patient 20mg of Astroten. He said that he was running late and would get there to sign the necessary paperwork shortly. Meanwhile, 22 different nurses not in the experiment were asked whether they would exceed the safe dose of a drug on the instructions of a doctor.

FINDINGS

Twenty-one out of 22 nurses surveyed said that they would not obey the doctor's instructions; however, 21 of the 22 nurses in the experiment did so. When interviewed, 11 of these said that they had not looked at the maximum dose. The other ten saw it but judged that it must be safe if the doctor ordered them to give it.

CONCLUSION

Nurses obey dangerous orders from doctors, although they do not believe that they would do so.

Figure 6.10 Studies have found that nurses tend to obey doctors' orders

Thinking practically about psychology

How might the training of nurses have been improved as a result of the Hofling *et al.* study?

Both Milgram and Hofling surveyed people about how obedient they believed people would be in the sort of situation their participants faced. Milgram asked students and psychiatrists how many people would give the maximum shock, and all the groups surveyed estimated that far fewer people would give the larger shocks than was actually the case. Note that Milgram and Hofling were investigating slightly different things here. Hofling's nurses were estimating how they *themselves* would respond, while Milgram's respondents were making estimates of obedience in *other* people. This raises an interesting question: is there a difference between how obedient people believe others to be and how obedient they believe themselves to be? Glenn Geher and colleagues addressed this in a recent study.

RESEARCH NOW

Geher G, Bauman KP, Hubbard SEK & Legare JR (2002) Estimates of obedience of self and others. *Journal of Social Psychology,* **142** 677–89

AIM

To see how large a voltage people believe they would give in the Milgram procedure, and to see whether this differed from their estimates of how big a shock other people would give. A secondary aim was to see whether people entering law enforcement would be more accurate in their estimates.

PROCEDURE

Eighty-five female and 17 male American psychology students were given a description of the Milgram procedure. They also received a questionnaire that asked them what voltage they believed they would have given, and what voltage they believed a typical person of the same gender would give. In a second study, 51 criminal justice students and 62 psychology students underwent the same procedure.

FINDINGS

In the first study the psychology students estimated an average of 139V for themselves and 210V for a typical other person. In the second study the criminal justice students estimated an average of 192 volts for themselves and 231 volts for other people.

CONCLUSIONS

All the average estimates were lower than Milgram's actual average of 368 volts. People typically estimated that other people would give a significantly higher voltage than themselves. Students entering law enforcement were more accurate in their estimates than psychology students, and the gap between their self-estimates and other-estimates was smaller.

For ethical reasons, you should not conduct student practicals that test people's actual obedience. However, you could survey people on what sort of voltage they believe they would give in a Milgram-type study. You could also replicate Geher *et al.*'s study and find out whether people tend to believe they would give a lower voltage than other people.

Recent research has continued to demonstrate our tendency for obedience in a variety of situations. Tarnow (2000) has investigated the role of obedience in accidents. It is possible that accidents happen because the people in a crisis situation have the best information on which to base decisions, but instead of using this information they follow orders from those in authority. Often, those giving orders from a distance have less information on which to base their judgements. Tarnow analysed the records from 37 plane crashes and suggested that 25 per cent of them were caused by pilots following orders from the ground even though they knew the orders were a mistake.

Milgram's own procedure is not normally run nowadays because of the serious ethical issues it raises. It is one thing to run a study when we do not know what will be found and when the results have profound implications for real life. Now we know what we would find were we to run the study again, so there is little justification for doing so. Recently, however, a multinational team of researchers have developed a way around some of the ethical issues associated with the Milgram procedure by conducting it in virtual reality.

Media watch: obedience can cause plane crashes

http://news.independent.co.uk/europe/article183479.ece

Russian pilot obeyed wrong instructions

The Russian pilot involved in last week's mid-air crash which killed 71 people was given conflicting orders by Swiss air traffic control and his automatic warning system, the German investigation team said yesterday.

Ground staff told [the pilot] to dive to avoid an oncoming cargo plane, but the TCAS on-board crash-avoidance device ordered the plane to climb. The pilot of the Tupolev 154 airliner, Alexander Gross, obeyed the second command from controllers to descend and 30 seconds later crashed into the Boeing 757 freight jet.

Voice recorders recovered from fragments of the two planes scattered across the Swiss–German border showed that the on-board system on the Boeing had told its pilot to dive. The systems are designed to communicate so that aircraft are sent in opposite directions to avoid a collision .... If the Russian pilot had obeyed the machine rather than the air traffic controller, the disaster might have been avoided.

Barrie Clement, *The Independent*, 9 July 2002

Figure 6.11 Up to 25 per cent of plane crashes may result from pilots mistakenly obeying orders

1 On the basis of studies by Milgram and Hofling, suggest two possible reasons why the pilot might have obeyed the air traffic controller rather than acting independently.

RESEARCH NOW

Slater, Antley, Davison *et al.* (2006) A virtual reprise of the Stanley Milgram obedience experiments. *PLOS One*

AIM

The aim of the study was to test whether people would respond to destructive orders in the Milgram procedure in virtual reality in the same way as they do in a real situation.

PROCEDURE

Thirty-four volunteer participants were recruited by advertisement from staff and students at University College London. The Milgram experiment was recreated with participants acting as teacher and interacting with a 'learner' avatar (shown in Figure 6.12). In 23 cases the participant had the full visual experience of virtual reality; in 11 they communicated with the avatar by text. As in the Milgram procedure, the avatar was given word pairs to learn. An experimenter ordered the participant to give a series of 20 ascending shocks whenever the avatar got an answer wrong. The avatar exhibited distress when 'shocked'. To assess their responses to the stress of the situation, participants had their skin conductance and heart rate monitored.

FINDINGS

Results were very much in line with those of Milgram's study. Seventeen of the 23 participants (73.9 per cent) obeyed the orders and gave all 20 shocks. However, skin conductivity, heart rate and interview responses all indicated that they suffered stress as a result of 'hurting' the avatar.

CONCLUSIONS

Participants respond to destructive orders in virtual reality like they do in real life. There is a strong tendency to obey but to suffer stress as a result.

Figure 6.12 The virtual reality apparatus and avatar used in the study by Slater *et al.* (2006)

LOOKING FURTHER

You can read the full text of the Slater *et al.* study in full at http://www.plosone.org/article/fetchArticle.action?articleURI=info per cent3Adoi per cent2F10.1371 per cent2Fjournal.pone.0000039. You can also hear an audiofile of the study discussed on Radio 4's *Today* programme at http://www.plos.org/cms/comment/reply/174. How convincing do you find this type of research?

KEY TERMS

virtual reality (VR) – a three-dimensional computer simulation in which participants wearing VR helmets perceive themselves to be inside the environment

avatar – a computer-generated 3-D representation of a person in a virtual reality environment

Studies like this are fascinating because they appear to show that we respond to people in virtual reality in much the same way as we do real people. This is important, because it suggests that our social behaviour is automatic rather than consciously thought-out. However, the situation is *not* real, and we should be cautious about applying any findings from virtual reality to real life.

Virtual reality aside, replicating the Milgram procedure is not considered ethically acceptable nowadays. However, there are other ways of investigating obedience, for example people's attitudes towards people's behaviour when acting under orders. At his trial the Nazi war criminal Adolf Eichmann famously said he was not guilty of anything because he was only following orders. Although this is not a defence in law, there is some evidence to suggest that people see crimes differently when they are committed under orders. Hamilton & Sanders (1995) presented participants from the United States, Japan and Russia with stories of crimes set in the workplace, some of which were the orders of superiors and some of which were the actor's own idea. When questioned about how responsible the actor was, respondents attributed little responsibility to them when they were acting under orders, but a lot of responsibility when they acted independently. Some cultural differences emerged, with the American respondents attributing more responsibility to criminals following orders than respondents from Russia and Japan.

LOOKING FURTHER

Look for more modern studies of obedience using databases like PubMed or search engines like Google Scholar. How do they fit in with the studies you have looked at? Tip: if you can use the advanced search features, try eliminating studies on dogs! Depending on the site you are using, you may have the option to eliminate studies with the key word 'dog' or choose studies on humans only.

OVER TO YOU

You can test the idea that people see criminals as less responsible for their actions when acting under orders using a procedure like that used by Hamilton & Sanders. You will need two versions of a fictional crime. In one condition the criminal or criminals will be acting independently and in the other they will be acting under orders. Corporate crimes like illegal waste-disposal work well because the bosses giving the orders will be legitimate authority figures.

You will also need a way for participants to rate how guilty they are. Test whether people are in fact rated as less guilty when acting under orders.

EXPLANATIONS FOR OBEDIENCE

Agency theory

Milgram (1974) proposed that our tendency to obey people in authority is a way of maintaining a stable society. In order to live in complex societies we need social rules. Sticking to these rules means that at least some of the time we have give up some of our free will. Milgram proposed that in order to accomplish this we have developed two social states.

In the *autonomous state* we are free to act as we wish, including how our conscience dictates. However, in our *agentic state* we surrender our free will and conscience in order to serve the interests of the wider group. When we are in an agentic state we see ourselves as primarily the agents of those in authority and only secondarily as individuals.

Figure 6.13 We need a degree of obedience to manage complex social situations such as driving on a busy road

KEY TERMS

agentic state – state in which we surrender free choice over our actions and act as an agent of society

moral strain – the unpleasant sensation of feeling obliged to follow an order that violates our own morals

denial – a psychological defence in which we refuse to admit an unpleasant fact to ourselves

We are socialised during childhood into developing the capacity for the agentic state. In school we learn to put aside our individual wishes in favour of maintaining order, and so putting the good of the class as a whole first. Milgram believed that, like children in the classroom, we are all constantly subordinating our own needs and wishes to those of society. We can see this tendency in our job-related behaviour. If asked, most people would probably say that they work for their own benefit and would not go out of their way for their employers. In reality, however, once people are in a job and identify themselves as part of an organisation, they have a tendency to put the needs of their employers above their own.

An important aspect of the agentic state is the strategies we use to deal with *moral strain*. Moral strain results when we have to do something we believe to be immoral in order to function as an agent of authority, and so benefit society. Milgram suggested that we use psychological defence mechanisms to avoid the distress of having to perform acts we would normally find abhorrent. *Denial* was found to be particularly common in participants in the Milgram studies, and in the Holocaust as perpetrators refused to confront what they were doing.

Discussion of agency theory

Agency theory explains a wide range of social behaviours, ranging from how we act at work to the way in which peaceful people can go to war, and of course how ordinary people become involved in atrocities such as the Holocaust. The idea of moral strain explains Milgram's finding that the minority of dissenters in his studies showed signs of stress while deciding whether to obey but not after making the decision to disobey.

Agency theory is also supported by studies showing that we attribute less responsibility to actors following orders than people acting of their own free will. Blass & Schmitt (2001) showed students a film of Milgram's study and asked them about the relative responsibility of Milgram and his participants in administering shocks. Participants identified Milgram in the role of authority figure and attributed responsibility for the treatment of Mr Wallace to him rather than the participant. This supports agency theory because the participants were apparently seen as being in an agentic state and therefore not to blame for their actions. Blass and Schmitt questioned participants about why Milgram had such power over his participants. Agency theory would predict that the main factor was Milgram's position of legitimate authority. In fact, participants identified two main factors: legitimate position as a scientist and expertise. This partially supports agency theory.

There is also support for the idea that we use denial to cope with moral strain. Gudjonsson & Sigurdsson (2003) gave 424 Icelanders a questionnaire to measure their tendency to go along with orders and a measure of coping styles. A positive correlation (+0.39) was found between the tendency to use denial and reported tendency to comply with orders. If people who use denial tend to be more obedient, this supports Milgram's idea that denial is part of the way we cope with the stress of acting against our conscience.

A limitation of agency theory is that it does not neatly explain individual differences in people's obedience or in the ability of leaders to command obedience from subordinates. It tells us little about people who did not obey in Milgram's study. Also, agency theory does not explain Hofling's findings particularly well. Remember that although the majority of Hofling's nurses did obey the doctor, they did not show signs of moral strain like Milgram's participants. Half did not notice that they exceeded the maximum dose and half thought it must be safe if the doctor gave the order.

Figure 6.14 The lack of moral strain in Hofling's nurses poses a challenge for agency theory

Thinking critically about psychology

How well does agency theory fare against the following issues:

1. The quality of the evidence on which it is based?
2. Real-world relevance?
3. Supporting evidence?
4. Things it cannot explain?

Media watch: abuse of prisoners

http://www.guardian.co.uk/international/story/0,,1333090,00.html

Eight years for US soldier who abused prisoners

A US soldier at the centre of the Abu Ghraib prisoner abuse scandal was yesterday sentenced to eight years for sexually and physically abusing detainees. Staff Sergeant Ivan 'Chip' Frederick, 38, who admitted carrying out a mock electrocution of a detainee, was also given a reduction in rank, forfeiture of pay and a dishonourable discharge. Frederick, an army reservist from Buckingham, Virginia, pleaded guilty at the court-martial on Wednesday to eight counts of abusing and humiliating Iraqi detainees.

It was the longest sentence in the three convictions so far related to the abuses at Abu Ghraib, exposed in April with the publication of photographs and video showing US soldiers abusing naked Iraqis. Frederick's lawyer, Gary Myers, called the sentence excessive and said he intended to appeal to seek a reduction. Frederick, a military policeman who is a prison officer in civilian life, acknowledged his part in the abuse but also blamed his chain of command, telling the court prisoners were forced to submit to public nudity and degrading treatment "for military intelligence purposes". During the court martial, Chief Warrant Officer Kevin Kramer, a military intelligence soldier called as a witness, referred to an email from the US command in Baghdad telling him to order his interrogators to be tough on prisoners. "The gloves are coming off, gentlemen, regarding these detainees", said the email. It added that the command "wants the detainees broken". Frederick, who was in charge of the night shift at the 'hard site' facility at Abu Ghraib, west of Baghdad, said military intelligence soldiers and civilian interrogators told guards how to treat detainees. That included stripping detainees, depriving them of sleep or taking away their cigarettes, Frederick said. Investigators wanted detainees "stressed out, wanted them to talk more", he added …

"Give me an image of the all-American boy, and it's this young man", said a San Francisco-based doctor, Philip Zimbardo. "He is a wonderful young man who did these horrible things."

Jamie Wilson, The Guardian, 22 October 2004

Figure 6.15 Social psychologist Philip Zimbardo defends individuals in Frederick's position

1. Using ideas from agency theory, explain why Frederick might have participated in the maltreatment of prisoners.
2. Google Philip Zimbardo. Where might his view that individuals in Frederick's situation are not to blame have come from?

Charisma

Agency theory gives us a partial explanation of our general tendency to be obedient. However, a different approach involves looking at the skills some individuals use to gain obedience. People in authority who are expert in influencing people are known as charismatic or transformational leaders. House *et al.* define charisma as 'the

Figure 6.16 Charismatic leaders must have a vision and the social skills to put it across. They don't have to be nice.

ability of a leader to exercise diffuse and intensive influence over the beliefs, values, behaviour and performance of others' (1991, p366). This unusual level of obedience can be a good or bad thing according to the situation. Charisma probably enhances people's tendency towards destructive obedience, and it is likely that Hitler's charisma may have contributed to obedience in Nazi Germany that permitted the Holocaust. Historically, many of the most unpleasant and destructive national leaders – including Hitler and Stalin – were charismatic leaders.

The original approach to explaining charisma was to identify personality characteristics of charismatic leaders. However, most contemporary social psychologists are more concerned with the social processes by which charismatic leaders obtain obedience from others. For example, charismatic leaders tend to establish a very clear vision of what they want to achieve and how they intend to achieve it. Hitler, for example, motivated the German people with a vision of a utopian Germany. Charismatic leaders tend to give orders in terms of achieving their goal, so that there is a clear reason to obey them. They also use highly emotive language. This seems to energise followers so that they tend to obey instructions without stopping to think about them.

Discussion

Studies have supported the idea that charisma can lead to greater levels of obedience. For example, De Hartog *et al.* (2007) looked at 115 manager-employee pairs in a Dutch government organisation. Employees rated their manager for charisma while managers rated the employee on their tendency to follow instructions. A positive correlation was found; charismatic leaders were more likely to be obeyed. Of course, charisma can never be a complete explanation of obedience because, as Milgram showed, we tend to obey when people are in a position of legitimate and expert authority. Milgram did not use charismatic experimenters.

Media watch: talking CCTV cameras

http://www.telegraph.co.uk/news/main.jhtml?xml=/news/2007/04/05/ncctv05.xml

Oi! Talking CCTV cameras will shame offenders

A system of talking CCTV cameras that allows operators to publicly shame offenders is to be extended across the country. The scheme was pioneered in Middlesbrough where loudspeakers are fitted to 12 of its 158 town centre cameras. Now another 20 councils are to follow suit, using £500,000 from the Government's 'Respect' budget.

John Reid, the Home Secretary, denied the plans were overly intrusive or marked the arrival of a 'police state'. "This is a hugely popular scheme in Middlesbrough and the vast majority of the people here are right behind it", he said. "It helps counter things like litter through drunk or disorderly behaviour, gangs congregating."

Philip Johnston, *Daily Telegraph*, 6 April 2007

Figure 6.17 In spite of their lack of charisma, talking CCTV cameras attract good rates of obedience

1 It seems that talking CCTV cameras attract quite good rates of obedience. Does this fit better with agency or charisma explanations for obedience?

Thinking creatively about psychology

How could you go about comparing the rates of obedience to talking CCTV cameras and human authority figures such as police officers and community support officers? Design an experiment to investigate this. Consider whether it would be better done in the field or a controlled environment and what sort of orders you might give.

INDEPENDENCE AND RESISTANCE

The study of social influence grew largely out of concern over the tendency for destructive obedience and conformity shown in the Holocaust. Asch and Milgram were influenced very much by the harm caused by obedience and conformity in Nazi Germany. However, a smaller body of research has been devoted to understanding independent behaviour and resistance to conformity and obedience.

Minority influence

We have established that authority figures and group majorities can influence people. However, minorities in a group and individuals who rebel against authority can also influence us. One reason therefore why we might refuse to conform or obey is because we are *more* influenced by rebels who are already not conforming or obeying. Early researchers in both conformity and obedience noticed that once one person refused to go along with orders or majority behaviour, others would follow. This was demonstrated in a classic variation on the Milgram procedure.

CLASSIC RESEARCH

Milgram S (1965) Liberating effects of group pressure. *Journal of Personality & Social Psychology,* **1** 127–34

AIM

To test whether the rate of obedience in the Milgram procedure would be affected by witnessing rebellious or obedient fellow participants.

PROCEDURE

Eighty male participants aged 20–50 took part in one of two conditions. Those taking part in each condition were matched for age and occupation with those in Milgram's original procedure. Milgram's original procedure served as a control condition. In one of the experimental conditions the participant worked with two rebellious stooges. At 150 volts one refused to give any further shocks and at 210 volts the other also refused. In the second experimental condition, two obedient stooges gave shocks without protest and offered mild rebukes when the participant expressed displeasure with the procedure.

FINDINGS

In the baseline condition all 40 participants gave at least 300 volts and 26 (65 per cent) gave the full 450 volts. In the rebellious stooge condition, 50 per cent refused to carry on past 150 volts, and only 6 of the 40 (15 per cent) gave the full 450 volts. In the obedient stooge condition, 29 participants (72.5 per cent) went to 450 volts.

CONCLUSION

The behaviour of fellow participants made a difference to the rates of obedience. The presence of rebellious stooges had a much larger effect on participants than that of obedient stooges; the majority felt able to refuse orders once one or both the others had done so.

Figure 6.18 Rebels are well placed to encourage people to internalise their beliefs

Asch (1955) similarly introduced a rebellious stooge into his conformity procedure, challenging the majority over the correctly matching line. The rate of conformity dropped from 37 per cent to nine per cent. We can see, then, that once justified rebellion begins, it soon gathers momentum. In both the Asch and the Milgram studies, participants who conformed or obeyed were *complying* with the social demands of the situation; they had not *internalised* the choices pushed by the group majority or authority figure.

Moscovici (1985) suggested this is typical of social influence by group majorities and authority figures. He believed that the power of rebels, as opposed to majorities, to persuade people to go along with them and defy the majority lies in their greater ability to get people to actually *internalise* their beliefs. Moscovici believed that this influence of a rebellious minority requires that their message is consistent, relevant to current circumstances and that the rebels appear committed but flexible rather than rigid.

Reactance

Sometimes when we believe a group or individual is trying to restrict our personal choice and freedom we respond by getting angry. This anger tends to make us want to rebel, a response known as *reactance* (Brehm, 1966). Reactance is best documented in children and adolescents, in their response to pressure to conform to adult rules. For example, young people are consistently told not to smoke. Hamilton *et al.* (2005) investigated the effect of this approach in a large Australian study of 4636 13- to 14-year-olds. In a condition designed to produce low reactance, children underwent a harm minimisation programme in which they were told that it was normal behaviour in a free society to try various drugs, but to be aware of the health risks. In a high-reactance condition they were told that they must never smoke. Smoking rates were significantly lower in the low-reactance condition. This suggests that many of the young people who were pressured to surrender their freedom of choice reacted by resisting.

Figure 6.19 Telling young people they must not smoke may provoke reactance

Thinking practically about psychology

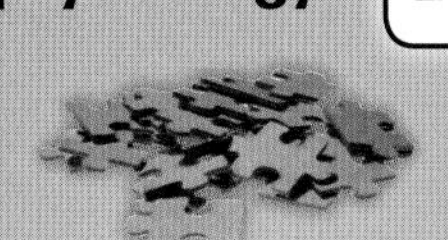

Many health professionals, including GPs, dietitians and physiotherapists, have to tell people to alter their behaviour for the sake of their health. Research tends to show that people tend to be quite poor at following their instructions. Explain, using the idea of reactance, why this might happen.

Attribution theory

When we are interacting with other people, we constantly make judgements about the reasons for their behaviour. These judgements are called attributions. When we see people conforming to group norms we make attributions about their reasons for doing so. These attributions can affect our own responses. If, for example, we witness people obeying an order and all behaving the same way, we attribute their behaviour to the order. If we believe the only reason people are conforming to a group norm is because they have been told to, then they lose their informational influence over us. This is called *ironic deviance*. Conway & Schaller (2005) investigated the role of ironic deviance in resisting conformity.

KEY TERMS

reactance – the angry response we experience when we sense that others are trying to restrict our freedom of choice

attributions – judgements about why people act in particular ways

ironic deviance – when we attribute majority behaviour to orders and so disregard it, meaning we do not conform

RESEARCH NOW

Conway LG & Schaller M (2005) When authorities' commands backfire. *Journal of Personality & Social Psychology,* **89** 311–26

AIM

To test whether people become less conformist when they believe that other group members are only conforming in response to an order.

PROCEDURE

Eighty Canadian students were given a scenario in which they imagined being a member of a large organisation and having responsibility to choose between two computer networks. They witnessed other employees agreeing unanimously that Wobblenet was the better network. In two conditions their boss told them to order Wobblenet, saying, "It seems to me that Wobblenet is the better system, so I think we should go with that. I don't want any disagreement." In the other two conditions he said, "I do not want to influence the vote." In one of these conditions the boss remained and in the other he left. Participants made a decision and gave their reasons.

FINDINGS

In the conditions where the boss ordered employees to choose Wobblenet, participants were much less likely to conform to the group norm and choose it. They gave their reason as believing that the majority behaviour was purely due to the boss' order. This was particularly the case in the conditions where the boss had left. Participants were strongly motivated to obey his order when he remained in a position of authority.

CONCLUSIONS

Orders to the group reduced conformity of participants to the group norm because participants believed the group behaviour was just the result of the orders.

Discussion

As we have seen, there is evidence that minority influence, reactance and attributions can all influence people's responses to orders and majority influence. Although these are quite different explanations, we should not see them as rival theories. They can all influence us to show independence and resist social influence; they just come into play under slightly different circumstances. Minority influence affects us when there is a rebellious minority to influence us, and when the rebels make their point relevant to us and put it across consistently but without appearing rigid. Reactance affects us in situations where we perceive that an individual or group is trying to restrict our freedom of choice. This is most likely when there is already resentment towards the majority or authority figure for doing this. Ironic deviance takes place when we believe that the behaviour of the majority is the result of unreasonable pressure from authority.

Thinking critically about psychology

Compare the different methods used by Conway & Schaller (p126) and Hamilton *et al.* (p175) to investigate resistance to social influence. What are the strengths and limitations of each study? Think about the samples they studied, the realism of the environment and what participants had to do, and the way resistance was measured.

Media watch: illegal downloading

Daily Mail, **11 August 2007 online email newsletter**

Illegal downloading is on the rise as fewer people pay for their music

Record numbers of people are illegally downloading music in Britain as the threat of prosecution fails to discourage consumers, according to a new study. A nationwide study of Internet users found that 43 per cent of people admitted to having illegally downloaded music tracks in the past 12 months, compared with 36 per cent last year and 40 per cent in 2005. Experts warned record labels must make legal buying easier and cheaper or face losing further sales as growing online social networks dominate the way Internet users buy and listen to music.

John Enser, a partner at media law firm Olswang, said: "As illegal downloading hits an all-time high and consumers' fear of prosecution falls, the music industry must look for more ways to encourage the public to download music legally."

Almost one of five people – 18 per cent – polled in the fourth annual Digital Music Survey said they would continue to download unauthorised music, up from less than one in ten last year.

The independent survey of 1,700 Internet users also found the number of people who have stopped legally downloading tracks has increased from nine to 11 per cent. Mr Enser added: "The trend towards piracy appears to be in real danger of accelerating as almost one in five people claim they will download more unauthorised tracks in the future."

Daily Mail online email newsletter, 11 August 2007

Figure 6.20 Many people refuse to conform or obey when it comes to illegal downloading of MP3 files

1 Explain how minority influence, reactance and ironic deviance could each explain why people are refusing to obey orders not to download music illegally or to conform to the majority who do not do so.

INDIVIDUAL DIFFERENCES IN INDEPENDENCE AND RESISTANCE

KEY TERMS

personality – the aspects of the person that make their behaviour consistent and distinct from that of other people

Minority influence, reactance and ironic deviance all explain why people resist social pressure in particular situations. However, there has always been a debate in social psychology about how important an individual's personality is as opposed to their situation in affecting their social behaviour. Although Milgram's research was concerned with the social situation in which people receive orders from an authority figure, he said himself, "I am certain there is a complex personality basis to obedience and disobedience, but I am certain I have not found it", (1974, p205). As Blass (1991) points out, in all the Milgram studies and in later replications by other researchers, some people were much more obedient than others, regardless of the situation. This suggests that individual differences as well as situation are important in affecting how people respond to social influence.

The authoritarian personality

There is some evidence to suggest that one personality characteristic, *authoritarianism*, is related to people's independence. The authoritarian personality is politically conservative, hostile, has rigid morals and hates challenges to authority or deviations from conventional social behaviour. The idea of authoritarianism was originally thought of in an attempt to explain the behaviour of the German people during the Holocaust. However, authoritarians exist in a wide range of cultures.

Because authoritarians value conformity and authority, we might expect that highly authoritarian people would be more conformist and obedient in their behaviour. In an early study of the role of conformity and authoritarianism, Elms & Milgram (1966) compared the personalities of 20 obedient and 20 disobedient participants from the Milgram experiments. They used a test of authoritarianism called the *Fascism Scale* (Adorno *et al.*, 1950) and a standard general personality test called the MMPI. The MMPI measures several aspects of personality, including neuroticism, extroversion, masculinity, paranoia, hysteria and symptoms of mental disorders including schizophrenia, depression and obsessive-compulsive disorder. No differences in the MMPI scores on any of these scales emerged between the obedient and disobedient groups. However, the obedient group were significantly higher in authoritarianism as measured by the Fascism Scale.

A limitation of the Elms & Milgram study was the use of the now old-fashioned Fascism Scale. However, more recent research using better measures of authoritarianism has continued to show that authoritarians are more obedient to authority. Altemeyer (1981) measured authoritarianism using a much more reliable and valid scale called the RWA (right-wing authoritarianism) Scale. In an experiment reported by Altemeyer in which participants were ordered to give themselves shocks when they got learning tasks wrong, a positive correlation was found between authoritarianism and the level shock they were willing to give.

The compliant personality

We have looked at compliance earlier in this chapter. People comply when they go along with the behaviour displayed by the majority or the behaviour demanded by an authority figure. Gudjonsson (1989) proposed that compliance is actually a personality characteristic, and that two factors make one person more compliant than another:

- eagerness to please
- avoidance of conflict.

These can both be measured using a questionnaire called the Gudjonsson Compliance Scale. Two of the twenty items from this scale are shown in Box 6.1. Both these aspects of behaviour make people susceptible to social influence. If we are naturally eager to please others, we are more likely to do as they do or what they tell us. If we hate conflict, we are unlikely to defy authority or risk upsetting a majority by deviating from their behaviour.

Box 6.1 *Items from the Gudjonsson Compliance Scale*

I tend to go along with what people tell me even when I know they are wrong
True ☐ False ☐

I give in easily to people when I am pressured
True ☐ False ☐

Gudjonsson & Sigurdsson (2003) suggest that in the Milgram studies it was more compliant participants who showed the highest level of destructive obedience. There is no direct evidence to support this; however, there is evidence to suggest that individual differences in compliance affect people's capacity to resist social pressure in other situations. This line of research has been particularly important in understanding the ability of suspects to resist pressure to confess to crimes. Gudjonsson & MacKeith (1997) examined the role of compliance in the false confessions of the Birmingham Six, one of the most notorious of all miscarriages of justice in Britain. The Birmingham Six were arrested following the bombing of a Birmingham pub in 1974 in which 21 people died. They were ordered to confess by the police and beaten until four of them obeyed. They were jailed from 1975 until 1990, when they were released on appeal. All six men were tested with the Gudjonsson Compliance Scale in prison. The four who confessed under police orders all scored higher in compliance than the two who resisted. Scores are shown in Figure 6.21.

Figure 6.21 Compliance scores for the Birmingham Six

Locus of control

Another aspect of personality that may affect individual differences in conformity and obedience is locus of control. We all tend to have either a broadly internal or a broadly external locus of control (Rotter, 1966). If it is internal, this means that we tend to see ourselves as in control of events. If we have an external locus of control, we tend to see ourselves as at the mercy of external events. We may thus feel generally in control of our lives or helpless depending on whether our locus of control is internal or external. Having an internal locus of control is generally associated with healthy behaviour (because internals believe they have control over their health) and good mental health (internals get less anxious and depressed because they do not feel threatened or helpless in the face of events).

LOOKING FURTHER There are various published questionnaires that aim to measure locus of control. Julian Rotter developed one of the earliest of these. You can find Rotter's scale at http://www.ballarat.edu.au/ard/bssh/psych/rot.htm. For each item, the scale requires you to select between two answers. For the first couple of items, decide which option, A or B, indicates internal locus of control and which indicates external locus of control. This should help you better understand the concept.

Rotter (1966) proposed that people with an internal locus of control are better at resisting social pressure. This makes sense; if we generally feel we are in control of situations, we are likely to believe that we have a choice over whether to obey or conform. Evidence for the idea is, however, actually rather mixed. In a study of conformity, Brehony & Geller (1981) assessed locus of control in four groups of 30 people. Two groups were male and two female. One group of each sex were stereotypically masculine and feminine respectively. The other two groups were *androgynous* – that is, they had a blend of masculine and feminine characteristics. The participants then took part in an Asch-style conformity experiment. This gave the researchers two measures of conformity: responses in the experiment and conformity to gender roles. Those with an external locus of control were more conformist on both measures, supporting Rotter's ideas.

Another approach to looking at the relationship between conformity and locus of control is to study changing social trends in each characteristic. Twenge *et al.* (2004) looked at changes in locus of control between 1960 and 2002, using archived data from existing studies. There is no doubt that people in general have become more independent and less conformist over the past 40 years. If Rotter were correct and people with an external locus of control are more conformist while more independent people have a more internal locus of control, we would expect to find that people have become steadily more internal in their locus of control. However, according to Twenge *et al.* the reverse is true. They found that people have become steadily more external in the past 40 years, at the same time as they have become less conformist. Results are shown in Figure 6.22.

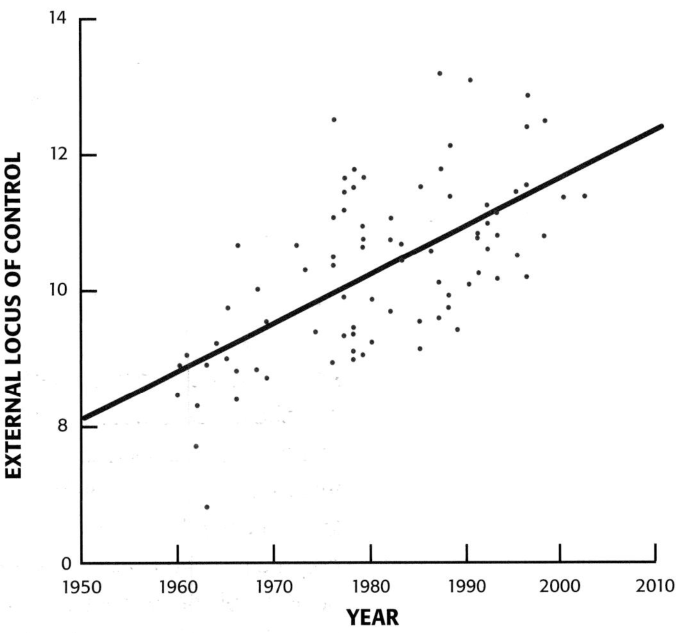

Figure 6.22 The increase in external locus of control since 1960
From Twenge *et al.* (2004)

Thinking critically about psychology

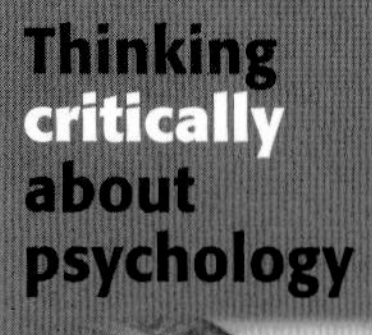

The studies by Twenge *et al.* and Brehony & Geller use very different methods and arrive at very different conclusions. Consider the strengths and weaknesses of each using the evaluation toolkit in Chapter 1. Which study do you see as more credible?

Thinking creatively about psychology

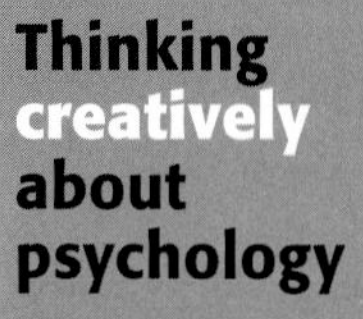

Design a study that would investigate whether there is a relationship between locus of control and conformity. Consider whether you would prefer to use an experimental method like Brehony & Geller or archived data like Twenge *et al.*

Evidence is similarly mixed when it comes to obedience. Some evidence for a link between locus of control and obedience comes from a study of ethics in American pharmacy students (Latif, 2000). Latif measured locus of control and level of moral reasoning. The lowest level of moral reasoning in the model of moral development Latif used (Kohlberg, 1966) is blind obedience. There was a correlation of +0.42 between belief that blind obedience is morally correct and external locus of control in Latif's participants. This does suggest a link between obedience and locus of control. However, note that the study is measuring only attitudes to obedience, *not* obedient behaviour. We cannot firmly say on the basis of a correlation like this that people with an external locus of control are actually more obedient. Other studies have found even less of a link between locus of control and obedience. In a Chinese study of the factors influencing obedience shown by diabetes sufferers to doctor's orders, Stewart *et al.* (2000) found only a weak correlation (+0.17) between obedience and external locus of control.

SOCIAL INFLUENCE AND SOCIAL CHANGE

According to Wikipedia, social change is a general term for change in the nature, social institutions, social behaviour or social relations of a society or community. Social change can take place quickly or slowly. It can be dramatic, as in armed revolution, but more commonly it takes the form of a gradual shift in attitudes. An example of the latter is the development of women's rights in Britain over the past 100 years. Prior to the First World War, women had no voting rights at all in Britain. In 1918 they were given limited rights to vote and in 1928 these were extended to the level of men's rights. In 1970 it became illegal to pay women less than men for the same work, and in 1974 the Sex Discrimination Act gave women further equal rights. In 2003, laws were further strengthened to make it harder to discriminate against women. Tracing the changes in legislation tells us how attitudes have gradually shifted in favour of sex equality.

Much social change takes place in the same way as the development of women's rights, beginning with the rebellious actions of a minority, who gradually increase their influence until they become the majority. It may seem

Figure 6.23 The suffragettes fought for the right for women to vote and paved the way for further social change around women's rights

strange now to think that environment campaigners, who now have huge support, were as little as 20 years ago regarded as a small group of irrational extremists. However, they have increased their influence until they have majority support. Once the views of a minority group are accepted by the majority, then conformity effects come into play, and those who resist social change become subject to normative and informational influences. If social change becomes enshrined in law, then orders are issued and obedience also comes into play.

The role of resistance and independence

Who initiates social change?

In the early twentieth Century a small group of women, the suffragettes, defied the majority and demanded the right of women to vote (suffrage means the right to vote). This is typical of the early stages of social change. At this point all women were subject to social pressure in the form of majority influence and, in some cases, direct orders to stick to their traditional gender role and not expect equal rights. The suffragettes defied this pressure. In terms of individual differences we might suspect, on the basis of modern research, that the suffragettes had some of the following characteristics:

- low in authoritarianism: suffragettes showed little regard for authority or tradition so they were probably not authoritarians
- not compliant personalities: suffragettes showed no desire to avoid conflict or eagerness to please so they were probably not compliant
- an internal locus of control: suffragettes must have believed they had the power to affect events and win the right to vote, so they probably had internal locus of control.

These characteristics are probably typical of the rebels who initiate social change.

What makes them rebel?

We can apply our explanations for resistance and independence to understanding the beginnings of social change. Rebels like the suffragettes almost certainly experienced reactance (see p174). They were told that they were not entitled to what they considered a basic right and so they responded much as we would if were denied a freedom we considered important. Just as telling young people not to smoke makes many more determined to do so, ordering the suffragettes to stop protesting just made them more determined.

Ironic deviance (p175) may also play a role at this point in social change. Once the suffragettes were ordered to conform and stop demanding suffrage, they may have begun to attribute the conformity of non-suffragettes to this sort of social pressure. At this point the conforming majority would have lost their influence over the minority, and the position of the latter would have become stronger.

Minority influence: changing the attitudes of the majority

Although minorities like the suffragettes were subject to social pressure from the majority, the reverse effect also comes into play and minorities also exert influence in the other direction. Studies like Milgram's and Asch's show that it becomes much easier to defy authority and the majority once others are already doing so. The existence of the suffragettes thus made it easier for other people to support women's rights. Moscovici suggested that minorities are particularly effective at getting people to internalise rather than just comply with behaviours and views, provided they are consistent and committed. The suffragettes and later campaigners for women's rights showed consistency and commitment in abundance, and over the last century most people have indeed internalised the idea of sex equality.

The role of conformity and obedience

When a minority successfully initiates social change, there comes a tipping point where the majority comes to support the change. At this point the processes of conformity come into play. Many of those who do not internalise the change nevertheless comply with it. For example, there are still people who do not agree with gender equality, but those individuals are subject to pressure to conform to it. They experience normative influence; anyone who now defies the norm of supporting sex equality is likely to be called a sexist and will suffer socially as a result. They may also experience informational influence; where the majority believe in sex equality, individuals who do not must constantly question why their views differ.

Obedience to orders also becomes a factor in social change once the tipping point has been reached and change has become sufficiently accepted to be supported by the law. Employers order employees to follow the new norm. In some cases the police and the courts also issue direct orders to comply with new behavioural norms. A recent example of this has followed the banning of smoking in public places in England in July 2007. According to the Department of Health, during the first month following the ban 97 per cent of pubs and clubs complied. Three hundred and twelve had to be issued direct orders to comply.

CHAPTER SUMMARY

- Conformity takes place when a majority of people behave in a particular way and this influences others to do the same. Their change of behaviour may take the form of compliance, or the new behaviour may be internalised.
- A classic study by Asch demonstrated that people will sometimes conform to a majority view even when this is obviously incorrect.
- People are subject to normative influence – that is, they wish to be part of a group and fear rejection if they do not conform to the norms of that group. Griskevicius *et al.* showed that when people are thinking about protecting themselves or finding a mate, normative influence increases and they conform more.
- People are also subject to informational influence. This means that we tend to believe that the majority must have better information than we have or be more competent than we are to make judgements. Related to this is cognitive dissonance. We feel uncomfortable when there is evidence that we are wrong about something, having a majority disagree with us is such evidence.
- Obedience is the following of direct orders. Psychologists are particularly concerned with destructive obedience: obeying orders that lead to harm. Studies like those of Milgram and Hofling *et al.* show that we are surprisingly obedient, even when following orders means behaving dangerously or immorally.
- Several studies have shown that we are largely unaware of how obedient people are. In particular, we tend to underestimate our own obedience.

- Milgram explained destructive obedience using the idea of agency. Under the influence of a legitimate authority figure we enter an agentic state and surrender free will in order to best serve the needs of our society or community.
- Some people, known as charismatic leaders, appear to be particularly skilled at getting people to obey their orders. Successful politicians and business leaders are often charismatic.
- Psychologists have also studied independent behaviour and resistance to obedience and conformity. We can be influenced as much by a rebellious minority as by a conforming majority or authority figure. Both Milgram and Asch found that the presence of a rebel sharply reduced conformity and obedience in their participants.
- People also show reactance and ironic deviance in response to pressure to obey and conform. Reactance occurs when we resent having our freedom of choice restricted. Ironic deviance occurs when we think that a majority are only behaving in a particular way in response to orders, so they lose their informational influence over us.
- Some people seem to be particularly resistant to social influence. These may be low in authoritarianism; this means that they do not overly respect authority or tradition. They may also be low in compliance; this means that they are unconcerned by conflict and have no need to please others. They may also have an internal locus of control, meaning that they feel in control of situations.
- We can apply our understanding of social influence to understand social change. Minority groups, who may have personal characteristics that make them particularly independent of social pressure, usually start social change. Minority groups are well placed to alter public opinions through the process of internalisation. Once they become the majority, then normative and informational influence come into play and most people conform to the new norm. Orders can be issued in support of this new norm.

What do I know?

1 (a) Draw a line between the terms on the left and their correct definitions on the right. (4 marks)

Compliance		Conforming to majority behaviour in the belief that the majority probably know best
Internalisation		Resisting the effects of group pressure
Normative social influence		Going along with the majority and becoming convinced that they are correct
Informational social influence		Conforming to the majority in order to avoid being rejected by the group
Authoritarianism		Going along with the majority without believing they are correct

(b) Outline what psychologists have concluded about why people conform. (5 marks)
(c) Outline one ethical issue that researchers into conformity have to take into account. (3 marks)

2 (a) Explain what is meant by informational social influence. (2 marks)
(b) Your school is having a dance competition. However, your judges are students and they are not experienced either in judging or in dance. What seems to be going wrong is that each judge is listening to what the other judges are saying and going along with it. Using aspects of this situation, explain how this conformity could result from informational social influence. (3 marks)

3 (a) Outline the findings of Milgram's study of obedience. (3 marks)
(b) Obedience can be studied by means of laboratory experiments and field experiments. Evaluate the usefulness of field experiments in studying obedience. (4 marks)
(c) Explain **one** conclusion from Milgram's research. (3 marks)

4 (a) (i) We usually do what someone in authority, for example a teacher or police officer, tells us to. Outline **one** explanation for why people are obedient. (4 marks)
(ii) Explain **one** way in which people resist pressures to obey authority. (3 marks)
(b) Give **one** explanation for why people resist pressure to conform. (4 marks)
(c) Explain the implications of research of obedience, conformity and independence can lead to social change. (4 marks)

5 In all the major studies of obedience and conformity, some participants have behaved independently in spite of the social pressure they were facing. Describe and evaluate the role of individual differences in independent behaviour. (12 marks)

CHAPTER 7
Individual Differences

Thinking ahead

By the end of this chapter you should be able to:

- explain and critically consider alternative ways of defining abnormality, including deviation from social norms, failure to function adequately and deviation from ideal mental health
- outline the key features of the biological approach to abnormality
- describe and evaluate biological treatments for mental disorder, including drugs and ECT
- outline the key features of the psychodynamic approach to abnormality
- describe and evaluate psychodynamic therapies including classical psychoanalysis
- outline the key features of the behavioural approach to abnormality
- describe and evaluate behavioural therapies including systematic desensitisation
- outline the key features of the cognitive approach to abnormality
- describe and evaluate cognitive therapies, including CBT

Most branches of psychology are mainly concerned with identifying general trends in human mind and behaviour. Although a minority of social psychologists are interested in individual differences in obedience and conformity, the bulk of research has been into how obedient and conformist we are in general. Similarly, although a few memory researchers have looked into why some people have better memories than others, the majority have focused more on how memory in general works. Some topics in psychology, however, are specifically concerned with how individuals differ. These include intelligence, personality and psychological abnormality. In this chapter we are concerned with the last of these, looking at the ways in which psychological abnormality can be defined, explained and treated.

DEFINING ABNORMALITY

We have probably all at some point looked at someone's behaviour and thought 'that's not normal'. What we mean by this is that the person's behaviour is outside the range of what we see as typical of people with good mental health. Individually and as a society we make decisions to declare some people to be mentally disordered or 'abnormal'.

As we will see in this chapter, there are several ways in which we can define an individual's mind and behaviour as abnormal. These matter for two reasons. First, there is a philosophical and ethical issue: at what point do we draw a line and say that someone is abnormal rather than simply unusual, eccentric or rebellious? When is it fair to call one person abnormal and another normal? Second, when we diagnose mental disorder we need some consistent and as far as possible objective ways to assess people and decide whether they qualify as abnormal. The following are some of the ways that have been used to define abnormality.

Deviation from social norms

A social norm is a behaviour or belief that most people within a society stick to. When someone simply follows the social norms of their culture it is very hard to use their behaviour to make judgements about them. However, when someone defies social norms it attracts our attention and provides us with the sort of information we can use to make judgements. We probably all therefore tend to notice and be a bit wary of people whose behaviour does not conform to social norms. In some cases where behaviour runs counter to the social norm but is clearly harmless we might think of people as eccentric or rebellious rather than abnormal. However, there are cases where behaviour runs counter to the moral values shared by whole societies. In these cases we can use deviation from social norms as a basis for defining someone as abnormal. An example is in the diagnosis of *antisocial personality disorder*. People with a diagnosis of antisocial personality are commonly known as psychopaths. The psychopath is impulsive, aggressive and irresponsible. One of the defining symptoms of antisocial personality disorder is 'failure to conform to social norms with respect to lawful behaviours as indicated by repeatedly performing acts that are grounds for arrest' (from the *Diagnostic and Statistical Manual of Mental Disorder-IV-TR*, 2000).

We would probably all agree that psychopaths are abnormal on the basis that they defy some important social norms. Other diagnoses, such as paedophilia (sexual attraction to children) and zoophilia (sexual attraction to animals), are also based largely on the social unacceptability of the individual's behaviour. However, although deviation from social norms is important in defining some mental disorders, it can lead to two problems.

KEY TERMS

social control – strategies to control the behaviour of particular groups in a society

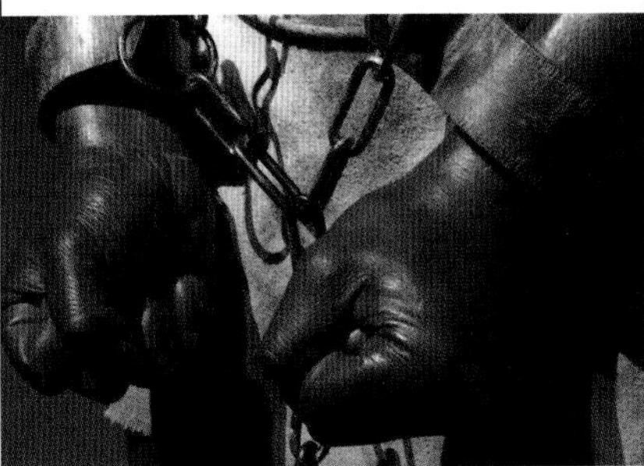
Figure 7.1 Escaping slaves were once regarded as abnormal

Personal liberty and social control

First, focusing on the ways in which an individual chooses to deviate from social norms can lead to severely restricting their freedom of choice. Table 7.1 shows some examples of real diagnoses that were given to people in the past because their behaviour defied social norms.

Table 7.1 Historical diagnoses made on the basis of deviation from social norms

'Condition'	'Symptoms'
Drapetomania	Slaves showed an irrational desire to escape from their owners
Nymphomania	Middle-class women were attracted to working-class men
Moral insanity	Women inherited money and irrationally wished to keep it
Unmarried motherhood	Unmarried women became pregnant
Homosexuality	Sexual attraction to members of the same sex

It is probably no coincidence that all these diagnoses have been aimed at groups that have always experienced discrimination. In these cases the main motivation for applying labels of mental disorder was probably a desire to maintain social control over women, black people and gay people. For example, by being able to get women diagnosed with nymphomania or moral insanity (with the cooperation of white, middle-class male doctors), nineteenth-century men were able to maintain strict control over women's economic and sexual lives. It is probably also no coincidence that standard treatments for most of the five 'conditions' in Table 7.1 included what we would now call cruel and unusual punishment. The diagnoses in Table 7.1 all appear absurd in twenty-first century Britain, but only because social norms have changed so much. As recently as the 1970s, gay men were given a psychiatric diagnosis and 'treated' by means of painful electric shocks. Even more recently, in the 1990s, audits of patient records revealed women who were still kept in psychiatric hospitals because they had had children out of wedlock some decades earlier.

Figure 7.2 Members of groups with distinctive appearances are still at increased risk of being labelled as abnormal

Cultural variations in social norms

Social norms are culturally specific. They differ, therefore, between any two groups with a different culture, including different ethnic, regional and socio-economic groups and different generations within the same community. This can cause huge problems when a mental health professional from one cultural group assesses someone from another. This is probably why in the United Kingdom black and Irish people are significantly more likely than others to receive a diagnosis of mental disorder, (Littlewood & Lipsedge, 1997). They illustrate this problem with the case of Calvin (Box 7.1).

This nightmarish case illustrates the difficulty a psychiatrist can have in assessing someone with a different cultural background. Calvin's appearance was described as eccentric, although for a Rastafarian it was entirely normal. Calvin is

Box 7.1 *The case of Calvin*

Calvin was a Jamaican man. A post office clerk had accused him of cashing a stolen postal order (it was not in fact stolen). An argument resulted and the police were called. Calvin was arrested. A prison psychiatrist assessed him for possible mental health problems. The following is an extract from his report:

> *This man belongs to Rastafarian – a mystical Jamaican cult, the members of which think they are God-like. The man has ringlet hair, a straggly goatee beard and a type of turban. He appears eccentric in his appearance and very vague in answering questions. He is an irritable character and has got arrogant behaviour.*

also described as 'irritable' – if either of us had just popped out to cash a postal order and been called a thief, arrested and found ourselves being assessed by a psychiatrist, we'd be bloody livid! Having never experienced this kind of discrimination, the psychiatrist clearly had difficulty appreciating this.

OVER TO YOU Under no circumstances should you try any practical work with anyone suffering from any form of psychological abnormality. You are not qualified for this sort of research and your teacher is probably not qualified to supervise it. What you *can* do, however, is to study people's attitudes to abnormality. Draw up a list of behaviours that might breach social norms in your community and find out what percentage of students think those behaviours are examples of psychological abnormality.

KEY TERMS

DSM – *Diagnostic and Statistical Manual of Mental Disorder*, the American Psychiatric Association's system of diagnosis. Now in its fourth edition with text revisions, so it is called *DSM-IV-TR*. *DSM* is the most popular system of diagnosis in Britain and the United States

Failure to function adequately

We have already said that using deviation from social norms as a way to define behaviour as abnormal causes problems because it restricts people's right to behave as they wish and according to the standards of their own culture or subculture. An alternative is to look at whether the person is able to live a 'normal' life. This may be a fairer approach because we are taking into account the individual's well-being rather than just imposing our standards on them. According to this way of defining abnormality, someone crosses the line and becomes abnormal when they can no longer cope with the tasks of day-to-day living. Thus, a person who hears voices occasionally when tired or stressed, but who can clear their head by having a walk and a good sleep, is *not* abnormal. However, if the voices become louder, more constant and more aggressive, the person might well start to have difficulty going about their daily life. They may well then receive a psychiatric diagnosis.

The adequacy criterion is important in psychiatric diagnosis. For example, a diagnosis of major depression requires that 'the person's symptoms are a cause of great distress or difficulty in functioning at home, work, or other important areas' (*DSM-IV-TR*, 2000). We all have fears, some sensible and some irrational. A fear is only classified as abnormal – that is, a phobia – if 'the avoidance, anxious anticipation, or distress in the feared situation(s) interferes significantly with the person's normal routine, occupational (or academic) functioning, or social activities or relationships, or there is marked distress about having the phobia' (*DSM-IV-TR*, 2000). Introducing this sort of element to diagnosis is very helpful because it defines where the cut-off point should be between unusual and abnormal, and because it ensures we take into account the welfare of the person as well as social norms.

Figure 7.3 This girl will only be diagnosed as phobic if her fear of spiders prevents her living a normal life

Global assessment of functioning

The *Diagnostic and Statistical Manual of Mental Disorder* (*DSM-IV-TR*) includes a scale of 1–100, measuring how adequately someone is functioning. This is called the Global Assessment of Functioning (GAF) scale and is shown in Table 7.2.

Table 7.2 The Global Assessment of Function

91–100	Superior functioning in a wide range of activities, life's problems never seem to get out of hand, is sought out by others because of his or her many positive qualities. No symptoms
81–90	Absent or minimal symptoms (e.g., mild anxiety before an exam), good functioning in all areas, interested and involved in a wide range of activities, socially effective, generally satisfied with life, no more than everyday problems or concerns (e.g., an occasional argument with family members)
71–80	If symptoms are present, they are transient and expectable reactions to psychosocial. stressors (e.g., difficulty concentrating after family argument); no more than slight impairment in social occupational, or school functioning (e.g., temporarily falling behind in schoolwork)
61–70	Some mild symptoms (e.g., depressed mood and mild insomnia) OR some difficulty in social, occupational, or school functioning (e.g., occasional truancy or theft within the household), but generally functioning pretty well, has some meaningful interpersonal relationships
51–60	Moderate symptoms (e.g., flat affect and circumstantial speech, occasional panic attacks) OR moderate difficulty in social, occupational, or school functioning (e.g., few friends, conflicts with peers or co-workers)
41–50	Severe symptoms (e.g., suicidal ideation, severe obsessional rituals, frequent shoplifting) OR any serious impairment in social, occupational or school functioning (e,g., no friends, unable to keep a job)
31–40	Some impairment in reality testing or communication (e.g., speech is at times illogical, obscure, or irrelevant) OR major impairment in several areas, such as work or school, family relations, judgment, thinking, or mood (e.g., depressed man avoids friends, neglects family, and is unable to work; child frequently beats up younger children, is defiant at home, and is failing at school)
21–30	Behaviour is considerably influenced by delusions or hallucinations OR serious impairment in communication or judgment (e.g., sometimes incoherent, acts grossly inappropriately, suicidal preoccupation) OR inability to function in almost all areas (e.g., stays in bed all day, no job, home, or friends)
11–20	Some danger of hurting self or others (e.g., suicidal attempts without clear expectation of death; frequently violent; manic excitement) OR occasionally fails to maintain minimal personal hygiene (e.g., smears faeces) OR gross impairment in communication (e.g., largely incoherent or mute)
1–10	Persistent danger of severely hurting self or others (e.g., recurrent violence) OR persistent inability to maintain minimal personal hygiene OR serious suicidal act with clear expectation of death. 0 Inadequate information

Reproduced from the *DSM-IV*

When someone is assessed for mental health problems using the DSM system they will receive a GAF score representing how well they are functioning. This is useful in planning treatment. In particular, it helps with decisions over how much support a patient needs. The lower the score, the more urgent it is that a patient receives treatment and the more support they will require.

Thinking practically about psychology

- Cressida is 14 years old. She has just failed her exams at school and is refusing to go back to school. Over the past year she has argued a lot with friends and is now completely isolated socially.
- Jeremy is 15 years old. He has made three serious suicide attempts in the last month, the first shortly before his end-of-year exams. He says he intends to carry on trying to commit suicide.
- Letitia is 17. She has good family relations and a good social life. However, in the run-up to her AS levels she has found herself suffering some anxiety.

In what GAF band would you place each of these students on the basis of what you know about their current functioning?

Adequacy and personal freedom

Figure 7.4 Should people who opt out of mainstream society be seen as abnormal?

There are still problems with defining abnormality in this way, however. Someone has to make the judgement about when an individual's behaviour has ceased to be adequate. This again introduces the problem of making allowance for an individual's personal freedom. It is tempting to say that if someone leaves their job, gives up their house or flat, lets their hair become matted into dreadlocks, wears dirty clothes and lives in a van they are not functioning adequately. However, they may simply be exercising their right to step outside mainstream society and live as a New Age Traveller. As a traveller, they *may* find themselves happier and more fulfilled than when they lived 'normally'. In this sort of case, two psychiatrists or psychologists might disagree over whether a person in this position was abnormal if adequate functioning were all they had to base their decision on. The reality is that judgements about how adequately someone is functioning will always be affected to some extent by social norms.

Ideal mental health

Marie Jahoda (1958) suggested a rather different approach to understanding normality and abnormality. She used the analogy of physical health to understand mental health. We start worrying that someone is physically abnormal and looking for a diagnosis of illness when the criteria for good health – such as normal temperature, blood pressure and energy levels – are not met. Jahoda suggested that we can look at mental health in the same way. We are thus abnormal when we fail to meet the criteria for good mental health. These include the following:

- healthy self-attitudes including good self-esteem
- personal growth – that is, fulfilling one's potential
- integration, the ability to cope with stress
- autonomy or independence
- accurate perception of reality
- environmental mastery: the ability to have relationships, manage work, enjoy leisure and adapt to changing circumstances.

Jahoda's criteria remain important in modern clinical practice. They are perhaps most helpful when assessing patients for psychological therapy. Most therapists begin with an assessment in which it is agreed not only that the individual is a suitable case for psychological treatment, but also what the therapy will focus on. Some patients work in therapy on their self-esteem, others on their ability to handle stress, others on their relationships. Another strength of the ideal mental health definition is that it is less likely to lead to restricting personal freedom of choice. With the exception of perception of reality, Jahoda's criteria are the sort of issues for which people seek help rather than have it imposed on them.

Cultural variations in ideal mental health

Figure 7.5 Autonomy is not considered a sign of mental health in Japanese culture

Marie Jahoda was writing in the 1950s, working in Britain and the United States. From a twenty-first century global perspective, some of her ideas seem rather culture bound. For example, many cultures do not value independence in the way American and Western European cultures do. More collectivist cultures, for example those found in Asia and Africa, are inclined to see people as functioning successfully when they are highly interdependent with their family, colleagues and local community. The idea of personal growth is also culture-bound. The American (and to a lesser extent British) ideal of striving for personal success is not actually particularly valued as a sign of mental health in most of the world.

Thinking practically about psychology

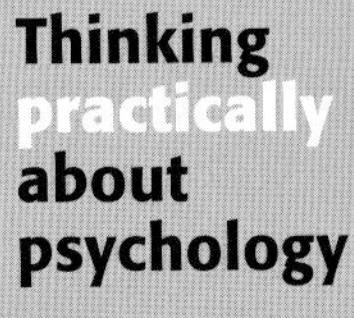

Consider the following cases.

- Edward is a married teacher of religious studies. Unknown to his colleagues, he wears women's clothes in the evenings and weekend.
- Plankton is a road protester. He does not have a permanent address but has moved from one road development to another. With fewer roads now being built, he sometimes finds nowhere to stay.
- Imogen suffers from severe exam stress. In the run-up to January exams this is currently preventing her attending school, and she is losing weight and not sleeping properly.

According to each of the three criteria we have looked at, which of these three people would you classify as abnormal?

EXPLAINING AND TREATING PSYCHOLOGICAL ABNORMALITY

Psychological abnormality can be explained in a number of different ways. These explanations can be grouped into *models*. In this context, a model or paradigm is a set of principles and assumptions within which there are particular explanations and theories. In this chapter we look at four of the most important models used to explain and treat mental disorder. These are the biological, psychodynamic, behavioural and cognitive models.

THE BIOLOGICAL MODEL

Biological psychology is concerned with the relationship between our biology and our mind and behaviour. Aspects of our biology that are particularly relevant to understanding psychology include our nervous system, our genetic make-up and the impact of the biological environment on our development. The biological model of abnormality thus focuses on abnormal functioning of the nervous system and genetic and environmental abnormalities that influence this.

KEY TERMS

schizophrenia – a serious mental disorder characterised by hallucinations, irrational beliefs and difficulty in thinking clearly

cannabis – a popular recreational drug

The genetic basis of mental disorder

There is considerable evidence to suggest that our genetic make-up makes each of us more or less vulnerable to developing certain mental disorders. It is important at this point to understand the relationship between genotype and phenotype. Our genotype is our genetic make-up. Our phenotype is our individual characteristics, including the physical and the psychological. Our phenotype is the product of both our genotype and our environment. When we talk about genetic influence we mean just that, *influence*. It is highly unusual for someone to have a gene or set of genes that doom him or her to definitely suffering a mental disorder. However, our genotype can make us particularly vulnerable to the effects of our environment. If, for example, we carry genes that make us susceptible to schizophrenia and we use cannabis, it may be that the cannabis alters our brain chemistry just enough to trigger the onset of schizophrenia (the cannabis–schizophrenia link is, of course, a debate, not a fact). In all probability, neither the genotype nor the cannabis alone would have directly led to schizophrenia.

It has been noted for several decades that mental disorder tends to run in families. However, this observation can be explained in various ways. From a biological perspective it *can* be explained by inheritance of genes that leave family members vulnerable to a particular mental disorder. From a behaviourist perspective, however (p202), it might equally be that children learn the symptoms of the disorder from older family members. From a psychodynamic perspective (p198) it is clearly harder for parents suffering serious symptoms to provide a stable and nurturing environment for children. Therefore, the fact that conditions run in families does not necessarily mean they are genetic.

There are, however, ways in which we can separate out the effects of genes and family environment. Adoption studies, in which children are brought up in a family who do not share their genetic make-up, provide one way to study genetic influence. If children born into a biological family with close relatives suffering a particular mental disorder but brought up in a different family go on to develop that disorder, this suggests that their genotype was important in developing the disorder. A classic adoption study by Heston (1966) demonstrated the importance of genotype in vulnerability to schizophrenia.

CLASSIC RESEARCH

Heston LL (1966) Psychiatric disorders in children of schizophrenic mothers. *British Journal of Psychiatry,* **112** 819–825

AIM

To investigate genetic influences on schizophrenia by comparing the incidence of schizophrenia in adopted children whose biological mother had schizophrenia with a control group of adoptees with no family history of the condition.

PROCEDURE

Forty-seven adults who had been adopted at birth because their mothers were suffering from schizophrenia took part in the study. A control group of 47 adults who had also been adopted but whose parents were believed to have good mental health also took part. The control group was important because it controlled for the possibility that the trauma of being adopted might influence the development of schizophrenia. The participants were interviewed about their history of mental health problems.

FINDINGS

Of the adults whose mother suffered from schizophrenia, five (10.6 per cent) had been hospitalised with schizophrenia themselves. Three of these were chronically ill. This is roughly the percentage of children who live with a parent suffering schizophrenia and go on to develop the condition. None of the control group had suffered schizophrenia.

CONCLUSION

Genotype is important in making some people particularly vulnerable to developing schizophrenia.

Go to http://www.pubmed.gov. Enter 'genes' and 'schizophrenia'. Do modern studies still point towards genetic vulnerability to the condition?

The biological environment

Figure 7.6 Recreational drugs such as cannabis form part of the biological environment and may trigger mental disorder

We often refer to the study of genes and environment as the nature–nurture debate, 'nature' referring to genes and 'nurture' to environment. This is actually slightly misleading, as it suggests that our environment is simply a question of how we are nurtured – that is, brought up.

Actually, as well as this psychological environment, our biological environment can also have a profound effect on us. We have already mentioned the possibility that certain drugs can trigger the development of schizophrenia in genetically vulnerable individuals. There is also evidence to suggest that other aspects of the biological environment also make people more vulnerable to schizophrenia. Bembenek (2005) looked at all patients discharged from hospital with a diagnosis of schizophrenia in Poland between 1997 and 2000. He worked out the coincidence between their birth dates and Polish flu epidemics. There was a significant statistical association between schizophrenia and flu epidemics when the patients were in the mid-trimester of their mother's pregnancy. Brown (2006) has reviewed evidence linking prenatal exposure to microbes and concluded that there is good support for the idea that a mother suffering flu, toxoplasmosis or herpes during pregnancy is at increased risk of having a child who will later go on to develop schizophrenia.

Another factor that has been linked to the later development of schizophrenia is having a difficult birth. Geddes *et al.* (1999) compared the births of 700 patients with schizophrenia and a matched control group. Premature birth and the use of resuscitation or an incubator were significantly more common in the schizophrenia group. Low birth weight and forceps delivery were also slightly more common in the schizophrenia group. The authors suggest that all these factors may be associated with oxygen starvation at birth and that oxygen starvation may thus be the factor in the biological environment that leads to schizophrenia.

LOOKING FURTHER **There has been considerable discussion in the news recently about the possible link between cannabis use and schizophrenia. It is, however, always unwise to take as fact anything scientific that you read in the press. Visit the website of the *British Medical Journal* at http://www.bmj.com/ and search it for related articles. How convincing do you find the evidence?**

Abnormal neurobiology and mental disorder

There is ample evidence showing that our central nervous systems do not function normally when we suffer from certain conditions. For example, depression is associated with reduced levels of monoamines in the brain. Monoamines are neurotransmitters – that is, chemicals that help transmit information from one brain cell to another. We can see this process in Figure 7.7. In particular, people with depression appear to have lower levels of serotonin and noradrenaline. Schizophrenia appears to be associated with unusually high levels of another monoamine, dopamine. There is evidence to suggest that one of the ways in which our genotype can make us more vulnerable to mental disorder is by leading to abnormal brain chemistry. For example, Dannlowski *et al.* (2007) analysed the genotype of 27 patients suffering from major depression. They found that abnormal variations in two genes involved in the production and breakdown of serotonin were more common in the depressed patients than in the general population.

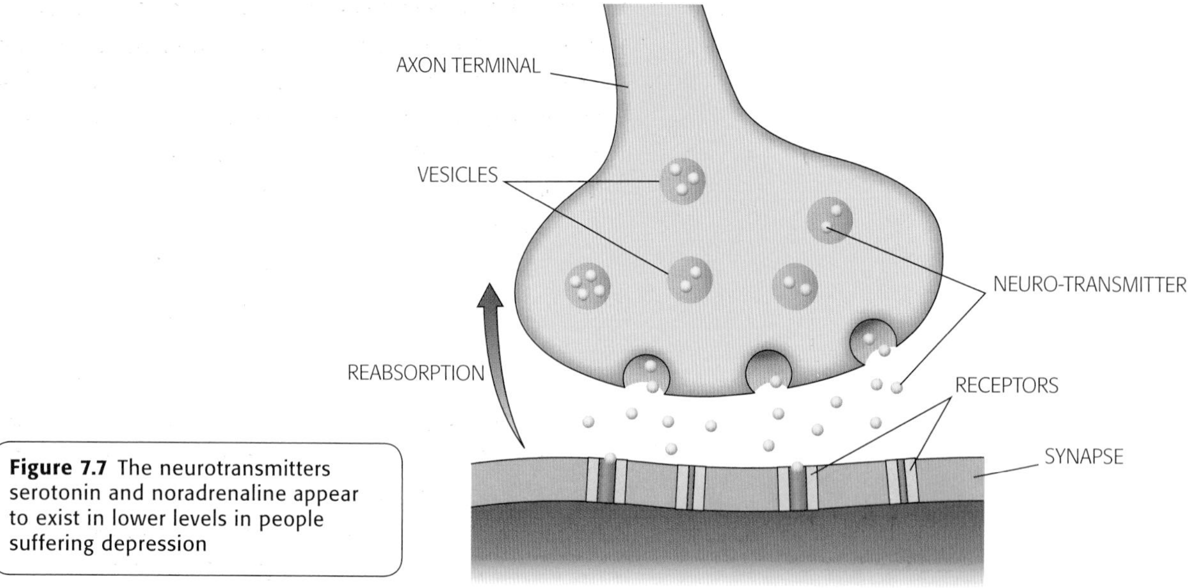

Figure 7.7 The neurotransmitters serotonin and noradrenaline appear to exist in lower levels in people suffering depression

Particular areas of the brain also appear to malfunction during mental disorder, although it is unclear whether this is simply due to the abnormal neurotransmitter levels or a separate phenomenon. It appears, for example, that in schizophrenia the left half of the brain does not function normally. In one study, Purdon *et al* (2001) compared the force applied with the right and the left hand in 21 patients with schizophrenia and a control group. Ten of the treatment group were then given anti-psychotic medication and tested again. The untreated group were significantly weaker in the right hand, though not the left. This effect disappeared after treatment. This suggests that schizophrenia involves a problem with the left brain, and that anti-psychotic drugs help correct this.

Biological Treatments

There are a number of ways in which biological principles can be applied to treating patients with mental disorder. The two most commonly used approaches are drugs and electroconvulsive therapy (ECT).

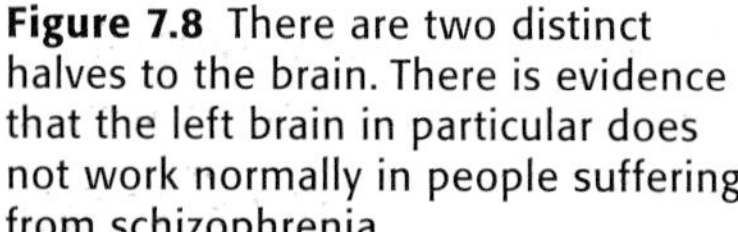

Figure 7.8 There are two distinct halves to the brain. There is evidence that the left brain in particular does not work normally in people suffering from schizophrenia

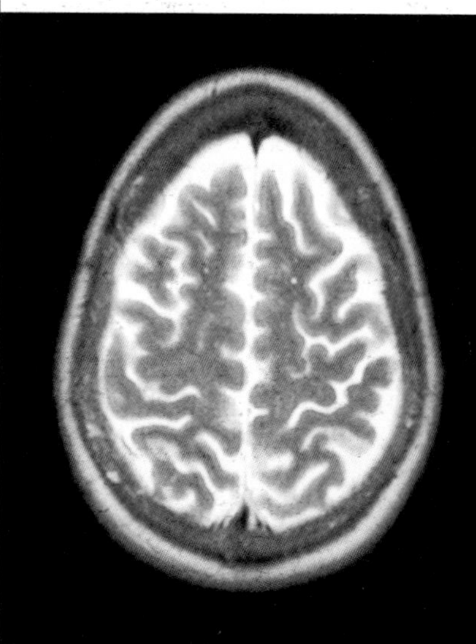

Drug treatments

We have already said that a number of mental disorders are associated with abnormally low or high levels of neurotransmitters. One way to tackle the symptoms of mental disorder is to use drugs to restore neurotransmitters to their normal level. Some newer psychiatric drugs have been specifically designed to target the action of particular neurotransmitters. These are known as rationally designed drugs. The benefits of others have been discovered accidentally. For example, the antipsychotic drug chlorpromazine was originally intended to treat hay fever and was then used as an anaesthetic. It was used to calm agitated patients with schizophrenia and only then was it discovered that coincidentally it also reduced psychotic symptoms. Most of the drugs used to tackle mental disorder fall into one of five categories:

- antidepressants: used to treat depression, anxiety and eating disorders
- mood stabilisers: used to treat bipolar disorder (manic depression)
- antipsychotics (or neuroleptics): used to treat schizophrenia and related conditions
- anxiolytics: used to treat anxiety disorders
- stimulants: used to treat attention deficit disorders and narcolepsy.

Each of these broad classes contains a number of different drugs. For example, antidepressants generally work on the monoamine neurotransmitters, but different antidepressants work in different ways and target all or particular monoamines. Monoamine oxidase inhibitors (MAOIs) stop all the monoamines being broken down so that levels build up. Tricyclics prevent serotonin or noradrenaline being reabsorbed after it has crossed a synapse, again increasing the level of these substances. However, because these old-fashioned antidepressants interfere with a number of neurotransmitters, they can have serious side effects. Tricyclics, for example, can cause drowsiness, dry mouth and constipation.

Newer antidepressants tend to work on one monoamine only. Selective serotonin reuptake inhibitors (SSRIs) such as Prozac and Seroxat stop serotonin being reabsorbed and broken down after it has crossed a synapse, and noradrenaline reuptake inhibitors (NRIs) do the same with noradrenaline. It is important to have a number of antidepressants available because individual patients vary in how they respond to each drug, in terms both of tackling their symptoms and of side effects. Different individuals also show variations in their symptoms, and this can influence the choice of drug. NRIs, for example, may be particularly useful for motivating patients whose depression has left them very inactive.

Antipsychotics can also be divided into traditional and newer, or first- and second-generation, drugs. The first antipsychotics were the phenothiazines, including chlorpromazine. These work by blocking the receptors in synapses that absorb dopamine. Effectively they reduce the action of dopamine, which is believed to be at higher than normal levels in patients with schizophrenia. Second-generation antipsychotics such as clozapine have fewer side effects. Each drug in this class is quite distinct in its chemistry, and in some cases we have no idea how they act on the brain to reduce psychotic symptoms.

Effectiveness of drug treatments

There is good evidence to suggest that drug treatments are effective in reducing symptoms. The standard procedure for testing the effectiveness of drugs is the random control trial with a placebo condition. A random control trial is an experimental procedure in which participants are randomly divided into two groups (or more than two if more than one treatment is being tested). One group is given the treatment and the other a placebo. In the case of drugs this is an inactive chemical. Each patient has no idea which condition they are in. The best random control trials are *double blind*. This means that as well as the patients, any researchers who meet them have no idea which condition they are in. This prevents them accidentally giving hints to patients about the chances of their improving as a result of the treatment.

Arroll *et al.* (2005) reviewed random control trials with placebo conditions that investigated the effectiveness of antidepressants prescribed by GPs. Ten studies were found that compared tricyclics with placebos, three comparing SSRIs with placebos and two comparing both with placebos. Overall, 56–60 per cent of patients treated with antidepressants improved, as opposed to 42–47 per cent of people given the placebo. SSRIs took longer to work but had fewer side effects. This study suggests that both tricyclics and SSRIs are moderately effective when prescribed by GPs. Similar results have been found with other psychiatric drugs. Generally there is support for the idea that drugs are reasonably effective at reducing symptoms. Of course, 'reasonably effective' covers a variety of effects for different patients. Some people find drugs extremely effective, others not at all. There are, however, potential downsides to drug treatment.

KEY TERMS

random control trial – a procedure in which patients are randomly allocated to a treatment or control condition and the outcomes compared

double blind – a procedure in which researchers who meet participants do not know which condition they are in

placebo – a substitute for a real treatment that is given as a control condition in a study of medical or psychological treatment

Figure 7.9 Many psychologists believe that drugs are overused in treating mental health problems

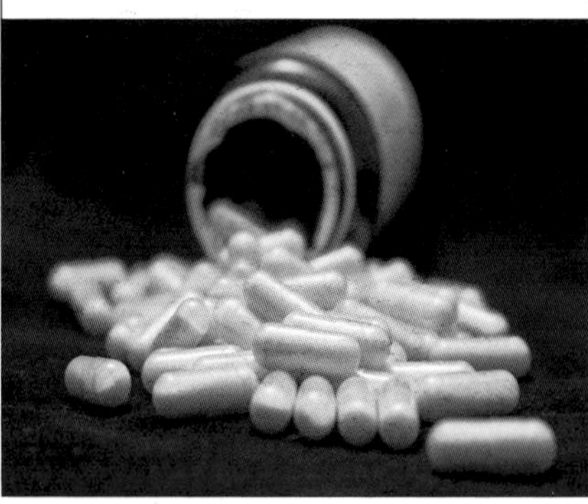

Ethical issues in the use of drugs

Although psychiatric drugs are generally reasonably effective at tackling symptoms, they remain controversial. One problem is that even though drugs work, they are not necessarily the most effective option, depending on the condition. Pinquart *et al.* (2006) reviewed studies of antidepressants and of psychological therapies used to treat depression. It emerged that psychological therapies were more effective overall. Drugs are, however, cheaper and can be provided instantly, whereas there is usually a waiting list for psychological therapies. In an ideal world these would not be considerations, and drugs would be used less often and psychological therapies more often. Many psychologists feel strongly that in spite of the cost, more psychological therapy should be made available to patients, and that we should rely less on cheap and easy drug treatment.

Drugs are also associated with side effects. Usually, newer drugs tend to produce fewer side effects than more traditional ones. However, the side effects do still exist. In a small number of cases (0.05 per cent of patients), antipsychotics can lead to *neuroleptic malignant syndrome*, while antidepressants can produce serotonin syndrome. These are similar serious neurological conditions, the symptoms of which include nausea, high blood pressure, confusion, coma and death. Up to ten per cent of cases lead to serious long-term neurological problems (Adityanjee *et al.*, 2005). These conditions are extreme and unusual; however, some milder but still unpleasant side effects are common. Antipsychotics can damage the immune system, depress mood and lead to *tardive dyskinesia*, repetitive involuntary movements of the face and limbs.

KEY TERMS

neuroleptic malignant syndrome – a rare complication of anti-psychotic drugs, a serious neurological problem, that can be fatal or lead to permanent brain damage

tardive dyskinesia – neurological damage from anti-psychotic drugs, leading to uncontrollable limb and facial movement

LOOKING FURTHER Some research has suggested that antidepressants increase the risk of suicide. The rationale for this is that they may relieve the inactivity associated with depression before they improve the patient's mood. Thus, the patient may therefore act on their mood. Evidence to suggest that antidepressants increase suicide risk is mixed. Search for studies using PubMed and the *British Medical Journal*, http://www.pubmed.gov and http://www.bmj.com/. What do you think?

Electroconvulsive therapy

Electroconvulsive therapy (ECT) is used primarily for treating depression. The procedure involves administering an electric shock for a fraction of a second to the head, inducing a seizure similar to that experienced in epilepsy. This seizure generally lasts between 15 and 60 seconds. In most cases the shock is bilateral – that is, given to both sides of the head. This is generally considered to be more effective than unilateral ECT (given to one side of the head), although also more likely to lead to side effects. ECT is generally repeated between six and twelve times, usually being administered two to three times per week.

Figure 7.10 Electroconvulsive therapy (ECT)

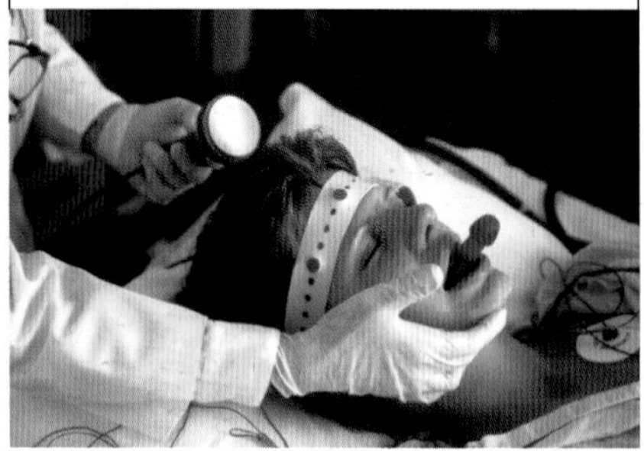

ECT has a fearsome reputation, largely a result of its early use, when the shock was relatively large and given without anaesthetic or muscle relaxants. The resulting fits sometimes resulted in broken bones and occasionally burns to the brain. Modern ECT involves small shocks given for short periods (typically 800 milliamps for 1 second), given under anaesthetic and using drugs such as succinylcholine to paralyse muscles and so prevent broken bones.

Effectiveness of ECT

Eranti *et al.* (2007) evaluated the effectiveness of ECT. Forty-six patients with major depression were randomly allocated to either ECT or a control condition in which they were exposed to powerful magnetic fields, which are also believed

KEY TERMS

major depression – a serious form of depression in which symptoms are extreme but intermittent, as opposed to the milder but constant minor depression

to benefit depressed patients. Depression was assessed immediately, after one month and after six months using standard depression scales. Fifty-nine per cent of the ECT patients went into remission, experiencing no symptoms immediately after treatment and at one-month follow-up. Only 17 per cent of the control group experienced similar remission. However, at six months follow-up most of the patients were suffering major depression again. This suggests that ECT is effective in the short term but not the long term. This pattern of good short-term gains but poor long-term effectiveness is typical of what is found in ECT research.

Ethical issues in the use of ECT

There are a number of ethical issues to consider in the use of ECT. One concerns side effects. The major side effect is memory loss. This is usually temporary, and a single treatment does not result in serious memory impairment. However, memory problems are cumulative – that is, they get worse over a course of treatment. Lisanby *et al.* (2000) randomly assigned 55 patients with major depression to either bilateral or unilateral ECT conditions. A standard memory test called the Personal and Impersonal Memory Test was administered before and in the week after ECT and two months later. A control group without ECT were also assessed for memory. In the week after ECT the patients forgot significant personal (relating to their own lives) and impersonal memories (of events not directly connected to themselves). This effect was greatest for those who had bilateral ECT. At two months follow-up they had recovered most but not all personal memories. They were still significantly worse than the control group at recalling impersonal memories. Generally, memory loss is not permanent, but neither is the remission from the symptoms of depression.

Another ethical issue concerns the ability of patients to give informed consent and the question of giving ECT against their wishes. This is tricky, because patients with severe depression may genuinely benefit from ECT but not really have the capacity to understand what it involves. In Britain, ECT requires the written consent of patients unless they have been sectioned under the Mental Health Act. Around 2000 patients a year in Britain are given ECT without their consent under the provision of the Mental Health Act. Given the side effects, this is a cause of concern to human rights campaigners. Even where consent is given, there are problems. According to a review of patient surveys by Rose *et al.* (2005), only around half of ECT patients believe they were given enough information before their treatment. Consent may thus not be truly informed.

Thinking critically about psychology

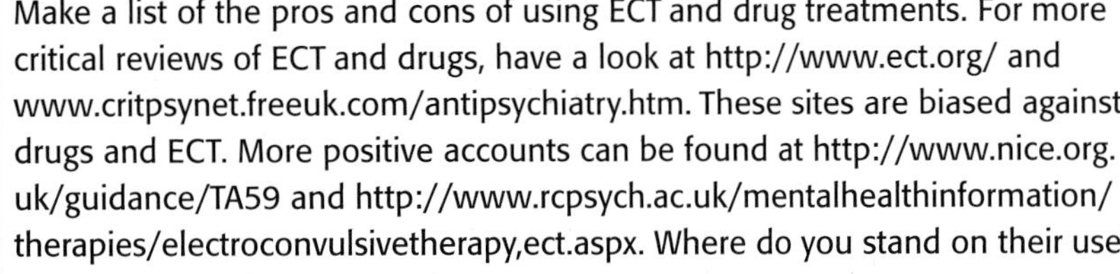
Make a list of the pros and cons of using ECT and drug treatments. For more critical reviews of ECT and drugs, have a look at http://www.ect.org/ and www.critpsynet.freeuk.com/antipsychiatry.htm. These sites are biased against drugs and ECT. More positive accounts can be found at http://www.nice.org.uk/guidance/TA59 and http://www.rcpsych.ac.uk/mentalhealthinformation/therapies/electroconvulsivetherapy,ect.aspx. Where do you stand on their use?

Thinking creatively about psychology

Put together a leaflet or Web page for students providing the sort of information you think they would like about psychiatric drugs and ECT. Use Internet sources to find any extra information you need.

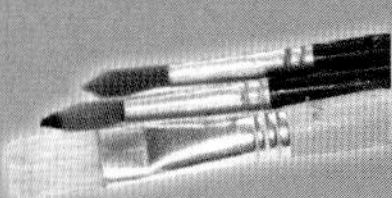

PSYCHOLOGICAL MODELS OF ABNORMALITY

The biological model has traditionally dominated the medical profession's response to psychological abnormality. Many psychologists feel that psychiatrists (medical doctors who specialise in mental disorder) and general practitioners have tended to overemphasise the biological aspects of mental disorder and to overuse biological treatments. Be careful not to oversimplify this issue, however; psychiatrists do not just use drugs and ECT. They are also trained in psychological therapies.

There are a number of psychological models that also aim to explain and treat mental disorder. In this chapter we are concerned with the three major psychological models: psychodynamic, behavioural and cognitive. Each of these offers a different way of explaining psychological abnormality and a way of treating it. It is important to say at this point that each of these models is useful for understanding particular mental disorders and for treating particular cases. Our task is *not* to choose a single correct psychological model, just to understand why we have them all.

The psychodynamic model

The psychodynamic model is the oldest of the psychological models of abnormality, first developed by Sigmund Freud at the end of the nineteenth Century. Freud was a neurologist, a medical doctor specialising in studying the nervous system. Although he believed that some mental disorders were biological in origin, he came to believe that many are the result of psychological factors. In particular, Freud believed that poor-quality early relationships and traumatic experiences in childhood led to the development of psychological abnormality.

Early relationships and mental health

To Freud and later psychodynamic psychologists, the child's developing personality, both normal and abnormal, is determined largely by its relationships with its parents. The poet Philip Larkin put it this way:

They f**k you up, your mum and dad.
They may not mean to, but they do.
They fill you with the faults they had
And add some extra, just for you.

Poor-quality relationships with parents generally make people more prone to mental health problems. Freud (1905) went on to speculate that childhood can be seen as a series of stages, each of which is dominated by particular aspects of the relationship with parents. As adults, we can regress to a childhood stage and behave in ways typical of that age. In the oral stage (0–1 year), children are forming their first close relationships. Problems at this stage can lead to problems in relationships such as over-dependence on others. This can manifest in adulthood as what is now called *dependent personality disorder*. In the anal stage (1–3 years) the child–parent relationship is centred on the first experiences the child has of having authority imposed on them. There can be conflict at this stage, for example over potty training. This can lead in turn to the anal personality characteristics of stinginess, stubbornness and *orderliness*, intolerance of mess or ambiguity. Freud believed that some anxiety disorders, in particular *obsessive-compulsive disorder* (OCD), can be explained in terms of this stage of development.

Figure 7.11 According to psychodynamic theory, the major factor affecting this child's mental health will be the quality of their relationship with their parents

KEY TERMS

dependent personality disorder – personality characterised by extreme dependence on and submission to others

obsessive-compulsive disorder – an anxiety disorder in which patients show repetitive thoughts or behaviours; a classic example is compulsive washing

Early trauma and mental health

According to Freud and later psychodynamic psychologists, traumatic experiences in childhood can also lead to later psychological abnormality. This is because, to Freud, emotion functions like physical energy. It can be transformed into another sort of energy or it can be discharged, but it does not simply disappear. This means that negative emotion resulting from traumatic experiences in childhood remains somewhere in the mind and later becomes transformed into symptoms. For example, Freud (1917) proposed that many cases of depression are the result of experiences of loss in childhood. Freud explained adult depression as delayed mourning for a childhood loss. Other childhood traumas may lead to later symptoms. A condition common in Freud's time, rather less common today, is conversion disorder. This involves physical symptoms that result from psychological factors. He illustrated this in the case of Anna O; see *Classic Research*.

CLASSIC RESEARCH

Breuer J & Freud S (1896) Studies on hysteria. *The Complete Works of Sigmund Freud, volume II.*

CASE HISTORY

Anna O was a 21-year-old woman. She was extremely intellectual in her interests. Her symptoms developed when nursing her father through a long illness. For the first five months of his illness Anna O devoted herself to caring for him; however, her own health then deteriorated and she suffered weakness, anaemia and lack of interest in food. She became bedridden, and so was unable to continue to nurse her father. It was at this point that further symptoms began, including headaches, a narrowing of the visual field, deafness, paralysis of the neck, and loss of sensation in the limbs. Just before her father died, she also suffered speech-related symptoms, forgetting words, then becoming mute for two weeks.

Following the death of her father, Anna's symptoms got worse. She suffered new symptoms, including prosopagnosia (inability to recognise faces). During this period, Anna also had symptoms of dissociation, displaying two personalities. One was anxious and depressed but aware of what was happening. The second was irrational and aggressive. At this point Anna was removed from the family home to a country sanatorium. Here she began what she called her 'talking cure'. Breuer noted that when allowed to speak unchecked, Anna tended to speak of events prior to the development of her symptoms, and that she would frequently link events to her symptoms. For example, she made an association between her deafness and an embarrassing childhood incident in which Anna's brother had caught her listening at her parent's door one night as they had sex. During this process the symptoms would often worsen; however, following the focus on each symptom it would disappear. Anna's deafness, for example, disappeared as soon as she had recalled the incident with her brother.

INTERPRETATION

Breuer and Freud explained Anna's symptoms and treatment in terms of Freud's understanding of emotion as physical energy. Her frustrated intellectual abilities and a series of childhood events such as hearing her parents having sex had led to a build-up of negative emotions. The trauma of her father's illness had triggered a process whereby this energy was converted into physical symptoms. When she talked to Breuer, she was able to discharge her feelings (this is called catharsis), and so her symptoms were relieved.

Figure 7.12 Anna O

KEY TERMS

conversion disorder – a condition in which stress leads to a physical symptom with no physical basis, such as paralysis, deafness or blindness

adult baby syndrome – a condition in which adults wish they were still babies and act as babies, for example wearing nappies and drinking milk

Figure 7.13 A scan of the left brain of Kanaan *et al.*'s conversion disorder patient

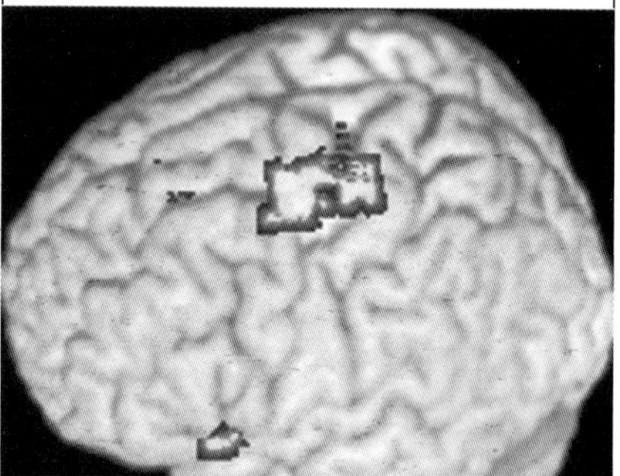

The general psychodynamic assumptions that childhood trauma and poor early relationships make us more vulnerable to mental health problems are borne out by modern research. In one study, Massie & Szajnberg (2002) followed the development of 76 people from birth to the age of 30. Quality of parental relationships was assessed in infancy, and traumatic events were recorded throughout the 30 years. At 30, mental health was assessed using standard psychiatric measures. Mental health problems were moderately associated with poor parental relationships and strongly associated with traumatic events during childhood.

There are also some conditions that may be best explained using psychodynamic ideas. One of these is conversion disorder. Kanaan *et al.* (2007) questioned a patient with conversion disorder (her main symptom was right-side weakness) about a range of events while scanning her brain. When she was asked about a particularly traumatic life-event (her partner leaving her), she denied that this was important. However, her scan revealed that activity in her left motor cortex (the area of the brain that controls movement of the right side; see Figure 7.13) declined. This suggests that Freud was correct to say that conversion symptoms result from traumatic events.

Another condition perhaps best explained by a psychodynamic approach is infantilism (adult baby syndrome). We can look at a case of adult baby syndrome; see *Research Now*.

Pate JE & Gabbard GO (2003) Adult baby syndrome. *American Journal of Psychiatry,* **160** 1932–6

CASE HISTORY

Mr A was a white male aged 35 years. He lived alone in a flat. He worked in law enforcement, keeping his unusual behaviour a secret. He described himself as heterosexual but had not dated women for some years and had never had sex. He had previously sought a psychiatric evaluation but never followed up for treatment because "the lady was mean" (p1932). Mr A described himself as a baby. He had wanted to be a baby since the age of 12. Since the age of 17 he had worn nappies, in which he would urinate, defecate and masturbate. He frequently ate baby food and slept in a crib. He described wanting to "be taken care of by a mommy who can hold me and rock me and give me a bottle" (p1932). Mr A was the older of two children, who had been adopted. He reported a good relationship with his adoptive parents, being generally closer to his adoptive father than his mother. He had never sought contact with his biological parents. In therapy, Mr A frequently missed or refused to schedule appointments. He was also very conflicted between wanting to grow up and remain a baby. Although he reported seeking treatment in order to stop wanting to be a baby, he demanded nappies on prescription and to be admitted by the psychiatrist to a nursery. Treatment ended when Mr A decided in the end that he liked being a baby and did not wish to change.

INTERPRETATION

Cases like this are most easily understood from a psychodynamic perspective. Mr A displayed regression to infantile behaviour, perhaps in response to the trauma of adoption or to his lack of a close maternal relationship in early childhood. His difficulty in forming relationships with women, shown by his virgin status and anger with a previous psychiatrist, can also be understood as the result of not having a close relationship with his mother.

There are, however, some criticisms of the psychodynamic approach and of Freud's work in general. Freud's ideas were based on self-analysis, informal observation and interpretation of what his patients said in therapy. By modern standards this is poor science, and some psychologists believe that any system based on such poor evidence should be abandoned. Even if we consider that to be extreme, there is no doubt that some of Freud's ideas, for example the oral and anal stages, are really just speculation. There is, for example, little evidence linking the anal stage to the development of OCD.

Psychoanalysis: a psychodynamic therapy

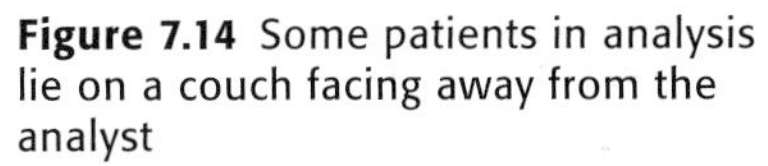

Figure 7.14 Some patients in analysis lie on a couch facing away from the analyst

The major application of the psychodynamic approach to psychology is in providing psychological therapy to help people suffering mental health problems or life difficulties. There are a number of variations on psychodynamic therapy, the most intensive and long-term being *psychoanalysis.* This takes place four to five times a week for several years. Psychoanalysis involves the patient (or *analysand*) sitting or lying comfortably and free-associating – that is, saying whatever comes into their mind, including childhood memories, dreams, current life situations and feelings towards the analyst. The analyst responds to this with interpretations of the links between past experience, current problems and symptoms, and nature of the patient–analyst relationship.

Early experience and catharsis

From a psychodynamic perspective we are all unconsciously influenced to a greater or lesser extent by the nature of our early experiences, in particular traumatic ones. One of the key aims of psychoanalysis is to loosen the hold these experiences have on us. Trauma can be remembered, re-experienced and worked through in the safety of the therapy room. In terms of Freud's theory, the emotion experienced as a result of a traumatic experience can be discharged. This process is called *catharsis*. Catharsis is undoubtedly one of the factors that make all psychological therapies helpful.

Early relationships and transference

A key factor affecting our mental health and our ability to relate to other people in adulthood is the quality of our early relationships. In psychoanalysis there is a tendency to play out the nature of our relationships with key people such as parents in our behaviour towards the analyst. This tendency is called *transference*, because feelings towards important figures like parents are bring *transferred* on to the analyst. To maximise the chances of transference developing, analysts tend to give away little or no information about their own lives. By feeding back to the patient how their current relationships are distorted by the influence of early relationships the analyst can give the patient insight into what goes wrong in their relationships. Transference interpretation is arguably the most important technique in classical psychoanalysis.

Reparenting

From the psychodynamic perspective, the single biggest influence on our development is the relationship with our parents. As well as developing insight into the ways our adult behaviour is linked to our relationship with parents and getting any lingering negative childhood emotions off our chests, we can also benefit from the experience in psychoanalysis of having a good-quality relationship with a responsible adult. In a sense, the analyst is 're-parenting' the patient. For patients who have never had a good-quality relationship before, this is an absolutely crucial aspect to therapy. For this reason, psychoanalysts take great care to maintain boundaries in their sessions, for example never being late or cancelling sessions.

Effectiveness of psychoanalysis

Early studies of psychoanalysis cast doubt on its effectiveness. Hans Eysenck (1952) reviewed early studies of outcomes of psychoanalysis. He concluded that there was no evidence that psychoanalysis increased the probability of patients getting better. Patients with and without analysis both showed a rate of improvement of around 66 per cent. However, the Eysenck study has some fairly serious weaknesses. He included some dubious studies that showed poor outcomes for therapy conditions yet ignored superior studies that found good outcomes. In addition, he counted only complete cure as improvement in analysis, but recognised even small improvements in patients who did not have analysis. Finally, he did not take account of how long patients took to get better, so a patient without treatment whose symptoms declined after several years was counted as equivalent to one whose symptoms declined in weeks during analysis. We would therefore be unwise to take too much notice of this study. Re-analysing Eysenck's data, Bergin & Garfield (1978) estimated that around 80 per cent patients in analysis and 30 per cent with no treatment got significantly better.

Modern research paints a much more positive picture of the effectiveness of psychoanalysis. Perhaps the best evidence comes from a recent systematic review by Leichsenring & Leibing (2007). The systematic review method is the standard procedure for deciding on the effectiveness of any medical or psychological treatment. Reviewers choose in advance what makes a published study of sufficient quality to include. They then search for any study they can find on the topic, in this case the effectiveness of psychodynamic therapies. Those that meet the inclusion criteria are reviewed and conclusions are reached based on the collective findings. In this review, twenty-four studies met the inclusion criteria, nine of psychoanalysis and the fifteen of brief dynamic therapy. Twenty-three of the twenty-four studies showed that psychodynamic therapies, including psychoanalysis, are as effective as the other standard therapies.

LOOKING FURTHER You can see the report of an influential study of the effectiveness of psychoanalysis in Sweden at http://www.ipa.org.uk/research/sandell.asp. What does this study suggest about the effectiveness of psychoanalysis?

Ethical issues in psychoanalysis

Although there is no longer any serious doubt that psychoanalysis is effective in treating mental disorder, its use is in decline in Britain, particularly in the National Health Service. This is because it is so intensive and long-term. Remember that classical psychoanalysis takes place four or five times a week for up to several years. This is tremendously expensive, and so in most cases psychoanalysis is not a particularly cost-effective treatment. While a minority of patients may really need this intensive and long-term treatment, most people can get better using much quicker and hence cheaper therapies. Also, as well as being expensive, having therapy most days for long periods is disruptive to patients' lives. An hour a day in therapy plus travelling time can interfere with work, child-rearing and social life. Being in analysis may also affect patients' lives in other ways. Some people may, for example, find that once they have insight into the ways their relationship with their parents has affected them, that relationship gets worse.

Thinking critically about psychology

Critically compare the use of drugs and the use of psychoanalysis to treat mental disorder. Consider rates of improvement, cost and ethical issues. Think, too, about whether they would be suitable for the same patients.

The behavioural model

The behavioural model is a radically different psychological model. Whereas the psychodynamic model is based on speculation about the deepest aspects of the unconscious mind, behavioural psychologists base their ideas on laboratory experiments that examine observable behaviour. Behavioural psychologists are concerned with the learning of behaviours through experience. The process of classical conditioning has been particularly well studied in relation to abnormality.

Classical conditioning

KEY TERMS

phobia – an irrational fear of an object or situation

paraphilia – a sexual disorder in which the patient becomes sexually aroused in response to non-sexual stimuli

Classical conditioning takes place when we come to associate something that initially does not produce any response (called a neutral stimulus) with something that already produces that response (called the unconditioned stimulus). This sort of association develops when the neutral and unconditioned stimuli are *paired* – that is, we experience them together. This leads us to respond to the neutral stimulus in the same way as we responded to the unconditioned stimulus. The neutral stimulus is no longer neutral because it does lead to a response, so it is called the conditioned stimulus.

Classical conditioning is particularly useful for explaining conditions in which the main symptom is a response to a stimulus. For example, in phobias we respond with fear to something, and in paraphilias (sexual fetishes) we respond with sexual arousal. Both phobias and paraphilias can be explained, at least in some cases, by classical conditioning. Watson & Rayner (1920) demonstrated the effect of classical conditioning, deliberately creating a phobia in a young boy, often called Little Albert.

CLASSIC RESEARCH

Watson JB & Rayner R (1920) Conditioned emotional responses. *Journal of Experimental Psychology,* **3** 1–14

AIM

To explore whether a fear response could be created by classical conditioning.

PROCEDURE

A nine-month-old infant was chosen and assessed for emotional stability. He was unafraid of a range of stimuli, including a white rat, a rabbit and some wooden blocks, although he was afraid of a loud noise (made with a hammer and a steel bar). Two months later he was shown the rat again, and when he reached for it, the loud noise was made, scaring him. This was repeated five times, one week later. After a further 31 days during which Albert was neither presented with the experimental objects (such as the rat or rabbit) nor exposed to the loud noise, he was tested again.

FINDINGS

Whenever the steel bar was struck, Albert displayed fear. By the second trial, he was cautious about the rat and leaned away when it was presented. A further five days later, Albert cried in response to the rat and various similar objects, including a fur coat, cotton wool and a Father Christmas beard, and these responses persisted until the final testing, seven weeks after the start of the study.

CONCLUSION

Albert was classically conditioned to be afraid of the rat and became afraid of other, similar white or furry objects such as cotton wool and a Santa Claus mask with a beard. This is a process called generalisation.

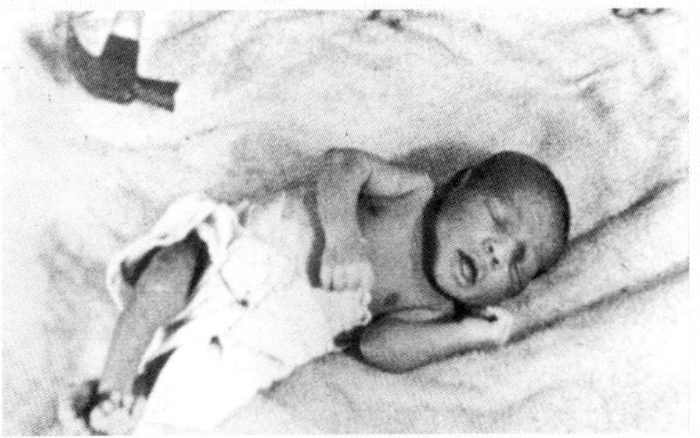

Figure 7.15 The bar is struck near Albert, frightening him

Thinking critically about psychology

What ethical issues does the Little Albert study raise? What ethical guidelines in particular would it breach today?

In the Little Albert study the loud noise was the unconditioned stimulus, frightening the boy. The rat was a neutral stimulus, but Albert became conditioned to associate it with the noise, so he came to fear it. This sort of irrational fear is a phobia. In the paraphilias, we come to associate an unconditioned stimulus (such as an attractive member of our target sex) with a neutral stimulus. The neutral stimulus can be something harmless such as sexy underwear or particular music (see *Media Watch*). However, it might be something potentially harmful like a school uniform. In the same way as Little Albert's fear of the rat generalised to other white, furry objects, a learned sexual response to school uniforms might become generalised to schoolgirls. This is at least a partial explanation of paedophilia. This is why Britney Spears and Baby Spice caused such controversy when they posed provocatively in school uniforms.

Media watch: conditioned response

Dr Vernon Coleman's Casebook, *The People*, 16 January 2000

The Barry White experience

Q My boyfriend and I tried an experiment that I'd like to tell you about. For two months, we made love every night with Barry White on continuous play on our CD player. Now, whenever either of us hears that music we become sexually aroused.

A A long-dead foreigner called Pavlov did much the same sort of experiment but used dogs, bells and food. Your research project sounds far more interesting and I suggest that you apply for a grant to help you continue with your studies. You might like to see if your boyfriend's enthusiasm can be triggered by constant exposure to the sound of Abergwili Male Voice Choir airing their tonsils.

Alternatively, try Seth Pitt and Eva Legova singing *Tonight's the Night*. Meanwhile, a warning. You could find yourself in a tricky situation if a Barry White track is played when you're in your local pub.

Figure 7.16 Barry White

Thinking practically about psychology

Explain how someone might acquire a sexual arousal response to schoolgirls through watching Britney Spears or Baby Spice by a process of classical conditioning. Use the terms *neutral stimulus*, *unconditioned stimulus*, *generalisation* and *conditioned stimulus* in your answer.

Systematic desensitisation: a behavioural therapy

We can use the principles of classical conditioning in various approaches to therapy. One of these is systematic desensitisation. The aim of systematic desensitisation is to unlearn conditioned responses, most commonly phobias. Mary Jones (1924), a student of John Watson of the infamous Little Albert study, treated a boy (Little Peter) with a phobia of rabbits by placing him in the same room as a caged rabbit and gradually moving the rabbit closer until eventually he was able to touch it. This gradual increase in the level of the fear-arousing stimulus is the basis of systematic desensitisation.

Modern desensitisation involves two processes: relaxation, and exposure to the conditioned stimulus. We cannot be relaxed and afraid at the same time; by definition, fear involves a high level of physical arousal. Patients learn in desensitisation that they can remain relaxed in the presence of the thing they fear. Relaxation can be achieved by hypnosis or meditation, or by anxiolytic drugs like Valium. The patient is then exposed to the thing they fear, working through an anxiety hierarchy. This starts with a form of exposure they feel reasonably comfortable with and building up to the one they most fear. An arachnophobic patient may thus start by being exposed to a small picture of a spider and end up with a Venezuelan tarantula on their face. Once the patient successfully remains relaxed with this sort of intense exposure to the object of their phobia, they will have learned not to fear it. In a recent study, Newman & Adams (2004) successfully treated a boy for a phobia of dogs – see *Research Now*.

RESEARCH NOW

Newman C & Adams K (2004) Managing dog phobia. *British Journal of Learning Disabilities*, **32** 35–8

CASE HISTORY

The patient, MV, was a 17-year-old boy with a moderate learning difficulty. The goal of therapy was to reduce his phobic response to dogs to the extent that he would remain still when he and his carer met a dog. MV was trained to relax using breathing exercises and by focusing his gaze away from dogs towards his mother. He was then exposed to dogs according to an anxiety hierarchy (shown in Table 7.3). This treatment was at first judged to be successful; however, 18 months after the initial treatment, MV's parents asked for further treatment because he was still afraid of dogs off their lead. This time, more time was spent achieving relaxation at the higher end of the anxiety hierarchy, including eight sessions with the most feared situation: meeting unfamiliar dogs off their lead in a park. At the end of 26 sessions, MV was able to remain relaxed in the presence of strange loose dogs.

INTERPRETATION

MV was desensitised to dogs, learning to stay relaxed at each level in the anxiety hierarchy in turn. The first course of treatment did not work enough on the situations at the top end of the hierarchy, so MV remained afraid of dogs off a lead. In the second course of treatment it took several exposures to achieve relaxation at the top end of the anxiety hierarchy.

Table 7.03 MV's anxiety hierarchy

Stage in hierarchy	Description
1	Introduction to our dogs via photographs
2	Dog introduced – no contact/access
3	Access to dog provided
4	Dog on lead brought into personal space
5	Loose dog introduced – no access (other side of window)
6	Loose dog introduced – limited access provided (in another room, entry door to client's room blocked by a waist-high object)
7	Loose dog introduced – complete access provided (loose dog in same room)
8	Generalise to other dogs (introduce new dogs to avoid familiarity) (stages 1–8 were at MV's home)
9	Generalise the environment (observe dogs loose and leashed from a distance at local parks)
10	Generalise the environment (close proximity to loose and leashed dogs at parks)

Source: Newman and Adams (2004)

Figure 7.17 Meeting a strange dog like this would cause MV considerable anxiety

Thinking critically about psychology

Compare the cases of Mr A (p200) and MV. After psychodynamic treatment, Mr A decided not to alter his behaviour but was happier about it. MV's behaviour was successfully altered.

1. What does this tell us about the differences between psychodynamic and behavioural models?
2. Do you see each of these outcomes as equally successful?
3. Could Mr A have been treated behaviourally? You may wish to Google 'aversion therapy'.
4. From a psychodynamic perspective, what might be the risk of treating Mr A behaviourally?

Thinking creatively about psychology

Imagine you are working with someone with a phobia of escalators. Put together an anxiety hierarchy that might help desensitise them.

Effectiveness of systematic desensitisation

Cases like that of MV show that systematic desensitisation can be effective in the treatment of phobias. There are many such cases, most commonly of treatment of phobias, but also for paraphilias. Martz (2003) has described the desensitisation of a 22-year-old woman who could only orgasm by the extremely dangerous practice of autoerotic asphyxiation (self-strangulation). By getting her to repeatedly write about autoerotic asphyxiation in ten sessions of therapy, in which she did not become sexually aroused, the therapist successfully desensitised her to asphyxiation. Behavioural treatments that reduce the sexual response in paraphilias are often accompanied by masturbatory reconditioning, so that patients learn to become aroused in response to normal sexual stimuli. In the Martz case, the patient was encouraged to use a vibrator to achieve orgasm without asphyxiation.

Case studies alone are not usually considered sufficient evidence for the effectiveness of a therapy. There is evidence, though, from studies with control conditions to show that people treated by desensitisation do better than those who do not get treatment. Brosnan & Thorpe (2006) used a ten-week desensitisation programme to help 16 technophobic students (who were afraid of computers) on an information technology course. As compared to a control group who had no desensitisation, their anxiety levels were significantly lower at the end of the course. Zettle (2003) treated 12 students with a fear of maths by desensitisation. They showed significantly reduced levels of anxiety, unlike a control group of students who were not desensitised.

KEY TERMS

autoerotic asphyxiation – a dangerous sexual practice in which partial strangulation is used in an attempt to heighten arousal

technophobia – fear of computers and/or related technology

flooding – a behavioural therapy in which patients are exposed to an extreme form of the thing they fear

Figure 7.18 Flooding is a traumatic alternative to systematic desensitisation

Ethical issues in systematic desensitisation

Behavioural therapies to treat phobias all raise ethical issues because they involve exposing patients to things they are afraid of and thus making them anxious. In deciding which behavioural treatment to use, there is a trade-off between effectiveness and ethics. Systematic desensitisation is the least traumatic option; however, alternative treatments that cause patients more anxiety are often more effective. *Flooding* is the most extreme form of exposure therapy. It involves exposing patients to the thing they fear in an extreme form for a small number of long sessions. Arachnophobics may thus find themselves face to face with a huge spider for two to three hours at a time. In a recent review, Choy *et al.* (2006) concluded that flooding was significantly more effective at tackling phobias than systematic desensitisation but that patients found it so traumatic that they frequently walked out of therapy sessions or did not return. There are clearly good reasons to go with systematic desensitisation!

The cognitive model

It is well known that people suffering a range of mental disorders, most obviously depression and anxiety, think about and perceive the world differently from the way most of us do. Anxious people tend to see the world as particularly threatening, while depressed people tend to see it as hopeless and unrewarding. The cognitive model focuses on the sort of thinking patterns that are associated with mental disorder. Two theorists have been particularly important in the development of the cognitive model, Albert Ellis and Aaron Beck.

Ellis' ABC model

Albert Ellis (1977b) was especially interested in how people overreacted to events, influenced by pre-existing irrational beliefs. He proposed the ABC model to explain this, where A = the activating event, B = beliefs and C = consequences. Palmer & Dryden (1995) have applied this to explaining a student's response to failing an exam (Table 7.4).

Table 7.4 An example of the ABC model

A	Activating event	Failing an exam
B	Beliefs	'I should have passed', 'I can't bear not passing'
C	Consequences	Depression

This sort of irrational belief makes people overreact to negative life-events with anxiety or depression. Abrams & Ellis (1996) identify two particularly important types of irrational belief.

- *Musturbation* is the tendency to think that we *must* always succeed in everything. This makes us very sensitive to failure.
- *I-can't-stand-it-itis* is the belief when something does not go smoothly this is a disaster. This makes us overreact to minor problems.

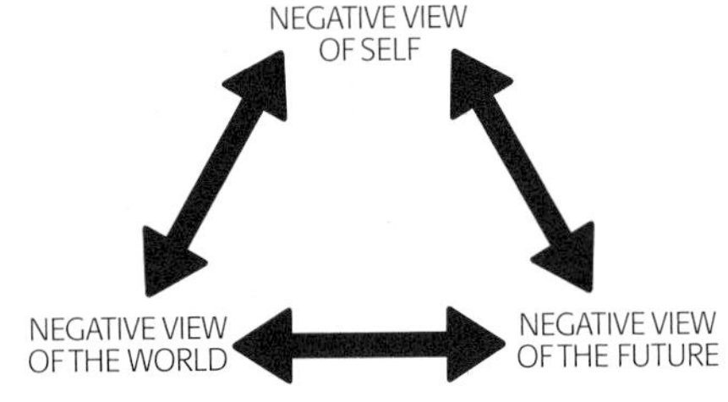

Figure 7.19 Beck's cognitive triad

Beck's negative thinking

Beck was particularly interested in the relationship between negative thinking and depression. Beck (1976) pointed out three types of negative thinking that are particularly common in people suffering from depression. The first of these is negative automatic thinking. The *cognitive triad* of negative automatic thoughts consists of a negative view of the self, a negative view of the world and a negative view of the future. The cognitive triad is shown in Figure 7.19.

Beck's second form of negative thinking involves attending to the negative aspects of a situation and ignoring the positive aspects. This causes us to overestimate the 'downside' of any situation and reach the most negative possible conclusions. To most people, half a glass of drink is a glass half-full. A depressed person will typically see it as half-empty instead.

Figure 7.20 A depressed person is likely to see a half-full glass as half-empty

The third form of negative thinking identified by Beck involves *negative self-schemas*. Our self-schema contains all our information about ourselves, including beliefs, feelings, etc. We acquire this negative set of beliefs about ourselves through criticism from our parents. When we meet a new situation, we interpret it using any relevant schemas, including our self-schema. If our beliefs about and feelings towards ourselves are negative, then so will be any interpretation we make about ourselves in a new situation. Say, for example, we meet someone we fancy and they are nice to us. If our self-schema contains the information that we are unattractive and unlovable, then we will not interpret the person being nice to us as meaning they fancy us. We might think instead that they feel sorry for us.

Both Beck and Ellis emphasised *cognitive vulnerability* to anxiety and depression. This means that we are more vulnerable to these conditions if we have particular patterns of thinking. There is plenty of evidence to support a role for cognitive vulnerability. Koster *et al.* (2005) examined the role of attention to negative stimuli in depression. Fifteen depressed and 15 matched non-depressed students were identified and given a selective attention task. They were presented with positive (e.g. successful, powerful), negative (e.g. loser, failure) or neutral words (e.g. crane, paper) for 1.5 seconds each on a computer screen. Half a second after each word, they saw a square on either the left or the right of the screen. Their task was to press Q if the square was on the left and 5 if it was on the right. How long they took to identify the location of the square was a measure of their attention to the words. The longer they took to locate the square, the harder they found it to disengage their attention from the word. The depressed participants took an average of 12 milliseconds to disengage from words like 'loser' whereas the non-depressed group took only two milliseconds. This shows that depressed people do attend to negative stimuli, as Beck suggested. There is also evidence to support the role of cognitive vulnerability in anxiety. Armfield (2007) demonstrated this with arachnophobia – see *Research Now*.

Armfield J (2007) Perceptions of spider characteristics and predicted spider fear. *Journal of Anxiety Disorders,* **21** 691–703

AIM

To test whether beliefs about how unpredictable, uncontrollable and dangerous spiders are affect how afraid people are of them.

PROCEDURE

One hundred and sixty-nine Australian students took part in the study. They were asked to imagine as vividly as possible that they were instructed to place their hand on a hinged divider of an aquarium. On the other side was a spider. They were shown a picture of a black house spider to help them imagine it. In different conditions they were given different information about the spider and the apparatus. In a high danger condition they were told it could give a painful bite. In the low danger condition they were told it could not bite. In a low uncontrollability condition they were told that they could remove the spider using a trap door if it approached their hand. In a high uncontrollability condition they were told they had to keep their hand still if the spider approached. In the high unpredictability condition they were told the spider made sudden movements. In the low unpredictability condition they were told that it did not. Participants were again assessed for spider phobia.

FINDINGS

Following the task, participants in the high uncontrollability, high danger and high unpredictability conditions were more afraid of spiders than those in the low conditions. Unpredictability had the biggest effect.

CONCLUSIONS

Manipulating people's beliefs about a spider affected how afraid they were of spiders in general. This shows that our beliefs make us more or less cognitively vulnerable to anxiety.

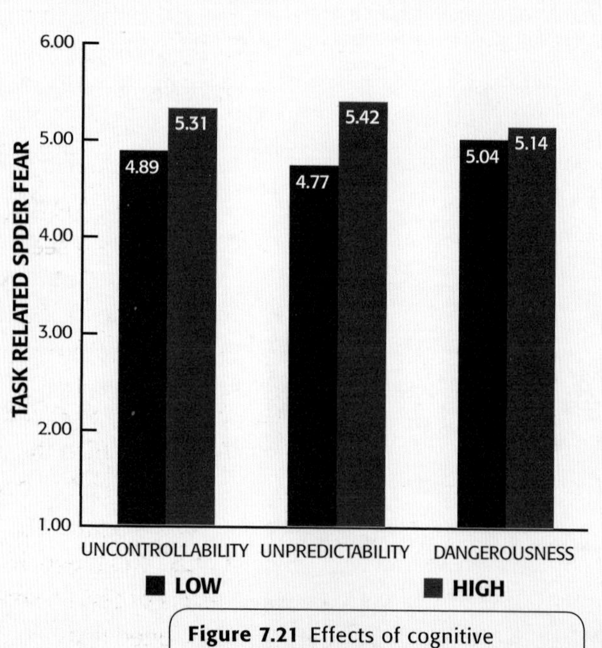

Figure 7.21 Effects of cognitive vulnerability on spider phobia
From Armfield (2007)

Cognitive behavioural therapy (CBT)

CBT is now the most commonly used form of psychological therapy, in particular among psychologists. It usually takes place once a week or fortnight for between five and twenty sessions. All CBT involves helping patients identify irrational and unhelpful thoughts and trying to change them. The rationale is that our thoughts affect our feelings and behaviour, so by changing our thoughts we can make ourselves feel better.

There are different varieties of CBT, using different techniques to change unhelpful ways of thinking. Ellis' approach, for example, focuses on identifying unhelpful beliefs and vigorously arguing against them. Beck's approach involves using *reality testing* experiments to test irrational beliefs, so someone who believed they never enjoyed socialising would be persuaded to go out and record in a diary that they had enjoyed it. Most cognitive behavioural therapists use a blend of techniques like this. They may also combine cognitive techniques with elements of behavioural therapies. A patient might, for example, be encouraged to desensitise themselves to something they fear by exposing them to it.

Thinking creatively about psychology

Design a study to find out which is the most effective treatment (psychological or biological) for arachnophobia. Look back to p195, which explains some of the features of good outcome studies.

Thinking practically about psychology

Brenda is suffering from severe anxiety over her university application. She has applied for Cambridge and is unlikely to get a place. She has also applied for the same course at a range of universities for which she expects to get the necessary grades, but to which she does not want to go.

1 Identify one way in which musturbation might be affecting Brenda.
2 Identify one way in which she might also be affected by I-can't-stand-it-itis.
3 How might Brenda be treated using CBT?

LOOKING FURTHER

CBT can be carried out via interactive websites. Most of these require a GP's referral, but if you are interested in seeing how they work this one is free: http://moodgym.anu.edu.au/. Note that if you have, or think you may have, a problem with depression or anxiety, you MUST seek help from a professional such as your family GP or college counsellor. DO NOT try to treat yourself using this or any other website. We recommend this site for demonstration purposes only.

Effectiveness of CBT

Although CBT is the most recently developed of the therapies discussed in this chapter it has been well researched and there is an impressive body of research supporting its effectiveness. Butler *et al.* (2006) reviewed studies of CBT and found 16 published meta-analyses, each of which included the results of several smaller studies. From this very large body of evidence they concluded that CBT was very effective for treating depression, generalised anxiety, panic disorder, social phobias, post-traumatic stress and childhood depressive and anxiety disorders. It was also moderately effective for marital distress, anger and chronic pain. The Royal College of Psychiatrists recommends CBT as the most effective psychological treatment for moderate and severe depression.

Although CBT is strongly supported by research and is increasingly dominating clinical psychology, there are some grounds for caution. Not all studies have revealed such positive findings, especially when CBT has been used to treat conditions other than depression and anxiety. In an outcome study of treatment for alcohol dependency, Sandahl *et al.* (1998) found that at 15-month follow-up significantly more patients were abstaining from alcohol after psychodynamic therapy than after CBT.

Review studies are always at risk of bias. Harrington *et al.* (1998) have pointed out that several published reviews of studies of CBT simply fail to mention studies where CBT was found not to work, so showing bias in favour of CBT. There is also an issue over the kind of research carried out on CBT. The vast majority of studies have focused on the short-term benefits for patients who only show symptoms of one condition. This means that we know much less about long-term effects of CBT or its effects on patients with a wider range of symptoms.

Ethical issues in CBT

CBT involves altering patients' thinking patterns. The therapist therefore has considerable power over the patient to determine how they think. This may be potentially open to abuse. A responsible therapist would negotiate any changes to a patient's cognitions, and only use cognitive techniques to make changes that the patient wanted to make. Ellis' brand of cognitive behavioural therapy raises particular ethical problems because it is so *directive* – it tells people exactly how they should think. Take, for example, a patient who experiences work-related stress because they believe their employers pay too little and work them too hard. A therapist using Ellis' approach might identify these as irrational beliefs. However, what if the patient's employers really were underpaying and abusing the rights of their workforce? The use of CBT might end up allowing them to continue to do so (Jarvis, 2003).

Trower & Jones (2001) surveyed CBT practitioners and found that they generally saw Ellis' style as too directive. Overwhelmingly, British cognitive behavioural therapists did not share Ellis' belief that we should be told how to think. Ellis' approach is more popular in the United States, where the culture generally places more emphasis on individual responsibility. Neenan (2004) suggests that Ellis' aggressive approach to CBT is offensive in Britain, not just because of its political implications but also because it is impolite, and we have a tremendous emphasis on politeness.

CHAPTER SUMMARY

- We can define abnormality in a number of ways. One of these is when behaviour deviates from social norms. However, this approach can restrict personal freedom, and makes it hard to judge abnormality in those from other cultures.
- We can also define abnormality as the failure to function adequately. This is an important part of psychiatric diagnosis. However, it still involves one person making a judgement about how successfully someone else is living.
- A third alternative is to judge how well someone matches up to standards of ideal mental health. However, these standards tend to vary between cultures.
- There are a number of theoretical approaches to understanding and treating psychological abnormality. The biological approach involves understanding the role of genetic vulnerability, environmental brain damage and abnormal brain chemistry.

- Biological treatments aim to correct brain malfunction by means of drugs or electroconvulsive therapy. Both these forms of treatment are effective but have a range of unpleasant side effects.
- The psychodynamic model emphasises the role of childhood experiences, including trauma and relationship formation, in the development of mental disorder.
- Psychodynamic treatments include psychoanalysis, an intensive and long-term therapy that involves revisiting and working through childhood experiences. Psychoanalysis is effective, but many patients may be able to benefit equally from quicker, cheaper therapies.
- The behavioural approach emphasises the role of learning abnormal behaviours, for example through classical conditioning.
- Behavioural treatments include systematic desensitisation, in which patients with anxiety disorders are gradually exposed to the thing that triggers their anxiety. Systematic desensitisation is reasonably effective, though less so than alternative behavioural treatments, but is less traumatic for patients.
- The cognitive model emphasises the role of abnormal thinking patterns that typically exist in patients with particular disorders.
- Cognitive behavioural therapy (CBT) involves identifying and challenging these abnormal thinking patterns. CBT is very effective for treating depression and anxiety. However, because it places responsibility on the patient rather than their environment, it can be politically misused.

What do I know?

1 (a) Outline what is meant by deviation from social norms. (4 marks)

(b) Explain one limitation of using deviation from social norms to define abnormality. (4 marks)

2 (a) In a copy of the table below, write in the following therapies next to the corresponding approach. (4 marks)

Psychoanalysis
Systematic desensitisation
CBT
ECT
PET scan

Approach	Therapy
Biological	
Psychodynamic	
Behavioural	
Cognitive	

(b) Describe **one** of these therapies.

(c) Evaluate the therapy you described in (b). (4 marks)

3 (a) Outline the key features of the behavioural approach to psychopathology. (6 marks)

(b) Explain **one** way in which this approach differs from the psychodynamic approach. (3 marks)

4 (a) Draw a line between each technique in the left-hand column and the therapy it corresponds to in the right-hand column. (4 marks)

FREE ASSOCIATION		SYSTEMATIC DESENSITISATION
ANXIETY HIERARCHY		ECT
BILATERAL		CBT
REALITY TESTING		PSYCHOANALYSIS
SSRIs		MEDICATION

(b) Evaluate psychoanalysis as a way of treating mental health problems. (4 marks)

5 Belinda has had a fear of birds since she was attacked by a seagull on a day trip to the seaside as a child. This fear is so extreme that she finds it hard to leave the house and she cannot visit parks or anywhere else where she believes she may encounter birds. She has consulted a clinical psychologist who favours a behavioural approach when it comes to explaining and treating phobias.

(a) Using the information given at the start of this question, how might the psychologist explain the way Belinda acquired her phobia using a behavioural approach? (5 marks)

(b) How might the psychologist use systematic desensitisation to treat Belinda? (5 marks)

6 Describe and evaluate the biological approach to explaining psychological abnormality. (10 marks)

CHAPTER 8
Your Examinations

Thinking ahead

By the end of this chapter you should be able to:

- understand the requirements of your AS examinations
- know how and what to revise
- understand what is good and bad examination practice
- develop strategies to improve your examination performance
- apply your learning to examination-style questions
- enter the examination process with motivation and confidence

There are many points of view about the best way to assess a student's value. However, whatever your personal viewpoint, the fact is that formal examinations remain the favoured form of assessment. Examinations can seem threatening regardless of how much work you have done; indeed, the very nature of formal assessment can be difficult for all types of students. So, ultimately how well you do will depend upon your performance on questions that you have never seen before on one particular day. What this means of course is that you need to be well prepared.

The prospect of this may fill you with such gloom that you feel like snapping your pen in two and giving up at once. Students who look forward to exams are rare, and for most of us exams are difficult to endure. But do not despair; help is at hand, for there are ways and methods of dealing with them. A lot of work goes into examinations to try to make them a fair process, and if you can understand what the exams require from you and revise thoroughly, then there is every chance that you will succeed. The golden principle in all this has two parts to it: be informed and be prepared.

THE AS EXAMINATIONS

You will be required to sit *two* AS examinations that will test your knowledge and understanding of the material covered in the specification. Both of the examinations will last one hour and thirty minutes.

Unit 1: Cognitive and developmental psychology and research methods

The Unit 1 paper will be divided into two sections, the first covering the Cognitive Psychology topic of memory and the second covering the Developmental Psychology topic of attachment. The Research Methods questions will occur within these two sections and will be centred on memory and attachment issues. The three topics that it covers are those featured in Chapters 2, 3 and 4 of this book.

This paper will account for 50 per cent of the total AS marks.

The first section, covering questions on the memory topic, will total 36 marks comprising 12 AO1 marks, 12 AO2 marks and 12 AO3 marks. The second section, covering questions on the attachment topic, will total 36 marks, comprising 12 AO1 marks, 12 AO2 marks and 12 AO3 marks.

You may sit this paper in either January or June.

Unit 2: Physiological and social psychology and individual differences

The Unit 2 paper will be divided into *three* sections, the first covering the Physiological Psychology topic of stress, the second covering the Social Psychology topic of social influences and the third covering the Individual Differences topic of abnormality.

This paper will account for 50 per cent of the total AS marks. The three topics that it covers are those featured in Chapters 5, 6 and 7 of this book.

The first section, covering questions on the stress topic, will total 24 marks comprising 10 AO1 marks, 10 AO2 marks and 4 AO3 marks. The second section, covering questions on the social influences topic, will total 24 marks comprising 10 AO1 marks, 10 AO2 marks and 4 AO3 marks. The third section, covering questions on the abnormality topic, will total 24 marks comprising 10 AO1 marks, 10AO2 marks and 4 AO3 marks. Research Methods questions will occur in all three sections.

You may sit this paper in either January or June.

ASSESSMENT OBJECTIVES

Both the AS examinations, Unit 1 and Unit 2, are designed to test your knowledge of *three* assessment objectives. Each of these assessment objectives tests a different skill.

AO1 (Assessment Objective 1) involves questions designed to test your knowledge and understanding. Candidates should be able to:

- recognise, recall and show understanding of knowledge
- select, organise and communicate relevant information in a variety of forms.

AO2 (Assessment Objective 2) involves questions designed to test your application of knowledge and understanding. Candidates should be able to:

- analyse and evaluate knowledge and processes
- apply knowledge and processes to unfamiliar situations, including those related to issues
- assess the validity, reliability and credibility of information.

AO3 (Assessment Objective 3) involves questions designed to test your knowledge and application of knowledge and understanding of how psychology as a science works. Candidates should be able to:

- describe ethical, safe and skilful practical techniques and processes, selecting appropriate qualitative and quantitative methods
- know how to make, record and communicate reliable and valid observations and measurements with appropriate accuracy and precision, through using primary and secondary sources
- analyse, interpret, explain and evaluate the methodology, results and impact of their own and others' experimental and investigative activities in a variety of ways.

EXAMINATION QUESTIONS

There are a number of different types of questions that will make up both your Unit 1 and Unit 2 AS examination papers:

- Questions that require you to make choices and organise information given to you – for example, selecting material and placing it in the correct parts of a table.
- Short answer questions worth a few marks – for example, describing or explaining knowledge concerning a set topic.
- Questions that involve being given information in the form of a scenario and then being asked questions about this scenario.
- Questions that assess your knowledge of Research Methods. These questions will be centred on the five topic areas covered in the specification.
- Long answer questions. On each of the two AS examination papers there will be one long answer question worth 12 marks that will assess AO1 and AO2 skills.

Examples of all these types of questions, with sample answers, examination guidance and examiner's comments, will be featured later on in this chapter.

REVISION STRATEGIES

There is no 'magic formula' for successful revision; there are many ways to revise, and some methods suit some students but not others. By a process of trial and error you will find which methods suit you best and which do not.

You may be tempted to use revision strategies that have served you well in the past, but remember, GCSE exams tend to be more knowledge based than AS exams. In the latter, not only your knowledge will be tested, but also your ability to use this knowledge in an analytical and evaluative way. That ability will be tested even further if you go on to study Psychology at A2 level.

There are those students who leave their revision to the last possible moment, and for most of us this is not to be recommended. It is stressful to work that way, and you will not perform to the best of your ability. A much better method is one that makes revision a regular part of your studying regime as well as part of your examination preparation.

- At the end of each week, revise the material you have been looking at in order to assist your learning.
- The best way to achieve this is to do something with the material, for instance read through it and record the important points – maybe highlight them in some way.
- Use the relevant section of your textbook to aid your understanding and to further your knowledge of the topic.
- After you have done this, it would be a good idea to attempt an examination-style question. There are examples of such questions at the end of each chapter of this book and later on in this chapter.
- Remember to practise not only AO1 questions that assess your knowledge and understanding, but also AO2 and AO3 questions that assess your ability to analyse and evaluate material and your knowledge and understanding of Research Methods.

At first when practising exam-type questions, you will probably need to have your learning materials, such as your notes and your textbook, immediately available to you. Ensure that in the answer you prepare, you have included enough detail to earn all the marks on offer. There is even a school of thought that advises including a little more than may be necessary in order to try to ensure that full marks will be gained. However, do not include what is clearly far too much material in an answer. It will not gain extra credit and you will have wasted valuable time that could have been better spent on another question. Also, do not include too little. For example, if a question asks for *two* limitations, make sure you have provided two and not just the one.

When you are comfortable and familiar with this method of regular revision, it will be time to move on and practise writing questions without using notes. A good way to do this is to read through the relevant material first and then put it out of view and write down your answer. In this way you will be gradually creating the actual environment of the examination that you will sit.

When you are used to writing answers without the topic materials in front of you, it will be time to put time constraints on yourself. It is difficult to judge how much time to spend on a particular question, but a general rule is that each mark is worth 1 minute and 15 seconds of the examination time available. Therefore, if a question is worth four marks, then you should be dedicating about 5 minutes to answering it. The longest questions you will encounter – and there will be one on each AS paper – are worth 12 marks, and so therefore should have about 15 minutes spent on them.

Using the forms of revision detailed above on a regular basis will not only aid your learning but will also prepare you well for your main revision period preceding the examination and will give you the confidence and motivation to do well.

REVISING FOR THE EXAMINATION

You will need to revise all topics, even those you don't like or have struggled with; they could still appear on the examination paper. It is also unwise to leave out something on the basis that it was on the examination paper last time; it could be there again this time. Therefore, when revising for your examinations ensure that you:

- Have got a copy of all the specification topics for each of the examination papers.
- Have all the necessary materials for revising each topic.
- Have created a realistic examination timetable. This needs to have all topics on it, with enough time dedicated to each separate topic to ensure they are revised thoroughly. Try to ensure there are a couple of 'spare' slots on your timetable in case extra revision of a topic is needed, or because through some unforeseeable circumstances you lose a timetable slot.

LOOKING FURTHER You will need a format for your revision timetable. You can download weekly and monthly planners from the BBC. The web address is http://www.bbc.co.uk/schools/revision/planners/.

When you revise, find somewhere you are comfortable working. For most of us this will be away from other people and possible distractions, but there are no hard and fast rules. For instance, some people work well with background music, while for others it is a distraction.

One distraction to be aware of is suddenly finding 'important' tasks to do. It is quite easy to use up all of a planned revision session by tidying your bedroom, arranging your books in size order and then sharpening 25 different-coloured pencils. Remember, a revision session is for revising and nothing else. Make necessary preparations beforehand and not during revision sessions.

Remember that you will need to revise over the Christmas period for a January examination and over Easter for the summer examination. There will be a lot of distractions to avoid at these times.

Ensure you have got your revision timetable and that you stick to it. Some students can work over protracted periods, but for most, an hour to 90 minutes a session will be best. During that time it is advisable that you use the revision methods you have been practising each week throughout the course.

- Read through the necessary materials for that topic.
- Record or highlight in some way the important points.
- Use previous examination questions and examination-style questions to construct practice answers. By this stage of your learning you should be used to doing these without having materials in front of you, and to time constraints.
- At the end of each planned revision session, as long as you achieve your goal, for example writing a satisfactory practice answer, then reward yourself in some way. The reward we choose will be different for each of us, but could take the form of a liked TV programme. Such rewards can even be written into your revision timetable as a form of motivation.

Indeed, motivation is very important, as is its close cousin confidence. If you have used revision techniques throughout the course and have prepared well for the examination revision period, then they you will feel confident that you can succeed and therefore will be motivated to revise well.

Figure 8.1 You are likely to be revising during the holidays when there is lots to distract you. Bear this in mind when planning your revision timetable.

Figure 8.2 Reward yourself with something you want (such as watching TV) but not until you have completed the work you had planned

One of the most demotivating things about taking exams is the sheer mass of material that needs to be revised. By constructing a realistic revision timetable you will be able to break down this material into manageable chunks.

Having a realistic revision timetable is very important to your confidence and motivational state of mind, as it allows you to see that everything can be covered in sufficient detail before the examination date rears its ugly head. There is no worse way of denting your confidence and motivation than in feeling a blind sense of panic and despair that it is all too much and there is not enough time, even if you knew where to begin. Feeling in control of the situation will help to keep you confident and motivated.

Another good way of ensuring that your confidence and motivational levels stay high is to remind yourself constantly why you are doing this, what your target is. This target should be important to you and not be one that someone else has imposed upon you.

Figure 8.3 Set your own targets and stick to them

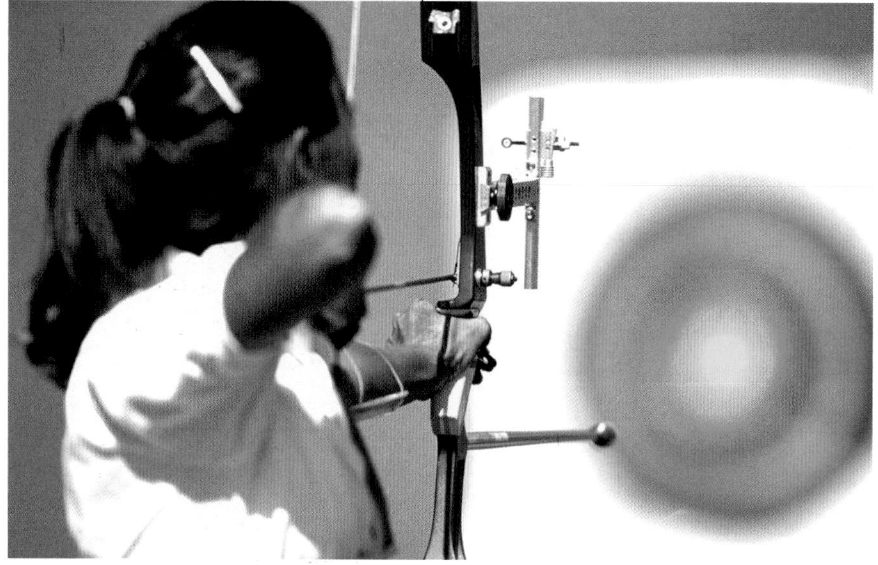

THE EXAMINATION

For a start, make sure you have got not only the date right, but the actual time of the examination too. Plan these details into your revision timetable; one of the authors once had a student miss an examination as she had an important revision session planned for that particular time!

Make sure you take everything you need with you to the examination; it is advisable to prepare a little bag containing the materials you will need. The inclusion of a couple of spare pens is especially recommended.

When you are told to begin, do not immediately start writing, but first of all read through the questions in order to ensure that you fully understand them and also as a way of mentally preparing yourself for the task at hand.

You may wish to begin with a question or questions that immediately appeals to you, though remember to spend only the necessary amount of time on them and no longer. You can then attempt the less appealing questions when you have settled into the examination.

If you finish before the allotted time is up, do not sit there looking smug. Instead, use that time to read through what you've written. In our experience, you may discover a mistake you've made, or at least an answer you could add a little more to.

EXAMINATION INJUNCTIONS

Examination questions make use of examination injunctions. These are simply the wording used in questions to instruct you what kind of answer is required. So, if you have an understanding of these terms, you will be more able to compose examination answers that are in line with what each individual question requires in order to gain the maximum amount of marks on offer.

There now follows an explanatory list of the most common examination injunctions for the AO1, AO2 and AO3 assessment objectives.

AO1

Identify = name
Define = what is meant by
Outline = give brief details without explanation
Describe = give a detailed account without explanation
Correctly complete = fill in the missing information
Select = choose the correct option

AO2

Analyse = examine in detail
Give = show awareness of
Explain = give clear account of why and how something is so
Evaluate = assess the value or effectiveness
Discuss = give a reasoned balanced, account
Apply = explain how something can be used

AO3

Outline = give brief details without explanation
Give = show awareness of
Identify = name
Explain = give clear account of why and how something is so
Write = compose your own example

EXAM-TYPE QUESTIONS

Throughout this book, towards the end of each chapter you will find examples of questions that relate to the material covered in a particular chapter. These questions are designed to facilitate your learning, in that by preparing answers for them you will have to engage with the material covered. The actual questions that you will be set in your AS examinations will be very like the questions included in this book, so by practising them you will not only be aiding your learning of the various topic areas, but also be preparing yourself for the real examination.

Actual examination questions can only be asked about subject material that is named specifically on the specification. So, for example, it would not be possible for you to be asked a question about Van IJzendoorn and Kroonenberg's meta-analysis of cultural variations in attachment, because this study is not directly named on the specification. However, you could be asked a specific question about Margaret Ainsworth's controlled observational study the 'Strange Situation' because it is explicitly named on the specification.

Figure 8.4 Don't spend too long on one question. Remember, you should spend only 1 minute 15 seconds per mark.

There are a number of differently styled types of questions that you may be presented with under examination conditions and it would be a good idea to familiarise yourself with each of these types of questions. A good way to help this process is to have a go at such questions yourself – only allowing yourself the amount of time that you would have for each question in the actual examination. This means in practice that for a long answer question worth 12 marks, you ought to be spending about 15 minutes writing your answer. Questions worth fewer marks should have less time dedicated to answering them. Probably the biggest mistake you can make is to spend too much time on some questions and then run out of time to complete the other questions. Only by practising examination-type questions under timed conditions can you really develop the ability to know how long to spend on each particular answer.

Also have a look at the sample answers that are presented with the questions in this chapter; they will allow you to see what is good practice and what is poor practice. If you can identify similar good and bad practices in your own work, then this will help you to form strategies to maximise your performance. Simply removing identified poor practices from your own work and accentuating and building upon identified good practices in your own work will provide you with a basis for self-improvement.

We shall now have a look at the different types of question that you may encounter in your actual AS examinations. Each question will be explained in terms of what kind of answer is being asked for. Provided with each question will be two sample answers; one of these will be of a moderate standard, while the other will be of a good standard. Both answers will include examiner's comments that identify good and bad practice and also indicate what would be needed to improve the answer. Therefore, whatever the current standard of your written work under examination-type conditions, you should be able, by studying these sample answers, to identify ways in which you can improve your own work and therefore gain higher marks.

Selection questions

First of all, let us have a look at a type of question in which you are given bits of information and asked to put them in the correct parts of a table. With this type of question you will always have to make a choice for each option that is required to be included in the table. So, for example, if such a question were to require you to place three descriptive phrases into the correct parts of a table, then you would actually be given four descriptive phrases, one of which was surplus to requirements, and would be required to select which three were the correct ones and place them in the desired part of the table. If you were given only three options, then you might know two of them, which naturally means that the third one would have only one place left to go in the table, which of course would be the right place and you would have got the question right without really knowing the answer. Having an extra option to choose from means that you always have to make an informed choice and display your knowledge and understanding.

Let us have a look at such a question that is drawn from the Individual Differences topic area of abnormality. This therefore would occur in Paper 2.

The following are descriptions of psychological therapies.

A A therapy that aims to uncover unconscious conflicts and anxieties that have their origins in the past in order to gain insight into the causes of psychological disturbance.
B A therapy whereby clients are taught relaxation techniques and are then gradually exposed to feared objects or situations until the fear diminishes.
C A therapy that involves passing a high current through the brain for approximately half a second to induce convulsions in order to combat severe depression.
D A therapy that involves helping clients to identify their negative, irrational thoughts and to replace them with more positive rational ways of thinking

(a) In the table below, write down which description, **A**, **B**, **C** or **D**, matches each of the psychological therapies in the table. (3 marks)

Type of psychological therapy	Description of the therapy
Psychoanalysis	
Systematic desensitisation	
Cognitive behavioural therapy	

Examination guidance

These types of questions are easy to assess, as each answer is either right or wrong. The three marks on offer are all AO1 marks as the requirement of the question is that you use your knowledge of psychological therapies to identify which description corresponds to which type of named therapy. You would therefore also have to assess which of the four options does not relate to a description of a named therapy.

Moderate answer by Nicola

Type of psychological therapy	Description of the therapy
Psychoanalysis	A
Systematic desensitisation	C
Cognitive behavioural therapy	B

Examiner's comments

Nicola has clearly identified the correct description of psychoanalysis, for which she receives a mark. However, she places the description of systematic desensitisation wrongly into the cognitive behavioural therapy option box and places the non-required description (it is a description of electro-convulsive therapy, a biological treatment) into the systematic desensitisation option box. What is clearly required here in order for Nicola to improve the quality of her answer is for her to know this subject area in more depth. Three psychological therapies, all of which are included here, are named on the specification, and so students must know each and every one of them. Just having a knowledge and awareness of one of them, even if it is a very detailed knowledge, will not be sufficient to ensure that students could answer an examination question on this topic area. Marks: 1/3

Good answer by Becky

Type of psychological therapy	Description of the therapy
Psychoanalysis	A
Systematic desensitisation	B
Cognitive behavioural therapy	D

Examiner's comments

Becky clearly merits all three of the marks on offer as she selects the three correct options from the four offered and she places them into the correct places in the table. She clearly knows this area of the specification sufficiently well and has not been fooled by the inclusion of a biological therapy, electro-convulsive therapy (option C). Marks: 3/3

Short answer questions

On both the AS examination papers there will be questions that are worth a few marks; exactly how many marks will always be stated in brackets after the wording of the question. It would not be possible within this short chapter to give examples of all possible examples of these types of questions, so we will now look at one such question that requires AO1 material to answer it and then will follow this with a similar question that requires AO2 material to answer it. Questions that deal with AO3 material will be dealt with separately.

These types of questions will be generally be very specific in their requirements and oriented towards specific areas of the specification. Therefore, when answering these types of question you should always take care that the material to be used is carefully chosen and is oriented towards the demands of the question; in other words, make sure you really are answering the question you have been set.

Let us now look at an example of such a short-answer question that requires AO1 content.

Describe how the factor of age can affect eyewitness testimony. (4 marks)

Examination guidance

The instruction to 'describe' is an AO1 requirement, as you will need to provide material that reflects your knowledge of this specific topic area. One mark of the four available would be gained by describing how the factor of age can affect eyewitness testimony, and the further three marks available would be gained by the elaboration of your description. The overall mark therefore would be determined by the quality of the elaboration provided.

Moderate answer by Sven

Lewis showed that young children are susceptible to the effects of leading questions.

Examiner's comments

This is the classic moderate answer; it is accurate and relevant, but scores poorly as it contains no elaboration. Sven should have gone on to provide details of the research quoted so that the point being made was illustrated by a lot more relevant detail. Look at the next example of an answer to this question by Winston for more guidance as to how to achieve this. Marks: 1/4

Good answer by Winston

Lewis conducted research that looked at the effect of leading questions on children aged between three and four years. The children were shown photos of men and one was misidentified as their 'daddy'. Some children then went on to mistakenly identify this individual as being 'daddy'. This shows that young children can be susceptible to leading questions, though it was a minority of the children affected.

Examiner's comments

A much better answer than Sven's and yet an answer that makes the same point and uses the same piece of research, but to much better effect. Winston provides us with the aim of the research and relevant details of the procedure and findings. From these he then presents us with a valid conclusion about how the factor of age affects eyewitness testimony, and the elaboration of this answer is even added to by the final point that only a minority of children were affected. Marks: 4/4

Let us now look at an example of a short-answer question that requires AO2 content.

> Explain **one** weakness of the multi-store model. (2 marks)

Examination guidance

The stipulation to 'explain' is an AO2 one, as it requires analysis in that you must not only provide a relevant weakness of the model but explain why it is a weakness. One of the two marks available would be earned by a relevant explanation of a weakness of the model and the second mark would be gained by an elaboration of this explanation.

Moderate answer by Olwynn

A weakness of the model is that there is possibly more than just one kind of short-term memory store as different types of task either interfere with STM or don't.

Examiner's comments

Olwynn provides a valid explanation of the fact that there may be more than one type of STM store, and thus gains a mark for this explanation. However, there is not sufficient elaboration of this explanation to gain the other mark available; the material used is not quoted clearly enough to illustrate the explanation further. Marks: 1/2

Good answer by Maria

A weakness of the multi-store model is that there may be more than one type of LTM. Research on an amnesic showed that he could acquire new skills such as mirror drawing, but not new facts. This suggests that there is a distinction between declarative memory and procedural memory, which are therefore different types of LTM.

Examiner's comments

Maria provides a valid explanation of the fact that there may be more than one type of LTM and thus gains the mark available for her explanation. However, unlike Olwynn, Maria gains the extra mark on offer too, as she provides an elaboration of her explanation that illuminates the explanation further. Marks: 2/2

Stem questions

Now let us have a look at another type of AS examination question. This particular type of question provides you with a 'stem' or 'scenario' containing information concerning a topic area. In this example there are two parts to the question, using information provided in two stems. This particular example is drawn from the Social Psychology topic area of social influence. This therefore would occur in Paper 2.

A) Identify the type of social influence illustrated in the situation described below. Refer to features of the situation to justify your answer. (3 marks)

Situation 1

David had recently left home to take up his place at university. However, he had found university life to be very different from that at home and he was having trouble fitting in. He noticed that a lot of students were members of the thriving Athletics Union, so he went along and took up membership, even though he had no real interest in or experience with sports. He also bought and wore the distinctive Athletics Union sweatshirt and was surprised to find that almost immediately fellow members of the club would greet him and ask him to join in their social activities.

Examination guidance

The stipulation to 'identify' is an AO1 requirement, and one mark would be available for correctly identifying normative social influence, a type of social influence that is explicitly referred to in the specification.

Two further marks are available and both of these are AO2 marks, as there is a requirement for you to analyse the information given in the stem in order to provide a relevant answer.

There is a quite clear instruction that features of the stem (situation) must be explicitly referred to in your answer to gain the AO2 credit on offer. One mark is available for a brief explanation, one further mark for an elaboration of the explanation.

B) Identify the type of social influence illustrated in the situation described below. Refer to features of the situation to justify your answer. (3 marks)

Situation 2

Carl has been asked out on a date by Fiona, a young lady he is very attracted to. Fiona has a passion for ballroom dancing and has asked Carl to be her partner at a dance. Carl is keen to make a good impression, but knows next to nothing about ballroom dancing. He decides upon adopting the strategy of observing and copying the other more experienced dancers so as not to embarrass himself.

Examination guidance

The stipulation to 'identify' is an AO1 requirement, and one mark would be available for correctly identifying informational social influence, a type of social influence that is explicitly referred to in the specification. Two further marks are available, and both of these are AO2 marks, as there is a requirement for you to analyse the information given in the stem in order to provide a relevant answer.

There is a quite clear instruction that features of the stem (situation) must be explicitly referred to in your answer to gain the AO2 credit on offer. One mark is available for a brief explanation, one further mark for an elaboration of the explanation.

Moderate answer by Jemima

A) David's behaviour is an example of normative social influence. David probably had lots of friends in his home town and would be keen to make some new friends.

Examiner's comments

Jemima correctly identifies the type of social influence illustrated as that of normative social influence and so she gains the AO1 mark available.

However, she does not, as instructed, refer to features of the situation to justify her answer. She makes a guess that David had friends at home and that he would like to make new friends at university, and indeed logically this may be true, but there is nothing stated in the situation to explicitly back up this claim.

What Jemima could have done is to have referred to David joining the Athletics Union even though he had no previous interest or experiences with sport. This, along with his purchasing and wearing of the Athletics Union sweatshirt, points towards David yielding to the majority position, but without actually accepting their point of view. It is public, not private, acceptance. Marks: 1/1 + 0/2 = 1/3

B) Carl demonstrates informational social influence. Carl has gone ballroom dancing for the very first time and looks to the behaviour of others so as not to embarrass himself.

Examiner's comments

Jemima correctly identifies Carl's behaviour as being that of informational social influence and thus gains the AO1 mark available. She then goes on to refer in part to features of the situation to justify her answer, when she talks about Carl looking to the behaviour of others so as not to embarrass himself. Jemima therefore earns one of the two AO2 marks on offer, but she would need a fuller answer that refers to features of the situation to gain the final mark. For instance, Jemima could elaborate the point she makes by referring to the fact that Carl observes and actually imitates the behaviour of other, experienced ballroom dancers. This amount of detail is not apparent in Jemima's answer. Marks: 1/1 + 1/2 = 2/3

Good answer by Jarvinder

A) David displays normative social influence. He has a desire to be accepted by the others and feels that if he has the same interests as them, then they will accept him.

Examiner's comments

Jarvinder correctly identifies the type of social influence as normative social influence and explains how David is attempting to be accepted by conforming to their group norms. However, Jarvinder does not refer to features in the scenario explicitly enough to get the third mark available. She would need perhaps to make reference to the purchase and wearing of the Athletics Union sweatshirt. Marks: 1/1 + 1/2 = 2/3

B) Informational social influence is the type of social influence apparent in the situation. Carl tries not to embarrass himself at the dance by copying more experienced ballroom dancers' actions. He is looking for information as to how to behave in this novel situation. He is likely to adopt this behaviour in the future too.

Examiner's comments

Informational social influence is correctly identified to gain the AO1 mark on offer, and this time enough reference is made to information contained within the situation to justify awarding both the AO2 marks available. Explicit reference is made to Carl attempting not to embarrass himself by copying the more experienced ballroom dancers, and Jarvinder goes so far as to elaborate this point by explaining that Carl is looking for information as how to behave in what for him is a new situation. Marks: 1/1 + 2/2 = 3/3

Research methods questions

Now let us have a look at a type of question that assesses your knowledge of Research Methods. These questions will always be centred on one of the five other topic areas set out in the specification. This type of question will be set on all *five* of these other topic areas. These questions are the ones that assess AO3 skills.

You will have seen this particular question before at the end of Chapter 6 on the Social Psychology topic of social influences. This question would therefore occur in Paper 2.

> **Obedience can be studied by means of laboratory experiments and field experiments. Explain *one* strength and *one* limitation of using field experiments in studying obedience. (2 + 2 marks)**

Examination guidance

As this is a question involving Research Methods, the marks available are AO3 marks. Therefore, your knowledge of how psychology works as a science is being assessed. You are required to explain a strength and a weakness of field experiments in studying obedience, therefore you must have a working knowledge not only of field experiments themselves, but also of how they pertain to the studying of obedience. One mark would be available for explaining a relevant strength and an additional mark would be available for an elaboration of this. One mark would also be available for explaining a relevant limitation and an additional mark would be available for an elaboration of this.

Moderate answer by Hyacinth

In a field experiment the participants are generally unaware that they are being studied and so their behaviour will be more representative of real life.

In field experiments, if participants are unaware they are being studied, this raises an ethical issue as they have not given consent to take part.

Examiner's comments

A valid strength of field experiments is explained. However, it is not really explained in terms of studying obedience. Perhaps Hyacinth could have used Hofling's study, where nurses in a real hospital were ordered to give a patient an overdose of a drug, to elaborate on the point she makes.

Hyacinth also supplies a valid limitation of field experiments, but again does not elaborate the point in terms of studying obedience. It might have been an idea to have used the study of Hofling, done in a real hospital, which, as the nurses were unaware of being tested, led to their feeling distressed at having given an apparent overdose to a patient. Marks: 1/2 + 1/2 = 2/4

Good answer by Euros

One strength of Hofling's study of obedience done on nurses in a real hospital is that it is high in ecological validity as it shows that obedience does occur in real-life settings. However, it has also been argued that the experimental procedure was so unlike real life – for example, it did not allow the nurses to confer, and it used an unfamiliar drug – that it therefore is not actually high in ecological validity.

A weakness of Hofling's field study is that it was unethical; the nurses were unaware they were in a study and so were deceived, not having been able to give

informed consent, and this led them to experience distress at their actions, even though they were debriefed later on.

Examiner's comments

Two good answers are supplied by Euros. He explains why Hofling's study may be high in ecological validity and then provides excellent elaboration of this point by explaining why it might not be so.

Euros gives the same weakness of Hofling's study as Hyacinth did, but explains it much better, combining several ethical points together to form an effective elaboration. Marks: 2/2 + 2/2 = 4/4

Long answer questions

Now let us have a look at a long answer question. There will be one of these questions on each of the two AS question papers, but they could occur in any of the topic areas on each paper. So, with Paper 1 you could be set a long answer question on memory, drawn from the material outlined in the specification, of course. However, you could just as easily be set one of these types of questions on the attachment topic. (Remember that in Paper 1 the research methods topic has its questions integrated into the memory and attachment topics.) Therefore, in Paper 2 a long answer question could occur on the stress topic, the social influences topic or the abnormality topic. For both papers it will not be possible for you to know beforehand or to predict which topics the long answer questions will be set on. This means, of course, that you must be prepared to answer such a question on any topic, and, especially as this question will involve a relatively large proportion of the marks available, it would be a good idea to have a look at and practise quite a few of these questions.

The long answer question will be worth twelve marks, six marks of which will be AO1 marks requiring a description of your knowledge in that specific area, and the remaining six will be AO2 marks requiring analysis and evaluation. The marks for AO1 and for AO2 will be determined by the use of mark band descriptors that remain fairly similar for all these types of questions. This is to your advantage, for it will be possible to familiarise yourself with the requirements needed to gain access to the higher band descriptors and to satisfy these requirements by attempting practice answers to such questions.

As six marks are available for both AO1 and AO2, it is advisable to create a balanced essay in terms of AO1 and AO2 content if you wish to gain good marks on this type of question. Previously, examiners have commented on a general student trend to concentrate on the AO1 part of these types of questions at the expense of the AO2 content. It is quite a skill to create a balanced answer, and one that to the majority of students becomes possible only by again practising these types of questions until you get it right.

There are two broad strategies you can employ to create a balanced answer. First, you can provide all your AO1 material, followed by your AO2 material. The trick here is knowing when you have provided sufficient AO1 material to be able to move on to the AO2 requirement. Remember, there are only six marks available for AO1, and if you provide material that is worth more than these six marks, you will not be awarded extra AO1 credit – and, of course, you will have wasted valuable examination time that could have been spent on providing relevant AO2 material.

Secondly, you could adopt the strategy of providing an AO1 comment followed by a relevant AO2 comment. This is a strategy that needs to be thoroughly practised to be useful to a student, but it does help to provide a balanced answer.

Let us now have a look at one such question. You will have seen this particular question before at the end of Chapter 3 on the Developmental Psychology topic of attachment. This question would therefore occur in Paper 1.

Critically discuss the possible effects of day care on children's social development. (12 marks)

Examination guidance

This question focuses in particular on the subject area of how day care affects children's social development. Your AO1 material therefore is going to be a description of possible effects that psychological research has demonstrated on this specific area of children's development. If you were to include AO1 material that focuses on the possible effects of day care on other areas of children's development, then you would gain no extra credit for such material, however accurately and well you were to use it, as it falls outside of what the question demands. There is, for example, a wealth of material available on the possible effects of day care on cognitive development, but it would not gain credit by its inclusion on this question.

If you are to gain high AO1 credit for this question, then you need to satisfy the demands of the higher mark band descriptors. (These are provided opposite.) Therefore, to earn all six AO1 marks on offer, your description of the possible effects of day care on children's social development would have to be accurate and reasonably detailed, demonstrating sound knowledge and understanding of the topic area. The demonstration of sound knowledge and understanding of the topic area would have to be conveyed in your description of the possible effects of day care on children's social development. This requires a great deal of sophistication in your writing style, but is a skill that can be practised and developed.

Again, if you are to earn high AO2 credit for this question, then once more you need to satisfy the demands of the higher mark descriptors. So, to earn all six AO2 marks on offer would require an effective evaluation. In order for you to provide one, you must make effective use of the material, with provision of an informed commentary. The question requires you to 'critically discuss', and it must be remembered that criticism can centre on weaknesses, but equally can centre on strengths. Therefore, a top-level answer would include an effective evaluation of strengths and weaknesses as it relates to this question. This could take the form of evaluating methodological aspects of research carried out on possible side effects of day care on children's social development, for example weaknesses in how research was carried out, or it could take the form of whether or not different research studies support or contradict each other.

If you explored a broad range of issues and/or evidence, then reasonable depth would be expected, whereas if you focused on a narrower range of issues and/or evidence, greater depth would be expected to gain access to the higher band of marks.

A final requirement of the six-mark AO2 mark band descriptor is to provide a clear expression of ideas, a good range of specialist terms and few errors in grammar, punctuation and spelling. This requires a degree of sophistication in your writing style, and is again a skill that can be practised and developed.

AO1: Knowledge and understanding	AO2: Application of knowledge and understanding
6 marks Accurate and reasonably detailed Accurate and reasonably detailed description of the possible effects of day care upon children's social development that demonstrates sound knowledge and understanding. There is appropriate selection of material to address the question. Presentation of material is clear and coherent.	**6 marks Effective evaluation** Effective use of material to address the question and provide informed commentary. Effective evaluation of strengths and weaknesses. Broad range of issues and/or evidence in reasonable depth, or a narrower range in greater depth. Clear expression of ideas, good range of specialist terms, few errors of grammar, punctuation and spelling.
5–4 marks Less detailed but generally accurate Less detailed but generally accurate description of the possible effects of day care on children's social development that demonstrates relevant knowledge and understanding. There is some evidence of selection of material to address the question. Information is presented in an appropriate form.	**5–4 marks Reasonable evaluation** Material is not always used effectively, but produces a reasonable commentary. Reasonable evaluation of strengths and weaknesses. A range of issues and/or evidence in limited depth, or a narrower range in greater depth. Reasonable expression of ideas, a range of specialist terms, some errors of grammar, punctuation and spelling.
3–2 marks Basic Basic description of possible effects of day care on children's social development that demonstrates some relevant knowledge and understanding, but lacks detail and may be muddled. There is little evidence of selection of material to address the question. Information is not presented in an appropriate form.	**3–2 marks Basic evaluation** The use of material provides only a basic commentary. Basic evaluation of strengths and weaknesses. Superficial consideration of a restricted range of issues and/or evidence. Expression of ideas lacks clarity, some specialist terms used, errors of grammar, punctuation, and spelling detract from clarity.
1 mark Very brief/flawed or inappropriate Very brief or flawed description of possible effects of day care on children's development demonstrating very little knowledge. Selection and presentation of information largely or wholly inappropriate.	**1 mark Rudimentary evaluation** The use of material provides only a rudimentary commentary. Evaluation of strengths and weaknesses is just discernible or absent. Expression of ideas poor, few specialist terms used; errors of grammar, punctuation and spelling often obscure the meaning.
0 marks No creditworthy material.	**0 marks** No creditworthy material.

Moderate answer by Paul

Day care is a form of temporary care provided by non-family members who are not well known to a child, and usually occurs outside of the family home. Financial and social factors have led to the norm being for both parents in this country to work, and therefore their young children have to be provided with day care.

If Bowlby is correct and separation disrupts the attachment process, then day care will have negative effects. However, Bowlby's work focused on long-term separation, while day care only concerns short-term separations.

Belsky found that babies in day care were at an increased risk of developing insecure attachments and showing aggressive behaviour. Other studies have supported this finding.

Andersson carried out a study on children who had been in day care for many years from infancy. Compared to children who had only received maternal care, the day care children were more popular and socially skilled.

Andersson also assessed babies' attachment patterns using the 'Strange Situation' and found that working mothers whose children received day care were more likely to have secure babies.

Ruhm found that day care could negatively affect children's development as it was found that children have lower verbal ability if their mother worked during the child's first year.

Figure 8.5 Try to maintain a balance between AO1 and AO2 in your essays

Examiner's comments

Paul provides us with an answer that demonstrates a wealth of desirable and poor practices. First of all he begins by explaining what is meant by day care, and although every student should have a clear understanding of what the term means in order to have a clear perception of this topic area and therefore to be able to construct high-quality answers to questions about it, the question set does not require such an explanation. Therefore, Paul's first sentence gains no credit at all, though it does not incur any negative value – that is, marks lost – as positive marking means that only relevant material of value is assessed. Any irrelevant material, such as Paul's first sentence, is just ignored. However, the time spent writing down this irrelevant material could have been spent on writing relevant material and thus would have improved the overall mark.

Paul's second sentence also falls into the trap of being irrelevant and not gaining any credit. This sentence explains why day care is popular, and although Paul's comments here are accurate and demonstrate an admirable understanding, they do not in any way answer the question, which, remember, requires a critical discussion of possible effects of day care on children's social development.

The comments about Bowlby's maternal deprivation hypothesis are relevant to the question and thus creditworthy, but the material is expressed in a very general or basic manner and could have been much more clearly focused on social development, rather than just stating that it would have negative effects. Paul could have developed this point by possibly outlining some effects of day care that have been found to affect children's social development negatively. The general comment about Bowlby earns AO1 credit, as it is a description of possible effects, albeit a basic description. However, the comment about Bowlby's work focusing on long-term separations rather than the short-term separations that day care incurs is a relevant AO2 comment, as it is an evaluative comment about Bowlby's hypothesis. This is again a basic comment, as it is not explicitly linked to day care, nor to children's social development.

Unfortunately, this AO2 comment is one of only two examples in the answer of relevant AO2 material. Indeed, that is the main negative criticism of this answer: that it is extremely unbalanced in favour of its AO1 content.

The following comment about Belsky's research is of a much better quality. It is accurate and relevant, focusing as it does upon areas of social development; attachment types and aggressive behaviour. This again is AO1 material and again could have been much improved by the provision of more relevant details concerning Belsky's work, for instance that her research was centred on babies who encountered day care in their first year of life and that such children were compared with a control group of similar children cared for at home in order to gain the results found. The last comment that Paul provides about the work of Jay Belsky, that other studies have supported her findings, is an AO2 comment, as it critically evaluates the creditworthiness of Belsky's findings by comparison with other research. The comment is, however, a fairly basic one, indeed almost rudimentary. The logical progression here of course would have been to go on and outline other relevant studies and to evaluate them in terms of how they supported Belsky's findings – for instance, Bates *et al.* (1994) study, which looked at teacher and peer ratings of social behaviour in 600 five- to six-year-old American children. Teachers rated children who had encountered a considerable amount of day care in their first five years of life as being less socially skilled than other children, while peers assessed them as being far from popular. This supports Belsky, as it also finds the effects of day care on children's social development to be negative ones.

Paul then outlines for us some comments concerning the possible positive effects of day care upon children's social development. These are focused upon the work of Andersson, performed on Swedish children. These comments are to be commended, because by providing evidence of both possible negative and possible positive effects of day care on children's social development, Paul is addressing the AO1 requirement to provide an appropriate selection of material to address the question. There is an increased amount of relevant detail here not apparent in the earlier parts of this answer, such as the reference to the fact that these children had been in day care from infancy for many years and that the results were found by comparing the sample to a control group of children who had only received maternal care. What these possible positive effects are is also outlined: that such children are more popular and socially skilled.

AO2 credit could have been earned here by the provision of evaluative commentary that focused upon the fact that the work was carried out on Swedish children and that Sweden is well known for its excellent day care provision. Therefore, the findings of possible positive effects of day care on children's social development could be in part due to the excellent day care provision in Sweden and that similar studies finding negative effects may be due to their being carried out in other countries where day care is not so excellent in its provision.

The second reference to the work of Andersson is flawed because Paul has confused the work of Andersson with that of Harrison and Ungerer (2002) carried out on Australian children. However, the comments made gain AO1 credit, as they are relevant and accurate. These comments, though, could have benefited from a lot more relevant detail – for example, that the findings came from the questioning of 145 mothers on their work behaviour and attitudes, and assessment of attachment types at 12 months of age. The finding was that mothers who returned to work when their baby was less than five months old were more likely to have a child with a secure attachment. AO2 credit could have been gained here by a consideration that the findings back up those of Andersson. Similar credit could also have been elicited by referring to relevant methodological considerations, for example that Harrison and Ungerer's study relied somewhat upon mothers' assessments of their own work behaviour and attitudes and that these assessments could have been faulty and thus negatively affected the results.

Paul's final contribution to his answer is the concluding sentence concerning the work of Ruhm. At first glance this seems to be a reasonable AO1 comment, and indeed the material is expressed in a clear manner and is accurate, demonstrating sound knowledge and understanding. Unfortunately, though, it receives no credit at all, for it concerns cognitive development rather than the required social development. Again, though, these irrelevant comments do not lose marks, as only correct and relevant material is marked. However, as was pointed out earlier, time used to express this material could have actually been spent providing material relevant to the question, which would have increased Paul's final mark for this question. Overall, the AO1 material fits into the wording of the basic mark band descriptor, being demonstrative of some relevant knowledge and understanding, but lacking in detail and being a little muddled. The mark gained comes from the top end of the mark band, as the quality of the answer is closer to the mark band descriptors in the mark band above than the one below. The two AO2 comments taken as a whole contribution are at the lower end of the basic mark band descriptor as they provide only a basic evaluation of strengths and weaknesses and there is also evidence of a superficial consideration

Figure 8.6 Including positive and negative points in your essays is a good way to achieve balance

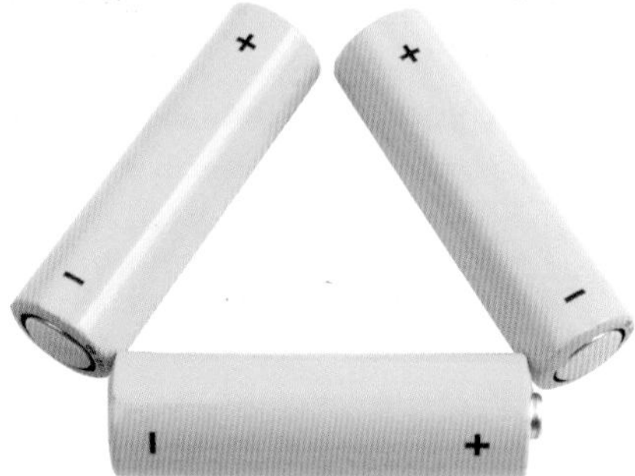

of a restricted range of issues and/or evidence. The mark gained is at the lower end of this mark band descriptor, for in quality the material provided is closer to the band below than the one above. Marks: AO1 = 3/6 + AO2 = 2/6 = 5/12

Good answer by Elidh

There is conflicting evidence to suggest that day care can either have positive or negative effects on children's social development. The whole idea of whether day care is beneficial or not is affected by bias from several sources, such as religious and political groups that see day care as anti-family and unnatural and also by feminist elements that see day care as being essential to mothers having the option to work. Psychology needs to conduct research that is free of such biases in order to gain valid results. Such valid results could lead to the formation of day care practices that do have a positive effect on social development.

Belsky suggested that babies placed in day care in the first year of life are at a higher risk of having an insecure attachment type and of being aggressive compared to children reared at home. The central point seemed to be the length of the day care provided, especially if the day care was full time, or close to it. Most studies support Belsky's view that day care can have negative effects on children's social development, such as Hofferth's study on over 500 American children, which found spending long hours in day care was associated with higher levels of aggression.

These are not proper experiments, though, that can determine causality. For instance, patterns of secure and insecure attachment may be due not to whether day care has been experienced, but rather to patterns of attachment being passed on from one generation to another.

There is some evidence that suggests day care can have positive effects on social development. Andersson assessed over 100 Swedish children who had been in day care from infancy to 13 years of life. Compared with a control group of maternal-care raised children, the day care children were seen to be more popular and socially skilled. Swedish day care is famous for its high quality, though, and this may be why day care had positive effects, whilst studies in other countries where day care isn't as high quality found negative effects on social development.

However, Harrison and Ungerer gave support to Andersson when their Australian study suggested that women who returned to work before a child was five months old were more likely to have a child with a secure attachment type.

Research needs to identify what are the important factors in positively affecting social development, such as length of care, type of care, etc., so that such factors can be generally utilised to positive effect.

Examiner's comments

Elidh's answer contains many examples of good practice. She begins by outlining the fact that there is evidence to suggest that day care can have both positive and negative effects on children's social development and that the whole topic area is affected by bias from many sources. The initial sentence of this is AO1 material as it describes the general findings of research in this topic area. However, the rest of this passage is AO2 material that is shaped into an informed commentary pertinent to the relevant issue that practical applications could be gained from bias free research. This general overlook of the topic area is quite a clever way to begin such an answer, especially as it is then followed by more specific material oriented around this general overlook.

Elidh then goes on to outline, as did Paul in the other example of an answer to this question, to use the relevant research of Jay Belsky. However, Elidh provides a lot more in the way of AO1 detail than did Paul, and this is accurately and clearly described. The fact that other studies tend to find similar results to Belsky is an AO2 evaluative point lending support to Belsky's claims. Such support is even given more credence by the supplying of Hofferth's findings. The material is used here in an AO2 manner, as it is shaped into an informed commentary upon the point being made.

The next passage is linked to the previous one and is all AO2 material centred on the methodological limitations of the research being conducted. This is well explained and is a legitimate strategy for gaining AO2 credit in these types of questions.

Elidh then goes on to present the other side of the argument, one that was introduced in her initial passage, that some research has found beneficial effects of day care upon children's social development. Paul, in the previous example of an answer to this question, also adopted this approach, but it is done much better here. For a start, a lot more relevant and accurate AO1 detail concerning Andersson's Swedish study is provided and this has the evaluative AO2 point added to it that the findings might be due to the high quality of Swedish day care and that in research conducted in other studies, which find negative effects of day care, those affects may actually be due to a lack of such high-quality day care.

Additional AO2 credit is then earned by the final comment of this passage, where Elidh points out that support is given to Andersson's findings by Harrison and Ungerer's Australian study. This again is AO2 material, because it is shaped into an informed commentary upon the point being made.

Elidh then concludes her excellent answer with a global AO2 point oriented towards implications and applications of this research. As this point is made in such a way that it is oriented to the demands of the question, it is a legitimate one and therefore creditworthy.

Overall, the AO2 content of Elidh's answer is at the top level; effective use of material is evident several times that provides an informed commentary. There is also evidence of effective evaluation and there is a broad range of issues covered in sufficient depth. Elidh also communicates her answer well and uses a good range of psychological terminology. The AO1 content is good, but not at the same level as her AO2 material. It is less detailed and generally accurate, and there is evidence of selection of material to address the question. The quality of the AO1 material is closer to the mark band descriptor below than the one above, and that is the criterion upon which the AO1 mark is decided. The AO1 credit is generally earned by description of relevant research and it is difficult to see how, in the time available, Elidh could realistically increase the AO1 content. What she could do is to cut down on the amount of AO2 material; there is more than sufficient here to get the six AO2 marks available. This would then free up time that could be dedicated to increasing the AO1 content, possibly by detailing more relevant research. To be able to create this kind of ideal AO1/AO2 balance in answers such as these is a skill that will come to most students only by the diligent practising of such answers. Even students as evidently talented and informed as Elidh can benefit from such a strategy.
Marks: AO1 = 4/6 + AO2 = 6/6 = 10/12

CONCLUSION

Hopefully, you now have a better understanding of the examination process, so know what you have to do to gain good marks. Working in a systematic and focused way, not only during the revision period but throughout your psychology course, will enable you to increase your understanding of both the subject content and the skills you need so that you can answer exam questions with confidence.

Remember to use the revision techniques regularly, and not just immediately before the exams. Use exam-type questions as a way to study and to revise. It will help if you try to create examination-like conditions while you do them – for example, by setting yourself a time limit.

By putting the ideas in this chapter into practice, you will increase not only your knowledge and confidence but also your motivation to study. All these will help to do well in your exams.

Good luck!

Epilogue: Want to explore psychology further?

Thinking ahead

By the end of this chapter, you should be able to:

- **understand what is involved in studying A2 psychology**
- **start researching possible careers in psychology**
- **find a degree course accredited by the British Psychological Society**
- **check out the entry requirements for a range of psychology degrees**
- **research the quality of psychology degrees you are considering**

If you hadn't already guessed by now, we love our subject! We would therefore love to see as many students as possible continue the subject to A2 level, go on to study psychology at university and go on to have careers in psychology. The aim of this very short epilogue is to give you some information to help you think about your options.

A2 PSYCHOLOGY

If you are reaching the end of your AS course, you have a couple of decisions to make about your future. Most immediately, should you continue to A2? Let us briefly take you through the content of A2 psychology and the ways you might find it different from your AS level.

The A2 content

A2 psychology aims to build on the knowledge and skills you have gained at AS level. There are two further units at A2. The first is Unit 3, Topics in Psychology. You or your teacher will select three topics to study in depth out of the following options:

- biological rhythms and sleep
- perception
- relationships
- aggression
- eating behaviour
- gender
- intelligence and learning
- cognition and development.

In Unit 4 you study psychopathology, the study of mental health and mental disorder. You also study one of the following three options:

- media psychology
- psychology of addictive behaviour
- anomalistic psychology (parapsychology).

In addition you will study research methodology, including statistical analysis. You can read the whole specification here: http://www.aqa.org.uk/qual/gceasa/psya. If the web address changes, go to http://www.aqa.org.uk/ and search or browse.

Figure E1 *Exploring psychology* for A2

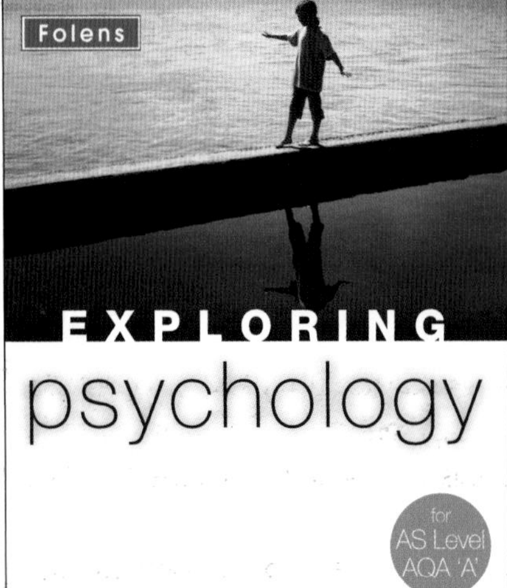

What else is different at A2?

AS levels are a fairly new idea, intended as a stepping-stone between GCSE and A level. Your stepping-stone stage is now over, and you can expect A2 to be at a higher level than AS. What does that mean in practice? It does *not* mean that all the psychology you have to study will be harder to understand than what you came across at AS level. However, exam questions will require some longer answers and there will be tougher testing of your high-level thinking skills such as evaluation. If you have completed our critical, practical and creative thinking exercises this year, then these thinking skills should come to you more naturally at A2. We also have an *Exploring Psychology* for A2 to continue to support you.

In addition, some areas of psychology, in particular research methods, get rather more technical at A2. You will have to study statistics. Try not to be too put off by this; the major difference from maths at school is that statistics in psychology is there to help us answer questions. In psychology it should always be clear *why* you are analysing data, and this makes stats easier to understand than maths at school, where you were expected to be interested in the mechanics of sums without knowing the point of them!

PSYCHOLOGY AT UNIVERSITY

As well as choosing whether to study A2 Psychology, you might also be thinking at the moment about making an application to university. Again, you won't be surprised to learn that we both heartily recommend going on to study psychology at degree level. There is no space in this chapter to talk through all the factors that might affect your decision, but we can point you in the direction of good advice. First, think about possible careers. Do you want to be a psychologist? If so, then you *must* start with a psychology degree. Also, think about the entry requirements of psychology degrees and the quality of the various courses you might apply for.

Finding out about careers in psychology

When people think of 'a psychologist' they usually think about clinical psychology, the application of psychology to understanding and helping with mental health problems. Actually, applied psychology is very broad, and psychologists work in many different fields, including health, sport, education, criminal justice and work.

You can read about careers in psychology here: http://www.bps.org.uk/careers/areas/areas_home.cfm. If the web address changes, go to http://www.bps.org.uk/ and search or browse.

If you have no idea what you want to do for a living but psychology is your favourite subject, our advice is to go for it! Most people with psychology degrees do not go on to become psychologists; a psychology degree will prove to a range of employers that you have a range of transferable skills, including conducting research, analysing information and report-writing. You are not limiting yourself to a career as a psychologist by taking a psychology degree.

Accredited psychology degrees

There are currently 348 degrees in the United Kingdom accredited by the British psychological Society. These include straight psychology and a range of joint and combined honours courses. If you are planning a career in psychology, it is important to choose an accredited degree.

You can view the accredited courses here: http://www.bps.org.uk/careers/accredited-courses/. If the web address changes, go to http://www.bps.org.uk/ and search or browse.

Entry requirements

Psychology is now the most applied-for undergraduate subject in the country. This means that entry requirements are very high, often on a par with law and medicine. For the most prestigious courses, this can mean up to three A-grades at A level.

You can find entry requirements for psychology here: http://www.ucas.com/students/coursesearch/coursesearch2008/. (The last 4 digits are the year of entry. You will need to change that according to the year you wish to start.)

However, before leaping for the most prestigious courses or getting downhearted because you can't see yourself getting those grades, consider the following:

- The most sought-after courses are not necessarily those that will suit you best as an individual learner. Go to some open days, meet some psychology lecturers and see where you feel comfortable.
- The most popular courses are often so sought-after partly for their location. If you are happy to study in Ireland, Scotland, Wales or London, you have a good chance of getting on to a highly rated course with lower grades.

If you would like to pursue psychology further but don't see yourself getting the top grades, do look at the UCAS website and check out the full range of entry requirements. Remember, there are over 300 accredited courses with a wide range of entry grades; there is a good chance you will find what you're looking for.

Measures of course quality

There are two major published figures that are used to define the quality of a university department:

- The Research Assessment Exercise (RAE) grade. This is a measure of how successful the department is in publishing research. The RAE scale goes from 1 to 5*, 5* being the highest.

You can read psychology RAE scores here: http://www.hero.ac.uk/rae/Results/

- The National Student Surveys. Statistics are recorded of how highly Psychology undergraduates rated their courses. Scores are out of 5 for several criteria, including quality of teaching and feedback.

You can read Student Satisfaction scores here: http://www2.tqi.ac.uk/sites/tqi/home/index.cfm

The Times also publishes a 'Good University Guide'. This includes RAE, student survey results and other measures such as graduate employment statistics.

You can view the *Times* guide here: http://extras.timesonline.co.uk/gug/gooduniversityguide.php

The same provisos apply as with looking at entry grades. Think about where you will be comfortable. Think as well about how important to you personally are student satisfaction scores and RAE grades.

A FINAL WORD

We really hope you have enjoyed your AS Psychology and this book. We would also love to see you carrying on with Psychology to A2 and perhaps at university. If that appeals to you and you think it is a possibility, check out the links in this chapter. See what courses you can realistically apply for and what career options may be open to you. Don't forget as well that we have an *Exploring Psychology* for A2. Happy exploring!

Matt & Julia

References

Abernethy EM (1940) The effect of changed environmental conditions upon the results of college examinations. *Journal of Psychology* **10**, 293–301.

Abrams M & Ellis A (1996) Rational emotive behaviour therapy in the treatment of stress. In S Palmer & W Dryden (eds) *Stress management and counselling*. London: Cassell.

Adityanjee M, Sajtovic M & Munshi KR (2005) Neuropsychiatric sequelae of neuroleptic malignant syndrome. *Clinical Neuropharmacology* **28**(4), 197–204.

Adorno TW, Frenkel-Brunswik E, Levinson DJ & Sanford RN (1950) *The authoritarian personality*: New York: Harper & Row.

Ahnert L, Gunnar MR, Lamb ME & Barthel M (2004) Transition to child care: associations with infant-mother attachment, infant negative emotions and elevated cortisol levels. *Child Development* **75**, 639-50.

Ahnert L, Pinquart M & Lamb ME (2006) Security of children's relationships with nonparental carers: a meta-analysis. *Child Development* **74**, 664–79.

Ainsworth MDS (1967) *Infancy in Uganda: infant care and the growth of love*. Baltimore: Johns Hopkins University Press.

Ainsworth MDS (1989) Attachments beyond infancy. *American Psychologist* **44**, 709–16.

Ainsworth MDS & Wittig BA (1969) Attachment theory and the exploratory behaviour of one-year-olds in a strange situation. In Foss BM (ed.) *Determinants of infant behaviour*, vol. 4, London: Methuen.

Aldridge AA & Roesch SC (2007) Coping and adjustment in children with cancer: a meta-analytic study. *Journal of Behavioral Medicine* 30(2), 115–29.

Allhusen V & NICHD (2003) Does quality of day care affect child outcomes at age 41/2? *Developmental Psychology* **39**, 451–9.

Altemeyer, B (1981) *Right-wing authoritarianism.* Winnipeg, Ontario: University of Manitoba Press.

Andersson BE (1996) Children's development related to day care, type of family and other home factors. *European Child and Adolescent Psychiatry* **5**, 73–5.

Armfield J (2007) Manipulating perceptions of spider characteristics and predicted spider fear: evidence for the cognitive vulnerability model of the etiology of fear. *Journal of Anxiety Disorders* **21**, 691–703.

Arroll B, Macgillivray S, Ogston S, Reid I, Sullivan F, Williams B & Crombie I (2005) Efficacy and tolerability of tricyclic antidepressants and SSRIS compared with placebo for treatment of depression in primary care: a meta-analysis. *Annals of Family Medicine* **3**, 449–56.

Asch SE (1955) Opinions and social pressure. *Scientific American* **193**, 31–5.

Atkinson RE & Shiffrin RM (1968) A human memory: a proposed system and its control processes. In KW Spence & JT Spence (eds) *The psychology of learning and motivation*, vol 2. London: Academic Press.

Atkinson RC & Shiffrin RM (1971) The control of short-term memory. *Scientific American* **225**(2), 82–90.

Baddeley AD (1966) The influence of acoustic and semantic similarity on long-term memory for word sequences. *Quarterly Journal of Experimental Psychology* **18**(4), 302–9.

Baddeley AD (1986) *Working memory*. Oxford: Clarendon Press.

Baddeley A (1996) The fractionation of working memory. *Proceedings of the National Academy of Sciences, USA* **93,** 13468–72.

Baddeley AD (2000) The episodic buffer: a new component of working memory? *Trends in Cognitive Sciences* **4**, 417–23.

Baddeley A (2003) Working memory and language: an overview. *Journal of Communication Disorders* **36**, 189–208.

Baddeley AD & Hitch G (1974) Working memory. In GA Bower (ed.) *The psychology of learning and motivation*, vol 8. New York: Academic Press.

Baddeley AD, Grant S, Wight E & Thomson N (1973) Imagery and visual working memory. In PMA Rabbitt & S Dornic (eds) *Attention and performance V*. London: Academic Press.

Baddeley AD, Thompson N & Buchanan M (1975) Word length and the structure of short-term memory. *Journal of Verbal Learning and Verbal Behavior*, **14**, 375–589.

Bahrick HP (1984) Semantic memory content in permastore: fifty years of memory for Spanish learned in school. *Journal of Experimental Psychology: General* **113**(1), 1–29.

Bahrick LE, Parker JF, Fivush R & Levitt M (1998) The effects of stress on young children's memory for a natural disaster. *Journal of Experimental Psychology: Applied*, 4: 308-31.

Bailey HN, Moran G, Pederson GR & Bento S (2007) Understanding the transmission of attachment using variable- and relationship-centered approaches. *Development and Psychopathology* **19**, 313–43.

Baker JR, Bezance JB, Zellaby E & Aggleton JP (2004) Chewing gum can produce context-dependent effects upon memory. *Appetite* **43**, 207–10.

Balevre P (2001) Professional nursing burnout and irrational thinking. *Journal for Nurses in Staff Development* **17**(5), 264–71.

Banse R (2004) Adult attachment and marital satisfaction: evidence for dyadic configuration effects. *Journal of Social & Personal Relationships* **21**, 273–82.

Bates J, Marvinney D, Kelly T, Dodge K, Bennett R & Pettit G (1994) Childcare history and kindergarten adjustment. *Developmental Psychology* **30**, 690–700.

Beck AT (1976) *Cognitive therapy and the emotional disorders.* New York: International Universities Press.

Belsky J (1986) Infant day care: a cause for concern? *Zero to Three* **6**, 1–9.

Belsky J (1999) Modern evolutionary theory and patterns of attachment. In J Cassidy & P Shaver (eds) *Handbook of attachment: theory, research and clinical applications*. New York: Guilford Press.

Belsky J (2002) Quantity counts: amount of child care and children's socioemotional development. *Developmental & Behavioral Pediatrics* **23**, 167–70.

Belsky J & Fearon RMP (2002) Infant–mother attachment security, contextual risk and early development: a moderational analysis. *Development & Psychopathology* **14**, 293–310.

Bembenek A (2005) Does the foetus exposition on influenza virus increase the risk of schizophrenia in adult life? *Psychiatry in Poland* **39**, 271-83.

Bergin AE & Garfield S (1978) *Handbook of psychotherapy and behavior change*. New York: Wiley.

Bettencourt BA, Talley A, Benjamin AJ & Valentine J (2006) Personality and aggressive behavior under provoking and neutral conditions: a meta-analytic review. *Psychological Bulletin* **132**(5), 751–77.

Billings AG & Moos RH (1981) The role of coping responses and social resources in attenuating the stress of life events. *Journal of Behavioral Medicine* **4**, 139–57.

Blades M & Krähenbühl S (2006) The effect of interviewing techniques on young children's responses to questions. *Child: Care, Health and Development* **32**(3), 321–31.

Blass T (1991) Understanding behaviour in the Milgram obedience experiment: the role of personality, situation and their interaction. *Journal of Personality & Social Psychology* **60**, 398–413.

Blass T & Schmitt C (2001) The nature of perceived authority in the Milgram paradigm: two replications. *Current Psychology* **20**, 115–21.

Boen F, Vanden Auweele Y, Claes E, Feys J & De Cuyper B (2006). The impact of open feedback on conformity among judges in rope skipping. *Psychology of Sport & Exercise* **7**, 577–90.

Bonanno GA, Galea S, Bucciarelli A & Vlahov D (2007) What predicts psychological resilience after disaster? The role of demographics, resources, and life stress. *Journal of Consulting and Clinical Psychology* **75**(5), 671–82.

Bowlby J (1955) Mother–child separation. In K Soddy (ed.) *Mental health and infant development.* London: Routledge.

Bowlby J (1957) Symposium on the contribution of current theories to an understanding of child development. *British Journal of Medical Psychology* **30**, 230–40.

Bowlby J (1969) *Attachment and loss*, vol 1. London: Pimlico.

Bowlby J, Robertson J & Rosenbluth D (1952) A two year-old goes to hospital. *The Psychoanalytic Study of the Child* **7**, 82–94.

Brazleton TB, Tronick E, Adamson L, Als H & Wise S (1975) Early mother–infant reciprocity: parent–infant interaction. *Ciba Symposium* **33**, 137–54.

Brehm, J. W. (1966) *A theory of psychological reactance*. New York: Academic Press.

Brehony KA & Geller ES (1981) Relationships between psychological androgyny, social conformity, and perceived locus of control. *Psychology of Women Quarterly* **6**, 204–17.

Brennan M & Brennan R (1988) *Stranger Language*. Wagga Wagga, New South Wales: Riverina Murry Institute of Higher Education.

Breuer J & Freud S (1896) *Studies on hysteria. The complete works of Sigmund Freud*, vol. 2. London: Hogarth Press.

Brimacombe CA, Quinton N, Nance N & Garrioch L (1997) Is age irrelevant? Perceptions of young and old adult eyewitnesses. *Law and Human Behavior* **21**(6), 619–34.

Brosnan MJ & Thorpe SJ (2006) An evaluation of two clinically-derived treatments for technophobia. *Computers in Human Behavior* **22**, 1080–95.

Brown AS (2006) Prenatal infection as a risk factor for schizophrenia. *Schizophrenia Bulletin* **32**, 200–2.

Budzynski TH, Stoyva JM, Adler CS & Mullaney DJ (1973) EMG biofeedback and tension headache: a controlled outcome study. *Psychosomatic Medicine* **35**(6), 484–96.

Butler AC & Beck JS (2000) Cognitive therapy outcomes: a review of meta-analyses. *Journal of the Norwegian Psychological Association*, **37**, 1–9.

Butler AC, Chapman JE, Forman EM & Beck AT (2006) The empirical status of cognitive-behavioral therapy: a review of meta-analyses. *Clinical Psychology Review* **26**, 17–31.

Cantero MJ & Cerezo MA (2001) Mother–infant interaction as predictor of attachment behaviours: two causal models. *Infancia y Aprendizaje* **24**, 113–32.

Carmichael LC, Hogan HP & Walter AA (1932) An experimental study of the effect of language on the reproduction of visually perceived form. *Journal of Experimental Psychology* **15**, 73–86.

Carter CA, Bottom BL & Levine M (1996) Linguistic and socioemotional influences on the accuracy of children's reports. *Law and Human Behavior,* 20: 335–58.

Choy Y, Fyer AJ & Lipsitz JD (2006) Treatment of specific phobia in adults. *Clinical Psychology Review* **27**, 266–86.

Clarke ADB & Clarke AM (1998) Early experience and the life path. *The Psychologist* **11**, 433-436.

Cohen J (2004) Parasocial break-up from favourite television characters: the role of attachment styles and relationship intensity. *Journal of Social & Personal Relationships* **21**, 187–202.

Cohen S, Tyrrell DA & Smith AP (1993) Negative life events, perceived stress, negative affect, and susceptibility to the common cold. *Journal of Personality and Social Psychology* **64**, 131–40.

Collins DL, Baum A & Singer J (1983) Coping with chronic stress at Three Mile Island: psychological and biochemical evidence. *Health Psychology*, **2**, 149–66.

Conners FA, Rosenquist CJ, Atwell JA & Klinger LG (2000) Cognitive strengths and weaknesses associated with Prader–Willi syndrome. *Education and Training in Mental Retardation and Developmental Disabilities* **35**(4), 441–8.

Conrad R (1964) Acoustic confusions in immediate memory. *British Journal of Psychology* **55**, 75–84.

Conway LG & Schaller M (2005) When authorities' commands backfire: attributions about consensus and effects on deviant decision making. *Journal of Personality & Social Psychology* **89**, 311–26.

Courtois R, Réveillère C, Paüs A, Berton L & Jouint C (2007) Links between stress factors, mental health and initial consumption of tobacco and alcohol during pre-adolescence. *Encephale* **33**(3 Pt 1), 300–9.

Crandall CS, Eshleman A & O'Brien L (2002) Social norms and the expression and suppression of prejudice: The struggle for internalization. *Journal of Personality and Social Psychology* **82**, 359–78.

Curtiss S (1977) *Genie: a psycholinguistic study of a modern day 'wild child'*. London, Academic Press.

Daneman M & Carpenter P (1980) Individual differences in working memory and reading. *Journal of Verbal Learning and Verbal Behavior* **19**, 450–66.

Daneman M & Carpenter PA (1983) Individual differences in integrating information between and within sentences. *Journal of Experimental Psychology: Learning, Memory, and Cognition* **9**, 561–84.

Dannlowski U, Ohrmann P, Bauer J, Kugel H, Baune BT, Hohoff C, Kersting A, Arolt V, Heindel W, Deckert J & Suslow T (2007) Serotonergic genes modulate amygdala activity in major depression. *Genes, Brain & Behavior* **6**, 672–76.

De Meuse KP (1985) The relationship between life events and indices of classroom preference. *Teaching of Psychology*, **12**(3), 146–9.

De Schipper JC, Van Ijzendoorn M & Tavecchio LWC (2004) Stability in center day care: relations with children's well-being and problem behavior. *Social Development* **13**, 531–49.

DeLongis A, Folkman S & Lazarus RS (1988) The impact of daily stress on health and mood: psychological and social resources as mediators. *Journal of Personality and Social Psychology* **54**(3), 486–95.

Den Hartog DN, De Hoogh AHB & Keegan AE (2007) The interactive effects of belongingness and charisma on helping and compliance. *Journal of Applied Psychology* **92**, 1131–9.

Denollet J (1998) Personality and risk of cancer in men with coronary heart disease. *Psychological Medicine* **28**, 991–5.

Desmond DM (2007) Coping, affective distress, and psychosocial adjustment among people with traumatic upper limb amputations. *Journal of Psychosomatic Research* **62**(1), 15–21.

Deutsch M & Gerard HB (1955) A study of normative and informational social influences upon individual judgment. *Journal of Abnormal and Social Psychology* **51**, 629-36.

D'Esposito M (2007) From cognitive to neural models of working memory. *Philosophical Transactions of the Royal Society of London B* **362**(1481), 761–72.

Dolcos F, Miller B, Kragel P, Jha A & McCarthy G (2007) Regional brain differences in the effect of distraction during the delay interval of a working memory task. *Brain Research* **1152**, 171–81.

Dollard J & Miller NE (1950) *Personality & psychotherapy*. New York: McGraw-Hill.

Donovan W, Leavitt L, Taylor N & Broder J (2007) Maternal sensory sensitivity, mother–infant 9-month interaction, infant attachment status: predictors of mother–toddler interaction at 24 months. *Infant Behavior & Development* **30**, 336–52.

Dykens EM (2002) Are jigsaw puzzle skills 'spared' in persons with Prader-Willi syndrome? *Journal of Child Psychology and Psychiatry and Allied Disciplines*, 43(3): 343-52.

Ellis A (1977a) The basic clinical theory of rational emotive therapy. In A Ellis & R Grieger (eds) *Handbook of Rational Emotive Therapy*. Monterey, CA Brooks/Cole.

Ellis A (1977b) *Anger: how to live with and without it*. Secaucus, NJ: Citadel Press.

Elms AC & Milgram S (1966) Personality characteristics associated with obedience and defiance toward authoritative command. *Journal of Experimental Research in Personality* **1**, 282–9.

Elsinger PJ & Damasio AR (1985) Severe disturbance in higher cognition after bilateral frontal lobe ablation: patient EVR. *Neurology* **35**, 1731–41.

Engels GI, Garnefski N & Diekstra RF (1993) Efficacy of rational-emotive therapy: a quantitative analysis. *Journal of Consulting and Clinical Psychology* **61**(6), 1083–90.

Epping-Jordan JE, Compas BE & Howell DC (1994) Predictors of cancer progression in young adult men and women: avoidance, intrusive thoughts, and psychological symptoms. *Health Psychology* **13**, 539–47.

Eranti S, Mogg A, Pluck G, Landau S, Purvis R, Brown RG, Howard R & Knapp M (2007) A randomized, controlled trial with 6-month follow-up of repetitive transcranial magnetic stimulation and electroconvulsive therapy for severe depression. *American Journal of Psychiatry* **164**, 73–81.

Erikson EH (1950) *Identity and the life cycle*. New York: Norton.

Erlandsson LK & Eklund M (2003) The relationships of hassles and uplifts to experience of health in working women. *Women & Health* **38**(4), 19–37.

Eysenck HJ (1952) The effects of psychotherapy: an evaluation. *Journal of Consulting Psychology* **16**, 319–24.

Eyssel F, Boehner G & Siebler F (2006) Perceived rape myth acceptance of others predicts rape proclivity: social norm or judgmental anchoring? *Swiss Journal of Psychology* **65**, 93–9.

Farah MJ, Hammond KM, Levine DN & Calvanio R (1988) Visual and spatial mental imagery: dissociable systems of representation. *Cognitive Psychology* **20**, 439–62.

Festinger LA (1957) *A theory of cognitive dissonance*. New York: HarperCollins.

Fisher RP, Geiselman RE, Raymond DS, Jurkevich LM & Warhaftig ML (1987) Enhancing enhanced eyewitness memory: refining the cognitive interview. *Journal of Police Science and Administration* **15**, 291–7.

Fisher RP, Geiselman RE & Amador M (1989) A field test of the cognitive interview: enhancing recollections of actual victims and witnesses. *Journal of Applied Psychology* **74**, 722–27.

Forde EM & Humphreys GW (2002) The role of semantic knowledge in short-term memory. *Neurocase* **8**, 13–27.

Forgays DK, Ottaway SA, Guarino A & D'Alessio M (2001) Parenting stress in employed and at-home mothers in Italy. *Journal of Family and Economic Issues* **22**, 327–51.

Freud S (1894) The defence neuropsychoses. In J Strachey (ed.) (1953) *The standard edition of the complete psychological works of Sigmund Freud*, vol. 1, London: Hogarth Press.

Freud S (1905) *Three essays on sexuality.* London: Hogarth Press.

Freud S (1917) Mourning and melancholia. *Collected works*, vol. 14. London: Hogarth Press.

Frydenberg E, Lewis R, Kennedy G, Ardila R, Fridte W & Hannoun R (2003) Coping with concerns: an exploratory comparison of Australian, Colombian, German and Palestinian adolescents. *Journal of Youth and Adolescence* **32**, 59–66.

Fuertes M, Santos PL, Beeghly M & Tronick E (2006) More than maternal sensitivity shapes attachment: the role of infant coping and temperament. *Annals of the New York Academy of Science* **1094**, 292–6.

Galan RF, Weidert M, Menzel R, Herz AV & Galizia CG (2006) Sensory memory for odors is encoded in spontaneous correlated activity between olfactory glomeruli. *Neural Computation* **18**(1), 10–25.

Gallardo M, Baños RM, Belloch A & Ruipérez MA (1999) Attentional biases and vulnerability to depression. *Spanish Journal of Psychology* **2**(1), 11–19.

Geddes JR, Verdoux H, Takei N, Lawrie SM, Bovet P, Eagles JM, Heun R, McCreadie RG, McNeil TF, O'Callaghan E, Stöber G, Willinger U & Murray RM (1999) Schizophrenia and complications of pregnancy and labor: an individual patient data meta-analysis. *Schizophrenia Bulletin* **25**, 413–23.

Geher G, Bauman KP, Hubbard SEK & Legare JR (2002) Self and other obedience estimates: biases and moderators. *Journal of Social Psychology* **142**, 677–89.

Geiselman RE & Fisher RP (1997) Ten years of cognitive interviewing. In DG Payne & FG Conrad (eds) *Intersections in basic and applied memory research.* Mahwah, NJ: Lawrence Erlbaum Associates.

Geiselman RE, Fisher RP, MacKinnon DP & Holland HL (1985) Eyewitness memory enhancement in police interview: cognitive retrieval mnemonics versus hypnosis. *Journal of Applied Psychology* **70**, 401–12.

Genco RJ, Ho AW, Grossi SG, Dunford RG & Tedesco LA (1999) Relationship of Stress, Distress, and Inadequate Coping Behaviors to Periodontal Disease. *Journal of Periodontology*, **70**(7), 711–23.

Ginet M & Verkampt F (2007) The cognitive interview: is its benefit affected by the level of witness emotion? *Memory* **15**(4), 450–64.

Glanzer M & Cunitz AR (1966) Two storage mechanisms in free recall. *Journal of Verbal Learning and Verbal Behavior* **5**, 351–60.

Godden DR & Baddeley AD (1975) Context-dependent memory in two natural environments: on land and underwater. *British Journal of Psychology* **66**, 325–31.

Griskevicius V, Goldstein NJ, Mortensen CR, Cialdini R & Kenrick D (2006) Going along versus going alone: when fundamental motives influence strategic (non) conformity. *Journal of Personality & Social Psychology* **91**, 281–94.

Groeger JA (1997) *Memory and remembering.* Harlow: Addison Wesley Longman.

Grossman KE & Grossman K (1990) The wider concept of attachment in cross-cultural research. *Human Development* **33**, 31–47.

Gudjonsson, GH (1989) Compliance in an interrogative situation: a new scale. *Personality and Individual Differences* **10**, 535–40.

Gudjonsson GH & MacKeith J (1997) *Disputed confessions and the criminal justice system*. London: Maudsley.

Gudjonsson GH & Sigurdsson JF (2003) The relationship of compliance with coping strategies and self-esteem. *European Journal of Psychological Assessment* **19**, 117–23.

Gupta MA & Gupta AK (2004) Stressful major life events are associated with a higher frequency of cutaneous sensory symptoms: an empirical study of non-clinical subjects. *Journal of the European Academy of Dermatology and Venereology* **8**(5), 560–5.

Haber RN & Haber RE (1964) Eidetic imagery: I. Frequency. *Perceptual and Motor Skills* **19**, 131–58.

Hadley CB & MacKay DG (2006) Does emotion help or hinder immediate memory? Arousal versus priority-binding mechanisms. *Journal of Experimental Psychology: Learning, Memory, and Cognition* **32**(1), 79–88.

Hair M, Renaud KV & Ramsay J (2007) The influence of self-esteem and locus of control on perceived email-related stress. *Computers in Human Behavior*, 23(6): 2791-803.

Hallberg UE, Johansson G & Schaufeli WB (2007) Type A behavior and work situation: associations with burnout and work engagement. *Scandinavian Journal of Psychology* **48**(2), 135–42.

Hamilton G, Cross D, Resnicow K & Hall M (2005) A school-based harm minimization smoking intervention trial: outcome results. *Addiction* **100**, 689–700.

Hamilton VL & Sanders J (1995) Crimes of obedience and conformity in the workplace: surveys of Americans, Russians and Japanese. *Journal of Social Issues* **51**, 67–88.

Hammarstrom A. & Janlert U (1997) Nervous and depressive symptoms in a longitudinal study of youth unemployment–selection or exposure? *Journal of Adolescence*, 20(3): 293-305.

Harlow H (1958) The nature of love. *American Psychologist* **13**, 673–85.

Harrington R, Campbell F, Shoebridge P & Whittaker J (1998) Meta-analysis of CBT for depression in adolescents. *Journal of the Academy of Child & Adolescent Psychiatry* **37**, 1005-1006.

Harrison LJ & Ungerer JA (2002) Maternal employment and infant–mother attachment security and 12 months post-partum. *Developmental Psychology* **38**, 758–73.

Heston LL (1966) Psychiatric disorders in foster home reared children of schizophrenic mothers. *British Journal of Psychiatry* **112**, 819–25.

Hodges J & Tizard B (1989) Social and family relationships of ex-institutional adolescents. *Journal of Child Psychology and Psychiatry* **30**, 77–98.

Hofferth S (1999) Child care in the first three years of life and language and preschoolers' behaviour. Paper presented at the Biennial Meeting of the Society for Research in Child Development, Albuquerque, NM, April.

Hofling KC, Brotzman E, Dalrymple S, Graves N & Pierce CM (1966) An experimental study in the nurse–physician relationship. *Journal of Nervous and Mental Disorders* **143**, 171–80.

Holmes TH & Rahe RH (1967) The social readjustment rating scale. *Journal of Psychosomatic Research* **11**, 213–8.

Holzhausen KG & Glyn RP (2001) Beyond compliance and acceptance: influence outcomes as a function of norm plausibility and processing mode. *Group Dynamics* **5**, 136–49.

Hosch HM & Cooper SD (1982) Victimization as a determinant of eyewitness accuracy. *Journal of Applied Psychology* **67**, 648–52.

House RJ, Spangler WD & Woycke J (1991) Personality and charisma in US presidents: a psychological theory of leadership effectiveness. *Administrative Science Quarterly* **36**, 364–96.

Howes C, Gallinsky E & Kontos S (1998) Child care sensitivity and attachment. *Social Development* **7**, 25–36.

Huang IN (1997) Recognition of student names past: a longitudinal study with $N = 1$. *Journal of General Psychology* **124**(1), 35–47.

Imbo I, Vandierendonck A & De Rammelaere S (2007) The role of working memory in the carry operation of mental arithmetic: number and value of the carry. *Quarterly Journal of Experimental Psychology* **60**(5), 708–31.

Jahoda M (1958) *Current concepts of positive mental health*. New York: Basic Books.

Jarvis M (2003) Can social representations theory explain negative responses from teachers to CBT-based stress management training? A case analysis. *Stress News: the Journal of the International Stress Management Association UK* **15**, 5–8.

Jepson E & Forrest S (2006) Individual contributory factors in teacher stress: the role of achievement striving and occupational commitment. *British Journal of Educational Psychology* **76**(Pt 1), 183–97.

Jones MC (1924) The elimination of children's fears. *Journal of Experimental Psychology* **7**, 382–90.

Kagan J, Kearsley RB & Zelazo PR (1980) *Infancy: its place in human development*. Cambridge, MA: Harvard University Press.

Kageyama T, Nishikido N, Kobayashi T, Kurokawa Y, Kaneko T, Kabuto M. (1998) Long commuting time, extensive overtime, and sympathodominant state assessed in terms of short-term heart rate variability among male white-collar workers in the Tokyo megalopolis. *Industrial Health*, **36**(3), 209-17.

Kanaan RA, Craig TKJ, Wesseley SC & David AS (2007) Imaging repressed memories in motor conversion disorder. *Psychosomatic Medicine* **69**, 202–5.

Kanner AD, Coyne JC, Schaefer C & Lazarus RS (1981) Comparison of two modes of stress measurement: daily hassles and uplifts versus major life events. *Journal of Behavioral Medicine* **4**(1), 1–39.

Karen R (1994) *Becoming attached: unfolding the mystery of the infant–mother bond and its impact on later life*. New York: Warner Books.

Kelman, H. (1958). Compliance, identification, and internalization: three processes of attitude change. *Journal of Conflict Resolution*, **1**, 51-60.

Kohlberg L (1966) A cognitive-developmental analysis of children's sex role concepts and attitudes. In EE Maccoby (ed.) *The development of sex differences*. Stanford, CA: Stanford University Press.

Köhler T, Theide G & Thöns M (2002) Kurz- und langerfristiges Vergessen von Wortassoziationen: Eine experimentelle Studie zur Freudschen Lehre von Widerstand und Verdrängung. *Zeitschrift für Klinische Psychologie, Psychiatrie und Psychotherapie* **50**(3), 328–33.

Koluchová J (1972) Severe deprivation in twins: a case study. *Journal of Child Psychology and Psychiatry* **13**, 107–11.

Koluchová J (1991) Severely deprived twins after 22 years observation. *Studia Psychologica* **33**, 23–8.

Koren-Karie N (2001) Mothers' attachment representations and choice of infant care: centre care vs home. *Infant & Child Development* **10**, 117–27.

Koster EHW, De Raedt R, Goeleven E, Franck E and Crombez G (2005) Mood-congruent attentional bias in dysphoria: maintained attention to and impaired disengagement from negative information. *Emotion* **5**, 446–55.

Krackow E & Lynn SJ (2003) Is there touch in the game of Twister? The effects of innocuous touch and suggestive questions on children's eyewitness memory. *Law and Human Behavior* **27**(6), 589–604.

Krähenbühl S & Blades M (2006) The effect of question repetition within interviews on young children's eyewitness recall. *Journal of Experimental and Child Psychology* **94**(1), 57–67.

Latif DA (2000) The relationship between pharmacy students' locus of control, Machiavellianism, and moral reasoning. *American Journal of Pharmaceutical Education* **64**, 33–7.

Lee JM & Watanuki S (2007) Cardiovascular responses of Type A and Type B behavior patterns to visual stimulation during rest, stress and recovery. *Journal of Physiological Anthropolology* **26**(1), 1–8.

Lee T, Toshiaki S, Megumi I, Kaoru O, Yuichiro Y & Shingo N (2006) Evaluation of psychosomatic stress in children by measuring salivary chromogranin A. *Acta Paediatrica* **95**(8), 935–9.

Leichsenring F & Leibing E (2007) Psychodynamic psychotherapy: a systematic review of techniques, indications and empirical evidence. *Psychology and Psychotherapy* **80**, 217–28.

Lewis C, Wilkins R, Baker L & Woobey A (1995) "Is this man your daddy?" Suggestibility in children's eyewitness identification of a family member. *Child Abuse and Neglect* **19**(6), 739–44.

Lindsay DS (1990) Misleading suggestions can impair witnesses' ability to remember event details. *Journal of Experimental Psychology: Learning, Memory and Cognition* **16**, 1077–83.

Linton M (1975) Memory for real-world events. In DA Norman & DE Rumelhart (eds) *Explorations in Cognition*. San Francisco: Freeman.

Lisanby SH, Maddox JH, Prudic J, Devanand DP & Sackeim HA (2000) The effects of electroconvulsive therapy on memory of autobiographical and public events. *Archives of General Psychiatry* **57**, 581–90.

Littlewood R & Lipsedge M (1997) *Aliens and alienists: ethnic minorities and psychiatry*. London: Routledge.

Loftus EF & Palmer JC (1974) Reconstruction of automobile destruction: an example of the interaction between language and memory. *Journal of Verbal Learning and Verbal Behavior* **13**, 585–9.

Loftus EF, Loftus GR & Messo J (1987) Some facts about 'weapon focus'. *Law and Human Behavior* **11**(1), 55–62.

Lorenz K (1935) The companion in the bird's world. *Auk* **54**, 245–73.

Lorenz KZ (1952) *King Solomon's ring*. London: Methuen.

Lüttke HB (2004) Experimente unter dem Milgram-Paradigma. *Gruppendynamik und Organisationsberatung* **35**, 431–64.

Main M & Solomon J (1986) Discovery of a disorganised disoriented attachment pattern. In *Affective development in infancy*. Norwood, Ablex.

Manes F, Hodges JR, Graham KS & Zeman A (2001) Focal autobiographical amnesia in association with transient epileptic amnesia. *Brain* **1243**, 499–509.

Marmot MG, Bosma H, Hemingway H, Brunner E & Stansfeld S (1997) Contribution of job control and other risk factors to social variations in coronary heart disease incidence. *The Lancet*, **350**: 235-9.

Martin-Loeches M, Schweinberger SR & Sommer W (1997) The phonological loop model of working memory: an ERP study of irrelevant speech and phonological similarity effects. *Memory & Cognition* **25**, 471–83.

Martz D (2003) Behavioral treatment for a female engaging in autoerotic asphyxiation. *Clinical Case Studies* **2**, 236–42.

Marucha PT, Kiecolt-Glaser JK & Favagehi M. (1998) Mucosal wound healing is impaired by examination stress. *Psychosomatic Medicine* **60**, 362–65.

Massie H & Szajnberg N (2002) The relationship between mothering in infancy, childhood experience and adult mental health. *International Journal of Psychoanalysis* **83**, 35–55.

Matz DC & Wood W (2005) Cognitive dissonance in groups: the consequences of disagreement. *Journal of Personality and Social Psychology* **88**, 22–37.

McCarthy G (1999) Attachment style and adult love relationships and friendships: a study of a group of women at risk of experiencing relationship difficulties. *British Journal of Medical Psychology* **72**, 305–21.

McClelland A, Kemps E & Tiggemann M (2006) Reduction of vividness and associated craving in personalized food imagery. *Journal of Clinical Psychology* **62**(3), 367–71.

McCutcheon E, Scott VB Jr, Aruguete MS and Parker J (2006) Exploring the link between attachment and the inclination to obsess about or stalk celebrities. *North American Journal of Psychology* **8**, 289–300.

Mead KML & Ball LJ (2007) Music tonality and context-dependent recall: the influence of key change and mood mediation. *European Journal of Cognitive Psychology* **19**(1), 59–79.

Melhuish EC, Mooney A, Martin S & Lloyd E (1990) Type of childcare at 18 months I. Differences in interactional experience. *Journal of Child Psychology and Psychiatry* **31**, 849–59.

Memon A, Holliday R & Hill C (2006) Pre-event stereotypes and misinformation effects in young children. *Memory* **14**, 104–14.

Menéndez Villalva C, Montes Martínez A, Núñez Losada C, Fernández Domínguez MJ, Gamarra Mondelo T & Buján Garmendia S (2002) Environmental stress and cardiovascular reactivity: the effect of stressful life events on hypertense patients. *Atención Primaria* **30**(10), 631–7.

Miles C & Hardman E (1998) State-dependent memory produced by aerobic exercise *Ergonomics* **41**(1), 20–8.

Milgram S (1963) Behavioral study of obedience. *Journal of Abnormal and Social Psychology* **67**, 371–8.

Milgram S (1965) Liberating effects of group pressure. *Journal of Personality & Social Psychology* **1**, 127–34.

Milgram S (1974) *Obedience to authority.* New York: Harper & Row.

Miller GA (1956) The magical number seven, plus or minus two: some limits on our capacity for processing information. *Psychological Review* **63**, 81–97.

Milner B (1970) Memory and the medial temporal regions of the brain. In KH Pribram & DE Broadbent (eds) *Biology of Memory*. New York: Academic Press.

Mitaishvili N & Danelia M (2006) Personality type and coronary heart disease. *Georgian Medical News* **134**, 58–60.

Moscovici S (1985) Social influence and conformity. In G Lindzey & E Aronson (eds) *Handbook of social psychology*. New York: Random House.

Murdock BB (1962) The serial position effect of free recall. *Journal of Experimental Psychology* **64**, 482–8.

Nakao M, Nomura S, Shimosawa T, Yoshiuchi K, Kumano H, Kuboki T, Suematsu H & Fujita T (1997) Clinical effects of blood pressure biofeedback treatment on hypertension by auto-shaping. *Psychosomatic Medicine* **59**(3), 331–8.

Newman C & Adams K (2004) Dog gone good: managing dog phobia in a teenage boy with a learning disability. *British Journal of Learning Disabilities* **32**, 35–8.

Newman E, O'Connor DB & Conner M (2007) Daily hassles and eating behaviour: the role of cortisol reactivity status. *Psychoneuroendocrinology* **32**(2), 125–32.

Nicholls AR, Polman R, Levy AR, Taylor J & Cobley S (2007) Stressors, coping, and coping effectiveness: gender, type of sport, and skill differences. *Journal of Sports Science* **27**, 1–10.

Oakhill JV, Yuill N & Parkin C (1988) Memory and inference in skilled and less skilled comprehenders. In MM Gruneberg, PE Morris & RN Sykes (eds) *Practical Aspects of Memory: Current Research and Issues*, vol. 2. Chichester: Wiley.

Oue W, Hakoda Y, Onuma N & Morikawa S (2001) The effect of negative emotion on eyewitness functional field of view. *Shinrigaku Kenkyu* **72**(5), 361–8.

Palesh O, Butler LD, Koopman C, Giese-Davis J, Carlson R & Spiegel D (2007) Stress history and breast cancer recurrence. *Journal of Psychosomatic Research* **63**(3), 233–9.

Palmer S & Dryden W (1995) *Counselling for stress problems*. London: Sage.

Parker JF, Bahrick LE, Fivush R & Johnson P (2006) The impact of stress on mothers' memory of a natural disaster. *Journal of Experimental Psychology: Applied* **12**(3), 142–54.

Parsons R, Tassinary LG, Ulrich RS, Hebl MR & Grossmann-Alexander M (1998) The view from the road: implications for stress recovery and immunization. *Journal of Environmental Psychology* **18**, 113–40.

Pate JE & Gabbard GO (2003) Adult baby syndrome. *American Journal of Psychiatry* **160**, 1932–6.

Perry AR & Baldwin DA (2000) Further evidence of associations of type A personality scores and driving-related attitudes and behaviors. *Perceptual Motor Skills* **91**(1), 147–54.

Peterson LR & Peterson MJ (1959) Short-term retention of individual verbal items. *Journal of Experimental Psychology* **58**, 193–8.

Pinquart M, Duberstein PR & Lyness JM (2006) Treatments for later-life depressive conditions: a meta-analytic comparison of pharmacotherapy and psychotherapy. *American Journal of Psychiatry* **163**, 1493–1501.

Purdon SE, Woodward ND, Flor-Henry P (2001) Asymmetrical hand force persistence and neuroleptic treatment in schizophrenia. *Journal of the International Neuropsychological Society* **7**, 606-14.

Rahe RH, Mahan JL & Arthur R (1970) Prediction of near-future health change from subjects' preceding life changes. *Journal of Psychosomatic Research* **14**, 401–6.

Rose D, Wykes T, Leese M, Bindman J & Fleischmann P (2005) Patients' perspectives on ECT: a systematic review. *British Medical Journal* **236**, 1363.

Rosenman RH & Friedman M (1958) The possible relationship of occupational stress to clinical coronary heart disease. *California Medicine* **89**(3), 169–74.

Rotter JB (1966) Generalized expectancies for internal versus external control of reinforcement. *Psychological Monographs* **80** (whole no. 609).

Rutter M (1981) *Maternal deprivation reassessed.* Harmondsworth: Penguin.

Rutter M (2006) The psychological effects of institutional rearing. In P Marshall & N Fox (eds) *The development of social engagement: neurobiological perspectives*. New York: Oxford University Press.

Rutter M and the English & Romanian Adoptees Study Team (1998) Developmental catch up and deficit after severe global early privation. *Journal of Child Psychology and Psychiatry* **39**, 465–76.

Rutter M, Colvert E, Kreppner J, Beckett C, Castle J, Groothues C, Hawkins A, O'Connor TG, Stevens SE & Sonuga-Barke EJS (2007) Early adolescent outcomes for institutionally-deprived and non-deprived adoptees I: Disinhibited attachment. *Journal of Child Psychology & Psychiatry* **48**, 17–30.

Samuel J & Bryant P (1984) Asking only one question in the conservation experiment. *Journal of Child Psychology & Psychiatry* **25**(2), 315–18.

Sandahl C, Herlitz K & Ahlin G (1998) Time-limited group psychotherapy for moderately alcohol dependent patients: a randomised controlled clinical trial. *Psychotherapy Research* **8**, 361-378.

Scher A & Mayseless O (2000) Mothers of anxious/ambivalent infants: maternal characteristics and child-care context. *Child Development* **71**, 1629–39.

Schmidt HG, Peeck VH, Paas F & van Breukelen GJ (2000) Remembering the street names of one's childhood neighbourhood: a study of very long-term retention. *Memory* **8**(1), 37–49.

Scoville WB & Milner B (1957) The loss of recent memory after bilateral hippocampal lesions. *Journal of Neurology, Neurosurgery and Psychiatry* **20**, 11–21.

Seitz K & Schumann-Hengsteler R (2000) Mental multiplication and working memory. *European Journal of Cognitive Psychology* **12**(4), 552–70.

Shaffer JW, Graves PL, Swank RT & Pearson TA (1987) Clustering of personality traits in youth and the subsequent development of cancer in physicians. *Journal of Behavioral Medicine* **10**, 441–7.

Sherif M (1935) A study of some factors in perception. *Archives of Psychology* **27**, 187.

Simantov E, Schoen C & Klein JD (2000) Health-compromising behaviors: why do adolescents smoke or drink? Identifying underlying risk and protective factors. *Archives of Pediatrics and Adolescent Medicine* **154**(10), 1025–33.

Slater M, Antley A, Davison A, Swapp D, Guger C, Barker C, Pistrang N & Sanchez-Vives M (2006) A virtual reprise of the Stanley Milgram obedience experiments. *PLoS One* December, n.p.

Smallbone SW & Dadds MR (2000) Attachment and coercive sexual behaviour. *Sexual Abuse* **12**, 3-15.

Smithson H & Mollon J (2006) Do masks terminate the icon? *Quarterly Journal of Experimental Psychology (Colchester)* **59**(1), 150–60.

Smythe JW & Costall B (2003) Mobile phone use facilitates memory in male, but not female, subjects. *Neuroreport* **14**, 243–6.

Sparks K, Cooper C, Fried Y & Shirom A (1997) The effects of hours of work on health : A meta-analytic review. *Journal of occupational and organizational psychology*, **70**(4) 391–408.

Sperling G (1960) The information available in brief visual presentations. *Psychology Monographs: General and Applied* **74**(11) (whole no. 498).

Stayton DJ & Ainsworth MDS (1973) Individual differences in infant responses to brief, everyday separations as related to other infant and maternal behaviours. *Developmental Psychology* **9**, 226–35.

Stewart SM, Lee PWH, Low LC, Cheng A, Yeung W, Huen K & O Donnell D (2000) Pathways from emotional adjustment to glycemic control in youths with diabetes in Hong Kong. *Journal of Pediatric Psychology* **25**, 393–402.

Takahashi K (1990) Affective relationships and their lifelong development. In PB Baltes (ed.) *Lifespan development and behavior* vol. 10. Hillsdale, NJ: Lawrence Erlbaum Associates.

Tarnow E (2000) Self-destructive obedience in the airplane cockpit and the concept of obedience optimisation. In T Blass (ed.) *Obedience to authority*. Mahwah, NJ: Lawrence Erlbaum.

Thomas LE & Irwin DE (2006) Voluntary eyeblinks disrupt iconic memory. *Perception and Psychophysics* **68**(3), 475–88.

Toda M, Makino H, Kobayashi H & Morimoto K (2006) Health effects of a long-term stay in a spa resort. *Archives of Environmental and Occupational Health* **61**(3), 131–7.

Toda M, Makino H, Kobayashi H & Morimoto K (2007) Health related lifestyle and patterns of behavior related to health effects of leisure travel. *Social Behavior and Personality: An International Journal* **35**(3), 287–94.

Treisman AM (1964) Verbal cues, language, and meaning in selective attention. *American Journal of Psychology* **77**, 206–19.

Trivedi MH, Rush AJ, Wisniewski SR, Nierenberg AA, Warden D, Ritz L, Norquist G, Howland RH, Lebowitz B, McGrath PJ, Shores-Wilson K, Biggs MM, Balasubramani GK & Fava M (2006) Evaluation of outcomes with citalopram for depression using measurement-based care in STAR*D: implications for clinical practice. *American Journal of Psychiatry* **163**, 28–40.

Trower P & Jones J (2001) How REBT can be less disturbing and remarkably more influential in Britain: a review of views of practitioners and researchers. *Journal of Rational-Emotive & Cognitive-Behavior Therapy* **19**, 21–30.

Tsai PS, Chang NC, Chang WY, Lee PH & Wang MY (2007) Blood pressure biofeedback exerts intermediate-term effects on blood pressure and pressure reactivity in individuals with mild hypertension: a randomized controlled study. *Journal of Alternative and Complementary Medicine* **13**(5), 547–54.

Tulving E & Pearlstone Z (1966) Availability versus accessibility of information in memory for words. *Journal of Verbal Learning and Verbal Behavior* **5**, 381–91.

Twenge JM, Zhang L & Im C (2004) It's beyond my control: a cross-temporal meta-analysis of increasing externality in locus of control 1960–2002. *Review of Personality and Social Psychology* **8**, 308.

Van Ijzendoorn MH & Kroonenberg PM (1988) Cross-cultural patterns of attachment: a meta-analysis of the Strange Situation. *Child Development* **59**, 147–56.

Van Ijzendoorn MH, Juffer F & Duyvestein MGC (1995) Breaking the intergenerational cycle of insecure attachment: a review of the effects of attachment-based interventions on maternal sensitivity and infant security. *Journal of Child Psychology & Psychiatry* **56**, 225-48.

Verkooijen KT, de Vries NK & Nielsen GA (2007) Youth crowds and substance use: the impact of perceived group norm and multiple group identification. *Psychology of Addictive Behaviors* **21**, 55–61.

Vidal A, Gómez-Gil E, Sans M, Portella MJ, Salamero M, Piqué JM & Panés J (2006) Life events and inflammatory bowel disease relapse: a prospective study of patients enrolled in remission. *American Journal of Gastroenterology* **101**(4), 775–81.

Waldrop AE, Back SE, Brady KT, Upadhyaya HP, McRae AL & Saladin ME (2007) Daily stressor sensitivity, abuse effects, and cocaine use in cocaine dependence. *Addictive Behaviors*, **32**(12), 3015–25.

Ward MJ, Lee SS & Polan J (2006) Attachment and psychopathology in a community sample. *Attachment & Human Development* **8**, 327–40.

Watson JB & Rayner R (1920) Conditioned emotional responses. *Journal of Experimental Psychology* **3**, 1–14.

Wicklegren WA (1968) Sparing of short-term memory in an amnesic patient: implications for strength theory of memory. *Neuropsychologia* **6**, 235–44.

Wijngaards-de Meij L, Stroebe M, Schut H, Stroebe W, van den Bout J, van den Heijden P & Dijkstra I (2007) Neuroticism and attachment insecurity as predictors of bereavement outcome. *Journal of Research in Personality* **41**, 498–505.

Wilson BA, Baddeley AD & Kapur N (1995) Dense amnesia in a professional musician following herpes simplex virus encephalitis. *Journal of Clinical and Experimental Neuropsychology* **17**(5), 668–81.

Wilson BA & Wearing D (1995) Prisoner of consciousness: a state of just awakening following Herpes simplex encephalitis. In R Campbell & MA Conway (eds) *Broken memories: case studies in memory impairment.* Oxford: Blackwell Publishing.

Wiswede D, Russeler J & Munte TF (2007) Serial position in free memory recall: an ERP study. *Biological Psychology* **72**(2), 185–93.

Wright AM & Holliday RE (2005) Police officers' perceptions of older eyewitnesses. *Legal and Criminological Psychology* **10**(2), 211–23.

Wright AM & Holliday RE (2007) Enhancing the recall of young, young-old and old-old adults with cognitive interviews. *Applied Cognitive Psychology* **21**, 19–43.

Wright DB, Loftus EF & Hall M (2001) Now you see it; now you don't: inhibiting recall and recognition of scenes. *Applied Cognitive Psychology* **15**, 471–82.

Yamada Y, Tatsumi K, Yamaguchi T, Tanabe N, Takiguchi Y, Kuriyama T & Mikami R (2003) Influence of stressful life events on the onset of sarcoidosis. *Respirology* **8**(2), 186–91.

Yuille JC & Cutshall JL (1986) A case study of eyewitness memory of a crime. *Journal of Applied Psychology* **71**, 291–301.

Zeanah CH, Smyke AT, Koga SF & Carlson E (2005) Attachment in institutionalised and community children in Romania. *Child Development* **76**, 1015–28.

Zettle RD (2003) Acceptance and commitment therapy (ACT) vs. systematic desensitization in treatment of mathematics anxiety. *Psychological Record* **53**, 197–215.

Zilbertstein K (2006) Clarifying core characteristics of attachment disorders: a review of current research and theory. *American Journal of Orthopsychiatry* **76**, 55–64.

Index

Acknowledgements

The authors and publishers are grateful to the following for permissions to reproduce copyright material.

p.11, © Simone van den Berg; p.13 (top), © ImageState/Alamy; p.13 (bottom), © ISIL; p.20, © Julia Russell; p.26 (top), © Andrea Zabiello/Shutterstock (top); p.26 (bottom), © Arne Trautmann/Shutterstock; p.27, © PhotoCreate/Shutterstock; p.30, © PA Wire/PA Photos; p.34, © courtesy of Soni Wright; p.30, © Corbis; p.35, © Betty LaRue/Alamy; p.43, © Mandy Godbehear; p.44 (top), © MaleWitch; p. 44 (bottom), © Anna Dzondzua; p.45, © Bubbles Photolibrary/Alamy; p.46, © Photo Researchers/Science Photo Library; p.48, © Christophe Testi; p.51, © Peter Baxter/Shutterstock; p.54 (top), © Kevin Lepp/Shutterstock; p.54 (bottom), © Yuri Arcurs; p.55 (top), © Howard Gray; p.55 (bottom), © Time & Life Pictures/Getty Images; p.56, © Getty Images; p.59, © PhotoCreate; p.62, © Mike Abrahams/Alamy; p.66, © Silvia Otte; p.67, © Picture Partners/Alamy; p.69, © Bubbles Photolibrary/Alamy; p.74, © Akela's Cubs; p.76, © Andresr/Shutterstock; p.78, © Junial Enterprises; p.79, © Vuk Vukmirovic/Shutterstock; p.82, © David Davis/Shutterstock; p.85, © Monika Wisniewska; p.93, © Jim Lopes/Shutterstock; p.97 (top), © Ros Drinkwater/Alamy; p.97 (bottom), *Genie: A Psycholinguistic Study of a Modern-day 'Wild Child'*, Academic Press 1977 © Elsevier; p.100, © Steve Lovegrove; p.103, © Darren Baker, Oleg Kozlov, Sophy Kozlova; p.105, © Getty Images; p.106, © Stephen Coburn; p.108, © Keystone/Corbis; p.109, © Tebenkova Svetlana; p.111, © Ilyssa Sky Tonnessen; p.112, © Peter Glass/Alamy; p.114, © PhotoCreate; p.118, © Andrew Gentry; p.125, © Photos 12/Alamy; p.132, © James Woodson; p.134 (top), © Losevsky Pavel; p.134 (bottom), © Rudolf Kotulán; p.139, © AFP/Getty Images; p.140, © 1125089601/Shutterstock; p.141, © Peter Dazeley; p.142 (top), © Ryan McVay; p.143, © Spauln; p.142 (bottom), © Carolina K. Smith, M.D; p.144, © Credit Line © Photos 12/Alamy; p.145, © Zoran Vukmanov Simokov; p.146 (top), © Phil Degginger/Alamy; p.146 (bottom), © PhotoCreate; p.147, © Julia Russell; p.148, © Galina Barskaya; p.159, © Julie DeGuia; p.160, © Andresr; p.161, © Paul Carstairs/Alamy; p.162, © Getty Images; p.163 (top), © Tim Pannell/Corbis; p.163 (bottom), © photogl/Shutterstock; p.164 From the film Obedience © 1968 by Stanley Milgram, © renewed 1993 by Alexandra Milgram, and distributed by Penn State Media Sales; p.166, © Cryptos; p.168 (top), © Tomasz Szymanski; p.168 (bottom), Figure 1 from Slater M et al. (2006) A Virtual Reprise of the Stanley Milgram Obedience Experiments. PLoS ONE 1(1): e39. doi:10.1371/journal.pone.0000039; p.170 (top), © Sean Gladwell/Fotolia; p.170 (bottom), © Dewayne Flowers; p.171, courtesy of Phillip Zimbardo; p.172 (top), © Getty Images; p.172 (bottom), © Alex Yeung/Fotolia; p.174 (top), © Joy Stein; p.174 (bottom), © Saniphoto/Fotolia; p.176, © Saniphoto/Fotolia; p.181, © ChipPix; p.187 (top), © Nathalie P/Fotolia; p.187 (bottom), © Lucian Coman; p.188, © Cheryl Casey; p.190, © kwest; p.191, © Tan Wei Ming; p.193, © Amihays; p.194 (top), © BSIP, Jacopin/Science Photo Library; p.194 (bottom), © Katrina Brown; p.196 (top), Gary Marshall/Fotolia; p.196 (bottom), © Will McIntyre/ Science Photo library; p.198, © Kurhan; p.199, © Mary Evans Picture Library/Alamy; p.200, courtesy of Richard Kanaan; p.201, © terekhov igor; p.203, © Archives of the History of American Psychology – The University of Akron; p.204, © Robert Trachtenberg/Corbis; p.205, © Mike Flippo; p.206, © Ben Heys; p.207, © GeoM; p.217, © Lane V. Erickson; p.218 (top), © Bob Pardue/Alamy; p.218 (bottom), © David Madison.